The Fragility of the 'Failed State' Paradigm

Developments in International Law

VOLUME 63

The Fragility of the 'Failed State' Paradigm

A Different International Law Perception of the Absence of Effective Government

By
Neyire Akpınarlı

MARTINUS NIJHOFF PUBLISHERS

LEIDEN • BOSTON
2010

This book is printed on acid-free paper.

Library of Congress Cataloging-in-Publication Data

Akpinarli, Neyire.
The fragility of the 'failed state' paradigm : a different international law perception of the absence of effective government / by Neyire Akpinarli.
p. cm. – (Developments in international law : v. 63)
Includes bibliographical references.
ISBN 978-90-04-17812-0 (hardback : alk. paper)
1. Failed states. I. Title.

KZ4029.A37 2009
341.5'84–dc22

2009030265

ISSN 0924-5332
ISBN 978 90 04 17812 0

PRINTED IN THE NETHERLANDS

Contents

Acknowledgements

This work on the absence of effective government was accepted as a PhD thesis by the University of Bremen in the summer of 2008. The subject is one of the most complex and important issues in international law, and the attempt to present the issue in a second foreign language compounded the difficulty. I am grateful to many people for their assistance throughout the process and would like to stress that any mistakes are my own.

If I learned how to think in the area of international law, it is mostly thanks to my two supervisors. I would above all like to thank my first supervisor, Prof. Dr. Thomas Giegerich. I regarded writing my thesis under his supervision as a privilege in many ways. I received endless support and knowledge from him and am grateful to him for everything.

I am also most grateful for the supervision of Prof. Dr. Gerd Winter, my second supervisor, with whom I also worked earlier. After my study of law in 2002 at the University of Bremen, he unhesitatingly supported my seminar work and master's thesis over many years.

Meeting Wendy Hammond while working on the writing brought me great happiness, not only because of her valued assistance in editing and the nuances of English but also because of her knowledge of and experience in different parts of the world. Her encouragement, energy, and enthusiasm was so empowering that I do not know how to acknowledge her adequately.

A sine qua non for writing a PhD thesis is the continuity of the work without having to worry about funds. I am very thankful to the Friedrich Naumann Foundation, which supported me generously between 2005 and 2008.

Being able to work at the library of the Max Planck Institute for Comparative Public Law and International Law while writing my thesis was a great privilege. I would like to express particular gratitude to the staff at the library for their assistance and efficiency.

Although I started this thesis in the summer of 2004, the writing was actually the last station on a long journey in Germany. Many people helped make this journey a pleasure. The first are my parents and my sister, Akgül Akpınarlı, who during my first year away from home sent letters, books, pocket money, and moral support when I was in a foreign country with no knowledge of the language. I am grateful to her for supporting me spiritually and materially whenever I have needed her help. I am also thankful to my cousin, Süheyla Kaya, and her family, who made me feel at home in Germany. Hans Scheulen has had a special place in my life there, making many things easier and pushing me forward. I would also like to express my gratitude to Reinhart Wolf, Richard Ortiz-Ortiz, and Carmen Timaru, others who have shared this time with me.

I dedicate the work to my mother, who suffered most from my move to Germany, and to my friend Ozan Zafer Ekin, who passed out of our circle in 2002 and is still the most important person lighting my way.

Berlin, January 2009

Abbreviations and Acronyms

ACP	African, Caribbean, and the Pacific
ADF	Allied Democratic Forces
AMISOM	African Union Mission to Somalia
APEC	Asia-Pacific Economic Cooperation
ARPCT	Alliance for the Restoration of Peace and Counter-Terrorism
ARSIWA	Articles on the Responsibility of States for Internationally Wrongful Acts
AU	African Union
CIA	Central Intelligence Agency
CPA	Coalition Provisional Authority
DDA	Doha Development Agenda
DRC	Democratic Republic of the Congo
DVPA	Democratic People's Party of Afghanistan
ECOSOC	Economic and Social Council
ECOWAS	Economic Community of West African States
GATT	General Agreement on Tariffs and Trade
GDP	Gross domestic product
IBRD	International Bank for Reconstruction and Development
ICISS	International Commission on Intervention and State Sovereignty
ICJ	International Court of Justice
IDA	International Development Association
IGAD	Intergovernmental Authority on Development
IGO	Intergovernmental organisation
IMF	International Monetary Fund
ISAF	International Security Assistance Force
ITO	International Trade Organization
MNE	Multinational enterprise
NAFTA	North American Free Trade Agreement
NATO	North Atlantic Treaty Organization
NGO	Nongovernmental organisation
NIEO	New International Economic Order
OAS	Organization of American States
OAU	Organization of African Unity
OECD	Organisation for Economic Cooperation and Development
OEEC	Organization for European Economic Cooperation
OSGAP	Office of the Secretary General for Afghanistan and Pakistan
SAP	Structural adjustment programme
SICC	Supreme Islamic Courts Council
SNM	Somali National Movement
SRRC	Somali Restoration and Reconstruction Council

SSF	Somali Salvation Front
TCC	Transnational capitalist class
TFG	Transitional Federal Government
TNG	Transitional National Government
U.S.	United States
UIC	Union of Islamic Courts
UK	United Kingdom
UN	United Nations
UNAMA	United Nations Assistance Mission in Afghanistan
UNCTAD	United Nations Conference on Trade and Development
UNDP	United Nations Development Program
UNGOMAP	United Nations Good Offices Mission in Afghanistan
UNHCR	Office of the United Nations High Commissioner for Refugees
UNICEF	United Nations Children's Fund
UNITAF	United Task Force
UNMIK	United Nations Interim Administration Mission in Kosovo
UNOSOM	United Nations Operation in Somalia
UNSMA	United Nations Special Mission in Afghanistan
UNTAET	United Nations Transitional Administration in East Timor
USC	United Somali Congress
USC/SNA	United Somali Congress/Somali National Alliance
WCED	World Commission on Environment and Development
WFP	World Food Programme
WTO	World Trade Organization

Introduction

The end of the Cold War shaped not only the international political context but also international law in many respects. In the following decades, however, two realities assumed a greater influence on the development of international law. The first was the hope for a more effective international legal order, which shifted international legal issues such as human rights and democracy on the one hand and the economy and the environment on the other from the internal to the external arena. In parallel with this change and also with the development of technology, international actors such as international organisations and multinational corporations have taken a more active role in relations both between and within states. The second reality was the disappearance of the shadow of the Cold War on international law after the demise of the Soviet Union in the 1990s. In its wake the United States has had a growing influence on global economic issues and international economic law.

In this context, the absence of effective government appeared on the international law agenda along with the concept of the 'failed state'. Under the leadership of the United States, the international community has intervened militarily in states such as Somalia, Iraq, and Afghanistan on the grounds that the chaotic situation in those countries threatens international peace.

For nearly 15 years, the notions of the 'failed state', the 'rogue state', and the 'war on terror' have been prominent features in international law. All these concepts were invented by the North to 'solve' problems in the South and invoked to justify military intervention to protect international peace and security. The devastating consequences of the military actions, characterised as 'collateral damage' by the interventionists, have made Somalia and Afghanistan two of the world's most critical cases of the absence of effective government. The international community abandoned early on its claim of state reconstruction in Somalia but remains in Afghanistan and Iraq to annihilate 'enemies' on the one hand and achieve an ambitious project of 'nation-building' on the other, at the expense of thousands of lost lives.

The absence of effective government is unquestionably one of the most important challenges in international law today. The international community's approach to the phenomenon under the paradigm of the 'failed state' since is at least as important because it has pervaded international law since the 1990s. Therefore, while the features and consequences of the absence of effective government are at the centre of this work, the international community's approach to dealing with the phenomenon determines the content.

It is true that the absence of effective government threatens international peace and security. But because its manifestations are different in each county, it is difficult to specify its features, Chapter 1 attempts to analyse the appearance of the phenomenon to draw its general outlines, bearing in mind this constraint. The case studies on Somalia and Afghanistan in Chapter 2 bring the picture into clearer focus and explore the phenomenon from a perspective ignored by the international community and international actors—the historical background. Both cases illustrate the diverse attributes and manifestations of the absence of effective government, as well as the reaction of the international community. The description of the situation in both states serves as the basis for a later discussion of the effectiveness of the international community's policies and efforts.

Chapter 3 places the issue in the global historical context, focusing on the link between the absence of effective government and important international historical, political, and economic trends. This chapter highlights the international community's disregard for this interdependency and points out the need to take external factors into consideration to address the phenomenon effectively. The three historical events analysed in detail in this chapter are colonialism, the Cold War, and the world order in the age of globalisation.

During and after the Cold War, public international law has dealt with several notions that appeared first in international politics and were translated into international law. These usually pejorative terms, including 'failed state' and 'rogue state', originated in the values, interests, and perspective of the powerful states of the North and were imposed on the South for their own ends. Chapter 4 analyses the term 'failed state' and its content in public international law to attempt to move closer to a definition of the absence of effective government. This analysis illuminates both the viewpoint of the international community and the extent to which international legal issues are determined by international politics.

Chapter 5 questions whether the notions of the 'rogue state' and 'failed state' are valid paradigms in international law, which considers all states sovereign and equal and is founded on the principles of non-force, non-intervention, and self-determination. These principles are examined following an analysis of the international legal issue of the subjectivity of states dealing with the absence of effective government. The international community's efforts in such states are shown to be limited to military intervention, humanitarian assistance, or development policy rather than addressing the root causes of the problem and to fuel charges of neo-colonialism.

The legal complications posed by states unable to take advantage of rights and fulfil duties under international law because of their lack of effective governments are highlighted in Chapter 6, which advocates for maintaining as normal relations as possible with these states to bring them back under the influence of international law

The international community's approaches to solving the problem of the absence of effective government, based on Chapter VII of the United Nations Charter, have included international territorial administration, 'nation-building', and 'state-building' to re-establish state institutions and impose human rights or democracy even through military measures. Chapter 7 discusses the dilemmas and fragile paradigms inherent in the legal basis and praxis of this approach.

Chapter 8 links peace to economic and social issues and argues that current international law offers an alternative to military intervention and external administration to maintain security in states dealing with the absence of effective government. An economic and social approach in a global context is both a long-term solution and a preventive measure. This chapter reviews the shape and trends of international law since 1945 to show how the North has imposed its model, including the liberalisation of the global economy, to address the problems of the South, which has in response demanded a more equitable role in setting global priorities. The hypocrisy of implementing policies to benefit the powerful states under the guise of bringing free trade and democracy to the less powerful is explored as an obstacle to the effectiveness of the international community in meeting economic and social needs.

The difficulty faced in this work was to remain within the parameters of international law while taking a fresh approach from that of the mainstream to a critical issue that affects all of our futures.

Chapter One

The Appearance and Features of the Absence of Effective Government

Public international law, political science, and sociology use different criteria to describe the appearance and features of the absence of effective government.[1] Robert Rotberg, a political scientist, describes the phenomenon as the inability of a state to bring positive political goods to its inhabitants. William L. Zartman, a social scientist, characterises the phenomenon as the disintegration of state structure, authority (legitimate power), law, and political order.[2] Some definitions are interdisciplinary. A political-sociological analysis by Ingo Liebach ascribes five characteristics to the absence of effective government: collapse of the state order, armed internal conflicts, substantial violations of human rights and humanitarian crises, an endogenous character, and social fragmentation.[3]

Different descriptions of the phenomenon also are found within disciplines. In public international law, for example, Jürgen Bartl identifies three criteria: the lapse of effective government, the increased use of privatised force, and an endogenous character.[4] Ingo Liebach, who uses Georg Jellinek's definition of the state as a basis for analysing the phenomenon from the perspective of public international law, considers the collapse of effective government to be the most important element.[5] Vis à vis Liebach, Robin Geiß pinpoints the dissolution of

---

1 Robert I. Rotberg, "The Failure and Collapse of Nation-States, Breakdown, Prevention, and Repair," in *When States Fail: Causes and Consequences*, ed. Robert I. Rotberg (Princeton: Princeton University Press, 2004), 2–4; William L. Zartman, introduction ("Posing the Problem of State Collapse") to *Collapsed States: The Disintegration and Restoration of Legitimate Authority*, ed. William. L. Zartman (Boulder: Lynn Rienner Publishers, 1995), 1; Gerard Kreijen, *State Failure, Sovereignty and Effectiveness: Legal Lessons from the Decolonization of Sub-Saharan Africa* (Leiden: Martinus Nijhoff Publishers, 2004), 86.

2 Rotberg, "The Failure and Collapse of Nation-States", 3–4; Zartman, "Posing the Problem of State Collapse", 1.

3 Ingo Liebach, *Die unilaterale humanitäre Intervention im "zerfallenen Staate"* (Cologne: Carl Heymanns Verlag, 2004), 25.

4 Jürgen Bartl, *Die Humanitäre Intervention durch den Sicherheitsrat der Vereinten Nationen im Failed State, Das Beispiel Somalia* (Frankfurt: Peter Lang Verlagsgruppe, 1999), 74.

5 Liebach, *Die unilaterale humanitäre Intervention*, 40.

effective government and the absence of law and order,[6] manifested in armed conflicts, displaced persons, devastation of internal infrastructure, and extreme human suffering.[7]

The State in Public International Law

Given this diversity of opinion about the features of the absence of effective government, it may be useful to start by defining the state in public international law. The definitions of Jellinek and Article 1 of the 1933 Montevideo Convention on the Rights and Duties of States are generally accepted as the legal criteria for the definition of statehood.[8] According to Jellinek's 'doctrine of the three elements' (*Drei Elemente Lehre*), a state is established as a social association through the three constitutive elements of defined territory, permanent population, and government.[9] Article 1 of the Montevideo Convention adds to Jellinek's doctrine the capacity to enter into relations with other countries:

> The state as a person of international law should possess the following qualifications: a) a permanent population, b) a defined territory, c) government, and d) capacity to enter into relations with other states.[10]

Some authors have interpreted the fourth element, 'capacity to enter into relations with other states', as independence.[11] However, whether this element is a constitutive element of the state is subject to dispute.[12] This capacity could be accepted either as a requirement of the government or as a requirement of independence, or even both. John Dugard considers it a consequence of inde-

---

6 Robin Geiß, *"Failed States". Die normative Erfassung gescheiterter Staaten* (Berlin, Duncker & Humblot, 2005), 58.

7 Ibid., 43.

8 In the literature of public international law, some international lawyers interpret Article 1 of the Montevideo Convention as a basic formulation of the criteria of statehood. James R. Crawford, *The Creation of States in International Law* (Oxford: Clarendon Press, 1979), 36; Ian Brownlie, *Principles of Public International Law*, 6th ed. (Oxford: Oxford University Press, 2003), 71. Others, especially in Germany, use Georg Jellinek's definition as the basis of the criteria of statehood. Karl Doehring, *Völkerrecht, Ein Lehrbuch*, 2nd edition (Heidelberg: Müller 2004), 28; Volker Epping, "Völkerrechtssubjekte" in *Völkerrecht*, ed. Knut Ipsen, 3rd edition (Munich: 1990, C.H. Beck), 56.

9 Georg Jellinek, *Allgemeine Staatslehre*, 4th edition (Berlin: Springer Verlag, 1922), 394.

10 "Montevideo Convention on the Rights and Duties of States", 26 December 1933, entered into force on 26 December 1934.

11 Brownlie, *Principles of Public International Law*, 71.

12 Peter Malanczuk, *Akehurst's Modern Introduction to International Law* (London: Routledge, 1997), 79; Otto Kimminich and Stephan Hobe, *Einführung in das Völkerrecht*, 7th edition (Tübingen, Germany: A. Francke Verlag, 2000), 67.

pendence,[13] while Torsten Stein and Cristian Buttlar take it as a requirement of government. James Crawford argues that the capacity to enter into relations with other states may be a 'conflation of the requirement of government and independence'.[14] In fact, there is no clear determination of the fourth criterion of Article 1 of the Montevideo Convention. In a newly established state, the capacity to enter into relations with other states can be interpreted as external sovereignty identified with independence. In an existing state, however, the same criterion could be interpreted as an external aspect of effective government. For all that, no interpretation satisfactorily clarifies the fourth criterion. Therefore, Jellinek's classical trilogy of government, people, and territory[15] will be taken here as the basic criteria for statehood[16] and used to explore the absence of effective government.

Government

Government is considered the central criterion of statehood, in spite of the constitutive equipoise of all three elements, because government is predicated on the criteria of defined territory and permanent population.[17] It is difficult to find a generally accepted definition of government in international law.[18] According to Max Weber's definition of statehood, government means

> [...] a compulsory political association with continuous organisation whose administrative staff successfully upholds a claim to the monopoly of the legitimate use of force in enforcement of its orders in a given territorial unit.[19]

Manfred Rotter described government as a 'minimal organisational structure' able to represent a country and its people in the international arena.[20] Volker Epping defines government through internal sovereignty—the ability to

---

13 John Dugard, *International Law, A South African Perspective*, 2nd edition (Capetown: Juta & Company Ltd Publishers, 2000), 74.

14 Crawford, *The Creation of States*, 74; Torsten Stein and Cristian von Buttlar, *Völkerrecht*, 11th edition (Munich: Carl Heymanns Verlag 2005), 90.

15 Bartl, *Die unilaterale humanitäre Intervention*, 41.

16 Kimminich and Hobe, *Einführung*, 67; Doehring, *Völkerrecht*, 27; Epping, "Völkerrechtssubjekte", 56; Dugard, *International Law*, 73–74; Crawford, *The Creation of States*, 47–48.

17 Georg Dahm, Jost Delbrück, and Rüdiger Wolfrum, *Völkerrecht*, Volume 1/3 (Berlin: de Gruyter Rechtswissenschaften Verlags, 2002), 128; Liebach, *Die unilaterale humanitäre Intervention*, 43; Epping, "Völkerrechtssubjekte", 57.

18 Martin Dixon, *Textbook on International Law*, 4th edition (Oxford: Oxford University Press, 2005), 107; Stein and von Buttlar, *Völkerrecht*, 98.

19 Max A. Weber, *The Theory of Social and Economic Organisation* (Oxford: Oxford University Press, 1947), 154.

20 Manfred Rotter, "Staat" in *Völkerrecht*, ed. Ignaz Seidl-Hohenveldern, 3rd edition (Neuwied: Luchterhand-Faschverlag, 2001), 380.

maintain order in the state territory—and external sovereignty—the ability to act independently according to international rule.[21]

Definition of Government in an Existing State

In order to define the range of inquiry, it is necessary here to clarify the difference between the notions of government in the establishment of a state and in an existing state. In international law, the definition of government in the establishment of a state is determined mainly through internal and external sovereignty.[22] While the internal sovereignty of a state is the highest authority over its territory, external sovereignty appears as independence in the international legal order.[23] There is no rule in public international law about the form of the government for the establishment of a state. Article 3 of the UN Charter appoints only states as members.

In an existing sovereign state, government is defined as the current political administration. Here, also, there is no special rule for the form of government. In Article 4/2 of the UN Charter, the only requirement for membership in the United Nations is that states be 'peace loving'.[24] This quality is far from clear and has no meaning for determining the form of government or ability of a state. Persistent violation of the Principles of the UN Charter can lead to expulsion from the United Nations, according to Article 6, but this does not take into consideration the legality and legitimacy of the government. It could be argued that General Assembly Resolution 36/162 (1981), which ruled on measures to be taken against totalitarian ideologies, especially Nazism, Fascism, and neo-Fascism, is an exception to this rule. Even if it is accepted as a criterion for government legitimacy, the resolution contains no sanction against totalitarian activities.[25]

According to the rule of pluralism of ideology, as well as Article 2/7 of the UN Charter, the question of how a country organises itself is an internal

---

21 Epping, "Völkerrechtssubjekte", 56.

22 Alfred Verdross and Bruno Simma, *Universelles Völkerrecht* (Berlin: Duncker & Humblot, 1984), 26; Epping, "Völkerrechtssubjekte", 56. In fact, the institution of the state and the notion of sovereignty are two different historical events. While discussion about the state took place in France, England, and Germany in the 13th and 14th centuries, the term "sovereignty" was first used in the 16th century by Jean Bodin (1530–1596).

23 Verdross and Simma, *Universelles Völkerrecht*, 30.

24 Article 4/1 of the UN Charter states, "Membership in the United Nations is open to all other peace-loving states which accept the obligations contained in the present Charter and, in the judgment of the Organisation, are able and willing to carry out these obligations".

25 GA Res. 36/162 of 16.12. 1981.

rather than an international issue.[26] The International Court validated this position in its report on the Western Sahara:

> No rule of international law, in the view of the Court, requires the structure of a State to follow any particular pattern, as is evident from the diversity of the forms of State found in the world today.[27]

Friedrich A. von der Heydte pointed out that the freedom of states to determine their forms of government is a fundamental principle unless this freedom damages the rights of other states.[28] In the 21st century however, public international law's increasing consideration of human rights and democracy as requisites of a valid government appears to contradict the fundamental principle of the freedom of the form of government.[29]

The Effectiveness of Government

As a subject of international law, the state has two capacities.[30] The first is the legal capacity—the rights and duties under international law—that the state automatically earns with its establishment.[31] The second is the capacity to exercise rights and fulfil duties under the international legal order.[32] While states implement or enforce their *capacity to act* through state organs such as legislative, executive, and juridical bodies, they can only exert their sovereignty over national territory and in international relations through effective institutions and organs.[33] The de facto ability to act with unrestricted capacity is the core of statehood and therefore extremely important for the practice of both international and state law[34]

---

26 Doehring, *Völkerrecht*, 199; Michael Schweitzer, *Staatsrecht III, Staatsrecht, Völkerrecht, Europarecht*, 7th edition (Heidelberg: C.F. Müller Verlag, 2000), 196; Epping, "Völkerrechtssubjekte", 58; Kimminich and Hobe, *Einführung*, 96.

27 *Western Sahara, Advisory Opinion*, I.C.J. Reports 1975, para. 94.

28 Friedrich August Freiherr von der Heydte, *Völkerrecht, Ein Lehrbuch*, Volume I (Cologne: Verlag für Politik und Wirtschaft, 1958), 201.

29 Epping, "Völkerrechtssubjekte", 58.; Doehring, *Völkerrecht*, 199.

30 Crawford, *The Creation of States*, 25.

31 Ibid.

32 Heike Krieger, *Das Effektivitätsprinzip im Völkerrecht* (Berlin: Duncker & Humblot, 2000), 89; Geiß, "*Failed States*", 127.

33 James Leslie Brierly, *The Law of Nations: An Introduction to the International Law of Peace* (Oxford: Clarendon Press, 1955), 55.

34 Krieger, *Das Effektivitätsprinzip im Völkerrecht*, 89; Dahm, Delbrück, and Wolfrum, *Völkerrecht*, 129; Karl Doehring, "Effectiveness," *Encyclopedia of Public International Law* 7 (1984), 71.

The effectiveness of government is, in fact, an extension of the principle of effectiveness in international law.[35] Although various aspects of the function and legal character of the principle of effectiveness are widely discussed in international law, effectiveness is widely accepted as a general principle of international law according to Article 38 I (c) of the Statute of the International Court of Justice.[36] International lawyers interpret differently the implementation of the principle of effectiveness as a criterion of 'government', largely because there is no strict definition of the principle.[37] However, it is generally accepted that the principle of effectiveness finds its implementation in existing statehood theoretically through the internal and external aspects of the effectiveness of the government.[38]

The internal aspect of effectiveness is the state's capacity to maintain order and govern the permanent population of the defined territory. The external aspect of effectiveness is the state's capacity to represent its people in the international arena, participate in international relations, and exercise its rights and fulfil its duties under international law.[39] In many cases the necessity of effectiveness is pointed out.[40] Because of the lack of clarity about the principle of effectiveness, the description of the internal and external aspects of the effectiveness of a state also differs from one international lawyer to another and from one period to another. Various Security Council resolutions directly or indirectly link human rights and non-democratic regimes to the threat to international peace and security. Resolution 688 (1991) on the Kurds in Iraq and Resolution 841 (1993) on Haiti are examples.[41] However, neither the legitimacy of government nor the violation of fundamental human rights can be classified as elements of the effectiveness of government. These can only be required by the international community for the recognition of new states and governments.[42]

---

[35] Krieger, *Das Effektivitätsprinzip im Völkerrecht*, 89; Eberhard Menzel, *Völkerrecht* (München: C.H. Beck 1962), 111.

[36] Georg Dahm, *Völkerrecht*, Volume I (Stuttgart: W. Kohlhammer, 1958), 19; Krieger, *Das Effektivitätsprinzip im Völkerrecht*, 53.

[37] Stein and von Buttlar, *Völkerrecht*, 100; Alfred Verdross, *Völkerrecht* (Vienna: Springer Verlag, 1964), 133.

[38] Rotter, "Staat", 381.

[39] Stein and von Buttlar, *Völkerrecht*, 99; Krieger, *Das Effektivitätsprinzip im Völkerrecht*, 88.

[40] Island of Palmas Case, Award7 of April 1928, UNRIAA II, 829 (839 et. seq.); Aaland Suppl. No. 3 (1920), 3. Island Case of 1920, L.N.O.J., Spec. Suppl. No. 3 (1920), 3.

[41] S/Res/688 (1991) and S/Res/841 (1993).

[42] Boleslaw A. Boczek, *International Law, A Dictionary* (Lanham, Maryland: The Scarecrow Press, Inc., 2005), 121.

The principle of effectiveness mainly determines the absence of effective government—a state's loss of capacity to act in its territory or in the international arena. In 1893 Frantz Despagnet described an ineffective state as follows:

> L'extinction de tout gouvernement par le fait d'une anarchie continue que rend impossible les relations internationales, aucune authorité n'est suffisement assise pour répresenter la collectivité des habitants de l'Etat.[43]

The Absence of Effective Government within a State Territory

International lawyers and institutions variously describe the appearance of the absence of effective government within a state territory. Boutros Boutros-Ghali described the internal emergence of the phenomenon as follows:

> A feature of such conflict is the collapse of state institutions, especially the police and judiciary, with resulting paralysis of governance, a breakdown of law and order, and general banditry and chaos. Not only are the functions of government suspended, but its assets are destroyed or looted and experienced officials are killed or flee the country. This is rarely the case in inter-state wars.[44]

The absence of effective government can emerge within a state in two ways: 1) the collapse of state institutions and 2) internal armed conflict and chaos. Each is a reason for and consequence of the other. The absence of law and order, the inability to provide political goods, and the fragmentation of authority are consequences of the collapse of state institutions. Humanitarian disasters are a consequence of both this collapse and the resulting conflict.

The Collapse of State Institutions

The collapse of state institutions and apparatus is the dominant element in the absence of effective government. This collapse should be understood in the broad sense and not restricted to the current governing authority, although the lack of a governing authority makes the phenomenon more visible and exacerbates the long-term ruin of the political, economic, and social structure. The common perception of the collapse of state institutions is seen clearly in both Security Council and General Assembly resolutions. When the Security Council described the 'rapid deterioration and widespread material damage' in Somalia in Resolution 733 (1992) and referred to the situation's 'unique

---

43 Frantz Despagnet, *Cours de Droit International Public*, 2nd edition (Paris, 1893), 128.

44 Boutros Boutros-Ghali, *Introduction, The United Nations and Somalia 1992–1996*, The United Nations Blue Books Series, Volume VIII (New York: United Nations Publication, 1996), 45–49.

character with its deteriorating, complex and extraordinary nature' in Resolution 794 (1992), the international community clearly did not limit the definition to the absence of a current government.[45] Similarly, the General Assembly described the 'widespread disruption of public facilities' in Somalia in Resolution 46/176 (1991).[46] After the assassination of Samuel Doe on 9 September 1990 the Secretary-General described the situation in Liberia as follows:

> The immediate origins of the three-year war can be traced to the complete breakdown of law and order and civil authority which accompanied the overthrow in 1990 of the regime headed by President Samuel Doe.[47]

The state can realise both its internal and external sovereignty through political institutions, legislative and executive apparatus, and independent jurisdiction. In the absence of effective government, these political institutions either do not exist or are not executable. In most African states established according to the Westphalia model after decolonisation and most states under the influence of the Cold War, the legislative institutions were the first to be affected by internal conflict. In many states in Africa, attempts at parliamentary democracy quickly came to an end with the abolition of the parliamentary system. Dictators such as Doe in Liberia and Barré in Somalia unified all state functions under their power. After only nine years of independence, Somalia's parliament was dissolved in 1969.[48]

The long-term lack of political decision-making power gradually ruins the administrative structure, causing difficulties for state enforcement of taxation and other duties.[49] The police and military are either abolished or highly politicised, as in Somalia, where military authority during the Barré regime was based on clanship.[50] The absence of a current governing authority is the last phase in the absence of effective government. The executive institutions—president and council of ministers—are either no longer in power or restricted

45 S/Res/733 (1992) of 23 January 1992; S/Res/794 (1992) of 3 December 1992.

46 GA/Res/46/176 of 19 December 1992, Also, Boutros Boutros-Ghali described the situation of Somalia as follows: '[...] hardly any governmental infrastructure, physical infrastructure is largely non-existent'; S/23829 of 21 April 1992 para. 56.

47 S/25402 5 of 12 March 1993.

48 Bartl, *Die unilaterale humanitäre Intervention*, 28.

49 Mary Kaldor, *Neue und alte Kriege: Organisierte Gewalt im Zeitalter der Globalisierung* (Frankfurt: Suhrkamp Verlag, 2000), 147.

50 David J. Harris, *Cases and Material on International Law*, 6th edition (London: Sweet & Maxwell, 2004), 101; Robert Rotberg, "Failed State in a World of Terror," *Foreign Affairs* 81 (2002), 4, 132; Liebach, *Die unilaterale humanitäre Intervention*, 26, 47; Bartl, *Die unilaterale humanitäre Intervention*, 78.; Daniel Thürer, "Der Wegfall effektiver Staatsgewalt 'the Failed State'", in *Der Wegfall effektiver Staatsgewalt: "The Failed State"*, Berichte der Deutsche

to a part of the country. A 1992 United Nations report described Somalia's 'barely existing administrative structure' already in mid-1991, shortly after the overthrow of Barré on 27 January.[51] Boutros-Ghali referred to the country's 'absence of a government and governing authority' in a letter of 24 November 1992.[52]

The absence of political institutions and long-term chaos and armed conflict disrupt economic and social infrastructure and vice versa. The Secretary General mentioned this in a report on Liberia on 30 August 1991:

> The civil conflict that raged across Liberia during most of 1990 completely disrupted the country's social, administrative and economic infrastructure. Over 1 million Liberians were forced to abandon their homes.[53]

Without a functioning legislature, there is little regulation of the national economy or external trade, and irrational decisions in favour of the conflict parties limit the state's capacity to act in the area of the economy. The state can neither take part in production nor perform infrastructural roles such as traffic control and information dissemination, minimal conditions for economic activities. A UNDP report described Liberia during the civil war as '[...] in the midst of a serious economic and financial crisis [with the result that the] standard of living has declined over the past 8–10 years'.[54] Seaports and international airports pass from government control to conflict parties, as in Somalia.[55]

The state's economic ineffectiveness produces, or at least reinforces, the criminal economy connected with illegal drugs and the arms trade or the exploitation of national resources. In much of sub-Saharan Africa, the black market rules state economies, and in many cases the remains of governments appear to be part of this activity.[56] Security Council Resolution 1653 (2006) clearly describes the links between the black market and the chaotic situation in the Great Lakes region:

Gesellschaft für Völkerrecht 34, ed. Daniel Thürer, Matthias Herdegen, and Gerhard Hohloch (Heidelberg: C.F. Müller Verlag 1996), 12; Samuel M. Makinda, *Seeking Peace from Chaos—Humanitarian Intervention in Somalia* (Boulder, Colorado: Lynne Rienner Publishers, 1993), 24.

51 S/23693 of 11 March 1992.

52 Letter of 24 November 1992 from the Secretary-General.

53 GA/46/403 of 30. Aug. 1991.

54 UNDP, *Fourth Country Program for Liberia of 8 October* 1986, DP/CP/LIR/4.

55 Geiß, "*Failed States*", 29.

56 Kaldor, *Neue und alte Kriege*, 161; Volker Matthies, "Regionale Anarchie als globales Problem", in *Weltpolitik in neuen Jahrhundert*, ed. Karl Kaiser and Hans-Peter Schwarz (Bonn: Bundeszentrale für Politische Bildung, 2000), 29.

> [. . .] the link between the illegal exploitation of natural resources, the illicit trade in those resources and the proliferation and trafficking of arms is one of the factors fuelling and exacerbating conflicts [. . .] especially in the Democratic Republic of the Congo.

A government without its minimal political and economic institutions and infrastructure is no longer able to maintain its social structure. Essential public services, which are basic political goods, and physical infrastructure such as roads, railways, and harbours are limited or disappear.[57]

The Absence of Law and Order

The usual consequence of the long-term collapse of political institutions is the end of law and order. Because parliament is the first institution dissolved in the chaos, no laws or rules can be made, changed, or revoked. Absent or ineffective executive organs make the state unable to enforce laws, and juridical independence is a rule but not a reality.

On 7 August 1990 the Economic Community of West African States (ECOWAS) described such a situation in Liberia:

> The result of all this is a state of anarchy and the total absence of law and order in Liberia. Presently there is a government in Liberia which cannot govern and contending factions which are holding the entire population hostage.[58]

Many reports and letters of the UN Secretary-General to the Security Council also mention 'the absence of law and order in Somalia'.[59]

As a consequence of diminished central authority and the absence of law and order, the state can no longer provide the basic political goods for its citizens.[60] In the hierarchy of political goods, security takes first place. The state's function is both to provide security for its inhabitants within its borders and to protect them from danger from outside. When effective government breaks down, the state cannot provide minimal security within its borders. Unable to govern its own territory, it cannot eliminate external threats or attacks on the state and

---

57 Kreijen, *State Failure*, 3; Rotberg, "The Failure and Collapse of Nation-States", 2 et. seq.

58 ECOWAS Standing Mediation Committee, *Final Communiqué of the First Session of 7 August 1990*, imprinted by Marc Weller, ed., *Regional Peace-Keeping and International Enforcement: The Liberian Crisis* (Cambridge, UK: Cambridge University, 1994), 72 and 89. The 1990 National Conference in Banjul organised by Liberian groups to establish an interim government remarked on the absence of law and order. *Final Communiqué of the National Conference of All Liberian National Parties, Patriotic Fronts, Interest Groups and Concerned Citizens of 29 August 1990*.

59 S/23693 of 11 March 1992, para 77; Letter of 24 November 1992; S/24859 of 27 November 1992.

60 Rotberg, "The Failure and Collapse of Nation-States", 3.

social order. Many Security Council resolutions have mentioned this issue. For example, Security Council Resolution 1653 (2000) invoked the responsibility of the governments of the Democratic Republic of the Congo and Burundi to protect their populations, pointing out the former's duty to enforce the arms embargo and the latter's duty to combat cross-border trafficking of illicit small arms.[61] In most cases, if there is any government, government forces threaten rather than protect the population.[62]

The state's inability to prevent outside attacks or deflect outside threats is evident mostly when other states interfere; the state can neither ensure its territorial integrity nor defend its territory.[63] With no central government to guarantee the security and protection of the population, these functions can be performed only by the private sector or ad hoc.[64] For example, after 25 years of civil war between 1975 and 1990, Lebanon had achieved some degree of stability by early 2006, but the war between Israel and Hezbollah in July 2006 clearly showed its limited ability to govern its territory and protect its people from outside threats.[65]

The political goods of essential education and health services deteriorate in the absence of effective government, functioning only in the capital city and surroundings and only with limited capacity. The General Assembly pointed out the 'widespread disruption of public facilities and services' in Somalia in Resolution 46/176 of 19 December 1991.[66] Poor education and low life expectancy fuel long-term problems. In Afghanistan illiteracy is estimated at 70 percent, and the average life expectancy is only 40 years (compared with 47 years in Africa).[67] Rising infant mortality and HIV prevalence rates are other markers of the absence of effective government. Approximately 71 percent—more than 28 million—of the world's population living with HIV or AIDS lived in sub-Saharan Africa in 2002.[68]

In the absence of effective government, the state's ability to fulfil its responsibility to maximise the welfare and personal prosperity of its citizens is strongly

61 S/Res/1653 (2000) of 27 January 2006. S/Res/1663 (2006) of 24 March 2006 concerning Sudan.

62 Kreijen, *State Failure*, 89.

63 Zartman, "Posing the Problem of State Collapse", 1–5.

64 Rotberg, "Failed State in a World of Terror", 132.

65 *Allison Leung*, "Lebanon, the History of a Failed State", *International Affairs Journal at UC Davis*, August 30, 2006, http://davisiaj.com/content/view/251/1/ (accessed October 9, 2006). Rotberg ("The Failure and Collapse of Nation-States", 48) described Lebanon as a weak state in 2003.

66 GA/R/46/176 of 19 December 1991.

67 Siegmar Schmidt, "Ambivalente Entwicklungen in Afrika und die internationale Gemeinschaft", *Jahrbuch internationale Politik* 25 (2004), 299.

68 Ibid.

compromised. It cannot supply even minimal public goods such as drinking water, public transportation, and energy.[69] Standards of living deteriorate even with abundant natural resources, as in Afghanistan and the Democratic Republic of the Congo. The population risks food scarcity, sometimes exacerbated by climatic conditions, and widespread hunger. Peter Penfold, former British High Commissioner to Sierra Leone, notes that 'The tragedy of Sierra Leone is that her people are among the poorest in the world while the country is among the richest'.[70]

The collapse of state institutions leads to the fragmentation of authority, which is manifest in two ways. The first is the presence of more than one governing authority, as in Liberia in 1992 and Zaire (later the Democratic Republic of the Congo) in 1993. Zaire had two concurrent governments and two concurrent parliaments between March and October of that year.[71] In Liberia five people declared themselves president and two different governments and parliaments coexisted.[72] Another type of fragmentation of authority is filling the power vacuum with different groups. With the collapse of state institutions and armed conflict, either no state institution controls the entire territory or a state institution is restricted to the capital city, as in Somalia, Liberia, and the Democratic Republic of the Congo.[73] The power vacuum that emerges[74] is filled by many groups, militias, or warlords governing different parts of the state territory. Lynda Chalker, former British Minister of State for Overseas Development, described the fragmentation of Somalia in 1992:

> There is no generally accepted government and the country has fallen into the hands of feuding clans. Each claims to represent the legitimate Government of Somalia, but in practice each represents only a specific sub-clan.[75]

Sometimes the government can control part of the territory. For example, the Congolese government was in control of one-third of the country, which consisted of four micro-states, between 1996 and the Sun City Convention

---

[69] Kaldor, *Neue und alte Kriege*, 161; Matthies, "Regionale Anarchie als globales Problem", 29.

[70] V.A.B. Davies, "Sierra Leone: Ironic Tragedy," *Journal of African Economies* 9 (2000), 3, 349. Rotberg, in *The Failure and Collapse of Nation-States*, 2 et seq., also mentioned enabling citizens to participate freely, openly, and fully in politics and the political process as a important political good.

[71] Kreijen, *State Failure*, 75.

[72] Thürer, "*Der Wegfall effektiver Staatsgewalt*"?, 25.

[73] Geiß, "*Failed States*", 42.

[74] Rotberg, "Failed State in a World of Terror", 132.

[75] Parliamentary Debates (Commons), vol. 205, col. 1089 of 12 March 1992, published by Stefan Talmon, "Recognition of Governments: An Analysis of the New British Policy and Practice," *British Yearbook of International Law* 63 (1992), 237.

of 2002–2003. Even if the main part of the territory is under the control of warlords, none is able to govern the whole.[76] After the rebellion against the Armed Forces of Liberia turned into fighting between different ethnic groups, the government could only control the capital city of Monrovia.[77] In Somalia opposition groups that had fought against Siad Barré under the United Somali Congress later fought each other, so that the capital and other parts of the country were divided between these groups.[78]

'Internal Armed Conflict' with a Trans-border Dimension

In the absence of effective government, the political, economic, and social ruin of the state is accompanied by long-term armed conflict, which has both internal and global dimensions.[79] Such conflicts first appear as classic civil wars, with an effective government still in place, and later take on a different dimension. Conflicts such as those in Afghanistan, the Democratic Republic of the Congo, Liberia, and Somalia have been described in the literature as 'a relapse to Hobbes 'primitive state',[80] 'new wars',[81] 'private wars',[82] 'post-national wars', 'ethnic-political conflicts', and 'complex emergencies'.'[83]

Conflict in the Case of the Absence of Effective Government

The most important difference between the armed conflicts described above and classic civil war is the clear aims of the conflict parties in a civil war. In the absence of effective government, no group is militarily organised, politically identified, or striving for the autonomy or independence of a territory of the state.[84] Neither the aims of the conflict parties nor their alliances are clear because the conflict is rarely triggered by a political issue. Sometimes it is impossible to identify even the number of conflict parties or the differences

---

76 Kreijen, *State Failure*, 87.

77 Ibid., 79.

78 Geiß, "*Failed States*", 29.

79 Liebach, *Die unilaterale humanitäre Intervention*, 3.

80 Daniel Thürer, "Der Wegfall effektiver Staatsgewalt 'the Failed State'", in *Der Wegfall effektiver Staatsgewalt: "The Failed State"*, Berichte der Deutsche Gesellschaft für Völkerrecht 34, ed. Daniel Thürer, Matthias Herdegen, and Gerhard Hohloch, 1996, 12.

81 Kaldor, *Neue und alte Kriege*, 200.

82 Erich J. Hobsbawm, *Das Gesicht des 21. Jahrhunderts, Hat der Staat noch einen Sinn* (Munich: Carl Hanser Verlag GmbH & Co, 2000), 89.

83 Raimo Väyrynen, *The Age of Humanitarian Emergencies* (Helsinki: WIDER Research for Action, 1996), 25.

84 Thürer, *Der Wegfall effektiver Staatsgewalt im Völkerrecht*, 13.

between them.[85] The fragmentation of the conflict parties is determined mainly along ethnic, religious, and cultural lines or as a battle over the distribution of resources.[86] There were more than 15 conflict parties during the civil war in Somalia in the 1990s[87] and 17 in the civil war in Bosnia-Herzegovina in 1992.[88] In almost every case of the absence of effective government, these groups' power to govern is restricted to one part of the country. On 13 September 1992 the European Political Co-operation noted that, 'In the view of the Community and its member States, none of the Somali factions can lay claim to speak as the legitimate authority in Somalia'.[89]

The second characteristic that distinguishes these conflicts from civil war is their duration. Internal armed conflicts last longer than civil wars—and are usually less intense—because of the absence of clear parties and aims. A 2001 World Bank study found that wars that started after 1980 lasted three times longer than those that began in the preceding two decades.[90] Violence is directed toward the government, if there is one. If not, groups fight each other, changing alliances over time. The opposition groups in Somalia fought together against Barré in 1990 but started to fight each other after his downfall in 1991.[91] The mudjaheddin groups in Afghanistan fought together against the Communist Party during the Cold War, but after the end of communism fought each other until the Taliban dominated most of the territory. The internal armed conflict between the Liberian Army and rebel groups in the 1980s turned into a conflict between ethnic groups in the 1990s; by 1995 more than seven major opposition groups were involved in the fighting.[92] Natural resources such as oil in the Sudan and diamonds in Sierra Leone also determine the duration and intensity of armed internal conflict.[93] Long-term and

---

85 Cristopher Daase, *Kleine Kriege—Große Wirkung. Wie unkonventionelle Kriegsführung die internationale Politik verändert* (Baden-Baden: Nomos Verlag, 2002), 53.

86 Kalala Ilunga Matthiessen, *Die Demokratische Republik Kongo, eine Analyse aus staatstheoretischer, verfassungsrechtlicher und völkerrechtlicher Sicht* (Münster, Germany: Waxmann Verlag GmbH, 2005), 16; Thürer, *Der Wegfall effektiver Staatsgewalt im Völkerrecht*, 13.

87 Daase, *Kleine Kriege—Große Wirkung*, 53.

88 Liebach, *Die unilaterale humanitäre Intervention*, 32.

89 Geiß, "*Failed States*", 30.

90 Paul Collier, Anke Hoeffler, and Mans Söderbom, "On Duration of Civil War", Policy Research Working Paper 2681 (Washington, DC: World Bank), www.econ.worldbank.org/programmes/conflict.

91 Kreijen, *State Failure*, 68.

92 Ibid., 79.

93 Michael L. Ross, "How Do Natural Resources Influence Civil War? Evidence from Thirteen Cases", *International Organisation* 58 (2004), 1, 35; Markus Goldmann, "Sierra Leone: African Solution to African Problems", *Max Planck Yearbook of United Nations Law* 9 (2005), 457.

low-intensity armed conflict can destroy the entire state structure, as happened in an extreme form in Sierra Leone in the 1990s.[94]

The third characteristic of armed internal conflict in the absence of effective government is internationalisation. Along with an increase in internal armed conflicts after 1949 came an increase in the quantity and complexity of foreign intervention. In some cases, the distinction between internal conflict and international war has blurred even when wars have been waged mainly within states.[95]

Internal conflict can be internationalised in different ways. First, armed conflicts are both the cause and result of the actions of neighbouring states and sub-state actors. Especially in sub-Saharan Africa, states interfere in the internal conflicts of their neighbours, a point that must be considered to understand the armed internal conflict in the Democratic Republic of the Congo. The conflict had absorbed Rwanda and Uganda by 1997 and Angola, Chad, Namibia, the Sudan, and Zimbabwe after 1997.[96] The internal armed conflict in Liberia that began in the 1980s spilled over into Sierra Leone by early 1991, and by 1995, Guinea and Côte d'Ivoire were used as bases of operation by some Liberian movements.[97] Internal armed conflicts in Guinea and Sierra Leone are so interdependent that their causes and consequences cannot be separated.[98] Second, the intervention of the international community can internationalise armed internal conflict, as in Afghanistan and Iraq.

The Place of Internal Conflict in International Law

In the literature of international law, some authors define internal armed conflicts as civil wars,[99] while others differentiate between civil war and non-international conflicts.[100] The Security Council uses different terms and does not clearly distinguish conflict situations in the absence of effective

---

94 Karl J. Holsti, *Political Sources of Humanitarian Emergencies*, Research for Action Paper no. 36 (Helsinki: UNU/WIDER, 1997), 165.

95 Dietrich Schindler, "Different Types of Armed Conflicts", *Recueil des cours/Académie de Droit International de La Haye*, 163 (1979), 2, 126.

96 Kreijen, *State Failure*, 76.

97 Ibid., 79.

98 Volker Böge, *Von Muschelgeld und Blutdiamanten. Traditionale Konfliktbearbeitung in zeitgenössischen Gewaltkonflikten* (Hamburg: Schriften des Deutschen Übersee-Institut, 2004), 8.

99 Doehring, *Völkerrecht*, 276; Robert Zischg, *Nicht-internationaler bewaffneter Konflikt und Völkerrecht, Zur Zulässigkeit der Konfliktparteien durch dritten Staaten* (Baden Baden: Nomos, 1996), 31.

100 Thomas Bruha and Markus Krajewski, "Bürgerkrieg", in *Völkerrecht*, ed. Ignaz Seidl-Hohenveldern (Neuwied, Germany: Luchterhand-Fachverlag, 2001), 46.

government. For example, the Somalia conflict was described as civil strife in Resolution 837 (1993) and an inter-clan conflict in Resolution 865 (1993).[101]

In modern international law, only Common Articles 2 and 3 of the four Geneva Conventions define war and the difference between international and non-international armed conflicts. However, the Geneva Conventions only rudimentarily grasped the complexity and legal implications of different kinds of conflict. The difference between war and the resort to force short of war vanishes in classical international law in Common Article 2, but in Common Article 3 'non-international armed conflict' is defined only as occurring within a territory and lacking an international dimension.[102]

Article 1 of Protocol II of 1979 ('Material field of application') additional to the Geneva Convention of 12 August 1949 more clearly defines non-international conflict and the question of the legal implementation of international humanitarian law in such cases, enlarging the material field to apply to conflicts which

> [...] take place in the territory of a High Contracting Party between its armed forces and dissident armed forces or other organized armed groups which, under responsible command, exercise such control over a part of this territory as to enable them to carry out sustained and concerted military operations and to implement this protocol.

Although Article 1 of Protocol II falls short of a clear definition of non-international armed conflict, the second paragraph points out that 'Situations of internal disturbances and tensions, such as riots, isolated and sporadic acts violence and other acts of similar nature' do not fall under international humanitarian law.[103]

In general, then, it could be said that armed conflict in the absence of effective government does not fail under international law. However, each case should be analysed individually. In practice, international law has mostly ignored the internationalisation of internal civil wars through intervention by a third country or deployment of UN forces.[104]

---

101 S/Res/865 (1993) of 22 September 1993.

102 Schindler, "Different Types of Armed Conflicts", 125–126; Boczek, *International Law, A Dictionary*, 420; Zischg, *Nicht-internationaler bewaffneter Konflikt und Völkerrecht*, 43.

103 Protocol Additional to the Geneva Conventions of 12 August 1949 and relating to the Protection of Victims of Non-International Armed Conflicts (Protocol II), 8 June 1977; Schindler, "Different Types of Armed Conflicts", 126; Zischg, *Nicht-internationaler bewaffneter Konflikt und Völkerrecht*, 1996, 43.

104 Schindler, "Different Types of Armed Conflicts", 127.

Human Casualities

The collapse of state institutions and internal armed conflict have an immediate impact on the humanitarian situation. Katarina Tomasevski's chronology of human rights violators between 1967 and 1999 shows that most of the states responsible for such violations had faced the breakdown of effective government.[105] Human casualties are higher in the absence of effective government than in a civil war, and civilians are the first to be affected when effective government breaks down. The link among the absence of effective government, massive loss of life, and displacement of the population in Liberia was emphasised at the First National Conference that begun under ECOWAS on 27 August 1990.[106]

Factors that play an important role in this relationship include the duration of the conflicts and the use of civilians as strategic instruments. Moreover, because most internal armed conflicts are only superficially political, people in the conflict territories are either active fighters or passive participants by virtue of their ethnic, religious, or clan identities. The lack or insufficiency of infrastructure to deliver the minimal political goods in such states has made it impossible to send humanitarian assistance.[107] The government, if there is one, is often actively responsible for the human disaster through its repression, as in Liberia and Somalia.[108] After Monrovia was divided by the troops of Samuel Taylor[109] and Charles Johnson,[110] government troops under Samuel Doe massacred the civilian population on the basis of ethnicity, with the claim that they helped the rebels at the beginning of 1990.[111]

---

[105] Katarina Tomaševski, *Responding to Human Rights Violations*, 1946–1999 (The Hague: Martinus Nijhoff Publishers, 2000), 27.

[106] *Final Communiqué of the National Conference of All Liberian National Parties, Patriotic Fronts, Interest Groups and Concerned Citizens of 29. August 1990*, (Weller, ed., *Regional Peacekeeping*, 89).

[107] S/Res/794 (1992) of 3 December 1992 stated that, '[...] the magnitude of human tragedy caused by the conflict in Somalia, further exacerbated by the obstacles being created to the distribution of humanitarian assistance, constitutes a threat to international peace and security'.

[108] Harold D. Nelson, *Somalia: A Country Study* (Washington., DC: American University Press, 1982), 186.

[109] The National Patriotic Front of Liberia (NPFL) under Charles Taylor.

[110] The Independent National Patriotic Front of Liberia under Prince Johnson.

[111] *Dirk van den Boom, Bürgerkrieg in Liberia: Chronologie—Protagonisten—Prognose* (Münster, Germany: Lit Verlag, 1993), 20. Global Security.org points out that although the Liberian conflict was on one level an attempt by Americo-Liberians to re-establish themselves as the dominant political force, the war was not about tribes seeking dominance over one another. Charles Taylor led the invasion in the name of addressing the ill treatment of the Gio and Mano tribes, which motivated these two groups to join his movement. When the Taylor rebels

The rate of civilian casualties worldwide rose from approximately 5 percent of the population at the beginning of the 20th century to 90 percent between 1990 and 1999.[112] Many Security Council resolutions mention the human disaster in Somalia.[113] As a consequence of the ethnic massacres in Rwanda, approximately half a million of a population of 7.8 million were killed, 2.6 million were internally displaced, and another 2.6 million fled to Burundi, Tanzania, and Zaire.[114] Between January 1991 and mid-1992, an estimated 300,000 Somalis died of starvation after the fall of the Barré regime.[115] Between 1988 and 1995, 17,000 people were killed in Colombia for political reasons, and 1,451 people disappeared.[116]

In many countries dealing with the breakdown of effective government, the recruitment of child soldiers has been an important human rights issue. Approximately 300,000 children are reported to have participated in military activities in more than 50 countries, including some 50,000 young solders in Myanmar and 10,000 in Sierra Leone. Child soldiers as young as eight have been used by both sides in the civil conflicts in Colombia[117] and Sri Lanka.[118]

Another consequence of the absence of effective government is an increase in external and internal refugees. According to UNHCR, by 1993 an estimated 1 million Somalis had fled their country, many to refugee camps in Ethiopia and Kenya, and 35,000 had been internally displaced. Pakistan has been the most important destination for refugees from Afghanistan. Since the 1990s there have been two refugee camps in Ghana, one occupied by refugees from the Liberian civil war and the other by people fleeing human rights abuses in Togo.[119] Tanzania shelters refugees from Burundi, the Democratic

---

entered their home county, the conflict drew in the mostly Muslim Mandingoes. The Gio tribe soon formed a separate rebel force under Johnson, and a bloody three-way civil war began.

[112] *Promotion and Protection of the Rights of Children, Impact of Armed Conflict on Children*, A/51/306 of 26 August 1996, 9.

[113] S/Res/767 (1992) of 24 July 1992; S/Res/775 (1992) of 28 August 1992; S/Res/794 (1992) of 3 December 1992.

[114] *Washington Post*, July 21, 1994, A1.

[115] Kreijen, *State Failure*, 69; Michael Birnbaum, *Krisenherd Somalia: Das Land des Terrors und der Anarchie* (Munich, Heyne Verlag, 2002), 180.

[116] Dario Azzellini, "Kolumbien: 100 Jahre Krieg gegen die Bevölkerung," in *Politische Ökonomie der Gewalt*, ed. Werner Ruf (Opladen: Leske + Budrich Verlag, 2003), 236.

[117] Karns, Margaret P., and Karen A. Mingst, *International Organizations: The Politics and Processes of Global Governance* (Boulder, Colorado: Lynne Rienner Publishers, 2004).

[118] http://news.bbc.co.uk/2/hi/southasia/6144200.

[119] Bolante Akande Adetoun, "The Role and Function of Research in a Divided Society: A Case Study of the Niger-Delta Region of Nigeria," in *Researching Conflict in Africa, Inside and Experience*, ed. Elisabeth Porter et al. (New York, United Nations University Press, 2005), 56.

Republic of the Congo, and Uganda, in addition to Hutus and Tutsis from Rwanda.[120] Refugee camps often turn into 'proxy internal conflict locations'.[121,122] For various reasons, these camps are also rife with human rights abuses, not to mention health problems. According to a report of the International Committee of the Red Cross (ICRC), 75 percent of the people in many refugee camps are undernourished.[123]

External Aspects of Statehood

In the modern international legal order, states are still the most important legal subjects.[124] The UN Charter and the 1970 Declaration on Principles of International Law concerning Friendly Relations and Cooperation among States in Accordance with the UN Charter could be accepted as the basis for the rights and duties of states.[125] Some authors have attempted to specify and classify these rights and duties in reference to Articles 2, 25, 55, and 56 of the UN Charter and the Declaration on Principles of International Law concerning Friendly Relations and Cooperation among States,[126] but the complexity of the international legal order and relations between states and international organisations, as well as the dynamic evolution of international law, make such a classification almost impossible. Therefore, the direct and indirect consequence of the absence of central and de-central organs in the international area is generally demonstrated here.

---

120 Roderic Alley, *Internal Conflict and the International Community: Wars without End?* (Aldershot: Ashgate Publishing, 2004), 71.

121 Ibid., 81; Marie-Janine Calic, "Die Jugoslawienpolitik des Westens seit Dayton", *Aus Politik und Zeitgeschichte* 34 (1999), 22 et. seq.

122 In *The Ends of the Earth: A Journey at the Dawn of the 21st Century* (New York: Random House, 1996), 45–46, Robert D. Kaplan describes the complexity of the refugee problem in Sierra Leone as follows: 'As a consequence of the mayhem, 400,000 Sierra Leonians were internally displaced; 280,000 more fled to neighbouring Guinea; and another 100,000 fled to war-torn Liberia, even as 400,000 Liberians fled to Sierra Leone. The third largest city in Sierra Leone, Gondama, was a displaced persons camp, whose inhabitants were generally healthier than the population at large. With an additional 600,000 Liberians in Guinea and 250,000 more in Côte d'lvoire, the border regions of these four countries had become largely meaningless'.

123 Birnbaum, *Krisenherd Somalia*, 180.

124 Rebecca M.M. Wallace, *International Law* (London: Sweet & Maxwell, 2005), 61.

125 GA/Res/2625 (XXV) of 24 October 1970; Doehring, *Völkerrecht*, 82.

126 Verdross and Simma, *Universelles Völkerrecht*, 272–321; Crawford, *The Creation of States*, 40–41.

Absence of Central and De-central Organs

States fulfil their duties to the international community and use and vindicate their rights through (or by) their agents or organs in the international arena.[127] In the words of the Permanent Court of International Justice, 'states can act only by and through their agents and representatives'.[128] These organs can be classified as central and de-central.[129]

The executive organs of the state, heads of state, heads of government, and ministers of foreign affairs are the central authorities responsible for state representation.[130] While the unlimited representation of the head of state[131] appears more formal than substantial, the current government and its head and minister of foreign affairs have the main responsibility to fulfil the rights and duties of the state.[132] In the internal law order, a state's legislative organs also play an important role in international affairs by affirming acts of government or ratifying international treaties.[133]

The de-central organs mainly assist diplomatic and consular facilities in representing the state to foreign states and international organisations. These organs and their legal status are defined by Article 1 of the Vienna Convention on Diplomatic Relations (1961) and the Vienna Convention on Consular Relations (1963). The 'right of legation' consisting of active and passive rights is in fact based on the consent of both the sending and receiving states, according to Article 2 of the Vienna Convention on Diplomatic Relations. The juristic act between the sending state and the receiving state could appear as an expressly declared notification or an agreement between the receiving and sending states.[134]

Impact on Bilateral Diplomatic Relations

In the absence of effective government, states suffer from either the absence or ineffectiveness of central and de-central organs, which leads to international

[127] Dahm, Delbrück, and Wolfrum, *Völkerrecht*, 245; Johan Kaspar Bluntschli, *Das moderne Völkerrecht der zivilisierten Staaten* (Nördlingen: C.H. Beck, 1868), 27 et. seq.

[128] German Settlers in Poland Advisory Opinion, 10 September 1923, PCIJ, Ser. B, No. 6, 1–22.

[129] Brierly, *The Law of Nations*, 55.

[130] Dahm, *Völkerrecht*, 297; Article 7-2-a of Vienna Convention on the Law of Treaties, UN Treaty Series, http://treaties.un.org/Pages/Home.aspx?lang=en.

[131] Doehring, *Völkerrecht*, 214–215. The status of the head of state is based on customary law and on Article 7/2 of the Vienna Convention on the Law of Treaties.

[132] Ibid., 215.

[133] Geiß, "*Failed States*", 129.

[134] Robert L. Bledsoe and Boleslaw Boczek, *The International Law Dictionary* (Santa Barbara, California: ABC-CLIO, 1987), 94; Doehring, *Völkerrecht*, 216.

legal complications.[135] For example, the UN Secretary-General remarked on the lack of 'representation of Somali people in intergovernmental and international fora' in 1999.[136]

The absence of a state's executive organs both directly and indirectrly affects its representation in bilateral diplomatic relations. The direct consequence is that the executive organs cannot represent the country in relations with other states. The indirect consequence is that with no central organs, it is impossible either for the sending state to accredit new diplomatic representatives or for the receiving state to consent to the accreditation. The central organs essentially determine the representational capacity and legitimacy of the de-central agents[137] and are responsible for decisions about accrediting diplomatic missions.[138] In the absence of effective government, the sending state cannot notify the receiving state to end the function of diplomatic agents in accordance with Articles 9/2 and 42 of the Vienna Convention on Diplomatic Relations or break off or suspend diplomatic relations in accordance with Article 45. The legal status of current diplomatic representation is also problematic when the central government no longer exists.[139]

Material impossibility likewise determines consular relations. In the absence of effective government the sending state has little or no capacity to finance its diplomatic and consular activities in other countries and must close its facilities. Sierra Leone closed 18 embassies in 1989 for this reason.[140] When the Embassy of Somalia in Bonn could not longer pay its diplomats in 1992, the Superior Administrative Court of North Rhine-Westphalia received an application for social security assistance from a Somali diplomat.[141]

The other negative impact of the absence of effective government on diplomatic relations is the receiving state's inability to provide security for the diplomatic and consular facilities of sending states. When a state cannot take measures regulated by Article 44 of the Vienna Convention on Diplomatic Relations in the case of armed conflict because of material impossibility, the sending states recall their representatives either temporarily or indefinitely. Almost all

135 Rolf Knubben, *Die Subjekte des Völkerrechts—allgemeine Lehre von der vollen und beschränkten völkerrechtlichen Rechts—und Handlungsfähigkeit* (Stuttgart: W. Kohlhammer, 1928), 263.

136 S/1999/882 (1999) of 16 August 1999, para 63.

137 Geiß, "*Failed States*", 130.

138 Ibid.

139 Ibid., 128 et. seq.

140 Dahm, Delbrück, and Wolfrum, *Völkerrecht*, 293; Geiß, "*Failed States*", 133.

141 *Somali Diplomat Case, Case No. 8 B536/92*, Federal Republic of Germany, Superior Administrative Court (OVG) of North Rhine-Westphalia, 11 February 1992,94 ILR (1994), 597–608, 602. This decision was cancelled by the decision of the Federal Administrative Court of 29 February 1996 (BVerwG 5 C 23.95) (BVerwGE 100, 300).

sending states recalled their representatives from Liberia and Somalia for this reason.[142] Bulgaria, France, and Italy also temporarily recalled their diplomats from Kabul in 1992.[143]

Finally, the absence of effective government negatively affects the activity of consulates.[144] According to Article 5 of the Vienna Convention on Consular Relations, consular functions include traffic between states, economic and commercial interests of the sending state, and protection of citizens in the receiving state. The inability of a state to fulfil its consular functions in the absence of effective government particularly jeopardises the protection of citizens.[145]

Impact on Representation in Inter-state Fora

In general, the representation of states in international or regional organisations, as well as in international conferences or fora convened under the auspices of international organisations regarding treaties and negotiations, plays an important role in multilateral relations in current international law. The lack of an effective government makes it difficult to sign or implement treaties and negotiations and complicates state representation in regional and international organisations. For example, states are represented at the United Nations through permanent missions and the General Assembly. The absence of effective government affects current representation not in the permanent missions in New York and Geneva but in the General Assembly and other specialised UN organisations.[146] Somalia did not have representation in the General Assembly sessions between 1992 and 2000.[147]

Absence of the Ability to Exercise Rights and Duties under International Law

Without an effective government, a state either is unable to exercise its rights and fulfil its duties as a subject of international law or has limited capacity to exercise its rights in the international sphere.

---

142 Dahm, Delbrück, and Wolfrum, *Völkerrecht*, 293; Geiß, "*Failed States*", 135.

143 Eileen Denza, *Diplomatic Law, Commentary on the Vienna Convention on Diplomatic Relations*, 2nd edition (Oxford: Clarendon Press, 1998), 395.

144 Geiß, "*Failed States*", 139; Normally the current situation of diplomatic relations has no influence on consular relations. The exception could be the situation foreseen in Article 70 of the Vienna Convention on Consular Relations. The end of the consular function ruled in Section II of the Chapter of the Vienna Convention on Consular Relations is mainly interpreted according to the interests of the receiving and sending state.

145 Ibid., 134.

146 Ibid., 143.

147 Riika Koskenmäki, "Legal Implications Resulting from State Failure in Light of the Case of Somalia," *Nordic Journal of International Law* 73 (2004), 1, 13; Geiß, *Failed States*, 147.

Lack of Capacity to Exercise Rights

Absent or ineffective central and de-central organs restrict states' capacity to exercise their rights. A state without an effective government still has the right to make treaties, but this is a physical impossibility. States without central organs can neither conclude international treaties under Article 6 of the Vienna Convention on the Law of Treaties nor ratify agreements.

This lack of capacity is especially important if the treaties are part of international development policy.[148] For example, with no authority to conclude the Lomé IV Convention and Cotonou Partnership Agreement, Somalia could not benefit from the European Development Fund.[149] Many programs under the World Bank's development framework cannot be implemented because no authority is available to conclude the treaties.[150] The absence of effective government is also an obstacle to exercising rights under treaties that have already been concluded.

International efforts to reconstruct a state with no effective government suffer in the absence of a partner. Such efforts by the international community range from providing information on the current situation in the country to implementing peace-keeping operations under Chapters VI and VII of the UN Charter. Article 2/7 of the UN Charter on the non-intervention of the United Nations requires state consent to humanitarian relief from international organisations and other states.[151] Security Council Resolution 387 (1976) of 31 March 1976 states that it is 'the inherent and lawful right of every state, in the exercise of its sovereignty, to request assistance from any other state or group of states'.[152] A state without an effective government cannot request such assistance. Resolution 794 (1992) illustrated this fact when it noted that 'in Somalia there is no government that can be the interlocutor of the United Nations for the purposes of agreeing upon a humanitarian-assistance operation'.[153]

---

[148] K. van Hippel and A. Yannis, "The European Response to State Collapse in Somalia" in *European Approaches to Cries Management*, ed. Knud Erik Jorgensen (The Hague: Kluwer Law International, 1997), 78. Geiß, "*Failed States*", 152.

[149] "Should Somalia ask to accede to this Convention, the Council of Ministers shall act on the request and take a decision on that State's accession". Concerning the Lomé Convention (Court of 1st Instance) Case C-316/91, European Parliament v. Council of the European Union, Judgment of 2 March 1994, [1994] ECR 1–625.

[150] *Report of the Secretary-General on the Situation in Somalia*, UN Doc. S/1999/882, 16 August 1999, Para 72.

[151] A/Res/S/51/194 (1997) of 10 February 1997: '[...] humanitarian assistance should be provided with the consent of the affected country and in principle on the basis of an appeal of the affected country'; also A/Res/46/182 v. 19 December 1991.

[152] S/Res/387 (1976) of 31 March 1976, http://www.un.org/documents/sc/res/1976/scres76.htm.

[153] S/Res/794 (1992) of 3 December 1992.

The absence of an effective government makes it impossible for a state to take part in judicial proceedings in a foreign or international court because there is no person or institution to represent the state.[154] As mentioned above, the absence of effective government deprives a state of the finances and personnel to represent its economic and political interests and protect its citizens in a foreign country, according to the Vienna Convention on Diplomatic Relations and Vienna Convention on Consular Relations.

The Lack of Capacity to Full Duties

The lack or restricted effectiveness of the central organs hinders the fulfilment of international duties in good faith. A state with no effective government cannot observe treaties according to the general principle of *pact sunt servanda* in Article 26 of the Vienna Convention on the Law of Treaties.[155] The state could appear to default on its payment or fail to fulfil multinational treaties on human rights or in international humanitarian law. Such a state cannot meet its obligation under the Vienna Convention on Diplomatic Relations and Vienna Convention on Consular Relations. For example, it cannot protect the facilities, archives, property, and accommodation of the sending state in the territory in accordance with Articles 44 and 45 of the Vienna Convention on Diplomatic Relations.[156]

Without an effective government, a state cannot fulfil its duties as a member of an international organisation to hold a permanent mission or meet its financial obligation. Many states fail to fulfil their financial obligations to the United Nations under Article 17/2 of the UN Charter. Somalia failed to pay its financial contribution between 1993 and 2001,[157] and Liberia defaulted on its payments for two years, as reported by the Contribution Committee in session from 27 May to 20 June 1997.[158] This failure can in turn obstruct the state's use of its veto power in the General Assembly under Article 19 of the UN Charter.

[154] *Republic of Haiti v. Duvalier*, 626 NYS2d 472 (AD 1st Dept. 1995).

[155] Friedrich Berber, *Lehrbuch des Völkerrechts*, Volume I, Allgemeines Friedensrecht (Munich: C.H. Beck, 1975), 44; Geiß, "*Failed States*", 153.

[156] Horst Fischer, "Diplomatische und konsularische Beziehungen", in *Völkerrecht*, ed. Knut Ipsen (Munich: C.H. Beck, 1990), 432, 439.

[157] Since 1993 Somalia has repeatedly failed to pay its financial contribution, as noted in A/47/870 of 1993, A/48/853 (1994) of 21 January 1994, A/50/888 (1996) of 28 February 1996, (1997) of 16 September 1997, and A/52/788 (1998) of 4 February 1998.

[158] Geiß, "*Failed States*", 149.

Complications of the Absence of Effective Government for the People and the Territory

Two other constitutive elements of the state, people[159] and territory,[160] are most affected by the absence of effective government even if they do not determine the phenomenon. The differences between people exploited by the sides in a civil war play an important role in internal armed conflict and are exploited by dictators such as Doe in Liberia or Barré in Somalia to keep themselves in power.[161] In some countries this fragmentation goes so far that one group declares independence or autonomy in a part of the country, as in the secession of Somaliland and Puntland in Somalia and Abkhazia in Georgia. The missing authority can also lead to complications in territorial boundaries. The nominal territory loses its meaning when warlords control their own fiefdoms in the absence of government authority. In many states with civil war or armed conflict, the national authority is limited to the capital city and one or more specific ethnic zones. In Afghanistan, the Democratic Republic of the Congo, Somalia, and the Sudan, warlords have emerged as leaders of clans or other groups to control zones where the state authority has no power.[162] Recent Security Council resolutions have called into question the issue of state territory in the absence of effective government in relation to the problem of piracy in the Gulf of Aden.[163]

---

159 Unlike in political and social science, in international law "the people" is defined as the people under a state's authority in a defined territory. Neither unity, a common identity, nor a common political will determines the definition of the "people" in international law. Liebach, *Die unilaterale humanitäre Intervention*, 37; Rudolf Geiger, *Grundgesetz und Völkerrecht, die Bezüge des Staatsrechts zum Völkerrecht und Europarecht*, 2nd edition, (Munich: C.H. Beck, 1994), 21; Reinhold Zippelius, *Allgemeine Staatslehre*, 14th edition (Munich: C.H. Beck 2003), 73; Dahm, Delbrück, and Wolfrum, *Völkerrecht*, 126; Kay Hailbronner, "Der Staat als primares Völkerrechtssubjekt", in *Völkerrecht*, ed. Wolfgang Graf Vitzthum, 2nd edition (Berlin: de Gruyter Rechtswissenschaftenverlags, 2001), 190; Liebach, *Die unilaterale humanitäre Intervention*, 37.

160 Crawford, *The Creation of States*, 36; The third element, territory, is defined as a juridical unity in international law.

161 Geiß, "*Failed States*", 35.

162 Kreijen, *State Failure*, 96.

163 S/Res/1816(200) of 2 June 2008.

Chapter Two

Case Studies

Somalia and Afghanistan are chosen as case studies to explore the absence of effective government for several reasons. One of the most important is that each country is sui generis, showing different features of the phenomenon. While Somalia is a chronic and classic case of the long-term absence of effective government, the picture is not so clear in Afghanistan. Many international lawyers and international organisations classify Afghanistan as a 'failed state', but it is debatable to which phases of its history this label applies.

Another important difference between the two states is the reaction of the international community to the breakdown of effective government. In the aftermath of the Cold War, the issue of human rights shaped this reaction in Somalia, where the efforts of the international community were the first and most far-reaching ever to be based on this concept.[1] In Afghanistan, however, until the 1990s the United Nations, other international organisations, and non-governmental organisations (NGOs) restricted their activities to humanitarian assistance. These bodies became seriously involved in the country only after the United States and its allies intervened in 2001 with the justification of fighting terrorism under the slogan 'You are either with us or against us'. Shortly afterward, the United States and its allies invaded Iraq under the aegis of protecting collective security. Today both Afghanistan and Iraq are stark examples of the absence of effective government, especially Iraq with its 'collateral damage' from 'fighting terrorism'.

Finally, the international community's involvement in the reconstruction of these two countries has differed in spite of the common use of military means. The United Nations established itself as the main actor in the reconstruction of Somalia in early 1993 but gave up this role two years later after 18 U.S. soldiers were killed. Although the United Nations declared that the Afghan people were

---

1 Boutros Boutros-Ghali, introduction to *The United Nations and Somalia 1992–1996*, The United Nations Blue Books Series, Volume VIII (New York: United Nations Department of Public Information, 1996), 45.

the main actors in the reconstruction of their country, for almost six years the international community has been in Afghanistan under the claim of helping to rebuild the state.

Despite these differences, Afghanistan and Somalia share certain similarities. Both were once wealthy nations that today are among the world's poorest.[2] Both were affected by colonialism and the Cold War. Although Afghanistan was never colonised directly, its buffer state status defined its history during the colonial period as well as during the Cold War.

Somalia

This section briefly describes the history of Somalia from its position as a rich trade centre in the 10th century to its impoverished status in the 21st, in order to understand the roots of the absence of effective government. The section then focuses on the international community's response to the phenomenon in Somalia.

A Rich Trade Centre

From the 10th to the 17th centuries, Somalia's relationship with the outside world was based exclusively on trade. Especially in the 10th century, the Somali coast was a trans-shipment centre between Somalia and the rest of Africa, Egypt and the Arab world, Persia, and China.[3] Because of its geographical position, waves of immigrants from the Arabian Peninsulas settled in Somalia over more than 2,000 years. Most of the immigrants were Arabs from Yemen, Oman, and Persia, who mixed with the Somali people and established their own clans and coastal cities. From the 13th century, many rich trade cities along the coast were involved in trading with the Arab world, India, China, and the coast of East Africa.[4] After the 16th century, the Portuguese began to play a larger role in trade with Somalia.[5]

---

2 Ibid., 13.

3 Ahmet I. Samatar, *Socialist Somalia, Rhetoric and Reality* (London: Zed Books Ltd, 1998), 12.

4 Hans Krech, *Der Bürgerkrieg in Somalia 1988–1996* (Berlin: Verlag Köster, 1996), 9. Ibn Battuta, an Arab world traveler of the 14th century, described Mogadishu as a large, rich harbor city in 1331.

5 Ibid.

The Colonial Era

In the 18th and 19th centuries, British, North American, German, and French traders came on the scene.[6] Their arrival was accelerated by the 1869 opening of the Suez Canal, which gave Somalia a geostrategic meaning for the European powers. Consequently, by the end of the 19th century, Somalia was divided among five different colonial regimes. The British officially protected northern Somalia and brought the southwest corner of the Somali Peninsula under their influence.[7] The French annexed the territory known today as Djibouti, which was designated as French Somaliland. In 1893 Italy formally established a colony in southern Somalia, and Ethiopia absorbed the city-state of Harar.

Somalia achieved the right of self-determination in 1960, when the former British protectorate declared its independence. The Italian Trust Territory soon joined the new state, and the independent Somali Republic was proclaimed in July 1961. Kenya retained northeast Somalia after the final decolonization, and the French held Djibouti, which eventually proclaimed its independence in 1977.[8]

When the first constitution was adopted in June 1961, the new state of Somalia was established as a parliamentary democracy based on the Italian system.[9] In spite of a common language, religion, and cultural traditions,[10] however, the new state never managed to unite the former British protectorate and the former Italian trust territory for a combination of internal and external reasons. One of the most important was the different political, legal, administrative, and economic structures established by Italy and Great Britain during the colonial period. Different education systems using different languages spoken exclusively by the elite, as well as diverse economic conditions in the two former colonial territories, made it more difficult to establish a uniform state.[11]

6 Samatar, Socialistt Somalia, 16.

7 Jürgen Bartl, *Die Humanitäre Intervention durch den Sicherheitsrat der Vereinten Nationen, im: 'failed state', Das Beispiel Somalia* (Frankfurt: Peter Lang Publishing Group 1999), 23. Later this area was known as the Northern Frontier District of Kenya.

8 Ibid., 23 et.seq.; Matthies Volker, "Die UNO am Horn von Afrika: Die Missionen in Somalia, (UNOSOM I, UNITAF, UNOSOM II) und in Äthiopien (UMEE)" in *Praxis-Handbuch UNO, Die Vereinten Nationen im Lichte globaler Herausforderungen*, ed. Sabine von Schorlemer (Heidelberg: Springer Verlag, 2003), 43 et.seq.

9 Heinrich Scholler, "Somalias langer Weg zur neuen Staatlichkeit", *Recht in Afrika* 7 (2004), 2, 229.

10 Boutros-Ghali, introduction to *The United Nations and Somalia*, 9. The Somali people are remarkably homogeneous, all of Somali origin, speaking the same language, adhering to the same religion (Islam), and following similar cultural traditions.

11 Samatar, Socialist Somalia, 17.

Moreover, the concept of a 'state' was foreign to the inhabitants. Originally Somali society was composed of clans. The clan elders and chiefs were the main authorities, wielding immense influence on social and political life. Despite almost a century of colonial rule, the colonial administrations were generally limited to the cities and established no lasting infrastructure. The clan structure therefore did not essentially change. The disparity between the traditional clan system and the Westphalian state system could be clearly seen during the parliamentary period in the 1960s, when the political party system was used to further the aims of the clans rather than to promote democratic choice. While 18 parties participated in the first national election in 1964, the number reached more than 60 in the election of 1969.[12]

On the other hand, the colonial period also initiated the destruction of the traditional economic structure. This process was already visible in the latter half of the 19th century, when Richard Burton, visiting the region in 1850, reported that the fine cotton clothing manufactured in Harar was being replaced by cheaper European and North American products.[13]

The Cold World Period

Attempts were made to establish a parliamentary democracy in Somalia between 1961 and 1969.[14] The assassination of the first president of the newly independent state, Abdirashid Ali Shermake, by a group of army officers led by General Siad Barré on 21 October 1969 was the end of the political party system. The coup was defined as a Marxist revolution. The military dictatorship of Siad Barré (1969–1991) established a new political order based on a single-party state. The radical transformation of Somali society, which the regime called 'scientific socialism', lasted only until Barré's defeat in the Ogaden War between Somalia and Ethiopia in 1978.[15]

To further complicate the situation, the Cold War was beginning to influence these events in Somalia. Alternating support for Siad Barré from the United States and the Soviet Union kept him in power for more than 20 years.[16] While the Soviet Union supported the regime until the Ogaden War, the United States

12 Bartl, *Die Humanitäre Intervention*, 27.

13 Samatar, *Socialist Somalia*, 13.

14 Abdulqawi A. Yusuf, "Government Collapse and State Continuity: The Case of Somalia", *Italian Yearbook of International Law* 13 (2003), 13.

15 Christiane E. Philipp, "Somalia—A Very Special Case", *Max Planck Yearbook of United Nations Law* 9 (2005), 1, 521.

16 Michael Birnbaum, *Krisenherd Somalia: Das Land des Terrors und der Anarchie* (Munich: Heyne Verlag, 2002), 181.

supported Barré against Ethiopia and the Soviet Union from 1978 to 1990.[17] Intensified by the intervention of the two superpowers, the Ogaden War was the cruellest armed conflict in Africa since the Second World War.[18] The arms and military advice of the Cold War powers exacerbated the brutality of this proxy war, leading to a humanitarian catastrophe in the 1980s.

The first civil war during the Cold War and the second immediately after the Cold War ended were supported not only by the superpowers but also by Italy, Egypt, Libya, and Saudi Arabia, which provided military and economic assistance to the Barré regime. Concurrently, the International Monetary Fund (IMF) and World Bank contributed loans to the acknowledged dictatorship in spite of the protests of Somali exiles and the purported democratisation policies of these bodies.[19]

After Somalia's military defeat by Ethiopia in the Ogaden War, Barré took brutal revenge against his opponents to stay in power. This marked the beginning of the first civil war, which subsequently influenced the political and economic structure of Somalia.[20] Two opposition movements arose to oust the Barré regime. Army officers who had tried to mount a coup against him established the Somali Salvation Front (SSF) in the northeast. Intellectuals, businessmen, and opposition ministers in London established the Somali National Movement (SNM) in 1981. Both movements had nationalistic goals supported by Ethiopia, which was under Soviet influence.[21]

By 1982 northern Somalia was rife with chaos, and the unrest spread to the central and southern regions. By the end of 1989, only the zone around Mogadishu was under the control of regular government troops, with warlords controlling the rest of the country.[22] As many as 50,000 people lost their lives in the fighting, and 500,000 Somalis left their homes seeking refuge in neighbouring states. The conflict left the national treasury bankrupt.[23] When Barré fled Kenya 1991 after 21 years of dictatorship, the country collapsed into anarchy.

After the Barré regime fell, the SSF and SNM joined forces to create a political-military organisation called the United Somali Congress (USC). The USC appointed Ali Mahdi Muhammad as president of an interim government

---

17 Scholler, "Somalias langer Weg", 230.

18 Mohammed D. Abdullahi, *Fiasco in Somalia: US—UN Intervention*: Occasional Paper 61 (Pretoria: African Institute of South Africa, 1995), 4.

19 Ibid.

20 Philipp, "Somalia—A Very Special Case", 523.

21 Bartl, *Die Humanitäre Intervention*, 34.

22 Birnbaum, Krisenherd Somalia, 179.

23 Boutros-Ghali, introduction to *The United Nations and Somalia*,11.

in January 1991. The rejection of this appointment by the military wing of the USC, led by General Mohammed Farah Aidid, was a portent of the second civil war. The two principal USC leaders, Ali Mahdi Muhammad and General Muhammed Farah Aidid, who had joined to oppose Barré, began to fight each other.[24] When all attempts by these two leaders and other opposition groups failed to oust Ali Mahdi Muhammed, battles followed among 14 different ethnic groups and clans. By the end of 1991, the second civil war had spread throughout the country, fought with arms that were the legacy of the Cold War.

With Somalia to all intents and purposes a state without a government at the end of 1991, the former British Protectorate of Somaliland declared independence under the name of Somaliland on 18 May.[25] The civil war, along with a drought and the dire economic crises, led to catastrophic rates of malnutrition.[26] During the second civil war 300,000 people lost their lives and approximately 1.7 million were displaced. Many people from the rural areas moved into Mogadishu and other cities such as Kismayo and Baidoa, where international organisations had established relief camps. Others sought refuge in the neighbouring countries of Djibouti, Ethiopia, Kenya, and Yemen.[27] Along with other Somali cities, Mogadishu, one of Africa's largest and richest harbours in the 14th century,[28] was completely dependent on economic aid by the beginning in the 1990s. The country could no longer feed its population. In 1992 Somalia was ranked among the world's 10 poorest nations, with a very low gross domestic product, rudimentary health care services, and diminished access to safe drinking water.[29]

The ideological confrontation between the two superpowers from the 1970s to the 1990s and the political and economic damage caused by both civil wars blocked Somalia's development and any potential for intellectual and political infrastructure. It was no coincidence that Barré immediately lost the civil war after the Cold War superpowers ceased to support his regime. Because of this support, the international community ignored the corruption, repression, and human rights violations in the country from the late 1970s until the beginning of the 1990s.

---

24 Philipp, "Somalia—A Very Special Case", 523.

25 Scholler, "Somalias langer Weg", 230.

26 Birnbaum, *Krisenherd Somalia*, 179.

27 Boutros-Ghali, introduction to *The United Nations and Somalia*, 15.

28 Krech, *Der Bürgerkrieg in Somalia 1988–1996*, 9.

29 Boutros-Ghali, introduction to *The United Nations and Somalia*, 13; Bartl, *Die Humanitäre Intervention*, 32.

Reflection of World Economic Policy

After 1980 world economic policies had various effects on the economic situation in Somalia. The important markets for Somalia's exports in the 1980s were broken through increasing international competition, leading to a dramatic decline in market prices.[30] Another reason for the country's economic crisis was the Structural Adjustment Program agreed between the IMF and World Bank and Barré in 1981. Under this program, Somalia was obligated to open its markets to foreign investors, who ended up profiting more than the Somali population.[31] In the end the economic planning measures of the Bretton Woods institutions, which were intended to improve the economic situation, made it worse than before, as explained in Chapter 8.[32]

In the early 1980s, after the Ogaden War, relief goods entered the country through bilateral and multinational relief programs. Given Somalia's weak economic capacity, this relief was an important component of the economy at the time.[33] The international community's misguided management of the famine relief, however, soon made Somalia dependent on imported food and destroyed the traditional local economy. Market prices for foodstuffs fell so low that local farmers abandoned production.

Response of the International Community

From 1978 to 1992 the international community restricted its role in Somalia to providing limited humanitarian assistance, in spite of the fact that the internal conflicts following the Ogaden War destroyed Somalia's political and economic infrastructure. The Office of the United Nations High Commissioner for Refugees (UNHCR), the World Food Programme (WFP), the United Nations Children's Fund (UNICEF), and other UN agencies and programmes began sending aid in the late 1970s, but their efforts were frequently disrupted by warring factions and armed bandits. Although the UN agencies and NGOs kept delivering relief despite the insecurity, only 30 percent of the aid was estimated to reach the people in need.[34]

---

30 Boutros-Ghali, introduction to *The United Nations and Somalia*, 13; Bartl, *Die Humanitäre Intervention*, 32.

31 Bartl, *Die Humanitäre Intervention*, 32.

32 Scholler, "Somalias langer Weg", 230.

33 Bartl, *Die Humanitäre Intervention*, 39.

34 U.N. Doc. S/23693, 11 March 1992, *Report of the Secretary General on the Situation in Somalia*; U.N. Doc. S/23829, 21 April 1992, *Report of the Secretary General on the Situation in Somalia*; Frank-Erich Hufnagel, *UN-Friedensoperation der zweiten Generation, vom Puffer zur neuen Treuhand* (Berlin: Duncker & Humblot, 1996), 158.

In fact, for 14 years the international community missed its chance to prevent conflict in Somalia. First, it did not recognise peace initiatives by the opposition groups. Neither the United Nations nor other international organisations showed much interest in April 1990 when various intellectuals, community leaders, business people, religious leaders, and elders presented their Somali Manifesto I, which called for a national reconciliation conference.[35] The international community also failed to support initiatives by neighbouring countries and regional organisations to find a solution to the civil war, including an attempt by Djibouti in July 1991 to discuss establishing peaceful and democratic relations with Somalia and early offers of assistance from Ethiopia and Eritrea.[36]

The first UN engagement in Somalia came on 23 January 1992,[37] after the end of the Cold War, following a letter sent by the Interim Prime Minister to the President of the Security Council citing the deteriorating situation in the country and the need for '[...] a program of effective action to end the fighting'.[38]

The situation in Somalia actually offered the United Nations an opportunity to assume the more effective role it had sought since the end of the Cold War. The United Nations first attempted to mediate a settlement between the Somali parties in January 1992, sending James Jonah, a special envoy from the UN Secretary-General, to Mogadishu. After this first engagement, the Security Council placed Somalia on its agenda. Resolution 733 was adopted on 23 January 1992, almost a year after Barré had been chased out of Mogadishu. In this resolution, the Security Council first cited the internal and regional consequences of

> [...] the rapid deterioration of the situation in Somalia and the heavy loss of human life and widespread material damage resulting from the conflict in the country and aware of its consequences on stability and peace in the region [...].[39]

---

35 Volker, "Die UNO am Horn von Afrika", 47; http://unhcr.org/home/RSDCOI/3ae6acc44.html.

36 Ibid.

37 Bartl, *Die Humanitäre Intervention*, 40. From December 1988 until 1992 the United Nations General Assembly was the only organ that placed the situation of Somalia on its agenda. However, the General Assembly dealt only with relief deliveries. A/Res/43/206 of the 20.12.1988, A/Res/44/178 (1989) of 19 December 1989, A/Res/45/229 (1990) of 21 February 1990, A/Res/46/176 (1991) of 19 December 1991.

38 Letter dated 11 January 1992 from the Prime Minister of Somalia to the President of the Security Council (UN Doc. S/23445 Annex I, 20 January 1992).

39 S/Res/733 (1992) of 23 January 1992.

From that point on the Security Council determined that the situation in Somalia was a threat to international peace and security under Article 39 of the UN Charter, opening the way for collective action.[40]

In Resolution 733 (1992) the Security Council focused on finding a solution to the civil war by ending hostilities, promoting reconciliation, and facilitating the delivery of humanitarian assistance. However, the United Nations mandate under Chapter VII of the UN Charter was restricted to '[...] a general and complete embargo on all deliveries of weapons and military equipment to Somalia'.[41]

As a result of the efforts of the Secretary-General, the League of Arab States, the Organisation of African Unity, and the Organisation of the Islamic Conference in February 1992, the two conflict parties, represented by Ali Mahdi Muhammad and General Muhammad Farah Aidid, signed an *Agreement on the Implementation of a Cease-Fire* in New York on 3 March 1992. Both parties also accepted a UN Security Component for convoys of humanitarian assistance and deployment of 25 military observers in their respective sections of Mogadishu to monitor the ceasefire.[42]

The first UN operation, the United Nations Operation in Somalia (UNOSOM I), was set up through Security Council Resolution 751 (1992) on 24 April 1992. In the beginning the Security Council directly linked the internal issue of 'the magnitude of the human suffering' to a threat to international peace and security without demonstrating the regional or international consequences of this threat.[43] UNOSOM I was established only in and around Mogadishu, and its main mandate was to deliver humanitarian relief to the civilian population. Although Resolution 751 also mentioned reconciliation and a political settlement, the United Nations focused on stabilising the situation rather than endeavouring to establish peace.[44] In the same resolution, the Security Council provided for 50 UN observers to monitor the ceasefire in Mogadishu and also mentioned establishing a security force to protect humanitarian relief activities in the future.[45]

The legal basis of the UN mandate in Somalia was not explicitly mentioned, but two features of Resolution 751 demonstrated that UNOSOM I was

40 Ibid.
41 Ibid.
42 Boutros-Ghali, introduction to *The United Nations and Somalia*, 18–19.
43 S/RES 751 (1992) of 24 April 1992.
44 Ibid., para. 7; Philipp, "Somalia—A Very Special Case", 531.
45 S/RES 751 (1992) of 24 April 1992, Para. 3 and 4.

conceived as a traditional peacekeeping operation.[46] The first was the need for consent from both conflict parties,[47] and the second was the non-use of force.[48] What differentiated UNOSOM I from traditional peacekeeping operations was that its primary purpose was to deliver emergency assistance.[49]

In spite of UNOSOM I, the situation in Somalia did not change. The outbreak of famine and the civil war had already destroyed the countryside, and the ceasefire agreement did not improve the situation. In fact, the agreement was stillborn for two reasons. First, there was no instrument to implement the agreement, although both parties accepted the implementation of measures through the United Nations.[50] Second, the conflict parties were insincere in accepting the agreement. Only two days after the ceasefire, on 5 March 1992, a ship with wheat donated by the WFP was shelled. During this period, according to the United Nations, 4.5 million Somalis required humanitarian relief, and 1.5 million were in danger because of the famine.[51] Shortly afterward, the situation escalated in the north, with fighting also threatening in the south.[52]

The Security Council expanded the UNOSOM mandate to the whole country through Resolution 767 (1992),[53] which laid the legal basis for Operation Provide Relief. This operation, which began on 21 August 1992, was actually a U.S. initiative,[54] concentrated on southern Somalia and Somali refugee camps in northern Africa.[55]

Shortly after the first peacekeeping forces, the Pakistani Blue Helmets, entered Somalia to protect relief deliveries, Boutros Boutros-Ghali informed the Security Council of the extraordinary difficulty of taking relief goods to the people and pointed out the urgent need to protect the transport of aid supplies through the United Nations.[56] As a result, the Security Council expanded the

---

46 Boutros-Ghali, introduction to *The United Nations and Somalia*, 24; Hufnagel, *UN-Friedensoperation der zweiten Generation*, 167; Yusuf, "Government Collapse and State Continuity", 530.

47 The consent of the conflict parties was demonstrated in paragraphs 4 and 5 of Resolution 751 of 24 April 1992 and paragraphs 4 and 5 of Resolution 767 of 24 July 1992.

48 The non-force character of UNOSOM I was demonstrated in paragraph 3 of Resolution 751 of 24 April 1992. In the Report of the Secretary-General of 21 April 1992, the use of force in UNOSOM I was restricted to deterring attacks and self-defence. UN-Doc. S/23829 para. 28.

49 Boutros-Ghali, introduction to *The United Nations and Somalia*, 24.

50 S/23693, 11 March 1992, *Report of the Secretary-General on the Situation in Somalia*, 121; S/Res/751 (1992) of 24 April 1992.

51 Boutros-Ghali, introduction to *The United Nations and Somalia*, 21.

52 Kathrin Eikenberg, "Die UNO in Somalia", *Blätter für deutsche und internationale Politik* 38 (1993), 1061; Boutros-Ghali, introduction to *The United Nations and Somalia 1992–1996*, 21.

53 S/Res/767 of 27 July 1992.

54 S/RES 767 (1992) of 27 July 1992.

55 Boutros-Ghali, introduction to *The United Nations and Somalia*, 2.

56 Doc. S/24480/24 August 1992.

number of UNOSOM I Blue Helmets from 500 to 3,500 through Resolution 775 (1992) on 28 August 1992. Because this resolution was adopted without the consent of the conflict parties,[57] it was a turning point for the efforts of the international community.[58] The UN and U.S. imposition of troops brought the operation to a point at which a massive military intervention seemed the only appropriate way to deal with the conflict in Somalia.[59]

However, there were many critics of UNOSOM I among the conflict parties and international organisations and even within the United Nations. One of the main criticisms was of the operation's switch from a peaceful solution to a solution through violence. UN Special Representative Mohamed Sahnoun attempted a diplomatic solution based on the consent of the conflict parties to bring in 3,000 troops. He resigned after four months, however, when his efforts were thwarted by the Security Council resolution to impose the troops without General Aidid's consent.[60] In reality, UNOSOM I was never given a chance.[61] The situation worsened, especially after the declaration of Resolution 775 (1992). As a result of attacks by General Aidid and Ali Mahdi Muhammad against the UN troops and food aid convoys, the mortality rate climbed to 300 people a day by the end of 1992.[62]

In response to the deteriorating situation, the Secretary-General sent a letter to the President of the Security Council on 24 November 1992, in which he asserted that the engagement of the United Nations in Somalia had to be reconsidered.[63] In an unofficial meeting on 25 November, the Security Council confirmed that the situation was worsening and instructed the Secretary-General to draw up a concrete proposal for an adequate response.[64] Already in this meeting, several participants voiced the opinion that military action under Chapter VII of the UN Charter was necessary, while U.S. Secretary of State Lawrence Eagleburger informed the Secretary-General that the U.S. Government was ready for a large military operation.[65]

In a letter to the President of the Security Council dated 29 November 1992, the Secretary-General presented five progressive gradual options.[66] The first two did not involve the use of force. The first option foresaw the continuation of

---

57 S/RES 775 (1992) of 28 August 1992; S/24674 of 16 October 1992.

58 Ibid.

59 Volker, "Die UNO am Horn von Afrika", 47.

60 Bartl, *Die Humanitäre Intervention*, 41–44.

61 Jonathan Steveson, "Hope Restored in Somalia?" *Foreign Policy* 91 (1993), 154.

62 Bartl, *Die Humanitäre Intervention*, 42–44.

63 S/24859 of 27 November 1992.

64 Boutros-Ghali, introduction to *The United Nations and Somalia*, 30.

65 Ibid., 30; Bartl, *Die Humanitäre Intervention*, 45.

66 Letter dated 29 November 1992 from the Secretary-General to the President of the Security Council, S/24868 of 30 November 1992.

the existing UNOSOM peace-keeping operations. The second option was more restricted, proposing humanitarian activities without using military personnel. The last three options, in contrast, proposed that the Security Council authorise the use of force to provide humanitarian assistance. Option three foresaw the use of force only in Mogadishu, and options four and five in the entire country. Option four foresaw the use of force authorised by the Security Council, commanded and controlled by a group of Member States, and option five proposed such military action under the command and control of the United Nations.

On 3 December 1992, the Security Council adopted the fourth option in Resolution 794 (1992), with the justification that '[...] the situation in Somalia is intolerable [...] and [...] UNOSOM's existing course would not in present circumstances be an adequate response to the tragedy in Somalia'.[67]

The result of this authorisation was the United Task Force (UNITAF). UNITAF was empowered by the United Nations as a military action under Chapter VII of the UN Charter but gave the United States and the other Member States the responsibility of organising and commanding troops.[68] While the centre of the operation was to establish '[...] as soon as possible a secure environment for humanitarian relief operations in Somalia [...]', the resolution's use of the phrase 'use all necessary means' implied the use of force based on Article 42 of the UN Charter.[69]

UNITAF was conceived as a temporary operation that would work in parallel with UNOSOM I.[70] The United States, as the largest contingent, assumed operational command of the UNITAF forces. Unlike in other peacekeeping missions, the United Nations was not involved in preparing the UNITAF budget, and the cost of the mission was financed through the Member States. UNITAF consisted of approximately 37,000 troops, 28,000 of them from the United States and 9,000 from more than 20 other countries. During this largest 'humanitarian-military' relief operation in UN history, UNITAF delivered 70,000 tons of food and medical supplies to Somalia.[71]

The expressed aim of UNITAF was to stop the famine in southern and central Somalia. UNITAF forces took control of nine key towns within three weeks.[72]

---

67 S/Res/794 (1992) of 3 December 1992.

68 Ibid., operative para. 10.

69 Ibid.

70 Ibid., operative para.6.

71 Madeleine K. Albright, *Statement before the Subcommittee on Foreign Operations, Export Financing, and Related Programs of the House Appropriations Committee*, March 12, 1993, Department of State Dispatch of 5 April, 1993, 207, 209.

72 Mogadishu, Baidoa, Baledogel, Kismayo, Bardera, Hoddur, Belet Weyne, Jalalaqsi and most of Merca. Letter dated 17 September 1992 from the United States to the President of the Security Council transmitting a report on the activities of the Unified Task Force (UNITAF), S/24976 of 17 December 1992.

Despite these efforts the militias did not dissolve, but left before the arrival of UNITAF and waited for the withdrawal of the UNITAF forces.[73] Although UNITAF was an enforcing power and UNOSOM a concurrent peace-keeping force, the international community interpreted logistical and operational problems between the two units as evidence that they did not operate effectively.[74] Moreover, in spite of the fact that UNITAF was conceived as a mandate for the entire country, only 40 percent of Somalia was under its control by March 1993. The UN Secretary-General's report of 3 March 1993 therefore concluded that UNITAF's effort was incomplete.[75]

Parallel with UNITAF, the United Nations coordinated a national reconciliation conference in Addis Ababa, Ethiopia, between 4 and 15 January 1993. The representative of one of the two main conflict parties, General Mohammed Farah Aidid, boycotted the conference on the grounds that Security Council Resolution 775 (1992)[76] increased the number of Blue Helmets against the will of the conflict parties. Only Ali Mahdi Muhammad and representatives of 14 other, smaller, clan groups attended.[77] At the end of the conference, the 15 conflict parties signed 3 agreements, which called for an immediate ceasefire in all parts of the country under their control, a handover of heavy weapons to the ceasefire monitoring group, encampment and disarming of the militias, and the release of prisoners of war. The conflict parties established an ad hoc committee to prepare for a second national reconciliation conference in Addis Ababa on 15 March 1993.[78]

In a report dated 3 March 1993, the UN Secretary-General proposed to expand the mandate of UNOSOM to authorise the use of force to avoid the failure of UNITAF.[79] As a result of this report, on 26 March 1993 the Security Council adopted the fifth option for the new UNOSOM operation through Resolution 814 (1993) for '[...] a country-wide enforcement operation to be carried out under the United Nations command and control'.[80]

UNOSOM II absorbed the operations of both UNOSOM I and UNITAF. Although the Security Council had mentioned different elements of the reconstruction of Somalia in Security Council Resolutions 733 (1992) to 814 (1993),

---

73 Bartl, *Die Humanitäre Intervention*, 47.

74 Christine D. Gray, *International Law and the Use of Force*, 2nd edition (Oxford: Oxford University Press, 2004), 226.

75 Boutros-Ghali, introduction to *The United Nations and Somalia*, 40; S/25354 of 3 March 1993.

76 S/Res/775 (1992) of 28 August 1992.

77 Boutros-Ghali, introduction to *The United Nations and Somalia*, 38.

78 Ibid.

79 Ibid., 40.

80 S/Res/814 (1993) of 26 March 1993; letter dated 29 November 1992 from the Secretary-General to the President of the Security Council, S/24868 of 30 November 1992.

Resolution 814 (1993) put reconstruction at the centre of its mandate. Therefore, the mandate of UNOSOM II consisted of a military component and a civil component, considered inseparable and interdependent.[81] The civil component under Part A focused on the administrative and political reconstruction of the state,[82] distinguishing UNOSOM II from previous actions of the United Nations.[83]

The Security Council expressly referred to Chapter VII of the UN Charter as the legal basis for the military mandate of UNOSOM II in Part B of the resolution. Although this reference caused confusion about the legal basis of the civil competent, most international lawyers considered Chapter VII to be the legal basis of both components of UNOSOM II.[84] The Security Council implicitly confirmed this assumption in its next resolution, 897 (1994),[85] which authorized the concomitant military and civil components of UNOSOM II under Chapter VII. The legal construction of the operation made UNOSOM II a milestone in international law because this was the first time the Security Council had directly organised and commanded a peace enforcement operation authorised under Chapter VII.[86] UNOSOM II also differed from other UN operations in being the largest and most expensive peacekeeping mission in the history of the United Nations, with 33,000 soldiers and an annual budget of US$ 1.5 billion.[87]

Part A of Resolution 814 (1993) identified the people of Somalia as the main actor for national reconciliation and reconstruction and defined the role of the Security Council as fundamentally based on assistance to '[...] the people of Somalia to create and maintain order and new institutions for their own governance'.[88]

The Security Council's reconstruction mandate was complex because it comprised many different elements of state reconstruction as well as maintenance of peace and stability. While Resolution 814 (1993) saw reconciliation as the first step in the reconstruction process, the Security Council also addressed the rehabilitation of political and economic institutions and the re-establishment of

81 Report of the Secretary-General of 19 December 1992, UN Doc. S/24992, para. 44.
82 Part B of S/Res/814 (1993) of 26 March 1993.
83 Udo Fink, *Kollektive Friedenssicherung, Kapital VII UN-Charta in der Praxis des Sicherheitsrats der Vereinten Nationen*, Volume II (Frankfurt: Peter Lang Publishing Group, 1999), 751.
84 Hufnagel, *UN-Friedensoperation der zweiten Generation*, 167.
85 S/Res/897 (1994) of 4 February 1994.
86 Sean D. Murphy, "Nation-Building: A Look at Somalia", *Tulane Journal of International and Comparative Law* 3 (1995), 1–2, 29; Boutros-Ghali, introduction to *The United Nations and Somalia*, 40.
87 Murphy, "Nation-Building", 29.
88 S/25354 (1993) of 3 March 1993.

national and regional institutions and civil administration such as the Somali national police force in the entire country, at local, regional, and national levels.[89] The United Nations held itself responsible for establishing

> [a] condition under which Somali civil society may have role, at every level, in the progress of political reconciliation and in the formulation and realization of rehabilitation and reconstruction programmes.

The United Nations support also included humanitarian assistance, repatriation of refugees and displaced persons within Somalia, and mine removal.[90]

In spite of its substantial civil component, the United Nations's reconstruction mandate was superficial. For example, there was no explanation of how these tasks would be implemented. The Security Council only generally referred to the report of the Secretary General of 3 March 1993,[91] especially the Relief and Rehabilitation Programme concerning the Relief and Economic Rehabilitation of Somalia,[92] as the basis for the civil competent. However, the Relief and Rehabilitation Programme lacked clearly determined provisions and a means for a long-term solution.[93]

The incompatibility between the measures foreseen in Resolution 814 (1993) and the practice of the international community in Somalia was another indication of the superficiality of the mandate. Because the Security Council made reconciliation the first precondition for the reconstruction process, the Secretary-General was entrusted with convening a Conference on National Reconciliation for Somalia[94] and all UN entities were entrusted with providing assistance to the Somali people to promote resettlement and national reconciliation.[95] However, even under UNOSOM I, the international community had been unable to act as a neutral party between the conflict parties. This impasse took on other dimensions in the events that followed. As explained later, in UNOSOM II the international community appeared as a conflict party.[96] Another example of the superficial character of the civil competent was the discrepancy between the US$ 836,000 budget for the military

89 S/Res/814 (1993) of 26 March 1993operative para. A (4)(c), (d).

90 Ibid., operative para. A (4) (b), (e), (g).

91 S/25354 of 3 March 1993.

92 Executive summary of "The 1993 Relief and Rehabilitation Programme for Somalia prepared by the United Nations Department of Humanitarian Affairs", in: *United Nations and Somalia, 1992–1996*, United Nations Blue Book Series, Volume III, (New York: United Nations Department of Public Information, 1996).

93 S/Res/814 (1993) of 26 March 1993.

94 Ibid., operative para. A (2).

95 Ibid., operative para. A (4) and A (4) (c).

96 Bartl, *Die Humanitäre Intervention*, 250–251.

component, contingent personnel, and other contingencies and lack of any direct expenditure budgeted for reconstruction.[97]

The second National Reconciliation Conference, foreseen in the Addis Ababa Agreement of January 1993, opened with logistical assistance from the United Nations on 15 March 1993. However, neither the Somali National Movement, the major faction controlling the northwest, which only sent observers, nor Aidid's United Somali Congress/Somali National Alliance faction participated in this conference. One day after the establishment of UNOSOM II, 15 other small factions at the conference signed the second Addis Ababa Agreement of 27 March 1993. The participant parties agreed to disarm the clan militias, build a new government within a two-year transition period, and co-operate with UNITAF/UNOSOM.[98]

On 5 June 1993, shortly after the establishment of UNOSOM II and the beginning of the implementation of the second Addis Ababa Agreement, conflict escalated between the UNOSOM II forces and local military groups when the former went to inspect five USC/SNA weapons storage facilities in and around Mogadishu. In the aftermath, Pakistani troops were attacked and 24 soldiers were killed.[99] The Security Council and Member States, especially the United States, held General Aidid and the USC/SNA accountable for the attack, with no clear evidence.[100] The Security Council authorised the Secretary-General under Resolution 837 (1993) to take '[...] all necessary measures against those responsible for the armed attacks on UNOSOM II'.[101]

This was the second turning point for the operation after the expansion of UNOSOM I without the consent of the conflict parties under Resolution 775 (1992) of 18 August 1992. After the attack on the Pakistani troops, UNOSOM appeared more clearly as a conflict party. UNOSOM II forces and the Quick Reaction Force of the United States focused their attention on General Aidid, destroyed USC/SNA weapons stockpiles with aerial bombardments and ground assaults, and bombed Radio Mogadishu and Aidid's command headquarters. The UN Special Representative for Somalia also called for Aidid's arrest.[102]

97 Annex of S/25354 of 3 March 1993.

98 Boutros-Ghali, introduction to *The United Nations and Somalia*, 46; Bartl, Die Humanitäre Intervention, 50.

99 Murphy, "Nation-Building", 29; Boutros-Ghali, introduction to *The United Nations and Somalia*, 50.

100 The United States representative warned that those who had challenged the authority of the Security Council would 'pay a heavy price'; Boutros-Ghali, introduction to *The United Nations and Somalia*, 51.

101 S/Res/837 (1993) of 6 June 1993.

102 Boutros-Ghali, introduction to *The United Nations and Somalia*, 51.

As a consequence of the focus on General Aidid and his party, the civil competent of Resolution 814 (1993) could not be implemented and military measures could be used to achieve UNOSOM II's aims. Therefore UNOSOM II was unable to control the entire country in spite of its aggressive military measures.[103]

After 18 UNOSOM II soldiers were killed and another 78 wounded in a battle on 3 October 1993, the United States changed its Somalia policy. President William J. Clinton announced on 7 October 1993 the withdrawal of U.S. combat forces by 31 March 1994. Following this decision, other countries decided to pull out their contingents, and more than 9,000 soldiers were withdrawn. Under these circumstances, the Security Council redefined its peace enforcement mandate as 'a more limited peacekeeping mission'[104] in Resolution 897 (1994) of 4 February 1994. This resolution justified action under Chapter VII of the UN Charter on the grounds that the situation in Somalia, especially the absence of a government, constituted a threat to peace and security and set March 1995 as the withdrawal for UNOSOM II. Resolution 897 (1994) called for the gradual reduction of the force level of UNOSOM II to 22,000.[105]

The redefined mandate mainly included humanitarian assistance, implementation of the terms of the second Addis Ababa Agreement, protection of the efforts of the international community, construction of major infrastructure needed for humanitarian assistance, and repatriation of refugees and displaced persons. Resolution 897 (1994) included some elements of reconstruction, but these were neither strongly emphasised nor identified as an instrument to achieve the stated goal.

The UN experiment in 'nation building' or 'state-building' came to an abrupt and unsuccessful end with the withdrawal of UNOSOM II on 3 March 1995. According to the UN Secretary-General,

> [...] the withdrawal of UNOSOM II marked the end of a major phase of the efforts of the international community to facilitate the search for peace and reconciliation and to deliver humanitarian assistance.[106]

The Post-UNOSOM Situation

The Republic of Somaliland declared its independence in 1991 in the northwest and adopted a constitution in 1995. This state today includes 6 of the 18 administrative regions of Somalia, with its capital in Hargeisa. Multiparty

---

[103] *Report of the Secretary-General of 6 January 1994*, UN Doc. S/1994/12, para. 23.
[104] Boutros-Ghali, introduction to *The United Nations and Somalia*, 61.
[105] S/Res/897 (1994) of 4 February 1994.
[106] Boutros-Ghali, introduction to *The United Nations and Somalia*, 77.

elections were held in 2005. Somaliland has been recognised neither by the United Nations nor by other states. In 1998 the leaders of Puntland, the northeast region of Somalia, declared autonomy, but unlike Somaliland, Puntland chose to remain within Somalia.[107] In 2002 clan leaders in southwestern Somalia come together to declare Southwestern Somalia an autonomous state.[108]

In South Somalia, the former Italian Somaliland, battles continued between the clans. General Aidid declared himself interim president in Mogadishu in June 1995, after the withdrawal of UNOSOM II. But this was not the end of the conflict, as several other people appointed themselves interim presidents soon afterward.[109] After the 12th National Reconciliation Conference in Djibouti in 2000, Abdikassim Salat Hassan was selected by the participants to set up a Transitional National Government (TNG). The opposition Somali Restoration and Reconstruction Council (SRRC), which mainly evolved from the SNA and was supported by Ethiopia, did not accept the new TNG and fought against it. Consequently, the new government failed to establish a state structure.[110]

In 2002 the United Nations and United States organised the 14th National Reconciliation Conference, at which the participants decided to establish a new state called the Republic of Somalia. As a result of this conference, a new transitional government called the Transitional Federal Government (TFG) and a transitional constitution called the Transitional Federal Charter were created. At the end of 2004, Abdullahi Jussuf became president of this state, with his capital in Baidoa.

However, this transitional government was unable to establish authority over the remaining territory, largely because of the struggle between the Alliance for the Restoration of Peace and Counter-Terrorism (ARPCT) and the Union of Islamic Courts (UIC). The war between the conflict parties escalated with the UIC's declaration of holy war against the ARPCT and attempt to overthrow the president of the transitional government on the one hand and Ethiopia's support for the transitional government and ARPCT and its affirmation of the deployment of troops to Somalia on the other. The SICC[111] and ARPCT agreed to a ceasefire at a mediation conference in Khartoum, Sudan, in the second

[107] Puntland State of Somalia, http://www.puntlandgovt.com/profile.php; Yusuf, "Government Collapse and State Continuity", 15.

[108] Konftliktentwicklung—Somalia, Zentrum für Internationale Friedenseinsätze, http://www.zif-berlin.org/Downloads/Analysen/Veroeffentlichungen/Somalia_Januar_2008.pdf.

[109] Ibid.; Yusuf, "Government Collapse and State Continuity", 11.

[110] Ibid., 17; Michael Birnbaum, *Somalia, Die Arabische Staaten, Geschichte, Politik, Religion, Gesellschaft, Wirtschaft*, ed. Walter M. Weiss (Heidelberg: Palmyra Verlag, 2007), 294.

[111] The Union of Islamic Courts (UIC) renamed itself the Supreme Islamic Courts Council (SICC) on 24 July, 2006.

part of 2006, but this ceasefire could not last.[112] The SICC's declaration of holy war on Ethiopia on 9 October 2006 in reaction to Ethiopia's support for the transitional government turned the conflict in Somalia into a regional conflict, in which the SICC was supported by Libya, Saudi Arabia, and Eritrea.

After UNOSOM II the United Nations did not authorise any UN operation in Somalia and mainly restricted its activities to supporting regional peacekeeping forces. The Security Council first authorized a regional peacekeeping force under the command of the Intergovernmental Authority on Development (IGAD)[113] and African Union (AU) to protect the transitional government at the end of 2006,[114] but this force was never realised. Almost three months later, on 20 February 2007, the Security Council authorized deployment of AU troops under Resolution 1744 (2007) regarding Chapter VII. This operation, called the African Union Mission to Somalia (AMISOM), was extended twice until 20 August 2008.[115] The 8,000 troops foreseen in the resolution reached more than 2,000.

Ethiopia officially intervened militarily in Somalia between 2006 and 2009 'to protect the sovereign of the Ethiopian's nation'.[116] The President of Ethiopia, Meles Zenawi, refused to withdraw his troops until sufficient numbers of African Union troops were deployed. By 2009 there were 3,000 African troops in Somalia. The power vacuum left after Ethiopia's withdrawal was filled by islamist fighters.[117]

Somalia's name reappeared on the Security Council Agenda in 2008 in the wake of 'increasingly violent acts of piracy'. Pirate attacks in the Gulf of Aden led to Security Council Resolution 1816 (2008) of 2 June 2008, which allows foreign warships to enter Somali waters 'for the purposes of repressing acts of piracy and armed robbery at sea' by 'all necessary means'.[118] The ransom money demanded by the pirates is said to be used to finance the war in Somalia.[119]

---

112 Birnbaum, *Somalia, Die Arabische Staaten*, 294.

113 The Intergovernmental Authority on Development (IGAD) in Eastern Africa was created in 1996 to supersede the Intergovernmental Authority on Drought and Development (IGADD), which was founded in 1986.

114 S/Res/1725 (2006) of 6 December 2006.

115 S/Res/1772 (2007) of 20.08.2007, and S/Res/1801 (2008) of 20 February 2008.

116 Jeffrey Gettleman, "Ethiopia Hits Somali Targets, Declaring War", *New York Times*, December 25, 2006.

117 Jeffrey Gettleman, Mohammed Ibrahim, "Officials Still Arguing over Leader for Somalia", *New York Times*, January 13, 2009.

118 S/Res/1838(2008) of 7 October 2008, S/Res/1814 (2008) of 15 May 2008 and S/Res/1816 (2008) of 2 June 2008.

119 Roger Middleton, "Piracy in Somalia Threatening Global Trade, Feeding Local Wars", *Chatham House Briefing Paper* (London: Royal Institute of International Affairs, 2008), www.chathamhouse.org.uk.

Today Somalia is still a state without an effective government. The phrase 'the situation in Somalia constitutes a threat to international peace and security in the region', acting under Chapter VII of the Charter of the United Nations' is sin a qua non of Security Council resolutions since the 1990s.[120] In its resolution of 16 January 2009, the Security Council expressed its intention to establish a UN Peacekeeping Operation in Somalia after AMISOM by, 1 June 2009. The same resolution added 'building the capacity of the Somali government at the federal, state and local level' to the security agenday.

Despite all these efforts, the situation in Somalia has not changed significantly since the 1990s, as the humanitarian situation inside the country, the instability in the region, and the proliferation of piracy clearly show. The Somalia example demonstrates not only the threat a state without an effective government poses to the international community, but also its inability to protect itself from outside intervention. In April 2009 Somalia's Parliement voted to institute Islamic Sharia law as a means for strenthening 'the popular support for the government and siphoning it away from the Islamic militias'.[121] For its part, the international community has not changed its praxis for most of the past two decades.

Afghanistan: From 'Buffer State' to 'the Absence of Effective Government'

> "They (the men and women of Afghanistan) do not understand why their country is being attacked, why what little infrastructure is there is being destroyed, and civilians, including children, are being killed by stray bombs".[122]
>
> Lakhdar Brahimi, 13 November 2001

Afghanistan is another instructive example of the breakdown of effective government. Many authors in international law and political and social science,[123] as well as representatives of international organisations, characterise the coun-

---

[120] S/Res/1863 of 16 January 2009, S/Res/1838(2008) of 7 October 2008, S/Res/1814 (2008) of 15 May 2008 and S/Res/1816 (2008) of 2 June 2008.

[121] Mohammed Ibraim, "Somalia Adopts Islamic Law to Deter Insurgency", *New York Times*, April 18, 2009.

[122] Lakhdar Brahimi, *Briefing to the Security Council*, Transcript from 13 November 2001, http://www.un.org/News/dh/latest/afghan/Brahimi-sc-briefing.html.

[123] Robert I. Rotberg, "The Failure and Collapse of Nation-States: Breakdown, Prevention, and Repair", in *When States Fail: Causes and Consequences*, ed. Robert I. Rotberg (Princeton: Princeton University Press, 2004), 49; Gerard Kreijen, *State Failure, Sovereignty and Effectiveness: Legal Lessons from the Decolonization of Sub-Saharan Africa* (Leiden: Martinus

try as a 'failed state',[124] but there is no clear consensus about when in history an effective government disappeared. Some authors identify this phase as the period before the Taliban regime, while others describe the Taliban regime itself as an absence of effective government. Robin Geiß singles out the period between 1992 and 1996, while Kofi Annan labels Afghanistan under the Taliban a 'failed state'.[125] Lakhdar Brahimi, Special Representative of the UN Secretary-General for Afghanistan, described the country as a collapsed state before 11 September 2001,[126] when the Taliban de facto controlled 90 percent of the territory.[127]

After five external interventions and three long civil wars, Afghanistan stands on the world stage as a prominent example of the absence of effective government.[128] The international community partly played along with and partly stood back and observed the long, internationalised civil wars in Afghanistan and their consequences but reacted swiftly after the military intervention of the United States and its allies. At present the international community is providing assistance for the 'peace and reconstruction process' parallel to the 'war on terror' led by the United States.[129]

Historical and Political Background

The entire history of Afghanistan can be interpreted on the basis of its geographical position and its longstanding 'Afghan' identity.[130] Because of its geopolitical situation, the country has been affected by outside power conflicts for

---

Nijhoff Publishers, 2004), 94; Robin Geiß, *"Failed State": Die normative Erfassung gescheiterter Staaten*. Berlin, Ducker & Humblot; Barnett R. Rubin, *The Fragmentation of Afghanistan: State Formation and Collapse in the International System* (New Haven: Yale University Press, 1995).

124 Kofi Annan, 1997, SG/SM/6412 of 3 December 1997, *Report of the Secretary-General on the Situation in Afghanistan and Its Implications for International Peace and Security*, S/1998/532 of 19 June 1998, para. 50; "World Bank Lists Failing Nations That Can Breed Global Terrorism", *Washington Post*, September 15, 2006, A13.

125 Geiß, *"Failed State"*, 97; SG/SM/6412 of 3 December 1997; S/1998/532 of 19 June 1998, para. 50.

126 Brahimi, *Briefing to the Security Council*.

127 Rüdiger Wolfrum and Christiane Philipp, "Die Taliban: Ein Subjekt des Völkerrechts?", in *Praxis Handbuch UNO: Die Vereinten Nationen im Lichte globaler Herausforderungen*, ed. Sabine von Schorlemer (Heidelberg: Springer Verlag, 2003), 149.

128 The external interventions have included the Anglo-Afghan wars (1840–1842, 1877–1879, and 1919), the military interventions of the Soviet Union (1979–1989) and the United States (7 October 2001), and the civil wars of 1929–1933, 1979–1992, and 1992–1996.

129 Tanya D. Bosi, "Post-Conflict Reconstruction: The United Nations Involvement in Afghanistan", *New York Law School Journal of Human Rights* 19 (2003), 3, 819.

130 Mohammed Sadiq Sarwari, *Afghanistan zwischen Tradition und Modernisierung* (Bern: Peter Lang Publishing Group, 1974), 29.

almost all of its history. In ancient times as well as in the Middle Ages, when the land now known as Afghanistan was a major stop on the famous Silk Road between India, China, and the Arab world, the territory was subject to rivalry among conquerors.[131] After the colonial powers appeared as a new wave of conquerors at the end of the 18th century, Afghanistan became a buffer state between Great Britain and Russia in the 19th and 20th centuries.[132]

With exposure to the Silk Road traders, the country became a well-developed cultural and social centre during the Ghaznavi Empire in the 10th and 11th centuries. The first state of Afghanistan was established by Ahmad Shah in 1747, but there had been attempts to consolidate and defend the 'national' character of the state since the 10th century.[133]

The colonial period and the expansionist politics of the Russian and British empires in India and Central Asia throughout the 19th century had a profound influence on the current situation in Afghanistan. Rivalry between the two powers gave the country little opportunity to exercise its external and internal sovereignty in the 19th and 20th centuries, in spite of its existence as a state, and Afghanistan spent more than 80 years as a political 'dead zone'. After Russia and Great Britain agreed to solve the conflict in Central Asia and especially in and around Afghanistan through negotiation, the country achieved internal sovereignty through the Petersburg Agreement between these two powers in 1907 and external sovereignty through a peace agreement with Great Britain in 1919.[134]

The 'Great Game' between Great Britain and Russia[135] influenced the history of Afghanistan in various ways. First, because of its buffer status, the country was isolated from the outside world until 1919. Second, British colonial politics exacerbated internal conflict, and the more Afghanistan moved into the centre of British colonial politics, the stronger the internal conflict became.[136] Third, every step the country took toward economic and social progress was suspected as a manoeuvre of one or the other of the rivals and consequently suppressed.[137] Finally, European colonialism helped preserve traditional Afghanistan until

[131] Sarwari, *Afghanistan*, 7.

[132] Rubin, *The Fragmentation of Afghanistan*, 19.

[133] Sarwari, *Afghanistan*, 29; Dieter Fröhlich, *Nationalismus und Nationalstaat in Entwicklungsländern, Probleme der Integration ethnischer Gruppen in Afghanistan* (Meisenheim am Glan, Germany: Hain Verlag, 1970), 135. The capital city was Kandahar.

[134] Sarwari, *Afghanistan zwischen Tradition und Modernisierung*, 70–76, 189.

[135] The 'Great Game' in British parlance began in 1830 and described the rivalry of Russia and England over Afghanistan.

[136] Sarwari, *Afghanistan zwischen Tradition und Modernisierung*, 41.

[137] Ibid., 161.

the 20th century and prevented the country from taking advantage of the economic, cultural, and political influence of the industrialised world.[138]

Afghanistan was an important place for the new powers that emerged during the Cold War: the Soviet Union and the United States.[139] When Soviet troops entered the country under the Soviet-Afghan Friendship Treaty on 27 December 1979, a new Great Game began. Under the Reagan Doctrine, the U.S. Government claimed the moral and political right to fight any government supported by the Soviet Union by all possible means.[140] During the 1979–1992 civil war against the Democratic People's Party of Afghanistan supported by the Soviet Union, the United States provided assistance to resistance fighters through Pakistan.[141] As a result, the civil war quickly turned into a proxy war between the Soviet Union and the United States.

On 14 April 1988 the Afghan government, the Soviet Union, the United States, and Pakistan signed the Geneva Accords to separate the Afghan conflict from bilateral United States-Soviet relations. However, shortly after the Geneva Accords, the U.S. Secretary of State declared that the U.S. Government reserved the right to support the Afghan resistance fighters (*mudjaheddin*) as long as the Soviet government supported the government in Kabul.[142] After the withdrawal of the Soviet troops, the United States supported the mudjaheddin, but when a civil war erupted among the mudjaheddin, the U.S. Government supported the extremist Taliban movement as a stabilising factor in the region. When it declared its support for Usama bin Laden, the United States turned its back on the Taliban. The U.S. and British attack on Afghanistan on 7 October 2001 in reaction to the 11 September 2001 attacks in the United States was the high point of U.S. interventionist politics in the country.

Besides the actors in the Great Game, the neighbouring countries of Iran, Turkmenistan, Tajikistan, Uzbekistan, India, and China have variously influenced or been involved in Afghanistan's civil wars for their own economic and political interests. A number of Security Council and General Assembly resolutions called for an end to such foreign interference, which intensified Afghanistan's internal conflicts.[143] These resolutions included the Geneva

[138] Fröhlich, *Nationalismus und Nationalsaat*, 158.

[139] Helmut Hubel, *Das Ende des Kalten Kriegs im Orient, die USA, die Sowjetunion und die Konflikte in Afghanistan, am Golf und im Nahen Osten, 1979–1991*, Auswirkungen für Europa und Deutschland (Munich: Oldenbourg-Verlag, 1995), 205.

[140] Ibid., 59.

[141] Christian Hacke "Amerikas Krieg gegen Terror—Die Operation 'Enduring Freedom' in Afghanistan", *Jahrbuch internationale Politik*, 25 (2004), 17.

[142] Hubel, *Das Ende des Kalten Kriegs*, 207.

[143] A/Res/50/88 of 19 December 1995, 22 October 1996; SC/6282 of 22 October 1996; SC/6315 of 22 January 1997; S/Res/1193 (1998) of 28 August 1998, preamble para. 7; S/Res/1214 (1998) of 8 December 1998.

Accord of 14 April 1988, the Declaration on the Situation in Afghanistan by the foreign ministers and other senior representatives of the Six Plus Two countries (six of Afghanistan's neighbouring countries—China, Iran, Pakistan, Tajikistan, Turkmenistan, and Uzbekistan—plus the United States and the Russian Federation) on 12 November 2001, and the Kabul Declaration on Good Neighbourly Relations of 22 December 2002.[144]

The Geneva Accord of 14 April 1988 was signed by the Kabul regime, the Soviet Union, the United States, and Pakistan.[145] The issue of non-intervention was one of the most important elements of the agreement for both superpowers, but also for Pakistan and Saudi Arabia. Pakistan, which had striven for political influence in Afghanistan during and after the Cold War, never saw itself as bound by the Geneva Accord and played a major role in the rise of the Taliban, which was established in Islamabad and trained in the Afghan refugee camps in Pakistan. During the war of the Taliban against the mudjaheddin after 1992 and afterwards, the Pakistani intelligence services continuously supported the Taliban with training, supplies, and weapons.[146]

In an attempt to solve the Afghan conflict, the United Nations supported the establishment of the Six Plus Two group in 1998.[147] This involvement of eight countries in determining the future of Afghanistan is another illustration of the dependency of civil wars on outside interference. Since the invasion of the United States and its allies in 2001, the Six Plus Two group has been an important economic and political actor in the rebuilding of Afghanistan.[148]

The State Structure of Afghanistan

Unlike other countries that have experienced the breakdown of effective government, Afghanistan has existed as a state for almost 300 years. This state can be classified as multinational, with cross-border ethnic networks. The population consists of four major ethnic groups (Pashtuns, Tajiks, Hazaras, and Uzbeks) and many smaller groups. Pashtun and Dari are the major languages.

---

144 www.un.org/Depts/dpko/co_mission/ungomap/background.html. www.un.org/apps/news/story.asp?NewsID=2116&cr=Afghan&Cr1, S/2002/1416.

145 http://www.un.org/Depts/dpko/dpko/co_mission/ungomap/background.html.

146 Hacke, "Amerikas Krieg", 17.

147 *Report of the Secretary-General on the Situation in Afghanistan and Its Implications for International Peace and Security*, S/1998/532 of 19 June 1998; S/Res/1214 (1998) of 8 December 1998; *Declaration on the Situation in Afghanistan by the Foreign Ministers and Other Senior Representatives of the 'Six Plus Two'* on 12 November 2001, www.un.org.pk/latest-dev/hq-press-011112.htm.

148 Ebrahim Afsah and Alexandra H. Guhr, "Afghanistan: Building a State to Keep the Peace", *Max Planck Yearbook of United Nations Law* 9 (2005), 401.

Although Afghanistan is almost exclusively Muslim, factionalism between Sunni and Shiite Muslims has often been used as an instrument of division during the civil war.[149]

Afghanistan does not have a state structure in the modern Western sense. The tension between predominantly tribal traditions and an embryonic form of a modern nation-state has played a major role in the political picture of the country.[150] Especially after the withdrawal of the Soviet Union, the motif of Islam became part of the state legal system, which is called Sharia.[151] Three civil wars have shaped the political structure of Afghanistan.

The process of modernisation, which began during the Ghaznavi Empire in the 10th and 11th centuries, was interrupted several times in Afghan history.[152] The modernisation movement resumed during the rule of King Amunaullah Khan in the 1920s, Nadir Khan from 1929 to 1933, and Zahir Shah from 1933 to 1973. King Amunaullah Khan declared the first constitution on 6 October 1923, and Zahir Shah brought a modern functional administrative structure—a constitutional monarchy—to the country in 1964. Conflict in Afghanistan between 1929 and 1979 has been characterised as a confrontation between traditionalism and modernism, and the first civil war (1929–1933) took place in this context.[153]

When the communist Democratic People's Party of Afghanistan (DVPA) assumed power in April 1978 and renamed the country the Democratic Republic of Afghanistan, this confrontation took on a different dimension. Shortly afterwards, the struggle against communism replaced the struggle against modernisation. The main platform of the mudjaheddin in its fight against communism between 1979 and 1992 was the defence of Islam. The second civil war (1979–1989) was rooted in this context.

With the withdrawal of Soviet troops in February 1989, internal religious and ethnic tensions came to the fore. Especially after the forced resignation of DVPA President Mohammed Najibullah in 1992, Islam began to assume a major role in politics. When the mudjaheddin came to power in 1992, they instituted Sharia and proclaimed the country the Islamic State of Afghanistan.

---

149 Ibid., 378; Citha D. Maass, "Der Afghanistan-Konflikt: Konfliktmerkmale als Ansatz für ein UN-Vermittlungskonzept" in *Afghanistan in Geschichte und Gegenwart, Beitraege zur Afghanistan*, ed. Conrad J. Schetter and Almut Wieland-Karimi (Frankfurt: Verlag für Interkulturelle Kommunikation, 1999), 153–156.

150 Neamatollah Nojumi, *The Rise of the Taliban in Afghanistan, Mass Mobilization, Civil War, and the Future of the Region* (New York: Palgrave Macmillan Ltd., 2002), 2.

151 Sharia ('way' or 'path') is a legal framework based on Islamic jurisprudence.

152 Sarwari, *Afghanistan zwischen Tradition und Modernisierung*, 29. The central administrative structures include a postal, tax system, and the first Islamic university (madrasa).

153 Nojumi, *The Rise of the Taliban*, 2.

After the radical Islamic Taliban took power after the third civil war (1992–1996), the country was renamed the Islamic Emirates of Afghanistan. The political structure of the Taliban regime was based on an interpretation of the Koran according to the Deobandi tradition of Sunni Islam on the one hand and the tribal code of honour of the Pashtuns on the other. After the U.S. invasion of 2001, the state was called the Islamic Republic of Afghanistan.

Ethnic tensions and different interpretations of Islam appeared as the motives for the third civil war from 1992 until the Taliban took control of Afghanistan in 1996. Shortly after the establishment of the Islamic State of Afghanistan, the mudjaheddin began to fight among themselves. Two peace accords that attempted to impose a ceasefire and initiate the political process did not change the situation.[154] This conflict caused the breakdown of the entire political system of the country, which was already fragile after the second civil war. In the mid-1990s, the conflict within the mudjaheddin transformed into a conflict between the mainly Pashtun und Sunni Taliban and the Northern Alliance, a military alliance of ethnic minorities, especially Tajiks, Uzbeks, and Shiite Hazaras. Security Council Resolution 1193 (1998) pointed out the '[...] increasing ethnic nature of the conflict, particularly against the Shiites'.[155] The brutal assassination of thousands of Shiites after the Taliban conquest of Mazar-i-Sharif in 1997 attested to this trend.

The administrative structure of Afghanistan is strongly decentralised. Ahmad Shah (1723–1773) was largely responsible for establishing this structure in the 18th century, based on the two principles of equal treatment of tribes *primus inter pares* (first among equals) and feudalism. As a consequence, Afghanistan is based not on the idea of a nation-state but rather on changing systems of rank. The system distinguishes between forms of tribal organisation and clan systems. While a tribal organisation is usually identified with larger, relational, organised units, a clan system is based on place of residence, such as a village. Widely dispersed villages and poor transport also favoured this factionalism.[156]

The economic structure of Afghanistan was determined by agriculture.[157] As mentioned above, Afghanistan was a rich country in the past and even now has the capacity to produce more than staple foods, but has become one of

---

[154] Rubin, *The Fragmentation of Afghanistan*, 271–273. The first accord was signed in Islamabad on 7 March 1993, the second in Jalalabad on 18 May 1993. The parties to these accords aimed to establish an interim government, draft a new constitution, and initiate an election process.

[155] S/Res/1193 (1998) of 28 August 1998; Resolution 1214 (1998) of 8 December 1998; A/Res/53/165 of 25 February 1999.

[156] Fröhlich, *Nationalismus und Nationalsaat*, 130.

[157] August Pradetto, "Internationaler Terror, forcierter Regimewechsel und die UNO: Der Fall Afghanistan", *Aus Politik und Zeitgeschichte* 51 (2001), 31.

the poorest countries on earth. Five major invasions, three civil wars, drought, and a dispersed population have greatly impoverished the country. According to a 2000 report of the UN Human Rights Commission, Afghanistan has the world's highest child mortality, at 27 percent, and the largest number of widows and orphans. The average life expectancy is 40 years, while illiteracy ranks at 70 percent. At least 10 percent of the population is threatened by starvation, and this proportion is growing.[158] In 25 years of civil war, more than 1.5 million people died and at least 6 million were displaced. Approximately 80 percent of the Afghan civil population were refugees in their own country, and up to 4 million people were forced into neighbouring states.[159]

With the cultivation and sale of opium the only profitable economic activity in the country, Afghanistan has become one of the world's largest producers of the narcotic. According to the United Nations Office on Drugs and Crime, the country produces three-quarters of the world's illegal trade. In 2003 Afghan opium farmers and dealers earned approximately US$ 2.3 billion, half of the gross domestic product, and production is growing.[160] While it suppressed opium cultivation in the early years of its rule, the Taliban, as well as the Northern Alliance, later cooperated closely with the international mafia that sells the drug in Europe and the United States. After the 2001 invasion of the United States and its allies, heroin and opium production rose dramatically. The following excerpt from the 2006 report of the United Nations Office on Drugs and Crime illustrates this reality:

> This year the largest cultivation took place in the south, especially in Helmand and Kandahar provinces, where governance has collapsed under the weight of insurgency, drugs, crime and corruption ... Around the country, the number of people involved in opium cultivation increased by almost a third to 2.9 million—12.6% of the total population. Only six of the country's 34 provinces are opium free.[161]

The 2008 Office on Drugs and Crime report noted that in spite of a slight decrease, opium cultivation levels remain formidably high. Both reports clearly

---

158 CIA, "World Fact Book 2000". Afghanistan, http://www.odci.gov/cia/publications/factbook/geos/af.html.

159 For more information about the situation in Afghanistan in 2000, see the *Report of the Secretary-General on the Situation in Afghanistan and Its Implications for International Peace and Security*, S/2000/1106, 20 November 2000 and Reports of the Secretary-General from 2000 until 2008, http://www.un.org/documents/repsc.htm.

160 Susanna Loof, "UN Agentur warnt Afghanistan vor Opium", www.rawa-germany.de/aktuel, October 29, 2003.

161 Afghanistan Opium Survey 2006, United Nations Office on Drugs and Crime, Vienna, http://www.unodc.org/pdf/execsummaryafg.pdf., 5.

illustrate the influence of the absence of effective government. The number of opium-free provinces is growing in the north and centre of the country, but cultivation is growing in the south and west, where the instability holds sway.[162]

The Efforts of the International Community

Although both Somalia and Afghanistan experienced the breakdown of effective government at the same time, the reactions of the international community were completely different. While Somalia was considered the prime example of a 'failed state', the international reaction to the situation in Afghanistan was mainly restricted to humanitarian assistance from the withdrawal of the Soviet Union in 1989 to the military operation of the United States and its allies on 7 October 2001.

The first reaction of the United Nations to the situation in Afghanistan was in response to Soviet intervention at the end of the 1970s.[163] The United Nations endeavoured to negotiate between Afghanistan and Pakistan, and also between the superpowers, but this bid for peace had no effect. As a result, the United Nations restricted its activity in Afghanistan in the 1980s to providing humanitarian aid.[164] It took a more active role during the drafting of the Geneva Accord on 14 April 1988, after the Soviet government resolved to separate the Afghan conflict from bilateral American-Soviet relations.[165] One of the most important negotiation issues in these accords, besides the withdrawal of Soviet troops, foreign interference, and the surge in refugees, was the political future of Afghanistan.[166] This issue, however, was left open because of the lack of participation of the opposition groups. The efforts of UN Secretary-General Diego Cordovez to promote a solution of the internal conflict were therefore unsuccessful.[167] Two UN mandates, the United Nations Good Offices Mission in Afghanistan (UNGOMAP) between 1988 and 1990 and the Office of the Secretary General for Afghanistan and Pakistan

[162] "Afghanistan Opium Winter Rapid Assessment Survey 2008", United Nations Office on Drugs and Crime, http://www.unodc.org/documents/crop-monitoring/Afghan-winter-survey-Feb08-short.pdf.

[163] S/Res/462 (1980) of 9 January 1980.

[164] A/Res/40/137 of 13 December 1985.

[165] Hubel, *Das Ende des Kalten Kriegs*, 207; Dieter Braun and Karlernst Ziem, *Afghanistan: Sowjetische Machtpolitik-islamische Selbstbestimmung, Innenafghanische Prozesse, Regionale Konfliktfolgen, Internationale Verflechtungen* (Baden-Baden: Nomos Verlagsgesellschaft, 1988), 207.

[166] Gray, *International Law and the Use of Force*, 81.

[167] Hubel, *Das Ende des Kalten Kriegs*, 207.

(OSGAP) between 1990 and 1994, were unsuccessful in ensuring the non-interference of the two superpowers and neighbouring countries.[168]

The United Nations organs responded differently to the situation in Afghanistan. The Security Council mainly ignored the situation between 1992 and 1998,[169] while the General Assembly put Afghanistan on its agenda from the end of the Cold War to 11 September 2001. During this period the General Assembly resolutions mainly dealt with the humanitarian situation, the refugee situation, and the reconstruction of the country.[170] For example, the General Assembly assessed the establishment of the Islamic State of Afghanistan in April 1992 as a '[...] new opportunity for the reconstruction of the country [...]' in Resolution 47/119 of 2 April 1993[171] and mentioned the link between the revitalization of the economy and reconstruction of the state in Resolution 48/208 of 21 December 1993.[172] The latter resolution adopted the establishment of the UN Special Mission in Afghanistan (UNSMA) to achieve this assisted reconstruction.[173]

In the years that followed, the General Assembly was consistently concerned with the humanitarian situation and reconstruction in Afghanistan, usually linking the two, but the language of its resolutions remained vague, especially concerning reconstruction. In fact, the General Assembly resolutions on international assistance were restricted to restoring basic services and financial and technical assistance, while the revitalization of the economy as a precondition for ensuring peace somehow disappeared.[174] In addition, because of its lack of law-making power, the General Assembly appeared in the resolutions not as an effective actor but an institution that appealed to the Afghan government and the international community to provide assistance.

When the Taliban came into power in 1996, the international community preferred to isolate the movement economically and politically instead of

---

[168] *Repertory of Practice of United Nations Organs*, Supplement No. 7, 1989, article 98, paras 364–372; *Report of the Secretary-General on the Situation in Afghanistan and Its Implications for International Peace and Security*, Doc. A/45/635-S/21879 of 17 October 1990, para. 21; Afsah and Guhr, "Afghanistan: Building a State", 399.

[169] In this period the only Security Council resolution was S/Res/1076 (1996) of 22 October 1996.

[170] A/Res/48/208 of 21 December 1993; A/Res/49/140 of 20 December 1994; A/Res/50/189 of 22 December 1995; A/Res/51/195 [A] and [B] of 17 December 1996; A/Res/52/211 of 27 February 1998; A/Res/203 [A] and [B] of 12 February 1999.

[171] A/Res/47/119 of 2 April 1993, Emergency International Assistance for the Reconstruction of War-Stricken Afghanistan.

[172] For example, A/Res/48/208 of 21 December 1993.

[173] A/Res/48/208 of 21 December 1993.

[174] A/Res/47/119 of 2 April 1993.

dealing with it.[175] This isolation policy posed a dilemma. On the one hand, the United Nations and most states did not recognise the Taliban government in spite of its control over 90 percent of Afghanistan and considered President Burhanuddin Rabbani of the Northern Alliance the only legitimate representative of the country.[176] On the other hand, many Security Council and General Assembly resolutions after 1998 were directed to solving problems in Afghanistan through the Taliban, in the capacity of a conflict party rather than a government.[177] The international community's policy of ignoring the Taliban as a government brought the counter-reaction of the Taliban's ignoring the international community and also international law.[178]

Besides non-recognition, the international community used economic sanctions in its policy of isolating the Taliban. The Security Council proceeded with sanctions step by step until 11 September 2001. Sanctions against the Taliban in 1999 were limited to restricting air traffic and freezing financial resources, but in 2000 economic sanctions were extended to cover Usama bin Laden and al Qaeda as well as the Taliban.[179] The international community thus faced a second dilemma. Improving the economic situation was ostensibly an important part of state reconstruction, but the policy of economic sanctions against the Taliban worsened the economy.[180] Secretary-General Kofi Annan and various international aid organisations opposed political and economic sanctions, largely because of their negative effects on the impoverished population, but their warnings had little impact on the policy of the international community.[181] On the other hand, they called attention to the extremely critical economic and social situation in Afghanistan, which was mentioned in a number of General Assembly resolutions.[182]

The international community's practice in Afghanistan clearly showed that this policy did not bring the Taliban into the sphere of international law

---

175 Wolfrum and Philipp, "Die Taliban", 149–153.

176 Ibid., 149. Only Pakistan, Saudi-Arabia, and the United Arab Republics officially recognised the Taliban.

177 A/Res/53/203 A–B of 12 February 1999; A/Res/53/165 of 25 February 1999; A/Res/54/189 A–B; A/Res/54/185 of 29 February 2000; S/Res/1214 (1998) of 8 December 1998; S/Res/1267 (1999) of 15 October 1999; S/Res/1333 (2000) of 19 December 2000.

178 For more information about the status and rights and duties of the Taliban, see Wolfrum and Philipp, "Die Taliban", 145–156.

179 S/Res/1267 (1999) of 15 October 1999; S/Res/1333 (2000) of 19 December 2000.

180 Wolfrum and Philipp, "Die Taliban", 149–153.

181 Koffi Annan, Frankfurter Rundschau, Dezember 21, 2000.

182 General Assembly resolutions dealing with the situation of human rights in Afghanistan; A/Res/50/189 of 22 December 1995; A/Res/51/108 of 12 December 1996; A/Res/52/14 5 of 12 December 1997; A/Res/53/165 of 9 December 1998; A/Res/54/185 of 17 December 1999; A/Res/55/119 of 4 December 2000.

but instead marginalised movement further and worsened the economic and political situation of the country. More important, the international community lost any means of dealing with the Taliban.

It is necessary here to stress the hypocrisy of the international community regarding Afghanistan and the role of power politics in international law during the past decade. The United States permitted the Pakistani Inter-Services Intelligence (ISI) service to support the Taliban but at the same time disseminated anti-Taliban propaganda based on the regime's repression of women and destruction of the Buddhist monuments in Bamiyan in 2001.[183] The United States was not alone in this duplicity. Among the U.S. allies, the Arab countries supported the Taliban financially and Pakistan furnished military supplies and advisers.[184]

The General Assembly acknowledged that the situation of Afghanistan was a threat to international security at the beginning of the 1990s, pointing out its social and economic consequences for the region. One of these consequences was the influx of Afghan refugees into Pakistan and Iran.[185] The Security Council first identified the military confrontation in Afghanistan as a threat to regional security because of the refugees and displaced persons in 1996.[186] Security Council Presidential Statements in April, July, and December 1997 stated that the continuing conflict fostered terrorism and exacerbated the drug trade.[187]

In 1998 the international community began to take a different position on Afghanistan, mainly as a result of the bombings of U.S. embassies in Nairobi, Kenya, and Dar es Salaam, Tanzania, on 7 August 1998. Security Council Resolution 1189 (1998) called the bombings acts of international terrorism and stressed the need to eliminate international terrorist acts to maintain international peace and security.[188] With Resolution 1193 (1998), the Security Council changed its policy regarding the Taliban.[189] While before the bombings the Security Council had considered the Taliban one of the conflict parties to

---

183 Michael Ignatieff, "State Failure and Nation-Building", in *Humanitarian Intervention: Ethnic, Legal, and Political Dilemmas*, ed. J.L. Holzgrefe and R.O. Keohane (Cambridge: Cambridge University Press, 2003), 316.

184 Hacke, "Amerikas Krieg", 17.

185 A/Res/45/12 of 7 November 1990; A/Res/46/23 of 5 December 1991; A/RES/51 of 13 February 1997.

186 S/Res/1076 (1996) of 22 October 1996.

187 S/PRST/1997/20 of 16.4.1997: S/PRST/1997/35 of 9.7.1997; S/PRST/1997/55 of 16 December 1997.

188 S/Res/1189 (1998) of 13 August 1998. In this resolution, the Security Council mentioned neither Al-Qaeda nor the Taliban as the perpetrators.

189 S/Res/1193 (1998) of 28 August 1998.

involve in finding a solution to the conflict, Resolution 1193 (1998) accused the Taliban of breaking the international rule of law, violating human rights, and protecting international terrorists.[190]

Several Security Council resolutions before 11 September 2001 mentioned international terrorism in and around Afghanistan.[191] Resolution 1214 (1998) of 8 December 1998 noted that Afghan territory, especially area controlled by the Taliban, was used 'for the sheltering and training of terrorists and the planning of terrorists acts'.[192] The language of the Security Council became sharper in subsequent resolutions. Resolution 1267 (1999) linked Usama bin Laden to the bombings of the U.S. embassies in Africa and accused the Taliban of sheltering bin Laden.[193] The United Nations supported U.S. demands that the Taliban deliver bin Laden and other members of terrorist organisations for criminal proceedings, referring to Chapter VII of the UN Charter.[194]

The international community's changing policy concerning the violation of human rights, however, contained an element of hypocrisy. In the same month as the bomb attacks, the Taliban massacred at least 2,000 people, mostly Hazara civilians, and killed an unknown number of people in aerial bombardments after the conquest of Mazar-i-Sharif in August 1998.[195] These events drew little reaction from the international community. Security Council Resolution 1189 (1998) of 13 August 1998, adopted after the massacre began in Mazar-i Sharif, mentioned only the bombing of the U.S embassies. In a subsequent resolution, Resolution 1193 (1998), the Security Council cursorily mentioned the massacre along with international terrorism and drugs. Ironically, the Security Council's human rights agenda focused on discrimination against girls and women during this time.[196]

The international community's attitude toward Afghanistan changed again quickly after 11 September 2001, when al Qaeda claimed responsibility for the attacks on the World Trade Centre and the Pentagon. The Security Council and the General Assembly reacted speedily.[197] Resolutions 1368 (2001) and 1373 (2001) called the terrorist attacks a threat to international peace and security

---

[190] Ibid.

[191] S/Res/1333 (2000) of 19 December 2000; S/Res/1267 (1999) of 15 October 1999.

[192] S/Res/1214 (1998) of 9 December 1998.

[193] S/RES/1267 (1999) of 15 October 1999.

[194] Cristian Schaller, *Internationales Sanktionsmanagement im Rahmen von Artikel 41 UN-Charta* (Baden-Baden: Nomos Verlagsgesellschaft, 2003), 135; S/Res/1267 (1999) of 15 October 1999.

[195] http://www.hrw.org/reports98/afghan/Afreporo.htm#P35_500 of 30 August 2007.

[196] S/Res/1193 (1998) of 28 August 1998.

[197] A/Res/56/1 of 12 September 2001; S/Res/1368 (2001) of 12 September 2001; S/Res/1373 (2001) of 28 September 2001.

and mentioned '[...] the inherent right of individual and collective self-defence in accordance with the Charter [...]' without mentioning the Taliban or al Qaeda as responsible.[198]

From that point until the invasion of Afghanistan by the United States and its allies, the United Nations and United States ran on two different tracks. The United States concentrated on military action based on the right to individual and collective self-defence. On 12 September President George W. Bush asked the U.S. Congress for US$ 26 million to fight the terrorist threat, and on 14 September the U.S. Senate and House of Representatives passed a resolution authorising the use of force against terrorists. After calling on the Taliban to hand over all al Qaeda members and provide access to their training camps on 20 September, Bush committed the United States to a long-term 'war on terror' in almost every speech and called for a world coalition with the slogan, 'Either you are with us, or you are with the terrorists'.[199]

The United Nations took a different approach. Security Council resolutions called the 11 September attacks a threat to international peace and cited the inherent right of individual and collective self-defence under Chapter VII of the UN Charter but did not link this right to the United States. Even in Resolution 1373 (2001), the Security Council invoked Chapter VII in calling for redoubled efforts to prevent and suppress terrorist acts without mentioning al Qaeda or the Taliban.[200] Resolution 1368 (2001) called on all Member States to bring the people responsible for those acts to justice and stressed that any state aiding, supporting, and harbouring them would be held accountable.[201] The Security Council President's press statements focused on the political, military, and humanitarian situation in Afghanistan and called on the Taliban to implement Security Council resolutions. The United Nations also expressed its willingness to resolve the crisis in Afghanistan and develop plans to rehabilitate the country.[202]

The United States and its allies mounted a military operation against the Taliban on 7 October 2001. Calling Afghanistan the first step in the 'war on terror',[203] the United States and Great Britain cited the Taliban's refusal to hand over bin Laden and other al Qaeda leaders, close the alleged training camps

---

[198] S/Res/1373 (2001) of 28 September 2001; S/Res/1368 (2001) of 12 September 2001.

[199] Hacke, "Amerikas Krieg", 11.

[200] S/Res/1368 (2001) of 12 September 2001, S/Res/1373 (2001) of 28 September 2001.

[201] S/Res/1368 (2001) of 12 September 2001.

[202] Press Statement on Afghanistan by the Security Council President, Press Release SC/7148 of 18 September 2001; Press Statement on Afghanistan by the Security Council President, Press release AFG/148 SC/7164 of 4 October 2001.

[203] Conrad Schetter, "Der Krieg in Afghanistan und seine regionale Dimension", *Jahrbuch Internationale Politik 1997/1998* (2000), 211 et. seq.

for terrorists, and release foreign prisoners as reasons for the military intervention.[204] U.S. Secretary of Defence Donald Rumsfeld's strategy of supporting the opposition with military assistance made the Northern Alliance an important part of the ground forces of this Coalition.[205] In a press statement, the Security Council President reported receiving a letter from the United States and Great Britain two days after the invasion that justified the action under Article 51, which was accepted as tacit approval of the intervention by the United Nations.[206] When Kabul, Kandahar, Jalalabad, Mazar-i-Sharif, and Herat fell to the United States and its allies by November 2001, Security Council Resolution 1378 (2001) endorsed the action to 'root out terrorism' and recognised '[...] the urgency of the security and political situation in Afghanistan in light of the most recent developments, particularly in Kabul'.[207]

As mentioned earlier, the solution of the internal conflict in Afghanistan remained an open question in the Geneva Accord. Immediately after the October 2001 invasion, the international community was faced with the same question. Actually, the United Nations found itself in a dilemma after the U.S. invasion. The way the United Nations was entrusted with rebuilding Afghanistan clearly illustrates this dilemma and complex problems of international law. First, the United Nations preferred to avoid military intervention after 11 September but found itself entrusted with the task of cleaning up after the military operation of the United States and its allies. Moreover, the ambivalence of much of the international community toward the military intervention in Afghanistan complicated the UN's role.[208]

The UN's reaction was poised between two approaches. U.S. Secretary of State Colin Powell called for sending international peacekeeping forces to Afghanistan after the invasion. Lakhdar Brahimi, the Special Representative of the Secretary-General for Afghanistan, in contrast, pointed out the Afghan people's well-known resentment of foreign troops and instead supported a multi-ethnic Afghan peacekeeping force with UN support.[209] Proposals for a post-Taliban government changed many times between a partition plan by the United States and ideas representing diverse interests of Afghans and dele-

---

[204] Hacke, "Amerikas Krieg", 13; www.un.org/News/Press/docs/2001/afg152.doc.htm.

[205] Ibid.

[206] Press release AFG/152 SC/7167 www.un.org/News/Press/docs/2001/afg152.doc.htm; Hacke, "Amerikas Krieg", 13.

[207] S/Res.1378 (2001) of 14 November 2001.

[208] Michael Bothe, "Militärische Gewalt als Instrument von Konfliktregelung: Versuch einer rechtlichen und politischen Ordnung zehn Jahre nach dem Ende des Ost-West-Konflikts", in *Praxishandbuch UNO, Die Vereinten Nationen im Lichte globaler Herausforderungen*, ed. Sabine von Schorlemer (Berlin: Springer-Verlag, 2003), 13, 24.

[209] Brahimi, *Briefing to the Security Council.*

gates of various international organisations and NGOs.[210] Brahimi proposed three security options: a multi-ethnic Afghan security force, a multinational force, and a UN peacekeeping force.[211] The Security Council adopted the first option.[212]

On 14 November 2001, the day after Kabul fell to the United States-supported Northern Alliance, the Security Council adopted Resolution 1378 (2001), calling for the international community's reconstruction of Afghanistan. The Security Council established the UN's mandate on the basis not of protectorship, as in East Timor and Kosovo, but of collateral power, the so-called 'light footprint' mandate.[213] The Afghan people were to be the main actors in establishing the new government, with assistance from the international community.[214] There were three main reasons for choosing such a limited task for the United Nations. First, the country's size and complexity made a protectorship unrealistic, especially given the United Nation's negative experience in East Timor and Kosovo. Second, the difficulty and failure of international reconstruction efforts in Kosovo and Somalia had shown that the United Nations lacked capacity to deal with such an overwhelming task. The third reason was the likely resistance of the Afghan people to any external intervention.[215]

In response to Brahimi's directive on 13 November 2001 and Resolution 1378 (2001), the United Nations convened an Afghanistan Conference in Bonn, Germany, between 27 November and 5 December 2001.[216] The Bonn Conference established the basis for the international community's mandate to reconstruct Afghanistan, but it also sowed the seeds of failure, in which the 'war on terror' played an important role.

The Bonn negotiations and resulting agreement led the international community to give up its opportunity to find a long-term solution to the conflict in Afghanistan for several reasons. First, reconciliation is generally accepted as the first step in a post-conflict situation, but the Bonn Conference failed to provide for such a process. The international community's policy of isolating the Taliban before 11 September took on a new dimension when the Taliban was identified as an enemy. Five Afghan groups participated in the Bonn conference, including the two main groups—the United Front for the Salvation of Afghanistan (Northern Alliance) and a Tajik-dominated military alliance—

[210] Pradetto, "Internationaler Terror", 26–27.
[211] Brahimi, *Briefing to the Security Council.*
[212] Pradetto, "Internationaler Terror", 26–34.
[213] Afsah and Guhr, "Afghanistan: Building a State", 382.
[214] S/Res/1378 (2001) of 14 November 2001; Ignatieff, "State Failure and Nation-Building", 309.
[215] Ibid., 383.
[216] Brahimi, *Briefing to the Security Council.*

and the so-called Cyprus group, Peshawar group, and Rome group of exiles.[217] Although it was almost as large as all these groups combined, the Taliban was not invited. Its absence meant that the large Pashtun ethnic group was not represented. Thus the international community took the first step toward ignoring part of the population of Afghanistan, even though Security Council Resolution 1378 (2001) called for a broad-based, multi-ethnic, fully representative government.[218] The entire reconstruction process was in fact based on the concepts of good and evil. The Security Council resolutions assigned the 'evil' role to the Taliban and the 'good' role to the Northern Alliance. The Petersberg Agreement described the mudjaheddin as follows:

> [...] the Afghan Mujahideen who, over the years, have defended the independence, territorial integrity and national unity of the country and have played a major role in the struggle against terrorism and oppression, and whose sacrifice has now made them both heroes of jihad and champions of peace, stability and reconstruction of their beloved homeland, Afghanistan [...].[219]

Second, time pressure made it almost impossible to initiate a reconciliation process among the participants in the Bonn Conference. The Afghan parties had just eight days to deal with their past and plan their future, although the roots of the complex Afghan conflict went back many decades. Many controversial issues—the demobilisation of the mudjaheddin, the roles of the former king and Rabbani, and an international security force for Kabul—were suppressed at the conference without giving the participants time to seek rapprochement. Europe, the United Nations, and the United States pressed the participants to end their divisions without understanding each other. The United States repeatedly conveyed messages to Rabbani that it would hold accountable anyone opposed to the peace process.[220]

Therefore, the success of the conference was measured by how quickly an agreement could be reached rather than the feasibility and effectiveness of that agreement. The participants were enjoined to adhere to the planned timetable even for such important stages of the process as the election of the Loya Jirga and the drafting of the new constitution. With the exception of a few substantive issues, the participants were pushed to accept a ready-made outline of a process.[221]

---

[217] Afsah and Guhr, "Afghanistan: Building a State", 410.
[218] S/Res/1378 1378 of 14 November 2001, Para. 1.
[219] Petersberg Agreement, *Agreement on Provisional Arrangements in Afghanistan Pending the Reestablishment of Permanent Government Institutions*, Doc. S/2001/1154.
[220] Afsah and Guhr, "Afghanistan: Building a State", 412.
[221] Ibid., 384.

The Petersberg Agreement was signed on 5 December 2001, at the end of the Afghan Conference in Bonn. Because the participants did not discuss the roots of the civil conflict, the agreement was based on neither social nor political consensus.[222] The preamble cites principles of international law such as the 'independence, national sovereignty, and territorial integrity of Afghanistan'. The agreement was based on acceptance of the Afghan people's responsibility for reconstruction and internal security and the need for the international community's assistance,[223] but it consisted mainly of a work plan and timetables to establish a freely chosen, full-fledged government within two or three years.[224] Besides a new constitution, the document envisaged three stages of progressively more representative forms of government: an interim authority for six months, a transitional authority for two years, and a fully representative government elected in free and fair elections.[225]

The 'war on terror' indirectly influenced the content of the Petersberg Agreement in several ways. Because both the 'war on terror' and the Bonn Conference were based on the concept of good vs. evil, the agreement did not deal with the critical past or need to include the transitional justice component common in post-conflict situations.[226] The agreement also divided the Afghan people, portraying the Northern Alliance as an ally in the 'war on terror' and the Taliban as the enemy. Other issues commonly dealt with in post-conflict situations—disarmament, demobilisation, and reintegration—had no chance of implementation. Instead of calling for its demobilisation and disarmament, the United States-led coalition provided the Northern Alliance with financial and military aid.[227] The Petersberg Agreement's aims of national reconciliation, lasting peace, stability, and respect for human rights, independence, and national sovereignty were aborted during the Bonn negotiations or stillborn because of the 'war on terror' against part of the population of Afghanistan.

The Petersberg Agreement, as well as many Security Council resolutions, showed that the UN mandate in Afghanistan, unlike its other peace-building mandates, was based on 'light footprint' assistance.[228] One day after the Bonn Conference, the Security Council adopted Resolution 1383 (2001) to endorse the Petersberg Agreement. The United Nations established two different

[222] Petersberg Agreement of 5 December 2001.

[223] Ibid.

[224] Afsah and Guhr, "Afghanistan: Building a State", 383.

[225] Petersberg Agreement of 5 December 2001.

[226] Afsah and Guhr, "Afghanistan: Building a State", 385.

[227] Ibid., 450.

[228] S/Res/1378 (2001) of 14 November 2001; Petersberg Agreement, Annex to S/Res/1383 (2001) I (International Security Force), II (The Role of the United Nations during the Interim Period), and III (Request to the Untied Nations by the Participants at the UN Talks on Afghanistan).

mandates, the International Security Assistance Force (ISAF) and the United Nations Assistance Mission in Afghanistan (UNAMA). Security Council Resolution 1386 (2001) established ISAF under Chapter VII. ISAF was initially envisaged for six months, with the primary task of ensuring security for the Afghan Interim Authority and UN personnel.[229] ISAF undertook its duties in Kabul on 2 January 2002 on behalf of the United Nations. When the situation failed to improve, the Security Council extended ISAF's mandate several times and expanded it to cover the whole of Afghanistan.[230] Security Council Resolution 1833 (2008) extended the UNAMA mandate beyond 13 October 2008 for a period of 12 months.[231]

UNAMA was shaped mainly by an 18 March 2002 report of the Secretary-General[232] and the Petersberg Agreement, which centred on humanitarian relief, reconciliation, and reconstruction,[233] and endorsed by Security Council Resolution 1401 (2002).[234] UNAMA's mandate was extended until 23 March 2010 by Security Council Resolution 1868 (2009).[235] There was no mention in these resolutions, however, of the legal basis of UNAMA.

The international community succeeded in achieving the targets in its timetable. In 2008 the Islamic Republic of Afghanistan has an elected government. The new constitution is a mixture of Islamic and liberal ideas, combining the 'principles of Islam, democracy, pluralism, and social justice'.[236] Article 3 on law and religion rules that 'In Afghanistan, no law can be contrary to the beliefs and provisions of the sacred religion of Islam', although there is no explicit ruling on Sharia. The state structure described in the constitution is based mainly on Western values. According to Article 60, Afghanistan has a presidential system like that of the United States. The president is the head of the state but also the head of government. In December 2002 the Petersberg II Conference also established a national army for Afghanistan.[237]

---

229 S/Res/1386 (2001) of 20 December 2001.

230 Hacke, "Amerikas Krieg", 15; S/Res/1413 (2002) of 23 May 2002; S/Res/1444 (2002) of 27 November 2002; S/Res/1510 (2003) of 13 October 2003; S/Res/1563 (2004) of 17 September 2004; S/Res/1623 (2005) of 13 October 2005.

231 S/Res/1833 (2008) of 22 September 2008.

232 Doc.A/56/875—S/2002/278 of 18 March 2002, Para. 98. http://www.unama-afg.org/docs/_UN-Docs/_repots-SG/2002/2002–278.pdf.

233 http://www.unama-afg.org/about/overview.htm of 5 December 2007.

234 S/Res/1401 (2002) of 28 March 2002.

235 S/Res/1868(2009) of 23 March 2009.

236 Article 34 (Expression, Press, Media), Article 22 (Equality), Article 2 (Religion).

237 Konferenz "Afghanistan im Wiederaufbau-Frieden und Stabilität", Petersberg, Germany, www.auswertiges-amt.de/www/de/aussenpolitik/Friedenspolitik/ afghanistan/konferenz-021201-html.

The current situation in Afghanistan has been influenced partly by the reconstruction efforts of the Afghan people and international community and partly by the 'war on terror'. After more than eight years of intervention by the United States and its allies, it can hardly be said that the 'war on terror' has been won or the country rebuilt. Nor does the country have stability which promises security and peace. Only Kabul is under the control of the current government, but as Brahimi has said, 'The control of the capital of the country has immense symbolic value.'[238] Resentment has grown against the Hamid Karzai government as well as against foreign intervention. Karzai's presidency of the Islamic Republic of Afghanistan does not mean that he is accepted by the Afghan people. Several ministers in his government have been killed, and his government is barely in control of the country outside of Kabul. More countries have been accused of harbouring al Qaeda, which has gained increasing sympathy and recruits in Islamic countries.[239] During the reconstruction process Afghan civilians have suffered human rights abuses in their own country and internment in the U.S. naval based in Guantanamo.[240]

Somehow, the international community lost its bearings during its engagement in Afghanistan. The Security Council and General Assembly declared in many resolutions before 11 September 2001 that the Afghan crisis could be settled only by peaceful means and that

> [...] territorial gains through military operation will neither lead to a durable peace in Afghanistan, nor contribute to a comprehensive settlement of the conflict in this multi-cultural and multi-ethnic country.[241]

However, because the main aim of the 'war on terror' was to gain territory through military intervention, the international community is far from finding a long-term solution for or in Afghanistan and is still concerned mainly with security despite efforts to rebuild the state.[242] Security Resolution 1746 (2007) of 23 March 2007 focused on

> [...] the security situation in Afghanistan, in particular the increased violent and terrorist activities by the Taliban, Al-Qaida, illegally armed groups and those involved in the narcotics trade, and the links between the terrorism and illicit drugs, resulting in threats to the local population, national security forces and international military and civilian personnel, and stressing the importance of security [...].[243]

238 Brahimi, *Briefing to the Security Council.*
239 Hacke, "Amerikas Krieg", 19.
240 Ibid.
241 S/Res/1193 (1998) of 28 August 1998; A/Res/51/195 of 13 February 1997.
242 Hacke, "Amerikas Krieg", 17.
243 S/Res/1746 (2007) of 23 March 2007.

As a consequence of this policy, the international community has mounted little effort to solve Afghanistan's economic problems. The difficulty of dealing with economic issues under current conditions is clear, but there has been no serious attempt to address the link made by the General Assembly between revitalising the economy and peace and normalcy in the country.[244]

The 2009 report "Afghanistan: Humanitarianism under Threat" gives the following overview of the international community's actions and the situation of the country between 2006 and 2008:[245]

> In our 2006 report, we noted that the global war on terror was the defining environment of the situation in Afghanistan. At the time, there was still widespread hope that the world-ordering experiment in Afghanistan (and Iraq), built around the imposition of a *Pax Americana*, would prove successful. No such optimism was recorded during our 2008 visits. 'Failure' and 'anxiety about the future' were frequent terms used by Afghans to describe the situation.

[244] A/Res/51/195 of 13 February 1997; A/Res/52/211 of 27 February 1998.

[245] Antonio Donini, "Afghanistan: Humanitarianism under Threat" (Boston: Tufts University Feinstein International Center, 2009), 5, available online at fic.tufs.edu.

Chapter Three

Internal Reflection of the World Historical Context

Historical background and the world political and economic situation determine the causality, appearance, and intensity of the phenomenon of the absence of effective government.[1] Many of the problems of African states have been ascribed to the imposition of colonial rule and the modern state system[2] But while colonialism set the stage, the end of the Cold War was are more important factor. The globalisation process, especially in the economic context, not only intensified the breakdown of effective government, but also increased its negative effect on the world order. This chapter explains these external factors and their effects on the internal context.

Colonialism

The six-century legacy of colonialism is one of the most important historical contexts for the absence of effective government.[3] Almost every state in sub-Saharan Africa, Asia, and Latin America that has dealt with the phenomenon has had a colonial inheritance,[4] but Africa is the only continent to have had its entire territory (with the exception of Ethiopia and Liberia) colonised by seven European countries.[5]

---

1 Ingo Liebach, *Die unilaterale humanitäre Intervention im 'zerfallenen Staate' ('Failed State')* (Cologne: Carl Heymanns Verlag, 2004), 37; Jürgen Bartl, *Die Humanitäre Intervention durch den Sicherheitsrat der Vereinten Nationen, im: 'Failed State', Das Beispiel Somalia* (Frankfurt: Peter Lang Publishers, 1999), 75; Daniel Thürer, "Der Wegfall effektiver Staatsgewalt 'the Failed State,'" in *Der Wegfall effektiver Staatsgewalt: 'The Failed State'*, Berichte der Deutsche Gesellschaft für Völkerrecht 34, ed. Daniel Thürer, Matthias Herdegen, and Gerhard Hohloch (Heidelberg: C.F. Müller Verlag, 1996), 13; William L. Zartman, introduction to *Posing the Problem of State Collapse to Collapsed States: The Disintegration and Restoration of Legitimate Authority*, ed. William L. Zartman (Boulder, Colorado: Lynne Rienner Publishers, 1995), 1.

2 Makau wa Mutua, "Why Redraw the Map of Africa: A Moral and Legal Inquiry", *Michigan Journal of International Law* 16 (1995), 4, 1115.

3 David K. Fieldhouse, *The Colonial Empires: A Comparative Survey from the Eighteenth Century*, 2nd edition (London: Macmillan Publishers Ltd., 1982), 3.

4 Ibid., 5.

5 A. Adu. Boahen, ed., *General History of Africa, Volume VII: Africa under Colonial Domination*

The outcomes of colonialism and decolonisation were manifested differently on every continent because of different historical backgrounds. The Ottoman Empire's hegemony from the western Mediterranean to the Indian Ocean, especially between the 16th and 19th centuries, Indian Hindu rule in South Asia from the 9th through the 14th centuries,[6] and European colonialism differ in many respects. Differences can also be seen between the first wave of colonisation in South and North America between the 15th and 19th centuries and the second wave in other parts of the world in the 19th and 20th centuries. One of the most important of these differences was the motive for colonisation, which was occupation in the Americas but exploitation of natural resources in Africa and Asia, where Europe largely remained on the periphery.[7] The time frame of decolonisation also differed, from one-and-a-half to three centuries in the American colonies but only 36 years (between 1945 and 1981) in most colonial territories of Africa, Asia, and the Pacific.

Today the colonial heritage still has a malign effect on the economic, social, and political structures of the former colonial territories.[8] Because of the complexity of this issue, this section focuses on colonialism in Africa.

Arbitrary Boundaries

European powers twice determined the boundaries of the colonial territories, first when they divided them among themselves and later when new states were formed in the colonial territories. The legal basis of colonisation and colonial borders in Africa was largely determined in the Berlin Conference of 1884–1885. European countries—France, Great Britain, Italy, and Germany—came together 'as a forum for the liberalization and internationalization of trade in Africa'. The main aim of the conference was however, to divide the African territories in order to eliminate potential conflict among them. While legalizing 'the partition and subordination of the continent to European states' was the centre issue for the Berlin conference, there was little consideration for ethnic, linguistic, religious, cultural, economic, and demographic features.[9]

1880–1935 (London: James Curry, 1990). At one point, 11 European imperial countries occupied Africa, but by 1914 the number was reduced to 7: Belgium, France, Germany, Great Britain, Italy, Portugal, and Spain.

6 Fieldhouse, *The Colonial Empires*, 3.

7 Ibid., 5.

8 Antony Parsons, *From Cold War to Hot Peace, UN Intervention 1947–1995* (London: Penguin Books, 1995), 77.

9 Antony Anghie, "Colonialism and the Birth of International Institutions: Sovereignty, Economy, and the Mandate System of the League of Nations", *New York University Journal of International Law and Politics* 34 (2002), 3, 549; Isaak I. Dore, "Constitutionalism and the

British Prime Minister Lord Salisbury (1830–1903) described the ignorance of the colonial powers in drawing up the boundaries of countries in West Africa as follows:

> We have been engaged in drawing lines upon maps where no man's foot ever trod; we have been giving away mountains and rivers and lakes to each other, only hindered by the small impediment that we never knew exactly where the mountains and the rivers and lakes were.[10]

Somalia, divided between England, France, and Italy into five parts between the mid-1800s and 1960, was one of the many examples of African victims of European colonial policy.[11]

Cultural, ethnic, and social factors also played little role in the creation of boundaries for the new states in the former colonial territories during decolonisation.[12] As a result, some territories remained completely or partly unified and some did not. Somalia, again, may be the most dramatic example of the artificial post-colonial creation of boundaries, as the new state contained only two-fifths of the former territory.[13] Some colonial territories, such as the Belgian Congo, were created as buffer zones to ward off inter-imperialist rivalry.[14] This arbitrary division of territories was the main cause of conflicts between neighbouring countries over the European-drawn boundaries shortly after the independence of the new states. The Ogaden War between Somalia and Ethiopia and border disputes between Nigeria and Cameroon, Algeria and Morocco, and Pakistan and India have their roots in this context.[15] Relationships among people with the same ethnic, social, historical, and cultural heritage in different countries persisted in spite of the new boundaries, as in Ethiopia, Djibouti,

Post-Colonial State in Africa: A Rawlsian Approach", *Saint Louis University Law Journal* 41 (1997), 4, 1303. Mutua, "Why Redraw the Map of Africa", 1127.

10 Dore, "Constitutionalism and the Post-Colonial State in Africa", 1303.

11 Bartl, *Humanitarian Intervention*, 23.

12 Dore, "Constitutionalism and the Post-Colonial State in Africa", 1305.

13 Bartl, *Humanitarian Intervention*, 23. As explained in Chapter 2, after independence from the United Kingdom in 1960, a new state was created from parts of the former territory—North Somalia, a British protectorate, and Italian Somaliland, a United Nations Trust Territory under Italian administration, while two other parts remained in Kenya and Ethiopia and the French protectorate later declared its independence as the state of Djibouti.

14 Yash Tandon, "Globalization and the Great Lakes Regional Crisis", in *Crisis in the Democratic Republic of the Congo*, ed. Mwesigu Baregu (Harare: SAPES Books, 1999), 42, 43. Bolivia, Ecuador, and Paraguay in South America, established as buffer zones, are now experiencing ineffective governments; Robert I. Rotberg, "The Failure and Collapse of Nation-States, Breakdown, Prevention, and Repair" in *When States Fail: Causes and Consequences*, ed. Robert I. Rotberg (Princeton: Princeton University Press, 2004), 46.

15 Daniel G. Partan, "Peaceful Settlement and the Cold War", *Cincinnati Law Review* 34 (1965), 293, 301.

and Kenya.[16] Arbitrary boundaries were also one of the most important reasons for the destruction of common values and traditional structures in the former colonial territories, where most of the new states retained little common socio-political identity.[17]

Destruction of Traditional Systems

Colonialism's destruction of traditional institutions, cultures, and heritage resulted in the lack of a common identity or social consensus for statehood that in large measure determined the failure of the first new republics and subsequent international (regional) conflicts in Africa.[18] Unfortunately, the establishment of constitutions was not enough to camouflage this deficiency. Colonialism's devastation can be summarised in three points.

First, even when former parts of a territory were joined after independence, they no longer had the same identity in spite of their shared pre-colonial heritage. Every colonial power imposed a different education system, language, and political, legal, administrative, and economic structures in its territories, sometimes different administrations in each part of one territory.[19] In many countries the pre-existing contrast between north and south was reinforced after the construction of the state.[20] This is one of the major reasons why Somalia had so many problems post-independence in spite of a common ethnic origin, nomadic tradition, and religion.[21] Italy and the United Kingdom governed

---

16 Bartl, *Humanitarian Intervention*, 26.

17 Dore, "Constitutionalism and the Post-Colonial State in Africa", 1303.

18 The mandate regimes contributed to this destruction of common values. The territory of Cameroon was first under the German Empire from 1870 until the defeat of Germany in First World War and then became two mandate territories, French Cameroon and British Cameroon, under the League of Nations in 1919. Togoland, a German protectorate between 1884 and 1914, was split into two administrative zones under Great Britain and France in 1916. These two zones were classified under the Class B mandate with the establishment of the Mandate System. The so-called Rhodesian territory was divided into Northern and Southern Rhodesia in 1911. After a short period of unification beginning in 1953, Northern Rhodesia declared its independence as the state of Zambia in 1964, and Southern Rhodesia became Rhodesia in 1965 and the country of Zimbabwe in 1980. "Trust and Non-Self-Governing Territories, 1945–1999", http://www.un.org/Depts/dpi/decolonization/trust.htm (accessed 14 February 2006).

19 H. Laurentie, "Recent Developments in French Colonial Policy", in *Colonial Administration by European Powers*, ed. José de Almada, Robert Godding, et al, (London: Royal Institute of International Affairs, 1947), 5.

20 Ahmet I. Samatar, *Socialist Somalia, Rhetoric and Reality* (London: Zed Books, 1988), 17.

21 Michael Birnbaum, *Krisenherd Somalia: Das Land des Terrors und der Anarchie* (Munich: Heyna Verlag, 2002), 178.

their colonial territories according to their own rules,[22] and these differences were shown in the declaration of independence of Somaliland in 1991.

Second, the colonial powers mainly restricted their rule to the political capitals to further their own economic and political interests. They had little interest in erecting costly judicial administrations in the entire territory.[23] While the British Raj in India employed 1,223 administrators and 938 police for roughly 43 million people, only 2,384 Belgian colonial administrators were installed in the Congo to govern 9.4 million people.[24] The native populations hesitated to accept colonial rule completely.[25] Because of the restrictive administrative structure and limitation of colonial rule to certain areas, most of the new states in Africa inherited a coexistence of the rule of the colonial powers and local customary law.[26] Because the education system and language imposed by the colonial powers had been accessible only to the elite in and around the capitals, colonial policies contributed to a new class system and exacerbated social divisions.[27]

Third, the indirect rule of the colonial territories played a decisive role in destroying traditional structures and exacerbating ethnic tensions. Choosing one social group to dominate others in their territories was a relatively inexpensive way for the colonial powers to govern. Many African scholars assert that current ethnic tensions in many African countries are rooted in the colonial policy of divide and rule.[28] The civil wars between the Tutsi and Hutu in Rwanda and Burundi are good examples of the effect of the indirect rule policy.[29] The German and Belgian colonial powers chose Tutsi kings in their territories to

---

22 Samatar, *Socialist Somalia*, 17.

23 Lauren Benton, *Law and Colonial Cultures: Legal Regimes in World History, 1400–1900* (Cambridge: Cambridge University Press, 2002), 27.

24 Jeffrey Herbst, "African Peacekeepers and State Failure", in *Peacekeeping and Peace Enforcement in Africa: Methods of Conflict Prevention*, ed. R. Rotberg, Ericka Albaugh, et al. (Cambridge: World Peace Foundation, 2000), 18.

25 Laurentie, "Recent Developments in French Colonial Policy", 6.

26 Mahmood Mamdani, "From Zaire to the Democratic Republic of the Congo", in *Crisis in the Democratic Republic of the Congo*, ed. Mwesiga Baregu (Harare, Zimbabwe: SAPES Books, 1999), 45–48.

27 Laurentie, "Recent Developments in French Colonial Policy", 5; Agibou Y. Yansané, *Decolonization in West African States with French Colonial Legacy: Comparison and Contrast: Development in Guinea, the Ivory Coast, and Senegal (1945–1980)* (Cambridge, Massachusetts: Schenkmann Publishing, 1984), 135.

28 Dore, "Constitutionalism and the Post-Colonial State in Africa", 1303.

29 It is a moot point whether Hutu, Tutsi, and Twa identities are real ethnicities or notional products of the colonial time. Mamdani, "From Zaire to the Democratic Republic of the Congo", 46; Dore, "Constitutionalism and the Post-Colonial State in Africa", 1303; Akiki B. Mujaju, "The Regional Response in Eastern and South Africa", in *Crisis in the Democratic Republic of the Congo*, ed. Mwesigu Baregu (Harare, Zimbabwe: SAPES Books, 1999), 83.

rule the Hutu, although the Hutu made up almost 85 percent of the population in both countries. Dividing the people and imposing decisions that served the interest of the colonial powers resulted in civil war between the ethnic groups that exploded into massacres and genocide decades later. Between 100,000 and 300,000 Hutu were murdered in Burundi in 1972 and 800,000 Tutsi in Rwanda in three months in 1994.[30] By the end of the civil wars, more than 3 million people had died in both countries.[31] These conflicts resulted in the absence of a government in Burundi at the end of 1993 and in Rwanda in 1994.[32]

Economic Destruction

Colonialism, especially its second wave, was based largely on the economic exploitation of the colonial territories.[33] The economic function of colonialism centred on cheap labour, rich mineral resources, and markets for goods manufactured by the colonial powers.[34] The capture and transport of African slaves to work on plantations in the New World was the first sign of European economic exploitation in Africa, but European capitalism, imperialism, and industrialism and the need for markets and materials meant it would not be the last.[35]

Northern Rhodesia (later Zambia) and the Belgian Congo (later Zaire), for example, were especially rich in copper, mined by local people under often miserable conditions for minimal pay by the colonial overlords.[36] The mercantile commercial enterprises and mine owners had broad rights over the African labour force that included sending workers from one colonial territory to another in search of richer natural resources. Labourers from the colonies of Bechuanaland (Botswana), Basotholand (Lesotho), Swaziland, and parts of Mozambique and Malawi were sent to Northern Rhodesia, Southern Rhodesia

30 Mutual, "Why Redraw the Map of Africa", 1116.

31 Helmut Strizek, *Ruanda und Burundi: Von der Unabhängigkeit zum Staatszerfall: Studie über eine gescheiterte Demokratie im afrikanischem Zwischengebiet* (Munich: Wetforum-Verlag, 1996), 37; Mark A. Drumbl, "Punishment, Post-Genocide: From Guilt to Shame to Civis in Rwanda", *New York University Law Review* 75 (2000), 5, 1221–222.

32 Strizek, *Ruanda und Burundi*, 1.

33 Mutua, "Why Redraw the Map of Africa", 1126.

34 Georg Scott, *The Rise and Fall of the League of Nations* (London: Hutchinson Publishers, 1973), 45; Fenner Brockway, *The Colonial Revolution* (London: Hart-Davis, 1973), 14; Sheikh Daramy, "Constitutional Developments in the Post-Colonial State of Sierra-Leone 1961–1984", *African Studies* 30 (Lewiston, New York: Edwin Mellen Press, 1993), 35; Aguibou Y. Yansané, *Decolonization in West African States, with French Colonial Legacy: Comparison and Contrast: Development in Guinea, the Ivory Coast and Senegal* (Cambirdge, Massachusetts: Schenkman Publishing Company, 1984), 36.

35 Mutua, "Why redraw the Map of Africa", 1126.

36 Rainer Tezlaff, "Der Wegfall effektiver Staatsgewalt in den Staaten Afrikas," *Internationale Politik* 55 (2000), 8–16.

(now Zimbabwe), and South Africa to work in the mines and on large farms.[37] The break-up of families that is the legacy of this migrant labour tradition resonates today and has contributed to the spread of HIV in Africa.

Especially after the Industrial Revolution, the European colonial powers needed foreign markets for their goods and looked abroad for new investment opportunities.[38] Cheap goods shipped to colonial territories by European traders replaced the local exchange systems and resulted in the decline of local industries in formerly wealthy countries such as Somalia.[39]

Uninterested in the economic development of their territories, the colonial powers limited the rudimentary infrastructure they built to serve the needs of colonial commerce,[40] as in the French colonies.[41] The European powers used financial assistance mainly to facilitate the export of wealth from their colonial territories.[42]

Another economic consequence of colonialism was the transformation of many colonies from a traditional to a capitalist production system. This process made the colonial territories markets for the colonial powers.

After decolonization the African states, with their distinctly artificial borders, had lost much of the character of their centuries-long political, social, economic, and cultural traditions. As a result of colonialism's disruptive effect on the most African states were unsuccessful in trying to adapt to the new nation-state paradigm.[43] Makau wa Mutua describes juridical statehood in West Africa as 'straightjackets with timebombs ready to explode'.[44] Since decolonization, corruption, military putsches, internal ethnic or religious rivalry, and the resulting loss of lives and livelihoods and economic, social, and physical misery have been common denominators of the modern states.[45] Mutua writes of the post-colonial state: 'Its normative and territorial construction on the African colonial state, itself a legal and moral nullity, is the fundamental reason for its failure'.[46]

---

37 Scott, *The Rise and Fall of the League of Nations*, 45; Brockway, *The Colonial Revolution*, 14; Yansané, *Decolonization in West African States*, 36.

38 Yansané, *Decolonization in West African States*, 2.

39 Samatar, *Socialist Somalia*, 13.

40 Id., 8, 135; Joe A. Alie, *A New History of Sierra Leone* (London: Macmillan Publishers, 1990), 10.

41 Yansané, *Decolonization in West African States*, 8, 23.

42 Roland Oliver, *The African Experience: Major Themes in African History from Earliest Times to the Present* (London: Harper Collins Publishers, 1991), 224; Basil Davidson, *Modern Africa: A Social and Political History* (London: Longman Publishers, 1994), 53.

43 Mutua, "Why redraw the Map of Africa", 1115.

44 Ibid., 1114.

45 Mutua, "Why redraw the Map of Africa", 1116.

46 Ibid., 1116, 1142.

The Cold War

Writers on the Cold War widely accept that this period lasted between the end of the Second World War and the collapse of the Soviet Union. In fact, conflict between the United States and first Russia and later the Soviet Union began just after the First World War. The conflict between the two countries that characterised the Cold War started after the Second World War when U.S. President Harry Truman (1945–1953) provided military and economic aid to the governments of countries such as Greece, Taiwan, Thailand, and Turkey to aid them in resisting communism.[47]

The Cold War expanded, however, through decolonisation. At the beginning of the anti-colonial movement in Africa, the United States generally left it to the European imperial powers to deal with the independence process.[48] In contrast, after the Second World War the Soviet Union supported the colonised nations in breaking away from the colonial powers in order to undermine Western influence and avert an anti-Soviet alliance. U.S. President Dwight D. Eisenhower's administration (1953–1961) was the first to respond to this Soviet policy. Eisenhower was therefore the most important actor in the expansion of the Cold War and the establishment of the anti-Soviet alliance.

When the Soviet Union supported the secessionist movement in the Congo in 1960, the Cold War expanded into sub-Saharan Africa. The U.S. administrations that followed Eisenhower's continued to expand the Cold War until the collapse of the Soviet Union in 1990. When U.S. President Ronald Reagan (1981–1989) assumed office, the Soviet Union had bases of power in Southern countries that it had established in the 1970s. The Reagan administration claimed a moral and political right to fight against governments supported by the Soviet Union.

While the Truman administration had mainly provided funding, equipment, and military force to the Southern countries, Reagan intervened more directly in their internal affairs. This policy sometimes went so far that the United States overthrew governments supported by the Soviet Union. The Central Intelligence Agency (CIA) mounted such takeovers in countries such as the

---

[47] Public Papers of Presidents of the United States: Harry Truman, 1947 (1963), 178–179; Brockway, *The Colonial Revolution*, 17; Ronald E. Powaski, *The Cold War: The United States and the Soviet Union, 1917–1991* (New York: Oxford University Press, 1998), 104, 300. The Truman administration also did not recognise Communist China, and the United States intervened under the UN Mandate in the Korean War according to its policy of containment.

[48] Powaski, *The Cold War*, 97.

Congo, Guatemala, and Iran.[49] Except for the prohibition against changing the boundaries of these countries, there were no rules in this game.[50]

After the Second World War, international economic institutions and rules increasingly shaped economic relations between states. The global extension of capitalism under the leadership of the United States enabled the United States and Europe to open the economic doors of the Southern countries. Therefore, while military and economic assistance were the main instruments of both superpowers at the beginning of the Cold War, managing the world economic order and facilitating the 'Open Door Policy' through international rules and institutions determined the progress of the Cold War.[51] Chapter 8 deals with this issue in detail. This section summarises the political, social, and economic impacts of the Cold War on the 'Third World' and the effectiveness of the United Nations.

The only point of agreement among the superpowers about the fate of Africa was the need to preserve the borders of the new states. Mutua compares the the new and colonial states as follow:

> The post-colonial state is, in concept and substance, the colonial state in another guise. Just as the colonial state was created by foreigners to benefit them, its existence over the last four decades was guaranteed by those same foreigners because it served the cruel logic of the Cold War.[52]

Obstruction of Political, Economic, and Social Development

The end of the Cold War showed both the fragility of the state structure and the consequences of the Cold War itself. The most important impact of the conflict was the obstruction of political, economic, and social progress in the South, especially in the new African states.

Attempts to build democratic systems or establish states according to the Westphalia system at short notice failed in many of the post-colonial countries, and military regimes and dictatorships took over. To secure ideological allies,

49 Dieter Braun and Karlernst Ziem, *Afghanistan: Sowjetische Machtpolitik-islamische Selbstbestimmung, Innenafghanische Prozesse, Regionale Konfliktfolgen, Internationale Verflechtungen* (Baden-Baden: Nomos Verlagsgesellschaft, 1988), 59; Powaski, *The Cold War*, 104.

50 In fact in Chad, Ethiopia, and the Congo, the Cold War actors intervened in order to maintain the borders. Herbst, "African Peacekeepers and State Failure", 19; Kalala Ilunga Matthiessen, *Die Demokratische Republik Kongo, eine Analyse aus staatstheoretischer, verfassungsrechtlicher und völkerrechtlicher Sicht* (Münster: Waxmann Verlag, 2005), 13.

51 Leo Panitch and Sam Gindin, "Theorizing American Empire", in *Empire's Law: The American Imperial Project and the War to Remake the World*, ed. Amy Bartholomew (London: Pluto Press, 2006), 21.

52 Mutua, "Why Redraw the Map of Africa", 1160.

both superpowers maintained these dictatorial regimes in power for long periods, although they often had no local base of support. Most states in Africa and Asia were dictatorships between the 1970s and 1980s. Siad Barré ruled for more than 20 years in Somalia, from 1969 to 1991, with alternating sponsorship by the United States and the Soviet Union. In Liberia Samuel Doe held power with U.S. support between 1980 and 1990, and in the Congo Mobutu Sese Seko came into power with the help of the CIA and held onto that power from 1965 to 1997.[53] It was no coincidence that Barré and Mobutu immediately lost power after the end of the Cold War. Nor was it a coincidence that effective government broke down in so many countries after this period.[54]

The economic interests of the Cold War parties, especially the United States, also spurred interference in post-colonial governments. The CIA was used directly or indirectly to stifle development and nationalist movements that were perceived to threaten U.S. political, social, and economic interests. The overthrow of Prime Minister Mohammed Mossadegh in Iran[55] and Jacobo Arbenz Guzmán, Guatemala's popularly elected president, in 1953[56] are examples of this interference. After the Republic of the Congo won its independence in 1960, legally elected Prime Minister Patrice Lumumba asked the United Nations for help in dealing with a secessionist movement in Katanga Province.

---

[53] Daramy, "Constitutional Developments", 35; Yansané, *Decolonization in West African States*, 145; Strizek, *Ruanda und Burundi*, 176. Niger, Rwanda. Sierra Leone, and Guinea are some other examples.

[54] Birnbaum, *Socialist Somalia*, 181.

[55] Iran was important for the United States because of its oil reserves. When the United States advocated for the territorial integrity of Iran and its independence from the Soviet Union in 1945, Truman clearly articulated the U.S. interest in Iran's oil, as well as the far vaster oil reserves of nearby Saudi Arabia, which he called '[...] a stupendous source of strategic power [...]'. After Iran gained its independence, Mossadegh nationalised the Anglo-Iranian Oil Company in 1951. In response, the international oil companies boycotted Irani oil, and Mossadegh asked the Eisenhower administration to help solve the problem. When the United States ignored Iran's request, which went counter to its own interests, Iran asked the Soviet Union for help. The U.S. and British intelligence agencies removed Mossadegh from power on 28 May 1953 to protect their oil interests and reinstated the Iranian monarchy under Shah Mohammad Reza Pahlavi. Harry S. Truman, *Memoires, Volume II: Years of Trial and Hope* (London: Hodder and Stoughton, 1956), 95; Powaski, *The Cold War*, 95, 105.

[56] Powaski, *The Cold War*, 106, 300. In Guatemala, where only 2 percent of the population owned 70 percent of the land, reformist President Arbenz attempted to initiate a land reform programme in the 1950s. As part of land redistribution, Arbenz offered to buy 234,000 acres of uncultivated land from the United States-owned United Fruit Company. The United Fruit Company found the price too low and demanded that the Eisenhower administration intervene. Shortly afterward, on 27 June 1953, Arbenz was overthrown by the CIA. With the approval of U.S. President John F. Kennedy (1961–1963), the CIA also prepared plans to overthrow Cuban Head of State Fidel Castro because of his (r)ejection of U.S. corporations and support for other revolutionary movements.

When the United Nations denied his request, Lumumba turned to the Soviet Union. Although Lumumba was pre-eminently a nationalist, CIA Director Allen Foster Dulles proclaimed that he had been 'bought by the Communists'. On 24 November 1965, Lumumba's government was deposed with the help and planning of the CIA.[57]

Proxy wars in many 'Third World' countries were another obstruction in their political, economic, and social development. The conflicts and civil wars in the new post-colonial countries were convenient arenas for the superpowers to fight each other. The rivalry between the Soviet Union and the United States was not the major reason for these conflicts, but because the two superpowers alternately supported the parties in the civil or border conflicts,[58] the Cold War largely determined their intensity and duration in Africa, the Middle East, and South America. During the Cold War, more than 100 major conflicts caused 20 million deaths and even more refugees and impoverishment.[59] Civil war or other brutal conflict left 2 million people displaced and 150,000 dead in El Salvador, Guatemala, and Nicaragua between 1962 and 1992.[60] The proxy wars left many countries with their political and economic structures in shreds.[61] Future civil wars and the absence of effective government in these countries had their roots in the Cold War's brutal and inept dictatorships, exacerbated ethnic rivalries, sub-regional tensions, and build-up of enormous weapons caches.

The Handicapping of the United Nations

Established by the international community to achieve world peace, the United Nations was emasculated by the vetoes of the two superpowers during the entire Cold War period.[62] Syed J.R. Bilgrami tellingly describes the situation

---

57 Richard D. Mahoney, *JFK: Ordeal in Africa, The Ordeal of Power* (New York: Oxford University Press, 1983), 217; Powaski, *The Cold War*, 130.

58 The Siad Barré regime in Somalia was supported by the Soviet Union between 1974 and 1977 and by the United States from 1977 until the collapse of the Soviet Union in 1990. Bartl, *Humanitarian Intervention*, 31.

59 *An Agenda for Peace*, A/47/277 S/24111 of 17 June 1992; Adekeye Adebajo, *Liberia's Civil War: Nigeria, ECOMOG, and Regional Security in West Africa* (Boulder, Colorado: Lynne Rienner Publishers), 1.

60 Peter Sollis, "Partners in Development? The State, NGOs, and the UN in Central America", in *NGOs, the UN, and Global Governance*, ed. Thomas G. Weiss and Leon Gordenker (Boulder, Colorado: Lynne Rienner Publishers, 1996), 189.

61 Ibid.

62 *An Agenda for Peace*, A/47/277 S/24111 of 17 June 1992. Powaski, *The Cold War*, 299 The capacity of the United Nations was already affected after the end of the Second World War by several issues relating to Germany and the control of nuclear energy.

as follows: "When the United States and the Soviet Union are in agreement, the United Nations is useless; when they are in disagreement, the Organisation is powerless."[63]

Three factors kept the United Nations from taking effective measures to promote international peace and security. First, the Cold War policy of interference made it impossible for the organisation to realise its main principles of independence, non-intervention, and equal sovereignty of states. Second, as a consequence of the two superpowers' protection of dictatorial regimes, the democratic legitimisation of new governments, human rights, and political corruption played subordinate roles in international law, diverting the attention of the United Nations to such issues. In fact, it can be claimed that the international community ignored repression and genocide throughout the 1970s and 1980s.[64] When Samuel Doe seized power in Liberia in 1980 through a military coup, the United States regarded him as a strategic Cold War ally in Africa and supported him militarily, economically, and diplomatically between 1980 and 1989 in spite of his corrupt and dictatorial regime and increasing human rights abuses.[65] After the overthrow of Lumumba in the Congo in 1960, Eisenhower and his successors worked closely with Mobutu until 1990 in spite of *his* record of human rights abuses and dictatorship.[66]

The final impediment to the United Nations' effectiveness was the failure of the collective security system. During the Cold War the organisation was barely able to act under Chapters VI and VII, either to prevent conflict in the South or to support peace initiatives of conflict parties, as in the Congo immediately after independence. Nor could the United Nations mediate during the Vietnam War, a typical proxy war, between 1965 and 1973 or the ethnic and religious tensions that ignited the Nigerian civil war and caused two million deaths from independence in 1960 to 1991.[67] Because weapons from both superpowers fuelled the internal conflicts, the United Nations could not implement Article 43 of the UN Charter, which calls on Member States to make armed forces available to the Security Council to maintain international peace and security.[68] The number of UN peace-keeping operations is an interesting

63 Syed J.R. Bilgrami, "United Nations: With and without Cold War", *Indian Journal of International Law* 35 (1995), 144.

64 Strizek, *Ruanda und Burundi*, 25.

65 Adebajo, *Liberia's Civil War*, 21. By 1989, Doe was said to have stolen $ 300 million in public funds; Mutua, "Why Redraw the Map of Africa", 1116.

66 Powaski, *The Cold War*, 105, 131, 223. In spite of the Shah's anti-democratic regime and appalling human rights record, the United States provided economic and military aid between 1954 and 1979, calling praised Iran under his reign 'an island of stability in one of the more troubled areas in the world'.

67 Brockway, *The Colonial Revolution*, 617.

68 Bilgrami, "United Nations: With and without Cold War", 144.

indicator of ineffectuality. There were only 13 such operations during the 40 years between 1948 and 1988, but the same number during the 4 years between 1988 and 1992.[69]

The World Order in the Age of Globalisation

Attempts to define the term 'globalisation' are complicated by the fact that the definition is so broad.[70] For example, no author seems sure when the trend began. Some think that it started at the end of the Cold War,[71] while others think it began in the 1980s and was accelerated by the technological revolution.[72]

There is greater consensus, however, on the different appearance and impact of globalisation in the North and the South. The North is seen as the architect of globalisation, with its advantages of technology, skills, and economic and political integration through international organisations such as the Asia-Pacific Economic Cooperation (APEC), European Union, and North American Free Trade Agreement (NAFTA), while the South is seen mainly as its target.[73] Globalisation and the end of the Cold War set the political, economic, and social context for the absence of effective government after 1990.

Political Impacts of the End of the Cold War

The end of the Cold War directly and indirectly accelerated the dissipation of effective government. One of the direct impacts was the declaration of independence of the territories of the former Communist regimes in the Soviet Union and Yugoslavia after their break-up. The 15 Soviet constituent or union republics from 1956 to 1991 became 15 newly independent states with the dissolution of the Soviet Union.[74] Six independent states were established in the

69 *An Agenda for Peace*, A/47/277 S/24111 of 17 June 1992.

70 Ivan Šimonović, "State Sovereignty and Globalization: Are Some States More Equal?", *Georgia Journal of International and Comparative Law* 28 (2000), 3, 381.

71 Cristopher Clapham, *Africa and The International System: The Politics of State Survival* (Cambridge: Cambridge University Press, 1996), 324; Philip C. Aka, "The Military, Globalization, and Human Rights in Africa", *New York Law School Journal of Human Rights* 18 (2002), 405.

72 Malcolm Waters, *Globalization* (New York: Routhedge Publishing, 1995), 1.

73 Ali A. Mazrui, *Address to the 19th Annual Meeting of the Association of Southern Studies*, http://igcs.binghamton.edu/jgcs_site/dirton7.html, 20 May 2006.

74 These states were Armenia, Azerbaijan, Belarus, Estonia, Georgia, Kazakhstan, Kyrgyzstan, Latvia, Lithuania, Moldova, Russia, Tajikistan, Turkmenistan, Ukraine, and Uzbekistan.

1990s after the disintegration of the Socialist Federal Republic of Yugoslavia.[75] Altogether 21 joined the world order after the end of the Cold War.

Many of these successor states have faced the absence of effective government, with different degrees of turbulence. Shortly after its independence on 9 April 1991, the Democratic Republic of Georgia contended with a civil war that lasted until 1995. Separatist movements in Abkhazia, Ajaria, and South Ossetia were accompanied by widespread inter-ethnic violence. The former Soviet Socialist Republics of Belarus, Kyrgyzstan, Moldova, Turkmenistan, and Tajikistan also have dealt with ineffective governments.[76] The Caucasus has seen six armed conflicts, over 10,000 deaths, and a half million refugees since the end of the Cold War. Several of the new states that arose from the former Socialist Federal Republic of Yugoslavia—Croatia, Bosnia-Herzegovina, Macedonia, and Serbia—have faced similar devastation.[77]

A wave of democratic movements in the South was another repercussion of the end of the Cold War. Eighteen multiparty elections were held in Africa in 1996.[78] The democratic process in Benin, Malawi, Namibia, and South Africa was relatively successful. Cameroon, Ghana, Nigeria, Senegal, and Zambia had some growing pains in their progress toward democracy, but many countries in Africa, Asia, and Latin America have faced intractable conflicts and civil war, accompanied by widespread human rights violations, increased poverty, or weak government. Afghanistan, Burundi, Colombia, Côte d'Ivoire, the Democratic Republic of Congo, Ecuador, Haiti, Liberia, Rwanda, Sierra Leone, Somalia, and Sudan are examples. Factionalism became a cliché in the new states. For example, after Mobutu allowed multi-party politics in the Congo in 1990, approximately 200 new political parties attended a constitutional conference in August 1991.[79] In the 1990s Africa became almost synonymous in the international news with the terms 'humanitarian catastrophe', 'crisis continent', 'clan warfare', and 'genocide'.[80] A 1998 report of the UN Secretary-General noted the following:

---

[75] Jens Reuter, "Die politische Entwicklung in Kosovo 1992/1993", *Südosteuropa* 43 (1994), 1–2, 18–30. The new states are Bosnia and Herzegovina, Croatia, Macedonia, Montenegro, Serbia, and Slovenia.

[76] Rotberg, "The Failure and Collapse of Nation-States", 48.

[77] Thürer, *Der Wegfall effektiver Staatsgewalt*, 11.

[78] Dore, "Constitutionalism and the Post-Colonial State in Africa", 1311; Howard W. French, "Despite Setbacks, Democracy Gains in Africa", *New York Times*, October 21, 2007, 43.

[79] Gerard Kreijen, *State Failure, Sovereigny and Effectiveness: Legal Lessons from the Decolonization of Sub-Saharan Africa* (Leiden: Martinus Nijhoff Publishers, 2004), 75.

[80] Matthiessen, *Die Demokratische Republik Kongo*, 13; Markus Goldmann, "Sierra Leone: African Solution to African Problems", *Max Planck Yearbook of United Nations Law* 9 (2005), 457; Nii Lante Wallace-Bruce, "Of Collapsed, Dysfunctional and Disoriented States: Challenges to International Law", *Netherlands International Law Review* 47 (2000), 63.

> The intra-state conflicts were made by the weapons of the Cold War powers. In 1996 alone, 14 of the 53 countries of Africa were afflicted by armed conflicts, accounting for more than half of all war-related deaths worldwide and resulting in more than 8 million refugees, returnees and displaced persons. The consequences of those conflicts have seriously undermined Africa's efforts to ensure long-term stability, prosperity and peace for its peoples.[81]

The final influence of the end of the Cold War was the appearance of the United States as the only superpower in the political world order. Since the 1990s, the United States has been the predominant influence on international political issues and international law, as explained later.

The World Economic Process

Globalisation has accelerated both the intensity and spread of the absence of effective government. Since 1990 the impact of the globalisation process has been especially evident in the economic world order: broad economic liberalisation, increased access of the North to international trade and investment and facilitaton of the imposition of the 'Open Door Policy' on the South through its technological dominance, and more poverty and indebtedness in the South.[82] The world economic picture in this period is explained in detail in Chapter 8.

The Development of International Law

U.S. dominance and globalisation have influenced public international law as well as international economic law. The impact of these factors on the absence of effective government is summarised below.

Since the end of the Cold War, concepts such as the 'failed state', 'rogue state', and 'war on terror' that appeared in and sometimes determined the international political arena through U.S. foreign policy have directly or indirectly appeared in international law. The term 'failed state' is considered more a part of international law notions or concepts than 'rogue state' and 'war on terror', which are mainly U.S. conflict definitions,[83] but the application of all of these concepts affects international law, as seen in Somalia, Afghanistan, and Iraq. At

81 *The Causes of Conflict and the Promotion of Durable Peace and Sustainable Development in Africa*, Secretary-General's Report to the United Nations Security Council, 16 April 1998, *RADIC* 10 (1998), 549.

82 Aka, "The Military, Globalization and Human Rights in Africa", 136.

83 Henry J. Richardson, "'Failed State', Self-Determination, and Preventive Diplomacy: Colonialist Nostalgia and Democratic Expectations", *Temple International and Comparative Law Journal* 10 (1996), 24.

the same time, the broad interpretation of international security and freedom under Chapter VII of the UN Charter and self-defence under Article 51 have affected states in the South, as explained in detail in Chapter 5.

Another influence on the phenomenon of the absence of effective government has been the appearance of increasingly effective new actors in the international law arena but also within states. While the international organisations as subjects of international law have taken on more authority in the international legal arena, multinational corporations and NGOs have had considerable influence on public international law in spite of their lack of international law subjectivity.[84] Because all these actors play an important role not only in the international order but also in the affairs of sovereign states, they now come under global governance in public international law.[85] Today states which had sole jurisdiction over their territories under the Westphalia System are no longer the only actors in their internal affairs. The issue of global governance has resulted in a new perception of the concept of sovereignty, non-intervention, non-use of force, and even self-determination.

Global governance also looks different in the North and the South. In the North this process, along with economic globalisation, seems a natural step from the Westphalia and capitalist systems, with multinational corporations and international organisations cooperating with the state. But because of its lack of social, economic, and technological capacity, the South could not take this step toward globalisation on its own. In the South the main actors in globalisation come from the North, sometimes with greater financial capacity than the states they work in. The broad influence of the multinational corporations and international financial institutions on the economic policies of Southern countries sometimes means that these countries are barely able to exert their sovereignty in economic affairs.

---

[84] It is even being discussed whether the multinational corporations are under the jurisdiction of the *jus gentium*. Otto Kimminich and Stephan Hobe, *Einführung in das Völkerrecht*, 7th edition (Tübingen, Germany: A. France Verlag, 2000), 123; Volker Epping, "Völkerrechtssubjekte", in *Völkerrecht*, ed. Knut Ipsen, 3rd edition (Munich: C.H. Beck, 1990), 71. Daniel Thürer, "Völkerrecht im Wandel und Wachstum-Gerechtigkeitsgedanke als Kraft der Veränderung", *Zeitschrift für ausländisches und öffentliches Recht und Völkerrecht* 60 (2000), 3–4, 557–604.

[85] David Kennedy, "New Approaches to Comparative Law: Comparativism and International Governance", *Utah Law Review* 2 (1997), 545.

Chapter Four

Determining the Absence of Effective Government in Public International Law

The social and political sciences were already dealing with the absence of effective government by the 1980s,[1] but international law first focused on the issue at the beginning of the 1990s. The notion of the 'failed state' arose in the post-Cold War context of high aspirations for democracy, human rights, a more active role for the United Nations in ensuring collective security, and the appearance of the United States as the main actor in setting the world political agenda. Petra Minnerop points out the defining role of the United States in propagating the concept of precarious states: 'Throughout the second half of the twentieth century the United States of America [...] developed a number of multifarious terms for states to which it ascribed a high threat potential as regards the United States and international security'.[2]

The term 'failed state' first appeared in the article "Saving Failed States" by Gerald Helman and Steven Ratner, published in the magazine *Foreign Policy* in 1992.[3] It was this article that established the basic concept and paradigm. International lawyers have reacted differently to the term. Some have attempted to incorporate "failed state" into international law and to analyse the concept from an international law perspective. Others have refused to admit the concept into public international law on the grounds that it is tainted with neo-colonialism.[4] Fifteen years after it first appeared, the term still has no clear definition.

---

1 Norman Yoffee and George L. Cowgill, eds, *The Collapse of Ancient States and Civilizations* (Tucson, Arizona: University of Arizona Press, 1988): J.A. Tainter, *The Collapse of Complex Societies* (Cambridge: Cambridge University Press, 1988); William. L. Zartman, ed., Collapsed *States: The Disintegration and Restoration of Legitimate Authority*, Boulder Colorado: Lynne Rienner Publisher, 1995.

2 Petra Minnerop, "The Classification of States and the Creation of Status within the International Community," *Max Planck Yearbook of United Nations Law* 7 (2003), 80.

3 Gerard Helman and Steven B. Ratner, "Saving Failed States", *Foreign Policy* 89 (1992–1993), 3.

4 Henry J. Richardson, "'Failed State', Self-determination, and Preventive Diplomacy: Colonialist Nostalgia and Democratic Expectations", *Temple International and Comparative Law Journal* 10 (1996), 7; Ruth E. Gordon, "Saving Failed States: Sometimes a Neo-colonialist Notion", *American University Journal of International Law and Policy* 12 (1997), 6, 906.

Because the absence of effective government is mainly identified in public international law with the concept of the 'failed state', the following section analyses the latter terminologically and then normatively and empirically to move closer to the phenomenon of the absence of effective government. Such an analysis also makes it possible to understand the increasing influence of international politics on international law and the potential harm from such influence. The next section tries to determine whether it is even possible to reach a universal definition of the absence of effective government.

The Notion of the 'Failed State'—Stigmatisation of States

The notion of the 'failed state' was a rallying cry for U.S. foreign policy and UN peace-keeping and peace enforcement operations in the 1990s.[5] The seminal article by Helman and Ratner[6] mainly defined the term and the approach of the international community to the concept. The same article described many features of the absence of effective government, classified states according to their effectiveness, pointed out the causes of state failure, and suggested solutions.[7] Somalia was chosen by the international community as an example of the operationalization of the policies that resulted from these discussions.

Since 1992 academics have used the term 'failed state' in English and other languages to describe the absence of effective government, but many other words have been used for the phenomenon. The choice of terms is sometimes determined by the need to find a local word or idea, but some authors are reluctant to use the term 'failed state' on the grounds that the word 'failed' is not only descriptive but valuational.[8] International lawyers instead use 'the breakdown of effective government' or the German 'der Wegfall effektiver Staatsgewalt'.[9] 'Failed state' was used by former Secretaries-General Boutros Boutros-Ghali and Kofi Annan as early as 1990,[10] but never by the General

---

5 Richardson, "'Failed State'", 4.

6 Helman and Ratner, "Saving Failed States", 3. Helman was U.S. Ambassador to the United Nations in Geneva and Deputy to the Under-secretary of State for Political Affairs. Ratner was an International Affairs Fellow at the Council on Foreign Relations, on leave from the U.S. State Department Office of the Legal Adviser.

7 Ibid.

8 Ingo Liebach, *Die unilaterale humanitäre Intervention im 'zerfallenen Staat'*, (Cologne: Carl Heymanns Verlag, 2004), 21; Richardson, "'Failed State'", 14.

9 Liebach, *Die unilaterale humanitäre Intervention*, 20.

10 Boutros Boutros-Ghali, introduction to *The United Nations and Somalia 1992–1996*, United Nations Blue Books Series, Volume VIII, New York, 1996, 45, 87; Kofi Annan, SG/SM/6325 of 15 September 1997; GA/9079 of 29 June 1996; SG/SM/6090 of 18 October 1996; UNDP Press Briefing on Somalia, 14 May 1998.

Assembly or Security Council. The United Nations described the situation even in Somalia, a typical case of the absence of effective government, without using the term.

The word 'failed' is not only an empirical but also a judgemental description.[11] Merriam Webster's Collegiate Dictionary lists 'unsuccessful', 'bankrupt', and 'insolvent' as synonyms and defines 'failure' as 'falling short' and 'neglect or omission'.[12] Webster's Third New International Dictionary lists the synonyms 'deficiency', 'absence', 'bankruptcy', and 'deterioration'.[13] The choice of the term 'failed state' in fact reflects the approach of U.S. foreign policy and the international community to the absence of effective government because it focuses almost exclusively on the incapacity of the state while ignoring the roots of the problem. Such a judgment has a pejorative meaning and sets a benchmark for stigmatising states dealing with the phenomenon.[14] For this reason, designating or classifying states as 'failed' in the first instance goes against the principles of the honour and equality of states and has consequences for the principle of state sovereignty.

The State's Right to Honour and the Equal Sovereignty of States

Over a century ago, in 1891, D.T. Woolsey described the state's right to honour as follows:

> [...] every nation has a right of reputation, every other therefore is bound to abstain from deeds and words which are calculated to wound its sense of character or to injure its good name, or that of its sovereign, before the world.[15]

---

[11] Richardson, "'Failed State'", 15.

[12] *Merriam Webster's Collegiate Dictionary* 10th edition (Springfield, Massachusetts: Merriam, 1996), 417; *The Concise Oxford Dictionary of Current English*, 9th edition (Oxford: Oxford University Press, 1995), 984.

[13] *Webster's Third New International Dictionary*, (Springfield, Massachusetts: Merriam, 1971), 815.

[14] Richardson ("'Failed State'", 14, 15) describes the term as an 'arrogant judgment' of the West, while Liebach (*Die unilaterale humanitäre Intervention*, 20) prefers *zerfallener Staat*; Alexandros Yannis, "State Collapse and Prospects for Political Reconstruction and Democratic Governance in Somalia", *African Yearbook of International Law* 5 (1997), 24; Daniel Thürer, Matthias Herdegen, and Gerhard Hohloch, *Der Wegfall effektiver Staatsgewalt: 'The Failed State'*, Berichte der Deutschen Gesellschaft für Völkerrecht, Volume 34 (Heidelberg: C.F. Müller, 1996); Minnerop ("The Classification of States", 98) focuses on the notion of the 'rogue state' from the same perspective.

[15] D.T. Woolsey, *Introduction to the Study of International Law*, 6th edition 1891, 83, cited by Friedrich Berber, *Lehrbuch des Völkerrecht, Allgemeines Friedensrecht*, Volume I (Munich: C.H. Beck Verlag, 1975), 206.

Friedrich Berber laments in his textbook on international law that 'the right to honour has largely become incomprehensible in a materialistic time and science'.[16] While the Preamble of the League of Nations described 'just and honourable relations between the nations' as a precondition for international peace and security in international relations, the United Nations Charter remains silence on this point.[17] As Berber mentions, this right may not be popular in current international law, but it is a supplemental principle of the sovereignty and equality of states in Article 2/1 of the UN Charter.[18]

The Permanent Court of International Justice plainly elucidated the principle of equality in a 1935 decision:

> Equality in law precludes discrimination of any kind; whereas equality in fact may involve the necessity of different treatment in order to attain a result which establishes equilibrium between different situations.[19]

Because the right to respect brings the expectation of equal treatment of states, it forbids any pejorative conduct and behaviour.[20] The notion 'failed state' therefore violates the right to honour and dignity of states and their people and the principle of equality of the states.[21]

The acceptance of such a notion in public international law automatically imperils the principles of the sovereignty of states, non-force, non-intervention, and self-determination. For example, Helman and Ratner called the principle of sovereignty in states dealing with the absence of effective government an 'ill-defined and amorphous notion of international law'.[22] The United Nations Conservatorship, described by these authors as a 'novel and expansive effort by the United Nations to undertake nation-saving responsibilities', is actually based on the limitation of state sovereignty.[23] From the same paradigm, Matthias Herdegen derived the view of the teleological reduction of the principle of non-force with regard to Article 2/4 of the UN Charter in the case of the absence of effective government.[24]

---

16 Berber, *Lehrbuch des Völkerrecht*, 205.

17 *Covenant of the League of Nations.*

18 Christian Gloria, "Die Grundprinzipien des Völkerrechts über die Beziehungen zwischen den Staaten", in *Völkerrecht*, ed. Knut Ipsen, 3rd edition (Munich: C.H. Beck Verlag, 1990), 334.

19 PCIJ Ser. A/B, No. 64 (1935), 19.

20 Berber, *Lehrbuch des Völkerrecht*, 206; Minnerop, "The Classification of States", 98.

21 Liebach, *Die unilaterale humanitäre Intervention*, 20–24; Richardson, "'Failed State'", 12–16.

22 Helman and Ratner, "Saving Failed States", 9, 11.

23 Ibid. 12; Minnerop, "The Classification of States", 98.

24 Matthias Herdegen, "Der Wegfall effektiver Staatsgewalt im Völkerrecht: 'The Failed State'", in Thürer, Herdegen, and Hohloch, *Der Wegfall effektiver Staatsgewalt*, 58.

Rejection of the Use of the Notion of the Failed State

As seen above, the appearance of the notion of the 'failed state' in public international law was actually a reflection of international policy. Henry Richardson describes the origin of the notion as follows:

> [...] from the superpower United States comes a proposed 'failed states' doctrine parallel to the official American sponsorship of a strong 'free enterprise' ideology that is to be applied through U.S. policy around the world wherever possible.[25]

Chapter 1 notes that the third constitutive element of the state—government—determines the absence of effective government. Therefore, any term used to define the phenomenon has to consider this fact. The notion 'failed state', however, defines not the government but the entire state. From the normative perspective explained above, the notion is unacceptable because states have the right to respect and protection of their dignity, sovereignty, and equality. For this reason and those explained above, the term 'failed state' should remain outside the sphere of international law. Therefore, this work uses the neutral empirical term 'absence of effective government' instead.

Overview of the Content of the Concept of the 'failed state'

As mentioned above, the article by Helman and Ratner mainly described the North's approach to the absence of effective government. Two features of the article in particular defined the concept of the 'failed state' for the international community: 1) basing the problem on the state's inability to function and 2) identifying the international community as the main actor to help these states under United Nations 'conservatorship'.[26] These and other important claims concerning the concept of the 'failed state' are examined below.

Stressing Defects and Ignoring Causes

The concept of the 'failed state' is based on the idea of the '[...] nation-state utterly incapable of sustaining itself as a member of the international community', in Helman and Ratner's words.[27] Much of the literature illustrates this idea with examples of states or conditions in states, citing civil war, ethnic strife, and unfulfilled economic and social goods as causes and consequences

25 Richardson, "'Failed State'", 25.
26 Helman and Ratner, "Saving Failed States", 12–20.
27 Ibid., 3.

of the conditions. The incapacity of these states is compared to infirmity. Helman and Ratner justified their conservatorship solution by comparing 'failed states' to people incapacitated by mental or physical illness, hapless and bankrupt.[28]

In reality, no cause has yet been identified for the absence of effective government. International lawyers go no further than to claim that consequences such as internal conflict and human rights violations result from state incapacity. But these consequences are only the first step in the causal connection. The importance of the lack of a causal connection between the reasons for and consequences of the absence of effective government is evident when solutions are sought to the problem.[29]

Chapter 1 described the long-term economic, social, and political causes of the absence of effective government and the critical role of external economic and political factors. The decay of the political order, economic infrastructure, and government institutions is therefore a historically continuous process.[30] The seeds of the absence of effective government in Somalia were sown long before the collapse of the Barré regime. The fact that the country has a government today does not mean that it has resolved the problem.[31] Lebanon was cited as an example of the absence of effective government in the 1980s.[32] Despite the minimal stability the country had achieved after the long civil war between 1975 and 1990, Israel's 33-day military operation in 2006 showed Lebanon's inability to protect its territory from either internal or external threats. More important, Lebanon is dealing with a high degree of the absence of effective government today.

The International Community as the Main Actor

The second paradigm, 'conservatorship', is based on the first paradigm of the 'failed state'.[33] Because the absence of effective government is mainly identified

---

[28] Ibid.

[29] Richardson, "'Failed State'", 18; Volker Böge, *Von Muschelgeld und Blutdiamanten. Traditionale Konfliktbearbeitung in zeitgenössischen Gewaltkonflikten* (Hamburg: Schriften des Deutschen Übersee-Instituts, 2004), 8.

[30] William L. Zartman, "Posing the Problem of State Collapse", introduction to *Collapsed States: The Disintegration and Restoration of Legitimate Authority*, ed. William. L. Zartman (Boulder, Colorado: Lynne Rienner Publishers, 1995), 2, 3.

[31] S/2002/722 of 3. July 2002, para. 34; Robin Geiß, *'Failed States': Die normative Erfassung gescheiterter Staaten* (Berlin: Duncker & Humblot, 2005), 34; *Report of the Secretary General on the Situation in Afghanistan and its Implications for International Peace and Security*, S/1998/532 of 19. June 1998, para. 50.

[32] Thürer et al, *Der Wegfall effektiver Staatsgewalt*, 11.

[33] Helman and Ratner, "Saving Failed States", 3.

by international lawyers with the incapacity of the state based on the model of illness, the international community portrays itself as coming to the rescue with military intervention and international administration. This perception is evident in the following description of military intervention in Somalia by Madeleine Albright, the former U.S. Ambassador to the United Nations who popularised the term 'failed state', in a *New York Times* article of 10 August 1993:

> The decision we must make is whether to pull up stakes and allow Somalia to fall back into the abyss or to stay the course and help lift the country and its people from the category of failed state into that of an emerging democracy.[34]

International administration has been compared to guardianship or trusteeship in domestic law, as shown in the following excerpt:

> In the domestic system, when the polity confronts persons who are utterly incapable of functioning on their own, the law often provides some regime whereby the community itself manages the affairs of the victim. Forms of guardianship or trusteeship are a common response to broken families, serious mental or physical illness, or economic destitution.[35]

Richardson, however, describes this reaction of the international community as 'oversized doses of doctrinal state-centrism'.[36]

The Dubious Claim of Novelty

A glance at world history does not bear out the claim that the 'failed state' is a relatively new phenomenon.[37] The international order confronted the problem after the First World War and especially after decolonisation. James R. Crawford noted that the Congo lacked an effective government from the beginning of its statehood,[38] and a UN Fact Finding Commission mentioned Rwanda's inability to function as an independent state in 1962.[39] Cambodia dealt with the problem for 20 years before the Paris Agreement of 1991, and Lebanon experienced it after the Israeli War in the 1980s.[40] Many states

---

34 Madeleine K. Albright, "Yes, There Is a Reason to Be in Somalia," *New York Times*, August 10, 1993, A19.

35 Helman and Ratner, "Saving Failed States", 12.

36 Richardson, " 'Failed State' ", 8.

37 Helman and Ratner, "Saving Failed States", 3.

38 James R. Crawford, *The Creation of States in International Law* (Oxford: Clarendon Press, 1979), 43–44; S/Res/142 of 7 July 1960; GA/Res/1480 (XV) of 20 September 1960.

39 Nii Lante Wallace-Bruce, "Of Collapsed, Dysfunctional and Disoriented States: Challenges to International Law", *Netherlands International Law Review* 47 (2000), 61.

40 Thürer et al, *Der Wegfall effektiver Staatsgewalt*, 11.

in Africa, including Angola, Chad, Ethiopia, Nigeria, Sudan, Uganda, and Zaire, lacked effective governments in the 1980s.[41]

The nature of the phenomenon has not changed since the end of the First World War, but it has become more complex in the current world political and economic context. According to a 30 September 2000 report of the State Failure Task Force, there were 114 state failure events between 1955 and 1998.[42] The end of the Cold War simply made the phenomenon more obvious. Any claim of novelty for the concept of the 'failed state' is therefore spurious.

The Arbitrary Labelling of 'Failed States'

There are several terminological uncertainties in the notion 'failed state'. Some authors claim that Germany was an example of the phenomenon after the end of the Second World War.[43] Geiss cites the Berlin Declaration of 1945, when there was

> [...] no central government or authority in Germany capable of accepting responsibility for the maintenance of order, the administration of the country and compliance with the requirements of the victorious powers.[44]

Although Germany during this period was marked by both internal anarchy and incapacity in international relations, the causes and effects were quite different from those in countries such as Somalia and Lebanon. Nor is the claim that China in the 1930s lacked an effective government entirely accurate.[45] The main problem in the absence of effective government is the lack of statehood and its economic, political, and social elements, but both China and Germany have long histories of statehood.

Some accounts cite the Soviet Union and the former Yugoslavia as examples of the phenomenon,[46] but it is necessary to differentiate their situations

---

41 Robert H. Jackson and Carl G. Rosberg, "Why Africa's Weak States Persist: The Empirical and the Juridical in Statehood", *World Politics* 35 (1982), 1, 1; Zartman, "Posing the Problem", 2, 3; Thürer et al, *Der Wegfall effektiver Staatsgewalt*, 11.

42 The State Failure Task Force is a body established and financed by the CIA and composed of people from six U.S. universities: the University of Maryland, the University of California, the U.S. Naval Academy, Columbia University, Harvard University, and the University of Minnesota, State Failure Task Force Report, www.yemenembassy.org/econmic/Reports/ColumbiaUniversity/StateCapacity, visited 30 March 2006.

43 Helman and Ratner, "Saving Failed States", 1; Geiss, '*Failed States*', 54.

44 Berlin Declaration of 5 June 1945, in: A Decade of American Foreign Policy: Basic Documents, 1941–1949 (1950), 506, cited in: Geiss, '*Failed States*', 55, footnote 164.

45 Thürer et al, *Der Wegfall effektiver Staatsgewalt*, 11.

46 Ibid., 2; Ernosto Kiza, "Polit-ökonomische Wege zur Analyse von Staatszerfall: Die Sozialistische Föderative Republik Jugoslawien", in *Politische Ökonomie der Gewalt. Staatszerfall und die Privatisierung von Gewalt und Krieg*, Werner Ruf (Opladen, Germany: Leske

from the absence of effective government. First, neither the Soviet Union nor Yugoslavia (nor Ethiopia/Eritrea) came to an end because of the collapse of state institutions, but rather because of the dissolution of the state.[47] International law provided for the disintegration of existing states, voluntarily or otherwise, while ignoring the absence of effective government and its consequences, such as the fragmentation of territory, in countries such as Somalia or Georgia.[48]

Other accounts, such as that of Rotberg, maintain that the states labelled as 'rogue states', including contemporary Belarus, Libya, North Korea, and Turkmenistan, Cambodia under Pol Pot, and Iraq under Saddam Hussein, lacked effective government at a low level.[49] The basis of this argument is that these countries were unable to deliver political goods to their citizens despite appearing to be strong states.[50] In contrast to Rotberg, Kreijen uses the criterion 'a lack of capacity to exert power' as the point of origin of state failure and therefore refuses to classify Nazi Germany, Iraq under Saddam, or other dictatorships under this rubric.[51] The argument that an undemocratic state is a 'failed state' per se cannot be supported because of the wide spectrum of states in the world and the general acceptance that a state's form of government is mainly an internal issue. As a result, U.S. politicians invented another pejorative term, 'rogue state'.

The Possibility of a General Definition

As noted above, while scholars have identified a growing number of countries as lacking effective governments and the 'failed state' concept has become more popular since 1992, international law still lacks a clear definition of the absence of effective government.[52] This section deals with the search for an adequate

2003), 184; State Failure Task Force Report, www.yemenembassy.org/econmic/Reports/ColumbiaUniversity/StateCapacity, visited 30 March 2006.

47 Gerard Kreijen, *State Failure, Sovereignty and Effectiveness* (Leiden: Martinus Nijhoff Publishers 2004), 95.

48 Wallace-Bruce, "Of Collapsed, Dysfunctional and Disoriented States", 66.

49 Robert I. Rotberg, "The Failure and Collapse of Nation-States, Breakdown, Prevention, and Repair", in *When States Fail: Causes and Consequences*, ed. Robert I. Rotberg (Princeton: Princeton University Press, 2004), 4.

50 Ibid.

51 Kreijen, *State Failure*, 94.

52 Thürer, *Der Wegfall effektiver Staatsgewalt*, 2, 3; The Congo in 1960–1961, Chad in 1980–1982, Uganda in 1979–1981, Ghana in 1979–1981, Somalia after 1990, and Liberia in 1990; Helman and Ratner, "Saving Failed States", 1, write "[...] from Haiti in the Western Hemisphere to the remnants of Yugoslavia in Europe, from Somalia, Sudan, and Liberia in Africa to Cambodia 3 in Southeast Asia, [...]"; Thürer (*Der Wegfall effektiver Staatsgewalt*, 11)

and generally acceptable definition that can cover all varieties of the absence of effective government. The difficulty of finding such a definition stems from 1) the use of diverse terms for the phenomenon, 2) its different manifestations, and 3) the variety of attempts to define it.

Definitions

Different languages depict the absence of effective government in terms other than 'failed state'. English uses 'quasi state',[53] 'fragile state', 'collapsed state',[54] 'state failure', 'weak state', and 'the breakdown of effective government'.[55] In German we find 'der Wegfall effektiver Staatsgewalt', 'gescheiterter Staat',[56] 'zerfallender Staat',[57] 'zerbrochener Staat', and 'prämoderner Staat',[58] and French uses 'état sans gouvernement', 'état faillé',[59] 'état mou', 'état faible', and 'état débile'.[60] The meanings of these terms differ in sometimes minor, sometimes significant ways. In addition to this multitude of expressions, the concepts 'anarchic state', 'phantom state', 'anaemic state', and 'rogue state' are not always easy to distinguish from the absence of effective government.

Another difficulty with terminology arises from the 'gradual' nature of the descriptions. In other words, some authors categorise the phenomenon accord-

---

mentions Somalia since 1991, Liberia, Bosnia Herzegovina, Rwanda with its genocide and massacre, Cambodia from 1970 until the Paris Agreement, Lebanon during the 1980s, Congo since its establishment as a state, and China during the 1930s; Yannis, "State Collapse", 25 lists Somalia, Liberia, Afghanistan, Bosnia, Cambodia, Zaire, Sudan, Angola, Albania, Tajikistan, and other countries; Helmut Strizek, in *Burundi and Ruanda von der Unabhängikeit in: Zum Staatszerfall: Studie über eine gescheiterte Demokratie im afrikanischem Zwischengebiet*, (Munich: Weltforum- Verlag, 1996), 21, describes Burundi and Rwanda in the 1990s as collapsed states; Gerry J. Simpson, in "The Diffusion of Sovereignty: Self-Determination in the Post-colonial Age", *Stanford Journal of International Law* 32 (1996), 2, 256, identifies a wide spectrum of countries from Yugoslavia to Rwanda to Sri Lanka; David Raič, in *Statehood and the Law of Self- Determination* (The Hague: Kluver Law International, 2002), 69, characterizes Albania as a failed state because of its civil war.

53 Robert Houghwout Jackson, *Quasi-States, Sovereignty, International Relations, and the Third World* (Cambridge: Cambridge University Press, 1993), 21.

54 Thürer et al, *Der Wegfall effektiver Staatsgewalt*,10.

55 Jackson and Rosberg, "Why Africa's Weak States Persist", 1.

56 Thürer, *Der Wegfall effektiver Staatsgewalt*, 11; Herdegen, "Der Wegfall effektiver Staatsgewalt", 49; Geiss, '*Failed States*', 21; Kreijen, *State Failure*, 92.

57 Liebach, *Die unilaterale humanitäre Intervention*, 20.

58 Peter-Michael Zenk, *Auf dem Weg zur Weltinnenpolitik? Zur Problematik militärischer Interventionen bei innerstaatlichen Konflikten* (Hamburg: Institut für Friedensforschung und Sicherheitspolitik, 1994), 57.

59 Liebach, *Die unilaterale humanitäre Intervention*, 21.

60 Ibid., 21; Geiß, '*Failed States*', 21.

ing to the *extent* of the absence of effective government. This is problematic first because each author uses different classifications. Helman and Ratner group states under three categories: 'failed states', 'failing states', and new states established from the former Yugoslavia and Soviet Union.[61] Rotberg classifies states under five progressive categories—strong, weak, failing, failed, and collapsed—while Herdegen proposes only two classifications—failed and failing.[62] Each author uses different criteria for the grades, or ranges, of state failure. For example, Helman and Ratner base the definition of a 'failed state' primarily on government structure, while Rotberg differentiates between strong and collapsed states according to their capacity to deliver the most important political goods effectively.[63] The differences between the various grades are sometimes so thin that it is difficult to distinguish one from another. Koskenmäki describes the difficulty as follows: 'The principal source of the ambiguity is under which criteria a state may be determined to be in a process of collapse or described as a collapsed or failed state'.[64]

Finally, because the ranges and definitions of the absence of effective government differ from one author to another, the same countries are often classified differently. For example, Helman and Ratner categorise Bosnia, Cambodia, Liberia, and Somalia as 'failed states',[65] while Rotberg describes Somalia as a 'collapsed state' and Cambodia as a 'weak state'.[66]

Different Definitions of the Absence of Effective Government

As we have seen, the difficulty of finding a common definition of the absence of effective government also arises from the fact that the phenomenon looks different in each state, depending on its historical background and political, economic, and social features. Moreover, different criteria are used to define the phenomenon, reflecting different definitions of the minimum requirements of government in international law. These range from the expansive to the narrow.[67] In the broad definition, the economic, political, and social approach determines the minimum requirement of a government, regardless of its form or extent, so that even non-democratic countries are included.

61 Helman and Ratner, "Saving Failed States", 2.
62 Rotberg, "The Failure and Collapse of Nation-States", 3, 5, 10, 48; Herdegen, "Der Wegfall effektiver Staatsgewalt", 52.
63 Rotberg, "The Failure and Collapse of Nation-States", 3, 5, 10, 48.
64 Richardson, "'Failed State'", 14.
65 Helman and Ratner, "Saving Failed States", 2.
66 Rotberg, "The Failure and Collapse of Nation-States", 46–49.
67 Yannis, "State Collapse", 85.

The narrow definition mainly focuses on the legal aspect from the perspective of international law.[68] These two types of definitions are explored below.

In the wide-spectrum definition of the absence of effective government, Western state values such as democracy and human rights or reference to a country's economic and social situation are used to determine the minimum requirements of government. The 2006 report of the State Failure Task Force defines 'state failure' as the presence of revolutionary wars, ethnic wars, adverse regime changes, genocide, assessed according to quality of life, regime type, international influences, and ethnic or religious composition.[69]

Some authors view the 'failed state' through the lens of democracy. From this perspective, states with dictatorships are also described as 'failed' or at least 'weak'. According to Rotberg's criterion of the ability of the state to deliver political goods to its citizens, dictatorships are weak states even if they appear strong, as did Iraq under Saddam.[70] Some authors use massive and serious violations of fundamental human rights as the basic criterion for the absence of effective government. Liebach and Strizek, Mutharika, and Thürer consider Rwanda an example of a 'failed state' based on genocide.[71] Other authors, such as Kreijen and Clapham, however, refute this categorisation of grievous violations of fundamental human rights—as in Afghanistan under the Taliban, Cambodia under the Khmer Rouge, and Rwanda—as examples of state failure.[72]

Internal conflict is another criterion for the broad definition of the absence of effective government, but in the sense of anarchy rather than civil war (in which the conflict parties are clearly distinguishable). The Democratic Republic of the Congo, Liberia, Sierra Leone, and Somalia have been cited as examples of the absence of effective government according to this criterion.[73] Here, too, there is a difference of opinion. While Kreijen differentiates between 'violent strife' in the absence of effective government and civil war—and considers Sierra Leone in 1997 an example of the absence of effective government because of

68 Riika Koskenmäki, "Legal Implications Resulting from State Failure in Light of the Case of Somalia", *Nordic Journal of international Law* 73 (2004), 1, 4.

69 State Failure Task Force Report.

70 Rotberg, "The Failure and Collapse of Nation States", 4.

71 Thürer et al, *Der Wegfall effektiver Staatsgewalt*, 11; Liebach, *Die unilaterale humanitäre Intervention*, 5; Strizek, *Ruanda und Burundi*, 238; Peter A. Mutharika, "The Role of International Law in the Twenty-First Century: An African Perspective", *Fordham International Law Journal* 18 (1995), 1706.

72 Kreijen, *State Failure*, 94; Christopher Clapham, "Failed States and Non-States in the Modern International Order", working paper submitted at the Third Conference on Failed States: Globalization and the Failed State, Purdue University 7–10 April 2000, available at www.purdue.edu/faileds_states/2000/papers/clapham.html.

73 Kreijen, *State Failure*, 95.

the enduring character of the violence—Geiss holds that chaos and violence alone do not define the phenomenon because government is not completely ineffective in such cases.[74] For Zartman, internal conflict is not a sufficient criterion for state collapse, primarily because he describes a collapsed state as experiencing a breakdown of structure, authority, law, and political order.[75]

The inadequacy of the broad definition of the absence of effective government is illustrated in reports of international organisations. The 13th meeting of the United Nations Committee on Economic Social and Cultural Rights in May 2000 recommended that the United Nations Development Program classify Egypt as a 'failed state' based on the following description:

> [...] one quarter of the population were poor by any standards and one quarter lived on the margins of poverty. Structural adjustment programs obviously affected the poor more than the rich, and women more than men [...] the gap between rich and poor was widening.[76]

Pakistan was described as a 'failed state' in another 2000 meeting of the same committee.[77] The 1994 UNDP *Human Development Report* used 'gaps in income and disastrous upheavals in society' as indicators of this status, classifying Brazil, Egypt, Nigeria, and South Africa as 'in danger of joining the world's list of failed states'.[78]

Thus a broad definition cannot help determine the nature of the absence of effective government because of the diversity of states in the world order and the criteria for statehood in international law. Current international law recognises 192 countries with widely different capacities; the welfare of their citizens, the existence of a constitution, their level of democracy, or their respect for human rights cannot be used to define their viability as states.[79] The legal difficulty is that the criteria for a state in current international law are limited to people, territory, and government and do not include values such as democracy and human rights, even if these are important in international law. The International Court of Justice demonstrated affirmed this point in a ruling on the Western Sahara question:

> No rule of international law, in the view of the Court, requires the structure of a State to follow any particular pattern, as is evident from the diversity of the forms of State found in the world today.[80]

---

[74] Ibid.; Geiss, '*Failed States*', 68.
[75] Thürer et al, *Der Wegfall effektiver Staatsgewalt*, 1.
[76] E/C.12/2000/SR.13 of 9 May 2000.
[77] E/N.4/2001/SR.17 of 3 December 2000.
[78] Paul Lewis, "UN Lists Four Nations at Risk because of Wide Income Gaps", *New York Times*, June 2, 1994, A6.
[79] Geiss, '*Failed States*', 48.
[80] Western Sahara, Advisory Opinion, I.C.J. Reports 1975, para. 94.

Attempts to define the absence of effective government narrowly according to the classical definition of the state are found in the literature of international law and statements of international organisations. The question arises whether it is possible to reach a general definition of the phenomenon through the narrow definitions analysed below.

The reaction of international lawyers to the phenomenon of the absence of effective government, and also to the concept of the 'failed state', is interesting. Many international lawyers refer only to the former when discussing other international legal matters, and several international law textbooks either mention it in reference to other issues or define it in a limited way.[81] For example, Doering's 2004 textbook comments on the absence of effective government along with the issue of the recognition of states but only briefly refers to a 'failed state' as an ungovernable state situation resulting from civil war.[82] Kimminich and Hobe (2002) mention the absence of effective government without giving a detailed explanation and settle for singling out Cambodia, Lebanon, Liberia, Rwanda, and Somalia as examples of 'failed states'.[83] Bruha and Krajewski (2001) identify two attributes of the absence of effective government—civil society marked by violence and a collapsed state government—without going into detail.[84]

Other references to the phenomenon appear in the context of military intervention in states without effective governments.[85] In reference to humanitarian intervention in such states through the United Nations, Bartl (1999), for example, identifies three criteria for state failure in this context: breakdown of

[81] Karl Doehring, *Völkerrecht, Ein Lehrbuch*, 2nd edition (Heidelberg: C.F. Müller Verlag, 2004), 415. Chinedu Reginald Ezetah, "Legitimate Governance and Statehood in Africa: Beyond the Failed State and Colonial Self-Determination", in *Legitimate Governance in Africa, International and Domestic Legal Perspectives*, ed. Kofi Edward Quashigah (The Hague: Kluwer Law International, 1999), 419 et. seq.; Tara Magner, "Does a Failed State Country of Origin Result in a Failure of International Protection? A Review of Politics Toward Asylum-Seekers in Leading Asylum Nations", *Georgetown Immigration Law Journal* 15 (2001), 4, 703 et. seq.

[82] Doehring, *Völkerrecht*, 415.

[83] Otto Kimminich and Stephan Hobe, *Einführung in das Völkerrecht* (Tübingen, Germany: A Francke Verlag, 2000), 103.

[84] Thomas Bruha and Markus Krajeweski, "Bürgerkrieg", in *Lexikon des Rechts—Völkerrecht*, ed. Ignaz-Seidl Hohenveldern (Neuwied, Germany: Luchterhand, 2001), 46–47; Torsten Stein and Christian von Buttlar, *Völkerrecht*, 11th edition (Munich: Carl Heymann's Verlag, 2005), 100; David J. Harris, *Cases and Material on International Law*, 6th edition (London: Sweet & Maxwell, 2004), 101–102.

[85] Liebach, *Die unilaterale humanitäre Intervention*; Jürgen Bartl, *Die Humanitäre Intervention durch den Sicherheitsrat der Vereinten Nationen, im: "failed state", Das Beispiel Somalia*, Schriften zum Staats-und Völkerrecht (Frankfurt: Verlag Peter Lang, 1999). While Bartl discusses collective humanitarian intervention in states dealing with the absence of effective government, Liebach focuses on unilateral humanitarian intervention in those states.

effective government, escalation of force, and endogenous character.[86] Very few international lawyers have dealt with the absence of effective government from a normative perspective. Thürer (1996) described the absence of effective government as characterised by the breakdown of the core of statehood and brutality and intensity of force.[87] Geiss (2005) attempted an abstract definition and concluded that the complete breakdown of government meant the absence of law and order. As mentioned earlier, only Afghanistan, Liberia, and Somalia at various stages in their histories met his criterion for 'failed states'.[88]

In summary, almost every international lawyer describes some key issues concerning the absence of effective government, but no common definition is found in the literature of international law.

Most international organisations prefer to describe the situation in countries dealing with the absence of effective government rather than attempting to define it. Former UN Secretary-General Boutros-Ghali saw the lack of government structure in its various manifestations as the main indicator of the phenomenon. He described Somalia as a country with 'hardly any governmental infrastructure' in a report of 21 April 1992[89] and with 'the almost total absence of central, regional or local government [...] fragmented along clan and family lines, without any recognised channels for political action' in a report of 22 July 1992.[90] Sometimes Boutros-Ghali cited multiple criteria for Somalia's lack of effective government, as in this 1995 excerpt: '[...] the collapse of state institutions, especially by police and judiciary, with resulting paralysis of governance, a breakdown of law and order, and general banditry and chaos'.[91]

Former Secretary-General Kofi Annan described Afghanistan as a failed state on 3 December 1997, when the Taliban controlled most of the territory:

> Most visibly, we have seen what happens in these states [...] when the center falls apart, when rival militias replace reason, when citizens are bereft of the most basic conditions of stable existence, when outside powers involve themselves in the running of the country. We have seen it in Angola, Somalia, Zaire, Bosnia [...].[92]

In a report of 19 June 1998, Annan wrote that 'Afghanistan itself shows typical "failed state" symptoms, in which the armed factions are unwilling to opt for

86 Bartl, *Die Humanitäre Intervention*, 75.
87 Thürer et al, *Der Wegfall effektiver Staatsgewalt*, 12.
88 Geiß, *'Failed States'*, 59.
89 S/23829 of 21 April 1992, para. 56.
90 S/24343 of 22 of July 1992, para. 54.
91 Supplement of *An Agenda for Peace*, UN Secretariat, New York, 1995, para. 13.
92 Kofi Annan, SG/SM/6412 of 3 December 1997.

peace'.[93] He also described Somalia as a failed state in a letter of 3 July 2002, even though the country had a government after June 2001.[94]The policy of the General Assembly and the Security Council vis-à-vis the absence of effective government is also interesting. Until today, neither of these organs of the United Nations has attempted to define the phenomenon conclusively, instead describing each case individually.[95] The Security Council detailed Somalia's rapid deterioration, heavy loss of human life, and widespread material damage in Resolution 733 (1992) of 23 January 1992, while describing the 'unique character' of the country with its 'deteriorating, complex and extraordinary nature' in Resolution 794 of 3 December 1992.[96] Some resolutions point out the failure to deliver public goods to citizens as an indicator of the absence of effective government, as in the 'widespread disruption of public facilities and services'[97] in Somalia described in General Assembly Resolution 46/176 (1991) of 19 December 1991.

Representatives of other international organisations such as the World Bank and IMF and regional organisations such as ECOWAS have referred to the phenomenon. ECOWAS described the situation in Liberia at a conference on 27 August 1990 as follows:

> [...] the total breakdown of law and order, the prevailing state of war, the massive loss of life, the displacement of the citizens, the collapse of the government of President Samuel K. Doe [...].[98]

There may be two reasons why the international and regional organisations identify common issues that define the absence of effective government but do not attempt to define the term itself. First, there is no generally accepted and satisfactory modern legal definition of statehood.[99] Second, because the attributes, causality, intensity, and consequences of the phenomenon differ in each country and sometimes in the same country at different times, it is difficult to settle on a common definition. Moreover, it is impossible to establish a

---

93 *Report of the Secretary General on the Situation in Afghanistan and its Implications for International Peace and Security*, S/1998/532 of 19. June 1998, para. 50.

94 S/2002/722 of 3. July 2002, para. 34: Geiß, *'Failed States'*, 34.

95 GA/46/457 of 19. Sept. 1991, II/7., GA/Res. 46/176 of 19. December 1991; S/23829 of. 21. April 1992 para. 56; S/24343 of 22. July 1992 para. 54 et.seq.

96 S/Res/794 (1992) of 3 December 1992.

97 GA/Res. 46/176 of 19. December 1991.

98 *Final Communiqué of the National Conference of All Liberian National Parties, Patriotic Fronts, Interest Groups and Concerned Citizens* of 29. August 1990, in *Regional Peace-Keeping and International Enforcement: The Liberian Crisis*, ed. Marc Weller (Cambridge: Cambridge University Press, 1994), 89.

99 Crawford, *The Creation of States*, 31; Kreijen, *State Failure*, 64.

classification system based on gradation because the discrete features of the absence of effective government cannot be clearly distinguished.[100]

Therefore, as Kreijen writes, '[...] as always, it may be difficult or even impossible to draw a clear line in distinct cases. Ultimately, each particular case will have to be judged on its own merits'.[101] Because it is impossible to find a common definition, the International Law Commission did not directly refer to the question of state responsibility in the absence of effective government in its 2001 Articles on the Responsibility of States for Internationally Wrongful Acts (ARSIWA). Instead, it noted various situations and issues concerning the phenomenon, including the responsibility of 'the person or group of persons [...] in the absence or default of the official authorities'.[102]

100 Herdegen, "Der Wegfall effektiver Staatsgewalt", 52.

101 Kreijen, *State Failure*, 93.

102 Article 8 of ARSIWA, adopted by the International Law Commission on 10 August 2001: *Report of the International Law Commission*, Fifty-Third Session, A/56/10, Chapter IV.

Chapter Five

International Legal Subjectivity

Modern international law has grown in scope and the number of actors but still considers the state the most important subject. For this reason, states dealing with the absence of effective government have compelled international lawyers as well as the international community to confront many difficult principles and rules of international law,[1] from subjectivity to the extinction of the state. The main challenges the phenomenon poses for international law are based on 1) the decentralised structure of international law vis-à-vis the necessity of continuity and stability of the international legal order, 2) the people as the real owner of sovereignty, and 3) the continued importance of the state as the main actor in international law. This part of the work first analyses the international legal issue of the subjectivity of states dealing with the absence of effective government through the question of the extinction of the state in the absence of effective government and then examines in detail the main principles of sovereignty, non-force, non-intervention, and self-determination.

The Subjectivity of States

The state as a subject of international law possesses two capacities: legal capacity and the capacity to act.[2] Existence as a state in international law automatically confers the legal capacity to assume rights and duties under international law.[3] The state earns this capacity with its establishment and retains it until it ceases to exist. The capacity to act, on the other hand, enables the state to acquire and exercise rights. Organs, agents, or institutions make it possible for the state

---

1 Ryszard Piotrowicz, "The Structure of the International Legal System," in *Public International Law: An Australian Perspective*, ed. Sam Blay, Ryszard Piotrowicz, and Martin Tsamenyi (Melbourne: Oxford University Press, 1997), 42; Friedrich August Freiherr von der Heydte, *Völkerrecht: Ein Lehrbuch*, Volume I (Cologne: Verlag für Politik und Wirtschaft, 1958), 94.

2 James R. Crawford, *The Creation of States in International Law* (Oxford: Clarendon Press, 1979), 25.

3 Ibid.

to assume rights and fulfil obligations both internally and under international law.[4] Therefore, the capacity to act requires an effective state government for action over the territory as well as in the international arena.[5]

The most important difference between legal capacity and the capacity to act is that subjectivity to legal rights and duties comes into effect with the existence of the state, but the capacity to act or the effectiveness of the capacity to act depends on the individual international law subject.[6] In regard to the diversity of states, every international law subject principally uses its rights and fulfils its duties in the international legal order according to its own capacity. In other words, international law leaves room for variety in the effectiveness principle. The incapacity to act, whatever its form, does not affect the capacity to acquire rights.[7]

States Dealing with the Absence of Effective Government

The problem in the case of the absence of effective government is explicitly demonstrated above: the lack of some or all state organs, institutions, and agencies. International law distinguishes between the organs, agents, and institutions of the state and 'government' as one of the important elements of the state.[8] The lack of current organs or state apparatus does not mean the absence of government as the main element of a state, but rather the absence of *effective* government. Hence the determining factor in decisions about the subjectivity of such states is their lack of capacity to act. For this reason, in the absence of a current government or an effective government, states continue to exist as subjects of international law with accompanying rights and duties.[9] The inability to act or restricted capacity to act does not detract from the international subjectivity of states.[10]

---

[4] Heike Krieger, *Das Effektivitätsprinzip im Völkerrecht* (Berlin: Duncker & Humblot, 2000), 89; Robin Geiß, *"Failed States", Die normative Erfassung gescheiterter Staaten* (Berlin: Duncker & Humblot, 2005), 127.

[5] Krieger, *Das Effektivitätsprinzip im Völkerrecht*, 89; Eberhard Menzel, *Völkerrecht* (Munich: C.H. Beck, 1962), 111.

[6] Von der Heydte (*Völkerrecht: Ein Lehrbuch*, 91) distinguishes between these two capacities by describing legal capacity as *actual* and the capacity to act as *potential.*

[7] Hartmut Schiedermair, "Effektive Herrschaftsgewalt und Rechtsfähigkeit im Völkerrecht", *Juristische Arbeitsblätter* 16 (1984), 638, 641; Geiß, *"Failed States"*, 127.

[8] Crawford, *The Creation of States*, 28; Von der Heydte, *Völkerrecht: Ein Lehrbuch*, 198.

[9] Robert L. Bledsoe and Boleslaw Boczek, *The International Law Dictionary* (Santa Barbara, California: ABC-CLIO, 1987), 35; Crawford, *The Creation of States*, 28.

[10] Volker Epping, "Völkerrechtssubjekte", in *Völkerrecht*, ed. Knut Ipsen (Munich: C.H. Beck, 1990), 58; Daniel Thürer, "Der Wegfall effektiver Staatsgewalt 'The Failed State'", in *Der Wegfall effektiver Staatsgewalt: "The Failed State"*, Berichte der Deutsche Gesellschaft für

International law historically has approved of the practice of the continuity of the international legal personality in spite of the incapacity to act. Different international lawyers have upheld the existence of the states in spite of their ineffectiveness for internal and external reasons. For example, Alfred Verdross (1964) writes that the right to acquire is protected by public international law even if the state cannot exercise it.[11] The international community has not hesitated to recognise the sovereignty of a state whose territory has been annexed illicitly. Estonia, Latvia, and Lithuania exemplify the continuity of subjectivity under international law. The Soviet Union occupied these three Baltic States between 1940 and 1991. Until the end of the occupation, they were unable to exercise their sovereignty and in fact lost their entire capacity to act. However, after 1991, these states were accepted not as new states that were the legal successors to the Soviet Union, but as intact states.[12] In this perception, the international community considers the exiled government of an annexed state to be the government of that state.[13]

Parallel to this practice, most international law literature accepts that states dealing with the absence of effective government are still subjects of international law and retain their legal capacity.[14] While some authors accept the subjectivity of such states in international law in spite of describing these states as 'faction states'[15] or 'quasi states',[16] few international lawyers are of the

---

Völkerrecht 34, ed. Daniel Thürer, Matthias Herdegen, and Gerhard Hohloch (Heidelberg: Müller Verlag, 1996), 13; Geiß, *"Failed States"*, 127; Von der Heydte, *Völkerrecht: Ein Lehrbuch*, 95.

11 Alfred Verdross, *Völkerrecht* (Vienna: Springer Verlag, 1964), 133; Von der Heydte, *Völkerrecht: Ein Lehrbuch*, 198.

12 Torsten Stein and Christian von Buttlar, *Völkerrecht*, 11th edition (Munich: Carl Heymann's Verlag, 2005),101.

13 Verdross, *Völkerrecht*, 133; Von der Heydte, *Völkerrecht: Ein Lehrbuch*, 198.

14 David J. Harris, *Cases and Material on International Law*, 6th edition (London: Sweet & Maxwell, 2004), 103; Thürer, "Der Wegfall effektiver Staatsgewalt", 9, 13; Matthias Herdegen, "Der Wegfall effektiver Staatsgewalt im Völkerrecht", in *Der Wegfall effektiver Staatsgewalt: "The Failed State"*, Berichte der Deutsche Gesellschaft für Völkerrecht 34, ed. Daniel Thürer, Matthias Herdegen, and Gerhard Hohloch (Heidelberg: Müller Verlag, 1996), 49, 50; Ingo Liebach, *Die unilaterale humanitäre Intervention im "zerfallenen Staate" ("Failed State")* (Cologne: Carl Heymanns Verlag, 2004), 58; Jürgen Bartl, *Die Humanitäre Intervention durch den Sicherheitsrat der Vereinten Nationen*, in *"Failed State", Das Beispiel Somalia* (Frankfurt: Verlag Peter Lang, 1999), 81; Stein and von Buttlar, *Völkerrecht*, 100; Robert Houghwout Jackson, *Quasi-States, Sovereignty, International Relations, and the Third World* (Cambridge: Cambridge University Press, 1993), 24.

15 Krieger, *Das Effektivitätsprinzip im Völkerrecht*, 173 et. seq; Dietrich Murswiek, "Souveränität und humanitäre Intervention", *Der Staat* 35 (1996), 1, 37; Malte Wellhausen, *Humanitäre Intervention, Probleme der Annerkennung des Rechtsinstitut unter besonderer Berücksichtigung Kosovo-Konflikts* (Baden-Baden: Nomos Verlagsgesellschaft, 2002), 224.

16 Jackson, *Quasi-States*, 24.

opinion that states without effective governments cease to exist and lose their subjectivity under international law.[17]

The international community has approved this legal situation in practice. It has not questioned the international law subjectivity of any state dealing with the absence of effective government, even Somalia, despite its long-term lack of effective government.[18] The Security Council has repeatedly stressed the sovereignty, territorial integrity, political independence, and unity of the states.[19] In international law practice regarding the absence of effective government, only Secretary-General Boutros-Ghali described Somalia as having 'lost its place as a member of the international community.'[20] However, this statement is found neither in Security Council resolutions nor in documents of other international organisations and international lawyers. The international community has developed the standard and consistent practice that statehood and international law subjectivity persist in states despite the absence of effective government.[21]

State Subjectivity through Continuity and Self-Determination

The international community's consensus that the state retains its international legal personality can be explained by two interdependent principles: the self-determination of a people and the continuity of the international legal order.

External self-determination determines the international law subjectivity of states dealing with the absence of effective government because it is not the organisation of the state, but the people organised under the government that is the subject of public international law.[22] The people are the only subjects who

---

17 Manfred Baldus, "Extraterritoriale Interventionen der Bundeswehr zur Rettung von fremden und deutschen Staatsangehörigen", in *Frieden und Recht*, ed. Ingo Erberich, Ansgar Hörster, Michael Hoffmann, Thorsten Kingreen, Hermann Pünder, and Rainer Störmer (Münster: Richard Boorberg Verlag, 1998), 259, 270; Robert Cooper, "Gibt es eine neue Welt-Ordnung," *Europa-Archive* 18 (1993), 507, 508 et. seq.; Ryan van Eijk, "The United Nations and the Reconstruction of Collapsed States in Africa", *African Journal of International and Comparative Law* 9 (1997), 573, 588; Nii Lante Wallace-Bruce, "Taiwan and Somalia: International Legal Curiosities", *Queens Law Journal* 22 (1997), 2, 453, at least for the Republic of Somalia.

18 Jackson, *Quasi-States*, 24; Harris, *Cases and Materials on International Law*, 103.

19 For example, SC Resolution 733 of 23 January 1992.

20 Boutros Boutros-Ghali, introduction to *The United Nations and Somalia 1992–1996*, United Nations Blue Books Series, Volume VIII (New York: United Nations, 1996), 45 and 87, and "Interviews", *Der Spiegel*, December 7, 1986, 169, and 19 July 1993, 18.

21 Claus Kress, *Gewaltverbot und Selbstverteidigungsrecht nach der Satzung der Vereinten Nationen bei staatlicher Verwicklung in Gewaltakte Privater* (Berlin: Duncker & Humblot, 1995), 283.

22 Verdross, *Völkerrecht*, 192. The Preamble of the Charter of the United Nations begins "We the Peoples of the United Nations have resolved to combine our efforts [...]".

can decide their future, but the loss of international personality or concomitant extinction of the state terminates all rights and duties of the state and its people. Therefore, as long as the people of the state exist, the state continues, regardless of the ineffectiveness of the government.[23] The international community has reinforced this principle over and over again, even in the absence of effective government.[24]

The other factor that determines whether a state retains its subjectivity under international law is the principle of continuity. Because the continuity of the state is important for the stability of the international legal order, it is more stringently applied than the effectiveness of government in international law.[25] The international community's position on the continuity of the state has two main consequences in international law. The first is when the international community ignores the absence of effective government, accepting this condition as temporary even if it lasts for decades, as in Somalia.[26] The second is when the international community ignores secession movements and tries to maintain state borders. The Security Council has consistently demonstrated this approach in many conflicts within states, recognising, for example, the integrity of the Federal Republic of Yugoslavia in Resolution 1244 (1999) regarding Kosovo.[27] In another example, the international community has not recognised the Republic of Somaliland in the territory of Somalia as a new state.[28] This issue will be explored later.

The Extinction of States in the Absence of Effective Government

The literature of international law approaches the extinction of the state through the syllogism of the criteria of statehood, so that if one of the three essential elements of statehood disappears, the state no longer exists.[29] Al-

23 Von der Heydte, *Völkerrecht: Ein Lehrbuch*, 198; Verdross, *Völkerrecht*, 192; Bledsoe and Boczek, *The International Law Dictionary*, 40.

24 Stein and von Buttlar, *Völkerrecht*, 110; Von der Heydte, *Völkerrecht: Ein Lehrbuch*, 198.

25 Stein and von Buttlar, *Völkerrecht*, 101.

26 Krieger, *Das Effektivitätsprinzip im Völkerrecht*, 173; Otto Kimminich and Stephan Hobe, *Einführung in das Völkerrecht* (Tübingen, Germany: A. Francke Verlag, 2000), 103; Thürer, "Der Wegfall effektiver Staatsgewalt", 9, 13; Bartl, *Die Humanitäre Intervention*, 80 et. seq.; Alexandros Yannis, "State Collapse and Prospects for Political Reconstruction and Democratic Governance in Somalia", *African Yearbook of International Law* 5 (1997), 27; Geiß, "*Failed States*", 109.

27 S/Res/1244 of 10 June 1999.

28 Peggy Hoyle, "Somaliland: Passing the Statehood Test", *IBRU Boundary and Security Bulletin* 8 (2000), 80; Bartl, *Die Humanitäre Intervention*, 83.

29 Ulrich Fastenrath, "States, Extinction", *Encyclopaedia of Public International Law* 10 (Heidel-

though 'merger, absorption, annexation, and dismemberment are accepted as 'classical' categories of state extinction',[30] in international law practice there are no clear criteria for the legal determination of state extinction.[31] Boutros-Ghali noted that there is no explanation for the reaction of the international community to states that lack one of the three constitutional elements.[32] International law practice has shown that answers to the question of the continuity or extinction of a state are diverse and dynamic in the historical-political context.[33]

International law assumes that the continuity of the state in the absence of effective government contains or implies the hope of the eventual recovery of the state. This recovery phase has differed in Albania, Bosnia, Cambodia, Liberia, and Somalia. Somalia, of course, has experienced the longest recovery period.[34] Public international law practice until now has proven this assumption and has never dealt with the question of the extinction of the state in the absence of effective government.

The question arises, what happens if a state cannot recover for a long period? Herdegen gives the implicit answer that if the reconstruction of the state is not evident in the near future, the state loses its international law subjectivity.[35] The generally accepted answer about the extinction of the state is found in the gap between the principle of effectiveness and the principle of continuity. In this context, a state is extinguished if there is no hope for its re-establishment.[36] The criterion of effectiveness alone, however, does not match the reality of international law.[37] In contrast, Doehring first posed the question whether the declaration of a state's extinction by other states, like the recognition of a new state by other states, can be an instrument of state extinction. He refused to accept this because of the character of the recognition of a state without a

berg: Max-Planck-Institut für öffentliches Recht und Völkerrecht, 1987), 465; Karl Doehring, *Völkerrecht, Ein Lehrbuch*, 2nd edition (Heidelberg: Müller Verlag, 2004), 70; Michael Schoiswohl, *Status and Human Rights: Obligations of Non-Recognized De Facto Regimes in International Law: The Case of Somaliland* (Leiden: Martinus Nijhoff Publishers, 2004), 29.

30 Schoiswohl, *Status and Human Rights*, 29.

31 Krystyna Marek, *Identity and Continuity of States in Public International Law* (Geneva: Librairie Droz, 1968), 7.

32 Boutros-Ghali, "Introduction", 87.

33 Von der Heydte, *Völkerrecht: Ein Lehrbuch*, 199.

34 Epping, "Völkerrechtssubjekte", 58; Marek, *Identity and Continuity of States* 162; Matthew C.R. Craven, "The Problem of State Succession and the Identity of States under International Law", *European Journal of International Law* 9 (1998), 1, 142, 159.

35 Herdegen, "Der Wegfall effektiver Staatsgewalt", 50–52.

36 Karl Doehring, "Effectiveness," *Encyclopedia of Public International* Law 79 (1984), 70 et. seq; Stein and von Buttlar, *Völkerrecht*, 100.

37 Geiß, *"Failed States"*, 99.

constitutive effect.[38] The criterion for the extinction of the state according to Epping is the establishment of a new state in the same territory by its people based on self-determination. Epping argues that until a new state exists in the territory, a state dealing with the absence of effective government is still a part of the international legal order.[39]

The outcome of this question is the reality that a state is a historical-social fact. Just as the juridical act of recognition of a state by the international community could come after the historical-social fact of the establishment of the state, the legal determination of the extinction of a state by the international community could come after the historical-social fact of the extinction of the state. The only actors in both situations are the people of the state. Therefore, in the absence of effective government, only the people of a state can avoid the extinction of the state, either by recovering the unity of the state, establishing a new state, or existing simultaneously in the former state and a new state within the territory.[40] Like recognition of an established state, confirmation of the historical-social fact of a non-existent state is not constitutive but declaratory.[41]

Applying the Basic Principles of International Law

The modern international legal order is based on the sovereignty and equality of states, non-intervention, and self-determination, the main elements of the Treaty of Westphalia of 1648.[42] These principles continue to be the cornerstones of international law but have changed with the historical and political world context, especially in the 20th and 21st centuries. Today, sovereignty, non-intervention, and self-determination are some of the most complex and interdependent issues in public international law. Crawford, for example, describes sovereignty as having 'a long and troubled history' and 'a variety of meanings'.[43]

The application of these main principles to states dealing with the absence of effective government mainly defines the reaction of the international com-

38 Doehring, *Völkerrecht, Ein Lehrbuch*, 416.

39 Epping, "Völkerrechtssubjekte", 58.

40 Ibid.

41 Von der Heydte, *Völkerrecht: Ein Lehrbuch*, 197–199.

42 Gene M. Lyons and Michael Mastanduno, "International Intervention, State Sovereignty, and the Future of International Society", introduction to *Beyond Westphalia? State Sovereignty and International Intervention*, ed. Gene M. Lyons and Michael Mastanduno (Baltimore: Johns Hopkins University Press, 1995), 6.

43 Crawford, *The Creation of States*, 26.

munity to the phenomenon. Thürer points out that the international community's reconstruction efforts in states dealing with the absence of effective government are mainly determined by the connection between sovereignty and self-determination.[44] Given the disputed meaning and implementation of these principles in international law, the following analysis focuses only on their implementation in the absence of effective government.

The Sovereignty and Equality of States

The basic principles of the sovereignty and equality of states in international law are expressed in Article 2(1) of the UN Charter. The principle of non-intervention mainly serves to realise these two principles. Actually, neither the League of Nations nor the UN Charter expressly mentions non-intervention. The reference in Article 10 of the League of Nations to the territorial integrity and political independence of states and the UN Charter's principles of non-force by states in dealing with each other in Article 2(4) and non-intervention of the United Nations in internal affairs of states in Article 2(7) are the only direct links to the principle of non-intervention.[45] Nonetheless, the general principle of non-intervention can be deduced from the spirit of the United Nations. The other principles in Article 2 of the UN Charter, self-determination of a people, territorial integrity, political independence, and the obligation to settle international disputes by peaceful means, are either conditions for non-intervention or based on the principle of non-intervention.[46]

The following 1986 judgement of the International Court of Justice (ICJ) in the case of Nicaragua confirmed the link between the principles of non-intervention and sovereignty:

> [...] the principle of non-intervention involves the right of every sovereign state to conduct its affairs without outside interference. It is part and parcel of customary international law.[47]

---

44 Murswiek, "Souveränität und humanitäre Intervention", 31; Thürer, "Der Wegfall effektiver Staatsgewalt", 16.

45 Josep Boyle, "Traditional Just War Theory and Humanitarian Intervention", in *Humanitarian Intervention*, ed. Terry Nardin and Melissa S. Williams (New York: New York University Press, 2006), 33.

46 Jost Berstermann, *Das Einmischungsverbot im Völkerrecht* (Frankfurt: Verlag Peter Lang, 1991), 33.

47 Military and Paramilitary Activities (*Nicaragua v. U.S.*), 1986 I.C.J.14, at 106 (June 27); Jennifer L. Czernecki, "The United Nations Paradox: The Battle between Humanitarian Intervention and State Sovereignty", *Duquesne Law Review* 41 (2002–2003), 396.

Sovereignty in the Absence of Effective Government

The question of sovereignty in the absence of effective government is determined through the correlation between sovereignty and international law subjectivity. Von der Heydte clearly describes this correlation: '[...] a state is not an international law subject because it is sovereign, but it is sovereign because it is an international law subject'.[48] Oppenheim describes the equality of the states 'before international law [as] an invariable quality derived from their international personality'.[49] Because states dealing with the absence of effective government are still subjects of international law, they retain their sovereignty and equality under the international legal order.

In practice, the international community has accepted the sovereignty of states lacking effective government or government institutions and organs.[50] The Security Council has mentioned the 'sovereignty, independence, territorial integrity and unity of the states' in almost every resolution concerning states dealing with the absence of effective government.[51] The principle of non-intervention is also valid in states without effective government[52] but is implemented parallel to the principle of equal sovereignty.

How far states can exercise their sovereignty depends directly on their economic, political, and social capacities, which also cannot be appraised without considering the historical context and the contemporary political and economic world order. Crawford describes the principle of sovereignty under international law as follows: 'The term "sovereignty" accurately refers not to the totality of powers which all States have, but to the totality of powers which States may, under international law, have'.[53]

Most states dealing with the absence of effective government have de facto a limited capacity to exercise their sovereignty. The reasons for this include the

48 Von der Heydte, *Völkerrecht: Ein Lehrbuch*, 97.

49 Lassa F.L. Oppenheim, *International Law*, ed. Sir Arnold D. McNair (London: Longman Publishing, 1928), 1.

50 Ignaz Seidl-Hohenveldern, "Souveränität", in *Völkerrecht, Lexikon des Rechts*, ed. Ignaz Seidl-Hohenveldern, 3rd edition (Neuwied, Germany: Luchterhand Verlag, 2001), 377; Thürer, "Der Wegfall effektiver Staatsgewalt", 16; Georg Dahm, Jost Delbrück, and Rüdiger Wolfrum, *Völkerrecht*, Volume 1/3 (Berlin: Walter de Gruyter, 2002), 144.

51 S/Res/1622 (2006) of 24 January 2006 on Côte d'Ivoire, which is described as a 'failing state' in Robert I. Rotberg, "The Failure and Collapse of Nation-States, Breakdown, Prevention, and Repair", in *When States Fail: Causes and Consequences*, ed. Robert I. Rotberg (Princeton: Princeton University Press, 2004), 47; S/Res/1653 (2006) of 27 January 2006 on Haiti, S/Res/1658(2006) of 14 February 2006, S/Res/1244 (1999) of 10 June 1999 on Kosovo, and S/Res/1483 (2003) of 22 May 2003 on Iraq.

52 Thürer, "Der Wegfall effektiver Staatsgewalt", 17.

53 Crawford, *The Creation of States*, 27.

former colonial territories' stillborn sovereignty without economic independence in a political world order dominated by powerful states, their economic and technological weakness in relation to the Northern states, and the changing concept of sovereignty.

The problematic issues arising from the principles of sovereignty and thereby non-intervention in the absence of effective government can be classified under two main categories: 1) economic and political interference by the international financial institutions and other international actors and 2) implementation of Chapter VII of the UN Charter.

Chapter 8 describes political and economic interference by the international actors. The next section examines implementation of Chapter VII of the UN Charter, especially concerning multilateral and unilateral military intervention and international administration.

International peace and security are the core of the spirit of the United Nations, demonstrated in the Preamble, Article 1, and several other articles of the UN Charter. Any crime of aggression undermines the collective peace and security of the world as well as the principles of sovereignty, self-determination, and territorial integrity. Chapters VI and VII of the UN Charter authorise the Security Council to take action to maintain collective security. Chapter VII notes that an important part of the function of the United Nations is to take 'action with respect to threats to the peace, breaches of the peace, and acts of aggression'.[54] There are only two exceptions, however, in which military means are legitimised in Chapter VII of the UN Charter. The first is Article 51, which sets forth the right of individual or collective self-defence of states. The second is the measures for collective security in Article 42.[55] Therefore, any use of force which is justified under neither Article 42 nor Article 51 of UN Charter is a breach of the UN Charter and international law.[56]

Since the end of the Cold War, however, public international law has tended to interpret Articles 39 and 51 of the UN Charter broadly. In accordance with this trend, Chapter VII of the UN Charter, written to apply to conflict between states, has been applied to intra-state conflicts since the 1990s.[57]

---

54 Chapter VII of the UN Charter.

55 Kurt Mills, *Human Rights in the Emerging Global Order: A New Sovereignty* (Basingstoke, UK: Macmillan, 1998), 130.

56 Emily Schroeder, "The Kosovo Crisis: Humanitarian Imperative versus International Law", *The Fletcher Forum of World Affairs* 28 (2004), 1, 179–197.

57 Boutros-Ghali's 1992 *Agenda for Peace* first called for implementing Chapters VI and VII of the UN Charter in the case of internal conflicts that appeared to threaten international peace after the end of the Cold War. *An Agenda for Peace*, A/47/277 S/24111 of 17 June 1992; Security Council Meeting on 31 January 1992, S/PV 3046.

The Security Council's 1992 description of the human tragedy in Somalia as a threat to international security was a milestone in international law because it identified an internal issue as a threat to peace without the need to mention the external dimension.[58] Afterwards, many states, including Albania, Bosnia, Haiti, Rwanda, and Somalia, experienced military intervention in the 1990s, justified on the legal basis of collective security, human rights, and democracy based on Article 39 of the UN Charter. International transitional administration was based on the principal of collective security.

Article of 51 of the UN Charter has been similarly invoked. The broad interpretation of individual and collective self-defence according to Article 51 appeared especially after 11 September 2001.[59] The United States and its allies intervened militarily in Afghanistan, Israel intervened in Lebanon in 2006, and Turkey intervened in Iraqi Kurdistan in 2007 and 2008 on the legal basis of Article 51.

Many states dealing with the absence of effective government have experienced intervention under one or the other of these articles. There are three arguments for interpreting the absence of effective government as such a threat. The first is its negative effect on human rights, health, and quality of life. The second is the regional effect of the extension of chaos over state boundaries and the problem of refugees. The last is the issue of terrorism, which has been debated heatedly since 11 September 2001. These issues will be examined in detail in the following section.

Non-Intervention under Article 2/7 of the UN Charter

Article 2(7) of the UN Charter rules on the non-intervention of the United Nations in matters under the domestic jurisdiction of states. The United Nations is allowed neither to intervene in domestic issues nor to require its Member States to undertake such intervention. The principle of the non-intervention of the United Nations is applied mainly in cases of the absence of effective government. However, a problem arises with the implementation of exceptions in Chapter VII to this principle in Article 2/7. Military intervention and international territorial administration are the most important issues for the implementation of Chapter VII in cases of the absence of effective government.

In parallel with the international community's broad interpretation of Article 39 of the UN Charter, as mentioned above, the Security Council has identified the absence of effective government with its internal, regional, and international consequences as a threat to international peace and security

[58] Bartl, *Die Humanitäre Intervention*, 54; S/RES 733 of 23 January 1992.

[59] Ibid., 179.

under various resolutions of Article 39 since the end of the Cold War.[60] Nonetheless, it is questionable whether the absence of effective government and its consequences should be handled as a threat to international peace and security concerning Article 39 and whether the preconditions in Chapter VI have been met in such cases.

In states dealing with the absence of effective government, the resulting low-level and long-term internal conflict, human rights violations, and regional or international effects appear to be long-term threats to international peace in many respects. However, whether such threats meet the conditions defined under Article 39 of the UN Charter is a very important question in international law. If so, military measures are justified under Chapter VII of the UN Charter to answer such threats.

One of the most important features of the measures under Chapter VII of the UN Charter is that they are a last resort after all other peaceful measures have been tried and found ineffective.[61] Article 1 describes the purpose of the United Nations broadly as maintaining international peace and security, but paragraph 1 points out that this is to be done by peaceful means. Paragraph 2 describes 'appropriate measures to strengthen universal peace [...] based on respect for the principles of equal rights and self-determination of peoples'. Paragraph 3 clearly elucidates the broad purpose of the United Nations as 'solving international problems of an economic, social, cultural, or humanitarian character' to maintain international peace and security. Under Article 42 of the UN Charter, the Security Council can take military measures only when none of the measures foreseen in Article 41 are adequate. In sum, taking military measures as 'a means of last resort to maintain international peace and security' implies first that all peaceful means have been tried and found insufficient and second, that the threat is so acute and harmful that it has to be eliminated through the military measures as soon as possible.[62]

The United Nations determines whether each case of the absence of effective government has consequences that threaten international peace and security and involves human rights violations, regional effects such as refuge problems, and international effects such as international terrorism and piracy. In addition, Article 39 of the UN Charter, which the international community invokes to justify an international transitional administration, determines the existence of the absence of effective government. Whether the existence and consequences

60 Many Security Council resolutions call the humanitarian, regional, and international effects of the absence of effective government threats to international peace and security. Security Council Resolution 1838 (2008) of 7 October 2008 notes that the threat of piracy is foreseen in Chapter VII of the UN Charter.

61 Article 1 of the UN Charter.

62 Article 42 of the UN Charter.

of such states as threats to peace and security have to be determined under Article 39 could be answered with another question, namely, what is the aim determining such a situation as a threat concerning Article 39? The aim is 'to maintain or restore international peace and security'. The following section on military intervention and international transitional administration discusses whether the international community can restore peace and security through the measures under Chapter VII.

Restoring Peace and Security through Military Intervention

The question whether military intervention can restore peace and security in the absence of effective government can be answered in two ways. First, if military intervention is seen as a precondition of the reconstruction of the state, the answer is clearly no, because military intervention is neither a legal nor an adequate means for restoring peace and security in such states. It is not a legal means because the two preconditions for military intervention are the exhaustion of all peaceful means and the existence of an acute and harmful threat. Instead, the conditions of the state appear to threaten peace. The international community has been faced with long-term threats to peace that are limited neither to a time nor a government.

Nor are military measures adequate to achieve the aim of restoring peace and security in the absence of effective government. As the economic, social, and political situation in states dealing with the absence of effective government appear as threats to peace, the solution can be found only through economic, political, and social measures.

The question whether military intervention is a legal and adequate means to avoid the consequences of the absence of effective government, human rights violations, or regional and international effects raises complex questions about humanitarian intervention[63] or the 'war on terror' in international law which cannot be discussed adequately. It is nonetheless necessary to mention some important issues. The first is that the international community considers military measures in case of the absence of effective government more legitimate than such measures in functioning states because of the humanitarian situation or regional and international effects. In fact, however, military intervention is less effective in the absence of effective government than in normal states. For example, the problem of piracy in the Gulf of Aden could be solved more easily if there were a functional government in Somalia. But if the

[63] Crawford, *The Creation of States*, 710. The notion and concept of humanitarian intervention was discussed in the late 19th century, but the concept appears in neither the League of Nations nor the United Nations.

international community does not judge any institution in the country to be responsible, military intervention alone cannot solve piracy but only expand it either in time or place.

Second, in the case of human rights violations, the problem has two aspects. On the one hand, in cases genocide, military intervention is easily justified in a state with effective government because of a threat of unavoidable hazards and the possibility that state institutions or organs are responsible for perpetrating or permitting violence.[64] On the other hand, in the absence of effective government, the international community is confronted not with a human rights violation with unavoidable hazards and known actors, but with a long-term threat to human rights.

In the absence of effective government, it could be postulated that the concept of 'just war'[65] might support military intervention, but this is not the case. 'Right intention' is closely related to just cause and action taken for that cause.[66] The elements of right intention are to 'satisfy the requirement of the necessity to act' and 'satisfy the requirement of proportionality'. Jeff McMahan writes that

> [...] military intervention will fail to satisfy the requirement of necessity if there is an alternative means of achieving the just cause that is less destructive but has comparable probability of success.[67]

---

64 There is currently a discussion in international law about whether perpetration of violence by an actor such as a government justifies humanitarian intervention. Some international lawyers classify all violations of human rights, regardless of the context and actors, as reasons for humanitarian intervention, while others consider government violations of human rights a main justification for such intervention; Boyle, "Traditional Just War Theory", 32; Terry Nardin, introduction to *Humanitarian Intervention*, ed. Terry Nardin and Melissa S. Williams (New York: New York University Press, 2006), 1; Ian Brownlie, in *Principles of Public International Law*, 6th ed. (Oxford: Oxford University Press, 2003), 710, describes humanitarian intervention as follows: 'A state which had abused its sovereignty through brutal and excessively cruel power, whether national or not, was regarded as having made itself liable to action by those within any state which was prepared to intervene'; Klinton W. Alexander, "NATO's Intervention in Kosovo: The Legal Case for Violating Yugoslavia's National Sovereignty in the Absence of Security Council Approval", *Houston Journal of International Law* 22 (2000), 3, 403–404.

65 Boyle, "Traditional Just War Theory", 35; Schroeder, "The Kosovo Crisis", 179–197. Today the just war theory is analysed under two categories, the 'ethical nature of the decision to wage war' and the 'just war strategy'. The ethical nature of a war is expressed through 'the morality of the decision to wage war' (*jus ad bellum*) and 'the morality of the means by which the war is conducted' (*jus in bello*). The just war strategy has four elements: the likelihood of achieving the main goals, sponsorship by a legitimate authority, the use of force as a last resort, and the proportionate use of force.

66 Boyle, "Traditional Just War Theory", 42.

67 Jeff McMahan, "Intervention and Collective Self-Determination", *Ethics & International Affairs* 10 (1996), 1.

In conclusion, there is no sufficient justification for military intervention in the absence of effective government for three reasons. First, military intervention in a state whose economic, social, and political situation constitutes a structural threat to international peace and security cannot eliminate human rights violations or the threat to peace. Second, the structural threat to peace of the absence of effective government can be eliminated only when the causes are eliminated. Finally, practice has shown repeatedly that military intervention causes more economic, social, and political damage than it alleviates. As McMahan writes, military intervention will fail 'if the probable harm it would cause exceeds the probable good involved in achieving the just cause'.[68]

Moreover, there are doubts about the capacity of the UN to play its role of intervener. In the current international law order, the Security Council is the proper authority to take military measures under Article 39 of the UN Charter.[69] However, if proper authority is determined by the ability to maintain order after a war,[70] it is questionable whether the United Nations can be considered to have this authority, as explained below. Given the complexity and chronic nature of the absence of effective government, the Security Council does not appear as a proper authority to undertake military intervention because it cannot address the causes of threats to peace, human rights violations such as famine and poverty, or direct regional and international effects. In the case of Somalia, the United Nations left the country more chaotic than it was before the military intervention.

International Transitional Administration

The international community invented international administration in the 1990s to address international legal situations such as new states, but it also used it to re-establish effective governments in states dealing with the absence of effective government. Richard Caplan describes international administration as 'an ad-hoc innovation with ambiguity'.[71]

The United Nations established an international transitional administration in Kosovo[72] and Timor Leste[73] in 1999 and—through the Coalition Provisional

68 Ibid., 1.

69 Boyle, "Traditional Just War Theory", 45.

70 Ibid., 35–36.

71 Richard Caplan, *A New Trusteeship? The International Administration of War-Torn Territories* (New York: International Institution for Strategic Studies, 2002), 13.

72 UNMIK/Reg/1999/1 of 25 July 1999; S/Res/1244 (1999) of 10 June 1999, para 11 (a).

73 UNTAET/Reg/1999/1 of 27 November 1999, section 3; S/Res/1272 (1999) of 25 October 1999.

Authority (CPA)—in Iraq in 2003.[74] International transitional administration takes over most of the authority of a sovereign state—legislative, executive, and juridical.[75] However, the UN Charter authorises neither the United Nations nor any single state or states to exercise sovereignty over another sovereign state territory. Therefore, the United Nation's competency to carry out such tasks is questionable.[76]

Given that current international law offers no adequate means for territorial administration, advocates of international administration justify it by invoking either the UN trusteeship system under Chapters XII and XIII of the UN Charter or the measures concerning international peace and security under Chapter VII. Chapter 7 discusses the implementation of international territorial administration and the link between aims and practice. The section below deals with the legal basis of international transitional administration.

The Trusteeship System succeeded the Mandate System, a 'natural evolution' in content as well as complexity in a different world political context.[77] Article 77 of the UN Charter describes territories in which the Trusteeship System is applicable as falling under three categories: 1) territories under the mandate system of the League of Nations, 2) territories 'detached from enemy states as a result of World War II', and 3) territories 'voluntarily placed under the trusteeship system by states responsible for their administration'.[78]

States without effective governments can be classified under neither the first two categories nor the third, which was established for the colonial territories. International lawyers who support political trusteeship for territories dealing with the absence of effective government claim that the third category could include sovereign state territories dealing with the phenomenon because 'the language is broad enough to include countries such as Afghanistan, East Timor, or Iraq being administrated by other states, whether or not authorized by the Security Council'.[79] Even if this argument is taken seriously, Article 78 of the UN Charter explicitly states that the 'trusteeship system shall not apply to

---

[74] CPA/Reg/16 May 2003/01, section 2.

[75] Jürgen Friedrich, "UNMIK in Kosovo: Struggling with Uncertainty", *Max Planck Yearbook of United Nations Law* 9 (2005), 237–240.

[76] Hans Kelsen, *The Law of the United Nations, A Critical Analysis of Its Fundamental Problems* (London: Steven & Sons, Ltd., 1950), 651. Andreas Zimmermann and Carsten Stahn, "Yugoslav Territory, United Nations Trusteeship or Sovereign State? Reflection on the Current and Future Legal Status of Kosovo", *Nordic Journal of International Law* 70 (2001), 435.

[77] Nele Matz, "Civilization and the Mandate System under the League of Nations as the Origin of Trusteeship", *Max Planck Yearbook of United Nations Law* 9 (2005), 50; Henry H. Perritt, "Structures and Standards for Political Trusteeship", *UCLA Journal of International Law and Foreign Affairs* 8 (2003), 396; Zimmermann and Stahn, "Yugoslav Territory", 436–437.

[78] Article 77 of the UN Charter.

[79] Perritt, "Structures and Standards", 398.

territories' of members of the United Nations because of the principle of the equality and sovereignty of states. While Article 78 uses the phrase 'members of the United Nations', it should also apply to non-member states. Therefore, the trusteeship system rule in Chapters XII and XIII of the UN Charter cannot be imposed on independent sovereign states.[80]

The final encumbrance for the trusteeship system is found in practice. The core of the system was the Trusteeship Council. After Palau, the last UN Trust Territory, became independent on 1 October 1994, the Trusteeship Council formally suspended its operation.[81] The High-Level Panel on Threats, Challenges and Change in 2004 recommended 'the final and formal abolition of the Trusteeship Council' in Chapter XIII for the following reasons:

> The Trusteeship Council of the United Nations performed an important task in helping the world emerge from the era of colonialism and steering many cases of successful de-colonization. The United Nations should turn its back on any attempt to return to the mentalities and forms of colonialism.[82]

Many international lawyers argue that Chapter VII of the UN Charter is an adequate legal basis for international territorial administration as well as humanitarian intervention.[83] They posit three reasons for this argument. First, those who consider the absence of effective government a threat to peace under Article 39 of the UN Charter argue for a broad interpretation of the Security Council's mandate to maintain or restore international security, to include the establishment of long-term and sustainable peace.[84]

The second argument is that the Security Council or its members have the authority under Chapter VII to take over the legislative, executive, and judicial authority of a state. Despite the lack of references to such measures in Articles 41 and 42 of the UN Charter, the proponents of this argument maintain that the measures listed in Article 42, which include the use of force, foresee such a mandate.[85] They also argue that the Security Council has the authority to decide on such measures and can take measures through its resolutions to maintain 'sustainable peace or its precondition' under Article 41 of the UN Charter.[86]

80 Zimmermann and Stahn, "Yugoslav Territory", 436–437.

81 Ibid.

82 *Report of the High-Level Panel on Threats, Challenges and Change: A More Secure World: Our Shared Responsibility*, Doc. A/59/565, para. 299, 92–93.

83 Simon Chesterman, *You, the People: The United Nations, Transitional Administration, and State-Building* (Oxford: Oxford University Press, 2004), 57. Friedrich ("UNMIK in Kosovo", 233) cites many references to using Chapter VII as the basis for international administration.

84 Friedrich, "UNMIK in Kosovo", 234.

85 Ibid., 234–235.

86 Rüdiger Wolfrum, "International Administration in Post-Conflict Situations by the United Nations and Other International Actors", *Max Planck Yearbook of United Nations Law* 9 (2005), 669.

The third argument is that the Security Council has the customary power to authorise the mandate of international territorial administration. The proponents of this argument invoke the two General Assembly resolutions (A/Res/53/241 of 28 July 1999 and A/Res/54/245 of 23 December 1999) as proof[87] and maintain that the 'implied power doctrine developed by the ICJ' displayed in Article 39 is the legal basis for the international trusteeship system.[88]

Some proponents accept that international administration could violate the principles of equal sovereignty of states, non-intervention, and self-determination but claim that such a mandate is necessary to enable these states to exercise their sovereignty and enable their people to exercise their self-determination.[89] Justifying international transitional administration under Chapter VII seems to be an arbitrary interpretation of the UN Charter by Northern international lawyers concerning states in the South.

As mentioned above, although the absence of effective government seems to be a long-term threat to international peace, it cannot be interpreted as a threat under Chapter VII or as falling under the responsibility of the Security Council. Just as with military intervention, the argument that long-term peace can be maintained through international administration needs to be discussed from many aspects, including its appropriateness, the capacity of the international community to implement it, and the question of accountability, which will be discussed in Chapter 7.

Another issue is the incompleteness of the list of measures in Article 41 of the UN Charter. Because the equal sovereignty of states, non-intervention, and self-determination are basic principles of international law, the broad interpretation that Article 41 can also cover the takeover of a state's legislative, executive, and juridical authority is invalid. Such an interpretation is against the spirit of the UN Charter. Self-determination and state sovereignty are clearly suspended under international administration.[90] By analogy, the trusteeship system in the UN Charter is an ad hoc exception for territories which do not exist as states. Only in this case can the United Nations take over states' legislative, executive, and juridical tasks. In summary, there is no justification for international administration on the legal basis of Chapter VII of the UN Charter.

---

[87] A/Res/53/241 of 28 July 1999 and A/Res/54/245 of 23 December 1999, cited by Friedrich ("UNMIK in Kosovo", 234–235).

[88] *Reparation for Injuries Suffered in the Service of the United Nations, Advisory Opinion*, ICJ Reports 1949, 174 et. seq (182), cited by Friedrich, "UNMIK in Kosovo", 234.

[89] Ruth E. Gordon, "Some Legal Problems with Trusteeship", *Cornell International Law Journal* 28 (1995), 316; Wolfrum, "International Administration", 651.

[90] Sebastian Weber, "Das Sezessionsrecht der Kosovo-Albaner und seine Durchsetzbarkeit", *Archiv des Völkerrechts* 43 (2005), 503.

Non-Force

Non-force in relations between states is ruled on in Article 2(4) of the UN Charter, but it is also a fundamental rule of customary law accepted as a principle of *ius cogens*.[91] The only exception to non-force is found in Article 51, which refers to 'the inherent right of individual or collective self-defence'. Therefore, any unilateral military intervention is forbidden except to protect the right of individual and collective self-defence under Article 51 of the UN Charter.

In the absence of effective government, the principle of non-force is valid but eroded in two ways. The first is the broad interpretation of self-defence under Article 51. The second is the teleological interpretation of the principle of non-force in the context of humanitarian intervention.[92] The unilateral military interventions in Liberia by ECOWAS in 1990 and in Yugoslavia by NATO in 1999 were implemented under humanitarian claims.[93] The interventions in Afghanistan by the United States and UK in 2001, in Lebanon by Israel in 2006, and in Iraqi Kurdistan by Turkey in 2007 and 2008 were implemented under the claim of individual or collective self-defence.

The Right of Self-Defence and the Absence of Effective Government

The right of self-defence already existed in customary law before the Second World War. With the establishment of the United Nations, this right was decreed in Article 51 of the UN Charter. Israel and the United States called the content and scope of Article 51 into question in the second half of the 20th century with their claims of pre-emptive self-defence,[94] but the debate about individual and collective self-defence came to the fore after 11 September 2001.[95]

---

91 *Case Concerning Military and Paramilitary Activities in and against Nicaragua: Nicaragua v. United States of America* (Merits) [1986] ICJ Rep 14 [188], 190; *Corfu Channel Case* (1949) ICJ Rep. 4; GA/Res/ 2131(XX) of 21 December 1965, *Declaration on the Inadmissibility of Intervention in the Domestic Affairs of States and the Protection of their Independence and Sovereignty*.

92 Bernd Grzeszick, "Staatsgewalt in der UN-Charta zwischen Gewaltverbot und Selbstverteidigung", *Archiv des Völkerrechts* 41 (2003), 484–486.

93 Caplan, *A New Trusteeship?*, 8.

94 Markus Krajewski, "Humanitarian Intervention and Other Use of Force? Preventive Use of Force and Military Actions against Non-State Actors: Revisiting the Right of Self- Defense in Insecure Times", *Baltic Yearbook of International Law* 5 (2005), 11; Andrew Garwood-Gowers, "Pre-Emptive Self-Defense: A Necessary Development or the Road to International Anarchy?" *Australian Year Book of International Law* 23 (2004), 61.

95 Albrecht Randelzhofer, "Commentary to Article 51", in The Charter of the United Nations, Vol. II, ed. Bruno Simma, 2nd edition (Oxford: Oxford University Press, 2002), 803; Christian Tomuschat, "Völkerrecht is kein Zweiklassenrecht, Der Iraq-Krieg und seine Folgen",

In the case of the absence of effective government, the right to self-defence and its wide interpretation are interesting issues in international law. First, because of the features of the lack of effective government, such states are claimed as actors in armed attacks. The main reasons for this are the exodus of refugees, the presence of non-state actors within the states, and the inability of the states to protect their borders.

Second, although international law has not yet dealt with it extensively, the right of self-defence of states dealing with the absence of effective government is an extremely important issue. One of the most obvious contemporary examples is the West Bank and Gaza, which are under the jurisdiction of the Palestinian National Authority but Israeli military occupation.

The following sections analyse the appearance of states dealing with the absence of effective government as actors in armed attack and discuss the issues of armed attack, imputability, and pre-emptive self-defence as covered in Article 51 of the UN Charter.

Article 51 does not explain the term 'armed attack'. In the case of Nicaragua, the ICJ distinguished between armed attack and a 'mere frontier incident'. According to the Court, an armed attack has greater 'scale and effects' (paragraph 195),[96] but this does not clarify the meaning of the term.[97] The changing world economic and political context and the evolution of technology make this ambiguity more visible. In spite of widely differing opinions, most international lawyers[98] acknowledge a difference between 'aggression' and 'armed attack' and hold that 'only a special form of aggression amounts to an armed attack justifying self-defence'.[99]

The degree and duration of such an operation is another question. Karl Zemanek writes:

Vereinten Nationen 51 (2003), 2, 41–42; Antonio Cassese, *International Law* (Oxford: Oxford University Press, 2001), 307–311; Richard N. Gardner, "Neither Bush nor the 'Jurisprudies'", *American Journal of International Law* 97 (2003), 585, 590. Johan C. Yoo, "International Law and the War in Iraq", *American Journal of International Law* 97 (2003), 563, 571; Krajewski, "Humanitarian Intervention", 7–8.

96 *Military and Paramilitary Activities in and against Nicaragua (Nicaragua v United States of America)*, Merits, ICJ, Reports 1986, 14–150.

97 Carsten Stahn, "Collective Security and Self-Defense after the September Attack", *Tirburg Foreign Law Review* 10 (2002), 1, 21.

98 Karl Zemanek, "Self-Defense against Terrorism; Reflections on an Unprecedented Situation", in *El Derecho Internacional en los albores del siglo XXI, Homenaje Al Profesor Juan-manuel Castro-rial Canosa*, ed. Fernando M. Mariño (Madrid: Editorial Trotta, 2002), 700.

99 Yoram Dinstein, *War, Aggression and Self Defense* (Cambridge: Grotius Publications Limited, 1994), 183; Albrecht Randelzhofer, "Commentary on Article 51", in *The Charter of the United Nations*, ed. Bruno Simma (Oxford: Oxford University Press 1994, 667); Zemanek, "Self-Defense against Terrorism", 700.

> Even [...] a single incident which leads to a considerable loss of life and extensive destruction of property is of sufficient gravity to be considered an 'armed attack' in the sense of Article 51 of the Charter, warranting defensive action, particularly if further attacks from the same source cannot be excluded.[100]

In light of the lack of a clear explanation of the term 'armed attack' and world political, economic, and social changes, the Security Council and its resolutions remain the most important authorities for determining the meaning of the term.[101]

Returning to the subject of the absence of effective government, some authors claim that states affected by a massive influx of refugees have the right to self-defence through a 'natural extension'.[102] Brian McCalmon, for example, finds erroneous the restriction of the right of self-defence to situations involving armed attack.[103] Some authors tried to justify the 1991 U.S. intervention in Haiti[104] under Article 51 of the UN Charter.[105] Many Security Council resolutions describe a massive exodus of refugees as a threat to international peace and security,[106] but it is impossible to compare this problem with armed attack for several reasons. It is neither aggression on the part of a state nor such a threat that the affected state has the right to resort to force. Moreover, intervention in states dealing with the absence of effective government cannot stop this threat. Therefore, the United States, one of the few states that has continually invoked the right of self-defence, did not directly claim this right in the case of Haiti. Instead, it intervened in the country under the catch phrase of 'democracy'.[107]

---

100 Zemanek, "Self-Defense against Terrorism", 702.

101 Stanimir. A. Alexandrov, *Self-Defense against the Use of Force in International Law* (The Hague: Kluwer Law International, 1996), 98; Zemanek, "Self-Defense against Terrorism", 700–701.

102 Brian K. McCalmon, "States, Refugees, and Self Defense", *Georgetown Immigration Law Journal* 10 (1996), 2, 239. There are many references to this issue in this article.

103 Ibid.

104 W.Q. Beardslee, "The United State's Haiti Intervention: The Dangers of 'Redefined' National Security Interests", *Denver Journal of International Law and Policy* 25 (1994), 1, 193. After the government of democratically elected President Jean-Bertrand Aristide was overthrown by a military junta led by Raoul Cedras in 1991, many Haitians fled to the United States. The United States imposed economic sanctions against the junta to deal with the refugee problem, but the sanctions increased poverty and repression and escalated the exodus of refugees.

105 Ibid., 189–195.

106 S/Res/688(1991) of 5 April 1991 on Iraq.

107 Beardslee "The United State's Haiti Intervention", 189–195. In response to an appeal by the United States to deal with the refugee problem, the Security Council authorised Member States 'to use all necessary means under Chapter VII of the UN Charter to facilitate the departure from Haiti of the military leadership'. Security Council Resolution 940 (1994) of 31 July 1994 called for the restoration of constitutional rule and Aristide's presidency. On the basis of this resolution, the United States mounted a military action under the claim of humanitarian intervention to restore democracy.

Because of the diversity of acts of non-state actors, every invocation of the right of self-defence in case of armed attack by non-state actors has to be assessed on its own merits. For example, if a terrorist action by non-state actors has the same effect as an armed attack, it could appear as a threat to international peace and security.[108] It is generally accepted that the 11 September 2001 hijacking of civil airlines and its consequences can be judged as an armed attack because of its scale. Zemanek describes the hijacked airlines below:

> They were used in the attacks of 11 September for the destruction of human life and property in the same way as bombs would have been, and bombs would qualify as conventional weapons. Hence the submission that the function and effect of 'arms' are decisive, not their designation.[109]

Nonetheless, it is difficult to classify Hezbollah's capture of two Israeli soldiers in July 2006 as an armed attack. Only two soldiers were captured, but Hezbollah's demand for the release of prisoners was clear, and it was responsible for border incidents and minor attacks only. Although there was no action which could be interpreted by the Security Council as an armed attack,[110] Israeli President Ehud Olmert declared the capture of the soldiers a violation of their sovereignty and therefore a 'reason for war'.[111] Nor can Lebanon's inability to protect its border during Israel's 33-day military operation in 2006 be accepted as an 'armed attack'.

Article 51 of the UN Charter contains no reference to parties responsible for armed attacks, but both before and after the UN Charter, states were traditionally accepted as the actors in armed attacks.[112] This perception of the international community has tended to change along with the changing world context, and imputability is now interpreted more broadly than before. Today not only a direct attack from the regular armed forces of a state, but also any attack by non-state actors with a clear link to the state, is considered an armed attack in the context of self-defence.[113]

---

108 Stahn, "Collective Security", 20.

109 Zemanek, "Self-Defense against Terrorism", 701; Ian Brownlie, "The Use of Force in Self Defense", *British Year Book of International Law* 37 (1961), 225–226.

110 Brownlie, "The Use of Force", 245.

111 Zaman, 13 July 2006, http://www.zaman.com.tr/webapp-tr/haber.do?haberno = 307538.

112 Zemanek, "Self-Defense against Terrorism", 703; Krajewski, "Humanitarian Intervention", 18.

113 Krajewski, "Humanitarian Intervention", 18; Zemanek, "Self-Defense against Terrorism", 703. This broad interpretation is found in several international documents. Article 3 (g): Definition of Aggression of General Assembly Resolution 3314 (XXIX), 14 December 1974 states that '[...] the sending by or on behalf of a State of armed bands, groups, irregulars or mercenaries, which carry out acts of armed force against another State of such gravity as to amount to the acts listed above, or its substantial involvement therein' is accepted as act of aggression. Article 8: Conduct Directed or Controlled by a State of the Responsibility of States for Inter-

In the absence of effective government, however, the international community has dealt with non-state actors with no clear links to the state, and even states have been unable to influence non-state actors.[114] For example, there was no clear direct link between the Government of Afghanistan and Al-Qaeda as a non-state group when the United States and its allies occupied Afghanistan on 7 October 2001 under the claim of self-defence.,[115116] However, many authors, as well as international organisations including NATO and the Organization of American States (OAS), claim that 11 September 2001 was an armed attack. The Security Council called the 11 September attacks a threat to international peace and security in Resolutions 1368 (2001) and 1373 (2001)[117] and invoked unilateral and collective self-defence in their preambles, but it neither made a link between the state and non-state actors nor clearly authorised the use of force.[118]

States are obligated not to allow their territories to be used for acts against the rights of other states,[119] but there is broad scope for interpretation between this obligation and armed attack. Supporting revolutionary groups logistically or otherwise cannot be classified as armed attack, but the action of a powerful organisation against a state whose territory it uses as a base and which protects it can.[120] Each case must be evaluated according to its unique circumstances.

The Taliban's logistical support of Al-Qaeda in Afghanistan was well known, as was such support in other states, especially states dealing with the absence of effective government such as Sudan. However, a link between the terrorists who planned and realised the destruction of the World Trade Center and the

---

nationally Wrongful Acts 2001 states, 'The conduct of a person or group of persons shall be considered an act of a State under International Law if the person or group of persons is in fact acting on the instructions, or under the direction or contract of, that State in carrying out the conduct' (annex to General Assembly Resolution 56/83 of 12 December 2001). This indirect link between armed attack and the state is also demonstrated in the Nicaragua case (para 86).

114 Tal Becker, *Terrorism and the State: Rethinking the Rules of State Responsibility* (Oxford: Hart Publishing, 2006), 353.

115 Letter dated 7 October 2001 from the Permanent Representative of the United States of America to the United Nations Addressed to the President of the Security Council, UN Doc. S/2001/946, 7 October 2001, www.un.int./usa/s-2001-946.htm. A similar letter was sent by the United Kingdom (see S/2001/947).

116 Krajewski, "Humanitarian Intervention", 7 et.seq.

117 S/Res/1368 of 12 September 2001; S/Res/1373 (2001) of 28 September 2001.

118 Efthymios Papastavridis, "Security Council Resolution 1368/2001 and 1378/2001: Collective Security or the Right of Self Defense?" *Reveu Hellénique de Droit International* 55 (2002), 502, 511; Zemanek, "Self-Defense against Terrorism", 696; Stahn, "Collective Security", 14–15.

119 *Corfu Channel Case*, Merits; ICJ, Reports 1949, 4–38, at 22; Cf. M.R. Garcia-Mora, *International Responsibility for Hostile Acts of Private Persons Against Foreign States* (The Hague: Martinus Nijhoff Publishers, 1962), 109–112, 130; Zemanek, "Self-Defense against Terrorism", 704.

120 Brownlie, *The Use of Force*, 245.

Taliban regime is disputed.[121] The United States and the UK claimed that Al-Qaeda was responsible for the 11 September 2001 attacks in a report to the Security Council[122] but presented no clear evidence:[123]

> The attacks on 11 September 2001 and the ongoing threat to the United States and its nationals posed by the Al-Qaeda organization have been made possible by the decision of the Taliban regime to allow the parts of Afghanistan that it controls to be used by this organization as a base of operation.[124]

In the current world political and economic picture, the broad interpretation of imputability in an armed attack complicates international law. Its meaning is still unclear, especially with the spectre of international terrorism, under which the slogan "war on terror" poses a threat to the international order in many respects. First, the many non-state actors such as Hamas, Hezbollah, and Al-Qaeda are not organised in any one state but in many states. Even though it is accepted that acts of such organisations have the dimensions of armed attacks, which states will the international community impute as responsible? The fact that many states are unable to control such organisations makes this issue even more complex.

There is a parallel between the absence of effective government and the appearance of such organisations, which claim to take on the main tasks of the state such as security. Therefore, as Brownlie (1961) clearly demonstrated, the imputability of indirect aggression should be narrowly interpreted. Otherwise, the requirement of proportionality goes beyond Article 51 of the UN Charter.[125] Support for a so-called terrorist organisation alone cannot logically be interpreted under Article 51 as justification for armed attack. There must be a proven connection between the aggression of such an organisation and the state. The International Court of Justice pointed out the necessity to prove 'the involvement in the attacks, direct or indirect, of the Government of the DRC' in the activities of Allied Democratic Forces (ADF) in the territory of the Congo in 2005.[126]

---

[121] Markus Krajewski, "Selbstverteidigung gegen bewaffnete Angriffe nicht staatlicher Organisationen: Der 11 September 2001 und seine Folgen", *Archiv des Völkerrecht* 40 (2002), 190–195.

[122] Letter dated 7 October 2001 from the Permanent Representative of the United States of America to the United Nations Addressed to the President of the Security Council, UN Doc. S/2001/946, 7 October 2001, www.un.int./usa/s-2001-946.htm.

[123] Christine D. Gray, *International Law and the Use of Force*, 2nd edition (Oxford: Oxford University Press, 2004), 166.

[124] Zemanek, "Self-Defense against Terrorism", 695.

[125] Brownlie, *The Use of Force*, 245.

[126] *Case Concerning Armed Activities on the Territory of the Congo (Democratic Republic of the Congo v. Uganda)*, International Court of Justice, December 19, 2005, General List. 116, paragraph 146.

A 2004 ICJ Advisory Opinion on the construction of a wall in the Occupied Palestinian Territory repeated the necessity of finding a link between the acts of the non-state actors and the state. While Israel claimed to justify the construction of the wall as an act of self defence under Article 51 of the UN Charter, the ICJ found the construction of the wall and its associated regime contrary to international law.[127] According to the ICJ, because Israel did not '[…] claim that the attacks against it are imputable to a foreign State […] Article 51 of the Charter has no relevance in this case'.[128] Article 51 states that there is no explicit 'requirement of State involvement or activity, and therefore, the non-state actors can be responsible for an armed attack'.[129] However such an argument is not acceptable either de jure or de facto. From a legal standpoint, this broad interpretation brings up many complicated legal issues ignored by international lawyers who claim that non-state actors can commit an armed attack.[130] When non-state actors are based in many states, it is difficult for the international community to act. Also, taking the examples of Al-Qaeda and Hezbollah, it is difficult to know where to attack such actors. Both Afghanistan and Lebanon are dealing with a serious absence of effective government after interventions that claimed to target only non-state actors.[131]

The use of force before an actual attack is defined synonymously as pre-emptive, preventive, and anticipatory self-defence, which cannot be clearly differentiated.[132] Especially after 11 September 2001, U.S. foreign policy clearly declared its aim to take preventive military action against specific new threats—weapons of mass destruction, rogue states, and international terrorism. This paradigm was implemented as the National Security Strategy under the 'Bush doctrine' in Afghanistan and Iraq.[133]

Both pro and con views on preventive self-defence are found in the literature. Some authors focus on the wording of Article 51 and advocate for a narrow interpretation of the right of self-defence, justifiable only in case of actual and imminent armed attack.[134] Hans Kelsen argues for this view as follows:

---

127 *Legal Consequences of the Construction of Wall in the Occupied Palestinian Territory*, Advisory Opinion, I.C.J. Reports 2004, 136.

128 Ibid., 194.

129 Krajewski, "Humanitarian Intervention", 21.

130 Ibid., 22.

131 Ibid., 24–25.

132 Ibid., 4.

133 *The National Security Strategy of the United States*, September 2002, 15.

134 Brownlie, *The Use of Force*, 183 et. seq; Krajewski, "Humanitarian Intervention", 11; Robert Kolb, "Self-Defense and Preventive War at the Beginning of the Millennium", *Zeitschrift für Öffentliches Recht* 59 (2004), 115.

> This article applies only in case of an armed attack. The right of self-defence must not be exercised in case of any other violation of the legally protected interests of a Member.[135]

Other authors broadly interpret Article 51, arguing that 1) such an interpretation is necessary in the current world order and international relations and 2) customary law allows a broad range of self-defence of the state.[136]

However, pre-emptive self-defence is unlawful under current international law for several reasons[137]

First, according to Article 51, self-defence is only valid in response to an actual or imminent armed attack, and the phrase 'if an armed attack occurs' leaves no space for preventive self-defence. Second, the claim that customary law allows a broader interpretation of the self-defence of the state is invalid because the principle of non-force in Article 2(4) also plays an important role.[138] Third, the spirit of the UN Charter does not allow the legalisation and legitimisation of preventive self-defence. The need for preventive self-defence appears when there is a belief in a threat to the state or international order. Chapter VII of the UN Charter gave the Security Council the responsibility of avoiding threats to collective peace and security.[139] In other words, the Security Council is the only body responsible for collective peace and security in the face of a wide spectrum of threats, from threats to peace to acts of aggression. According to Article 39, the Security Council has the authority to determine the existence of any threat to the peace, breach of peace, or act of aggression and to decide on measures to maintain or restore international peace and security.[140] Therefore, self-defence is an exception to be used only when the Security Council is unable to deal with such a situation.

Actually, the text of Article 51 as a whole clearly demonstrates the purpose of the UN Charter. The measures which a state can take in self-defence are temporary, until the Security Council can assume its responsibility. States

[135] Hans Kelsen, "Collective Security and Collective Self-Defense under the Charter of the UN", *American Journal of International Law* 42 (1948), 4, 792.

[136] McCalmon, "States, Refugees, and Self Defense", 239.

[137] Mary Ellen O'Connell, "The Myth of Preventive Self-Defense", The American Society of International Law Task Force on Terrorism, August 2002: 2–3.

[138] Krajewski, "Humanitarian Intervention", 11; Derek W. Bowett, *Self-Defense in International Law* (Manchester: Manchester University Press, 1958), 191.

[139] Yoram Dinstein, "Sovereignty, the Security Council and the Use of Force", in *Redefining Sovereignty, The Use of Force After the Cold War*, ed. Michael Both, Mary Ellen O'Connell, and Natalino Ronziti (Aldershot, UK: Transnational Publishers, 2005), 120.

[140] Article 39 of the UN Charter.

invoking the right of self-defence must report immediately to the Security Council after they exercise this right.[141]

However, there is a necessity here to distinguish preventive self-defence from the 'anticipatory self-defence' or 'incipient self-defence'[142] just before the armed attack. Neither the UN Charter nor the ICJ decisions enlighten us about where self-defence begins. Humphrey Waldock writes that if there is 'convincing evidence not merely of threats and potential danger but of an attack being actually mounted, then an armed attack may be said to have begun to occur, though it has not passed the frontiers'.[143]

Despite the lack of a clear explanation of the beginning of self-defense, the similarities between self-defense in municipal law, the general principles of law, and the practice of states enables us to determine the beginning of self-defence in each case.[144] It is generally accepted that '[...] a state need not to wait to suffer the actual blow before defending itself, so long as it is certain the blow is coming'.[145]

International law practice since the end of the Second World War has demonstrated that the principle of self-defence is implemented mostly in accordance with Article 51 of the UN Charter.[146] As mentioned above, only Israel, the United States, and the UK have invoked the right of preventive self-defence.[147] However, international practice has not supported this paradigm. When Israel destroyed an Iraqi nuclear reactor on 7 June 1981, most states refuted its claim of preventive self-defence. The Security Council condemned the attack in Resolution 487 (1981) of 19 June 1981 and defended Iraq's demand for compensation.[148] The International Court of Justice also has upheld the reaction of the international community to the claim of preventive self-defence, as shown in the case of Nicaragua.[149]

[141] Bowett, *Self-Defense in International Law*, 195.

[142] Yoran Dinstein, *War, Aggression, and Self-Defense*, 3rd edition (Cambridge: Cambridge University Press, 2001), 172.

[143] C.H.M. Waldock, "The Regulation of the Use of Force by Individual States in International Law", Recueil des Cours 081 (The Hague: Martinus Nijhoff Publishers), 498.

[144] Kolb, "Self-Defense and Preventive War", 115.

[145] O'Connell, "The Myth of Preventive Self-Defense", 8.

[146] Krajewski, "Humanitarian Intervention", 11–12; Alexandrov, *Self-Defense against the Use of Force*, 165, 172; Dinstein, "Sovereignty", 120.

[147] Examples are the U.S. invasion of the Dominican Republic in 1956 and Grenada in 1983, the U.S. offensive in Libya in 1986, and the Israel offensives in Iraq in 1981 and Tunis in 1982. For more detail on these cases, see Sean D. Murphy, "Terrorism and the Concept of Armed Attack in Article 51 of the UN Charter", *Harvard International Law Journal* 43 (2002), 45; Kolb, "Self-Defense and Preventive War", 113.

[148] Louis René Beres and Yoash Tsiddon-Chatto, "In Support of Anticipatory Self-Defense: Israel, Iraq and International Law", *Contemporary Security Policy* 19 (1998), 2, 111.

[149] Garwood-Gowers, "Pre-Emptive Self-Defense", 51.

Actually, the paradigm of preventive self-defence arises because neither a terrorist act, an influx of refugees, nor the consequences of an inability to protect a border can justify self-defence. Either a terrorist attack occurs or it is blocked before it can happen. Self-defence is not justified in either case. If the attack occurs, it is over, and there is no place to speak about self-defence. What remains is to find those responsible and bring them to justice. To maintain otherwise is simply to call for an eye for an eye, and international law is based on finding an alternative to this mentality. Blocking a terrorist attack before it happens appears as a criminal act rather than self-defence. Because the time and place of a terrorist attack are unpredictable, advocating preventive self-defence in such a case is nothing less than a violation of the principle of non-force.

How to protect states dealing with the absence of effective government against armed attack is one of the most important questions on which international law remains silent. Such states are at a disadvantage because they cannot protect themselves from outside threats, like situation of Lebanon during Israel's military intervention in 2006 or the situation of Iraqi Kurdistan during Turkey's military intervention in 2008. The question is answered in the international political context if not in international law, like the role of the United States for ceasing the intervention in each example.

Teleological Interpretation of Non-force in Humanitarian Interventions

The proponents of the teleological interpretation of non-force claim that the principle applies only to military intervention and that it violates the territorial integrity and sovereignty of a state to serve the political and economic interests of the intervening state.[150] However, where there is no responsible government or the government is ineffective, the people suffer from a chaotic situation and human rights violations. Because the violation of human rights is no longer a domestic issue, the teleological interpretations holds that any state can intervene in another to stop such violations and protect its exercise of self-determination.[151]

Some authors go a step further and claim that unilateral intervention is not unlawful if it aims to restore a democratically elected government.[152] The

[150] Bowett, *Self-Defense in International Law*, 152; Antony D'Amoto, "The Invasion of Panama Was a Lawful Response to Tyranny", *American Journal of International Law* 84 (1990), 2, 516, 520. Karsten Nowrot and Emily W. Schbacker, "The Use of Force to Restore Democracy: International Legal Implications of the ECOWAS Intervention in Sierra Leone", *American University International Law Review* 14 (1998–1999), 336.

[151] Stein and von Buttlar, *Völkerrecht*, 310.

[152] Fernando R. Tesón, *Humanitarian Intervention: An Inquiry into Law and Morality* (Dobbs Ferry, New York: Transnational Publishers, 1997), 151.

legality of unilateral military intervention, as well as humanitarian intervention, was discussed during the negotiation of the UN Charter in 1945, but the issue was not included in the Charter because its main aim was to prevent aggression *between* states.[153] In the current international legal order, only the Security Council is the competent authority to decide on the use of force to achieve collective security under Chapter VII.[154] Therefore, any unilateral intervention under the claim of protecting human rights or collective security is unlawful under international law.[155]

Nor is unilateral military intervention justifiable by the theory of just war in the teleological interpretation. The obstacles to legitimising multilateral military intervention also apply to unilateral military intervention, but there are two additional obstacles. The first is the question of right intention, in other words, the difficulty of differentiating one just cause from another. The second is the difficulty of redressing the problems that are cited to justify the intervention. Any act with an intent different from the predicated intent, according to the theory of just war, is unjustifiable because of the requirement of right intention.[156] While right intention is questionable even in the case of multilateral military intervention, the risk of different intentions than the purported ones is even higher in the case of unilateral military intervention.[157] The U.S. intervention in Panama in 1989 was a typical example of disguising political interests as humanitarian intervention to protect the fundamental right of democratic governance.[158]

The probability of success is one of the conditions of *jus ad bellum*. Given the difficulty of the task for the United Nations itself in the absence of effective government, fulfilment of the most important requirement of proper authority—the ability to take care of the people and the country after the war—is almost impossible in the case of unilateral intervention.[159] NATO's 1999 action in Kosovo illustrated this. When the military intervention ended after 78 days, it was clear that NATO had not thought through the next steps to protect the people in the short or long term.[160]

---

153 Nowrot and Schbacker, "The Use of Force", 373.

154 Dinstein, "Sovereignty", 115–116.

155 Sean D. Murphy, *Humanitarian Intervention: The United Nations in an Evolving World Order*, Procedural Aspects of International Law (Philadephia: University of Pennsylvania Press, 1996), 393; Schroeder, "The Kosovo Crisis", 179–197, 181.

156 Boyle, "Traditional Just War Theory", 42.

157 Mills, *Human Rights*, 134–145; Boyle, "Traditional Just War Theory", 46–47.

158 Nowrot and Schbacker, "The Use of Force", 370.

159 Boyle, "Traditional Just War Theory", 35–36; Mills, *Human Rights*, 137.

160 Schroeder, "The Kosovo Crisis", 179–197, 185.

The Right of Self-Determination

The principle of self-determination appeared as a political concept during the French and American revolutions of the 18th century. At the beginning of the 20th century, Vladimir Lenin (1870–1924) and Woodrow Wilson (1913–1921) advocated for the principle from different standpoints. Lenin recognised the political concept of self-determination as part of the concept of universal socialism and described the principle as a 'general criterion for the liberation of peoples', while Wilson formulated the principle from the internal aspect of self-determination based on Western democracy, popular sovereignty, self-government, and human rights.[161] Nevertheless, the principle did not acquire a legal dimension under the League of Nations but instead remained a 'political and philosophical concept' until the Second Word War.[162] Different parts of the UN Charter describe the principle of self-determination,[163] but many international documents and resolutions of the UN organs and other international organisations concentrate on the content of the right of self-determination.[164]

Modern international law accepts self-determination as central to human rights. The relation between human rights and self-determination is clearly shown in Article 1 of both the International Covenant on Economic, Social and Cultural Rights and the International Covenant on Civil and Political Rights of 1966.[165] However, statutes on self-determination in international law variously interpret the principle as a right with the identity of a general principle of customary law[166] or a legal principle.[167] For example, in the case of East Timor,

---

[161] Antonio Cassese, *Self-determination of Peoples, A legal Reappraisal* (Cambridge: Cambridge University Press, 1995), 13–15, 20; David Raič, *Statehood and the Law of Self- Determination* (The Hague: Kluwer Law International, 2002), 184.

[162] Bereket Habte Selassie, "Self-determination in Principle and Practice: the Ethiopian-Eritrea Experience", *Columbia Human Rights Law Review* 29 (1997–1998), 92.

[163] Articles 1 (2) and 55 of the UN Charter. Articles 73 and 76 also contain a reference to self-determination.

[164] International documents and resolutions of the international organisations, the two International Covenants on Human Rights, the International Covenant on Economic, Social and Cultural Rights the International Covenant on Civil and Political Rights of 1966, the Declaration on Granting of Independence to Colonial Countries and People (G/Res/1514 of 14 December 1960), the Declaration on Friendly Relations and Cooperation among States (G/Res/ 2625 of 24 October 1970), the Final Act of Helsinki of the Conference on Security and Cooperation in Europe of 1975, the Universal Declaration of Human Rights (not explicitly, in Article 21), and the Banjul Charter on Human and Peoples' Rights of 1981.

[165] Bartram S. Brown, "Human Rights, Sovereignty, and Final Status of Kosovo", *Chicago-Kent Law Review* 80 (2005), 245. Selassie, "Self-determination", 94.

[166] Benedetto Conforti, *The Law and Practice of the United Nations* (Leiden: Martinus Nijhoff Publishers, 2005), 263.

[167] Brownlie, *Principles of Public International Law*, 553.

the ICJ determined that the principle of self-determination was 'one of the essential principles of contemporary international law', 'a peremptory norm of international law', and a 'right of an *ergo omnes* character'."[168]

Self-determination remains one of the most difficult and controversial principles of international law.[169] Current international law perceives the principle as having both internal and external dimensions. The internal aspect is linked to the democratic form of government, and the external aspect to the relation between the people in the state and other countries.[170] The external aspect has two dimensions: an instrument to protect a state from outside interference, and the right of secession.[171]

In the absence of effective government, both internal and external self-determination pose important questions for international law. The external aspect raises the questions of subjectivity and the right of secession, while the internal aspect becomes an important argument to justify the legality of unilateral and multilateral military intervention. The link between subjectivity under international law and the external aspect of self-determination of states dealing with the absence of effective government was touched on earlier. The following section describes the right of secession and the internal aspect of self-determination in relation to unilateral and multilateral military intervention.

The Right of Secession in the Absence of Effective Government

The right of secession has been one of the most interesting issues in international law since the First World War because the international community's reaction to the issue has been influenced by the international political situation, in which the political and strategic interests of the powerful states play an important role.[172] The international community has accepted secession movements only during the breakdown of the Ottoman and Austro-Hungarian empires after the end of the First World War, the decolonisation process after

---

168 East Timor, 1995, ICJ 102; Brown, "Human Rights", 245.

169 Crawford, *The Creation of States*, 89; Mills, *Human Rights*, 68; Conforti, *Law and Practice*, 263; Kamal S. Shehadi, "Ethnic Self-Determination and the Break-up of States: The Power of Ethnic Responses to Creating New States, Redrawing International Borders and Salvaging Failed States", (London: Brassesy's Ltd., 1993), 4.

170 Shehadi, "Ethnic Self-Determination", 4.

171 Sarah Joseph, "Resolving Conflicting Claims of Territorial Sovereignty and External Self-Determination, Part 1: A Proposed Formula", *International Journal of Human Rights* 3 (1999), 1, 42–43.

172 Raič, *Statehood and the Law of Self- Determination*, 184; Cassese, "Self-Determination Revisited", 13–15, 20.

the Second World War, and the dissolution of the Soviet Union and Yugoslavia after the end of the Cold War.[173] In each case, the international community restricted the right of self-determination in terms of time, territories, or movements with no legal explanation.[174] Most other secessionist movements have been regarded with scepticism. By 2008 only the secession of Eritrea from Ethiopia, East Timor from Indonesia and Kosovo had been recognised by the international community.[175] The international community has largely ignored Hamas in the West Bank and Gaza and the Liberation Tigers of Tamil Eelam in Sri Lanka, citing the importance of the stability of the international order and the territorial integrity and sovereignty of states. The strategic and political interests of the permanent members of the Security Council, such as Russia in the case of Chechnya and China in the case of Tibet, play an important role in this reaction.[176]

Current international law offers no special ruling on the secession of states. Only two General Assembly resolutions in the context of decolonisation appear as legal sources.[177] In Resolution 1514 (XV) of 14 December 1960, the General Assembly saw itself as responsible for assisting the independence movements of the trust territories and non-self-governing territories and defined 'non-self-governing territory' as 'geographically separate' and 'distinct ethnically and/or culturally from the country administrating it' in what was called the 'saltwater theory of colonialism'.[178] The 1970 Declaration on Principles of International Law concerning Friendly Relations and Cooperation among States mentions self-determination, but along almost the same lines as General Assem-

[173] Raič, *Statehood and the Law of Self- Determination*, 3, 184; Shehadi, "Ethnic Self-Determination", 4. Because international law consistently ignored external self-determination throughout the Cold War, the recognition of the new states that arose from the dissolution of the Soviet Union and Yugoslavia can be explained mainly in terms of politics.

[174] Raič, *Statehood and the Law of Self- Determination*, 184; Cassese, "Self-Determination Revisited", 20.

[175] Joseph, "Resolving Conflicting Claims", 40. The discussion after the independence of Kosovo in February 2008 and its recognition by 54 states, Russia's recognition of the independence of Abkhazia in July 1992, and the recognition of the Republic of Abkhazia in August 2008 by first Russia and then Nicaragua show how closely the issue depends on international policy.

[176] Brown, "Human Rights", 244; Margaret Moore, "The Self-Determination Principle and the Ethics of Secession", introduction to *National Self-Determination and Secession*, ed. Margaret Moore (Oxford: Oxford University Press, 1998), 1.

[177] G/A/1514 of 14 December 1960 on *The Declaration on the Granting of Independence to the Colonial Territories* and G/A/1541(XV) of 15 December 1960 on *Principles which should guide members in determining whether or not an obligation exists to transmit the information called for under Article 73e of the Charter*.

[178] Paragraph VI of General Assembly Resolution1541 (XV) of 15 December 1960.

bly Resolutions 1514 (XIV) and 1541 (XV) in the context of decolonisation.[179] After decolonisation, international lawyers advanced the view that the safeguard clause 'saltwater theory of colonialism' precluded the right of secession by states that did not fulfil its criteria. However, as mentioned above, the General Assembly adopted both of these resolutions concerning colonial territories in the context of decolonisation. Therefore, the safeguard clause cannot be accepted as a legal reason to oppose the right of secession.[180]

The international community has similarly ignored secessionist movements in cases of the absence of effective government. In its resolutions regarding such states, the Security Council has consistently invoked the territorial integrity and sovereignty of the state and international stability. Self-determination is invoked only in its internal aspect regarding self-government, democracy, and human rights. Typical examples are Somaliland and Puntland in Somalia and Abhkazia in Georgia. Somaliland declared its independence in 1991 and Puntland in 1998.[181] South Ossetia declared its independence from Georgia in 1991, and Abkhazia in 1992, just after the Republic of Georgia declared its independence on April 9 1991.[182] Steve Kibble describes Somaliland, which has survived for more than 16 years in contrast to the absence of effective government in the rest of Somalia,[183] as follows:

> Somalilanders pointed out to me on a recent visit there that the Somalia model of development has had its success. It could, indeed, be seen as a first indigenous modern African form of government. This entails a fusion of traditional forms of organization within a democratizing framework containing an emphasis on self-reliance, as a legitimate post-colonial option for Africa. The Somaliland 'nation-building' process was more bottom-up and does actually function as a state. It is the one place in Somalia where peace with security has been established, unlike the south of the country, and it could be the basis of state-building.[184]

Many Security Council resolutions describe the question of secession as an important part of peace and security within states. For example, Resolution 971

---

179 General Assembly Resolution 2625 (XXV) of 24 October 1970; James Crawford, "State Practice and International Law in Relation to Unilateral Secession", in *Self-Determination in International Law, Quebec and Lessons Learned*, ed. Anne F. Bayefsky (The Hague: Kluwer Law International, 2000), 32.

180 Mills, *Human Rights*, 69–70.

181 Steve Kibble, "Somaliland: Surviving without Recognition: Somalia: Recognized but Failing", *International Relations* 15 (2001), 5, 13.

182 Russia declared its recognition of the Republic of Abhazia in August 2008.

183 Ismail I. Ahmed and Reginald Herbold Green, "The Heritage of War and the State: State Collapse in Somalia and Somaliland: Local-Level Effects, External Interventions and Reconstruction", *Southern Quarterly* 20 (1999), 1, 113–127, 126.

184 Kibble, "Somaliland", 18.

(1995) of 2 January 1995 maintained that a 'comprehensive political settlement of the conflict, including the political status of Abkhazia', was the only way to secure peace.[185]

The constitution of a state is a social-historical fact with no time limit. David Raič points out that 'the same forces of national feeling certainly have not ceased to operate, nor have they become weaker in the course of the twentieth and twenty-first centuries'.[186] A secessionist movement is in fact an issue between the people who attempt to establish a state and the parent state whose territorial integrity is threatened. In this respect, the rights of secession and territorial integrity under international law contradict each other. Crawford notes this issue in a report on the Quebec question: '[...] even where there is a strong and sustained call for independence; it is a matter for the government of a state concerned to consider how to respond'.[187]

Secessionist movements may 1) be provided the right of secession by the constitution of the parent state,[188] 2) gain the parent state's approval of the right of secession, or 3) conduct a war of secession.[189] While the first two pose no problem in international law, fighting for a new state through war pits the interests of the separatist movements and parents states against each other. The international community has perceived wars of secession, the third option, as domestic issues of the parent states, also out of concern for international stability, ignoring the Biafran movement against Nigeria, the struggle of Bangladeshis in Pakistan, and Eritrea's war against Ethiopia until these movements were recognised by the parent states.[190]

Without legal approval, secessionist movements as social and historical facts gain independence as states once they meet the three conditions of statehood and immediately acquire an international legal personality. As explained above, recognition by other states has no constitutional effect, but rather a declaratory

---

[185] S/Res/971 (1995) of 12 January 1995.

[186] Raič, *Statehood and the Law of Self- Determination*, 3.

[187] Crawford, "State Practice and International Law", 31–32.

[188] Constitution of the Union of Burma, 1947, Chapter X, Article 201–206, reprinted in *Constituent Assembly of Burma, Constitution of the Union of Burma*, 1948; 1977 Constitution of the former Soviet Union, Sowjetunie, Verchovnyj Sovet SSSR, Constitution of the Union of Soviet Socialist Republics Adopted at the Seventh (Special) Session of the Supreme Soviet of the USSR, Ninth Convocation, 7 October 1977, Article 72, cited in Raič, *Statehood and the Law of Self-determination*, 313.

[189] Raič *Statehood and the Law of Self- Determination*, 315; viz. the secession of Singapore from Malaysia in 1965 and Eritrea from Ethiopia in 1993.

[190] Gerry J. Simpson, "The Diffusion of Sovereignty: Self-Determination in the Post-colonial Age", *Stanford Journal of International Law* 32 (1996), 2, 283; Raič, *Statehood and the Law of Self- Determination*, 316.

effect.[191] However, in international law the international community has often moved in a series of steps when faced with the question of recognising a new state: 1) reluctance to meet a people's demand to exercise external self-determination and refusal to recognise the new state,[192] 2) attempts to change the recognition of the state from declaratory to constitutive, or 3) advocacy for the replacement of the right of secession with the right of internal self-determination.

In the first step, the international community at first reluctantly and sometimes even arbitrarily recognises a new state born from a secessionist movement. This practice in international law is justified by the necessity of 'permissive recognition' by the parent country rather than state criteria. Following this reasoning, the international community waits to recognise the new state until the parent state recognises it or transfers sovereignty in order to recognise it. But while recognition by the parent state was a condition for the international community's recognition of new states in the 18th and 19th centuries, the practice of contemporary international law has shown that there is no need for permissive recognition for a new state to be recognised by the international community.[193] In many cases, mostly in the context of decolonisation, such as Algeria's recognition by France and Guinea-Bissau's by Portugal, other states have recognised new states before the parent states have. This was true during the dissolution of the former Yugoslavia and the establishment of Slovenia, Croatia, Bosnia-Herzegovina, and Macedonia, without regard to their effectiveness as states.[194] As seen above, the recognition of any state in public international law is not a legal question but rather a question of international policy.[195]

The second step is to attempt to change the character of recognition of a new state from declaratory to constitutive. However, the dominant position is that the nature of this recognition is declaratory. The implicit attempt to change the nature of recognition is seen clearly in the notion of a 'de facto regime'. Many

---

191 Raič, *Statehood and the Law of Self- Determination*, 48, 57.

192 Antonio Cassese, "Self-Determination Revisited", in *International Law in an Evolving World, Liber Amicorum, Tribute to Eduardo Jiménez De Aréchaga* (Montevideo, Uruguay: Fundación de Cultura Universitaria, 1994), 235.

193 Cristine Haverland, "Secession", *Encyclopaedia of Public International Law* 10 (1987), 385, 388.

194 Raič, *Statehood and the Law of Self- Determination*, 93–95; Danilo Türk, "Recognition of States: A Comment", *European Journal of International Law* 4 (1993), 66; David O. Lloyd, "Succession, Secession, and State Membership in the United Nations", *New York University Journal of International Law and Politics* 26 (1993–1994), 788–789.

195 Hersh Lauterpacht, *Recognition in International Law* (Cambridge: Cambridge University Press, 1948), cited in: Lloyd, "Succession, Secession", 763. This is also valid for the recognition or non-recognition of the independence of Kosovo and Abkhazia.

states that have been in existence for more than a decade are still described by the international community as de facto regimes.[196] This means that they have the responsibilities but not the rights of states.

The final step is the international community's advocacy of replacing the right of external self-determination (secession) with the right of internal self-determination. This tendency, especially since the end of the Cold War,[197] is based on a false assumption that if internal self-determination can be implemented perfectly, there is no need to resort to secession.[198] It is true that there is a link between internal self-determination and the right of secession, but the two are not interchangeable. As Lea Brilmayer writes, 'Secessionist demands, unlike claims about domestic political fairness, cannot be satisfied through domestic political reforms'.[199]

The most important discussion of the right of secession in international law concerns the principle of the territorial integrity of the state and the stability of the international order.[200] The territorial integrity of the parent state is one of the main legal issues through which the international community attempts to legitimise or show cause for ignoring the right of secession.[201] The principle of territorial integrity is described in Article 2(4) of the UN Charter, as well as in many international law documents and customary international law.[202]

---

[196] The other example is the Turkish Republic of Northern Cyprus, a de facto independent republic within still internationally accepted borders of the Republic of Cyprus since its independence in 1983. In spite of its 24-year existence and the absence of the domestic jurisdiction of the Republic of Cyprus over this territory during this time, no state except Turkey has recognised the Turkish Republic of Northern Cyprus. The Security Council called on states not to recognise the independence of Northern Cyprus in Resolutions 541 (1983) of 18 November 1983 and 550 (1984) of 11 May 1984.

[197] This approach of the international community is clearly seen in the decision on the Aaland Island question in 1921. The Commission of Jurists spoke for the sovereignty of Finland over Aaland Island, precluding the claim of the right of secessionist on the one hand and guaranteeing autonomy, demilitarization, and minority and language rights, through which they focused on internal self-determination, on the other. *Aaland Islans Question*, 2 League of Nations O.J. 691, 699 (1921). The Report of the International Committee (sic) of Jurists entrusted by the Council of the League of Nations with giving an advisory opinion on the legal aspects of the Aaland Island question, League of Nations O.J. Special Supplement No. 3, 5 Oct. 1920, cited in Brown, "Human Rights", 244.

[198] Crawford, "State Practice and International Law", 32; Simpson, "The Diffusion of Sovereignty", 283.

[199] Lea Brilmayer, "Secession and Self-Determination: A Territorial Interpretation", in *Self-Determination in International Law*, ed. Robert McCorquodale (Aldershot, UK: Dartmouth Publishing Co., Ltd., 2000), 177.

[200] Brown, "Human Rights", 244, 256; Crawford, "State Practice and International Law", 31–32; Mills, *Human Rights*, 73.

[201] Joseph, "Resolving Conflicting Claims", 40.

[202] Ibid.

Concerning the right of secession, premature recognition could violate territorial integrity. However, if the new state achieves its independence, or the people cannot live together under the notion of 'we', as in Kosovo, then it is impossible to speak of territorial integrity. The spirit of territorial integrity is a determining factor for the recognition secession movements.[203] From this perspective, ignoring the independence of a state and forcing people to live together in fact threatens international security and refutes the argument of territorial integrity.[204]

The other main legal justification for ignoring external self-determination is the stability of the international legal order.[205] It is claimed that once the right of secession is recognised, every nation can claim the right of self-determination, and this can change the 'political geography of the world' and threaten the existing world order and stability.[206] After the Cold War, Boutros-Ghali's *Agenda for Peace* stated that

> [...] the United Nations has not closed its door. Yet if every ethnic, religious or linguistic group claimed statehood, there would be no limit to fragmentation, and peace, security and economic well-being for all would become ever more difficult to achieve.[207]

In fact, this argument is an overreaction divorced from reality. First, not every nation is able to establish a state, nor is it in the interest of every nation to do so.[208] Secessionist movements often appear in the context of unresolved political and historical questions. Second, the international community's ignoring the right of secession has caused more instability than stability. In other words, if a new state exists for more than a decade and the formal state does not have de facto sovereignty due to the absence of effective government, recognition is a stabilising rather than a destabilising factor in international relations and international law.[209] More interesting is the fact that the international community invokes international stability to argue against secession today but used the same argument as an instrument to protect decolonisation in General Assembly Resolution 1514 (XV) of 14 December 1960.[210]

---

203 Umozurike Oji Umozurike, *Self-Determination in International Law* (Hamden, Connecticut: Shoe String Press, 1972), 236; Simpson, "The Diffusion of Sovereignty", 283.

204 Weber, "Das Sezessionsrecht", 512.

205 This was also an important argument in the Aaland Island case (see note 197).

206 Mills, *Human Rights*, 91.

207 *An Agenda for Peace*, A/47/277 S/24111 of 17 June 1992.

208 Shehadi, "Ethnic Self-Determination", 12.

209 Friedrich, "UNMIK in Kosovo", 265.

210 Simpson, "The Diffusion of Sovereignty", 283; *Declaration on the Granting of Independence to Colonial Countries and Peoples*, General Assembly Resolution 1514 (XV) of 14 December 1960.

In summary, the right of secession is a sensitive issue in international law. The international community's interference in a people's attempt at secession or early recognition of a declaration of independence could appear to violate territorial integrity, but ignoring the right of secession can violate the principle of self-determination and destroy international stability.[211]

The Justification of Military Intervention to Protect Internal Self-Determination
Military intervention has been justified on the basis of protecting internal self-determination. Woodrow Wilson was the father of the concept of internal self-determination as the basis of Western democracy and popular sovereignty,[212] but the concept was linked to democracy, self-government, and human rights after the end of the First World War and especially after the end of the Cold War. At the beginning of the 1990s, democracy was classified as a fundamental human right. Many international lawyers, states, and international organisations supported the use of force to establish or restore democracy and advocated for military intervention in non-democratic governments to enable their people to exercise internal self-determination.[213] This view was also demonstrated in the 1980s by the UK's claim in the General Assembly that not only occupation by a foreign power but also a non-democratic government jeopardised the exercise of self-determination.[214] Democracy was claimed as the main justification for military intervention in Panama and Haiti.[215]

In the absence of effective government, military intervention is sometimes justified by the need to protect self-determination. It is argued that military intervention in the absence of effective government or in case of an arbitrary

[211] Brown, "Human Rights", 249.

[212] Raič, *Statehood and the Law of Self- Determination*, 184; Brown "Human Rights", 240–241.

[213] Lois E. Fielding, "Taking the Next Step in the Development of New Human Rights: The Emerging Right of Humanitarian Assistance to Restore Democracy", *Duke Journal of Comparative and International Law* 5 (1995), 329; W. Michael Reisman, "Coercion and Self-Determination: Construing Charter Article 2 (4)", *American Journal of International Law* 78 (1984), 642; Thomas M. Franck, "The Emerging Right to Democratic Governance", *American Journal of International Law* 86 (1992), 46–47.

[214] Cited in Geoffrey Marston, "United Kingdom Materials on International Law", *Baltic Yearbook of International Law* 56 (1985), 460.

[215] Fielding, "Taking the Next Step", 329; Domingo E. Acevedo, "The Haitian Crisis and the OAS Response: A Test of Effectiveness in Protecting Democracy", in *Enforcing Restraint: Collective Intervention in Internal Conflicts*, ed. Lori F. Damrosch (New York: Council on Foreign Relations Press, 1993), 119, 141; Nowrot and Schbacker "The Use of Force", 370–371; David Wippman, "Defending Democracy through Foreign Intervention", *El Papel del Derecho Internacional en América, La Soberania Nacional en la El Integración Regional* (México City: Universidad Nacional Autónomo de México Instituto de Investigaciones Jurídical, 1987), 122.

military regime does not violate international law.[216] The legal and moral aspects of unilateral and multilateral intervention were discussed earlier. This section focuses on the use of internal self-determination to legitimise the right of intervention.

In the absence of effective government, it is difficult from a theoretical point of view to advocate for such intervention to promote the right of people to 'choose their own legal and political institutions in the community of nations'.[217] It is true that people cannot exercise internal self-determination as a whole in the absence of effective government, but people also cannot exercise their right to self-identity in the case of military intervention or international administration.

The Security Council mentions in different resolutions on cases of the absence of effective government that the people of the state have the ultimate responsibility for their own future, Resolution 814 (1993), for example, recognises that 'the people of Somalia bear the ultimate responsibility for national reconciliation and reconstruction of their own country'.[218] However, the reality is different in every case. Military intervention and international territorial administration have always been 'an imposition of an external will on those subject to it, a usurping of the people's right to shape and direct their own collective life'.[219] The people of Afghanistan were pushed by Europeans and North Americans to accept this concept.

Military interference cannot resolve a people's inability to exercise internal self-determination. Rüdiger Wolfrum advocates for territorial administration by claiming that 'without assisting activities from the outside the population would not be able to exercise its rights of self-determination due to lack of representative institutions'.[220] However, military intervention in the case of international transitional administration suspends the right of self-determination.[221] The undemocratic approach of the international community was clearly seen in the United Nations Mission in Kosovo (UNMIK). During the nearly 10-year existence of UNMIK, the North, under the auspices of the United Nations, first replaced the self-determination of the people of Kosovo and second, delayed a decision on the status of the state.

---

216 Raič, *Statehood and the Law of Self- Determination*, 239.
217 Bledsoe and Boczek, *The International Law Dictionary*, 54.
218 S/Res/814 (1993) of 26 Mach 1993.
219 McMahan, "Intervention and Collective Self-Determination", 2.
220 Wolfrum, "International Administration", 651.
221 Weber "Das Sezessionsrecht", 503.

Chapter Six

Handling the Legal Complications of the Absence of Effective Government

The absence of effective government brings into focus many important problems in international law because it involves states' inability to take advantage of rights and fulfil duties under international law. Because public international law differs from other law orders in its lack of a central control mechanism, the principle of accountability in a decentralised legal order plays a more important role in ensuring stability and effectiveness.[1] In the absence of effective government, the state, but also the international community, suffers either from ineffectiveness or a lack of organs or agencies to fulfil its duties and exercise its rights, which Herdegen described as 'subjective impossibility'.[2]

Because government incapacity differs from one state to another in appearance and implementation, no general rule, for example, *ulta posse nemo obligatur*, can be applied in the case of the absence of effective government. The Articles on Responsibility of States for Internationally Wrongful Acts of the International Law Commission (ARSIWA)[3] bring into public international law the reality that not only *de lege lata* but also *de lege ferenda* perceive the phenomenon not as unique but rather as a combination of complications.[4] The answer to the question of the responsibility of states dealing with the absence

---

1 Robin Geiß, *"Failed States". Die normative Erfassung gescheiterter Staaten* (Berlin, Duncker & Humblot, 2005), 251.

2 Matthias Herdegen, "Der Wegfall effektiver Staatsgewalt im Völkerrecht: 'The Failed State'", in Daniel Thürer, Matthias Herdegen, and Gerhard Hohloch, *Der Wegfall effektiver Staatsgewalt: "The Failed State"*, Berichte der Deutsche Gesellschaft für Völkerrecht 34, (Heidelberg: C.F. Müller Verlag, 1996), 77.

3 The Article on the Responsibility of States for Internationally Wrongful Acts by the International Law Commission (ARSIWA) was adopted at the Fifty-Third session of the Commission in 2001 (annex to General Assembly Resolution 56/83 of 12 December 2001).

4 Article 8 on Conduct Directed or Controlled by a State of the Responsibility of States for Internationally Wrongful Acts of 2001 states, "The conduct of a person or group of persons shall be considered an act of a State under international law if the person or group of persons is in fact acting on the instructions, or under the direction or contract of, that State in carrying out the conduct".

of effective government, complications, consequences of violations, and the capacity to implement public international rules depends on the situation in each state.[5]

The practice of public international law, like that of other law orders, is determined between two axes: the current political, economic, and social world order and the rules of positive international law. In this context, the reaction of international law to the complications of the absence of effective government is influenced on the one hand by the subjectivity of states and their consequent rights and duties and on the other by the state's limited ability or lack of ability to enjoy rights and fulfil duties under international law. The international community's handling of the legal complications of the absence of effective government is a research subject of its own.[6] The present work maintains only that the reaction of the international community to the lack of effective government should be understood as part of its reconstruction efforts.

International law overcomes the difficulties of states dealing with the absence of effective government both actively and passively. Passively, other states ignore and tolerate the lack of effectiveness as much as possible and attempt to maintain normal diplomatic relations with those states. The international community applies different principles and criteria such as 'continuity, identity, practicability, [and] stability of the law' to justify ignoring or tolerating the lack of effectiveness. These principles are sometimes used alone and sometimes combined to decrease complications in practical international law.[7]

In practice the international community also actively tolerates the absence of effective government. This is clearly seen in its acceptance of warring parties as respondent parties because of the ad hoc necessity of reconciling these parties.[8] For example, the UK had contact with the warring parties in Somalia when there was no government,[9] and many countries and international organisations

---

5 James R. Crawford, "The ILC's Articles on Responsibility of States", *American Journal of International Law* 96 (2002), 874–876.

6 Geiß, "*Failed State*", 251 et. seq. and Riika Koskenmäki, "Legal Implications Resulting from State Failure in Light of the Case of Somalia", *Nordic Journal of international Law* 73 (2004), 1, 1 et. seq, mainly deal with this issue.

7 Heike Krieger, *Das Effektivitätsprinzip im Völkerrecht* (Berlin: Duncker & Humblot, 2000), 174; Herdegen, "Der Wegfall effektiver", 53; Georg Dahm, Jost Delbrück, and Rüdiger Wolfrum, *Völkerrecht*, Volume 1/3 (Berlin: Walter de Gruyter, 2002), 129, 144; James R. Crawford, *The Creation of States in International Law* (Oxford: Clarendon Press, 1979), 42; Torsten Stein and Christian von Buttlar, *Völkerrecht* (Munich: Carl Heymann's Verlag, 2005), 100; Daniel Thürer, "Der Wegfall effektiver Staatsgewalt: 'The Failed State' ", in Daniel Thürer, Matthias Herdegen, and Gerhard Hohloch, *Der Wegfall effektiver Staatsgewalt: "Failed State"*, Berichte der Deutschen Gesellschaft für Völkerrecht 34 (Heidelberg: Müller Verlag, 1995), 16–17.

8 Koskenmäki, "Legal Implications", 8; Herdegen, "Der Wegfall effektiver", 56.

9 Letter of the Foreign and Commonwealth Office of 20 February 1992, printed in The Weekly Law Reports of 6 November 1992, 754.

joined the warring parties in the Djibouti Conference for the Reconciliation of Somalia in June 1991.[10] The United States had contact with the Liberian factions between December 1989 and the summer of 1990,[11] and international organisations such as the United Nations, ECOWAS, and the OAU took part in the National Conference of All Political Parties.[12]

An example of active tolerance is the right of treaty making. This right under Article 6 of the Vienna Convention on the Law of Treaties theoretically remains in the absence of effective government. But the ability to make treaties depends on the capacity of states, and this capacity is almost totally destroyed in the absence of a current government. This creates many problems for the efforts of the international community to establish a development framework and provide humanitarian relief. The inability of a state to make treaties on the one hand and the need for a development framework on the other has led to different solutions. The failure to ratify the Lomé Convention on Somalia brought the African, Caribbean and Pacific (ACP)–European Union Council of Ministers to the following conclusion on 28 June 1996:

> The ACP-EU Council of Ministers 1 confirms the political accession of Somalia to the Lomé Convention, despite the fact that Somalia has not been able to ratify the Convention for reasons beyond its control [...].[13]

Paragraph 6 of Article 93 addressed the absence of any authority to ratify the Cotonou Partenrship Agreement as follows:

> [...] the Council of Ministers may decide to accord special support to ACP states party to previous ACP—EC conventions which, in the absence of normally established government institutions, have not been able to sign or ratify this agreement [...].[14]

In 1999 the UN Secretary-General called for flexibility on the part of the international financial institutions concerning administrating the Lomé IV Convention.[15]

---

10 Geiß, "*Failed State*", 138. The countries included Germany, the United States, France, Italy, and China, and the international organisations included the OAU and European Union.

11 U.S. House of Representatives, Subcommittee on Africa of the Committee on Foreign Affairs, 101st Congress, 2nd Session, Hearing on U.S. Policy and the Crisis in Liberia of 19 June 1990 and Subcommittee on African Affairs of the US Senate Foreign Relations Committee, Statement by H.J. Cohen, Assistant Secretary for African Affairs of 27, November 1990, printed in Marc Weller, ed., *Regional Peace-Keeping and International Enforcement: The Liberian Crisis* (Cambridge: Cambridge University, 1994), 47, 109.

12 Geiß, "*Failed State*", 138.

13 Case C-369/95, 27 November 1997, para. 11.

14 Cited in Geiß, "*Failed State*", 153.

15 S/1999/882 of 16. August 1999, para. 72.

The final example of the international community's active tolerance of the consequences of the absence of effective government is seen in measures taken to remedy the physical impossibility of diplomatic relations. The 1992 decision of the Superior Administrative Court of North Rhine-Westphalia in the face of Somalia's inability to ensure salaries and social security for its diplomats is a good example.[16] The Court decided that Germany, as the receiving state, could 'provide financial assistance to diplomatic agents in cases of urgent distress in accordance with its legislation'.[17] This decision was cancelled, however, by the Federal Administrative Court.[18]

As seen above, the international community mostly limits its active reaction to the consequences of the absence of effective government to humanitarian assistance or development policy. Nonetheless, taking active measures to maintain as normal relations as possible with states dealing with the phenomenon should be a major part of efforts to rebuild such states and bring them back into international law. For example, because the absence of effective government limits the international representation of a state and its people, as explained above,[19] host states should compensate for the lack of diplomatic relations stemming from financial incapacity. The international community should establish new institutions and measures to protect or address the grievances of people from states dealing with the absence of effective government who are living in other countries. The decision of the Superior Administrative Court of North Rhine-Westphalia should be taken as a precedent for this.

[16] *Somali Diplomat Case*, Case No. 8 B536/92, Federal Republic of Germany, Superior Administrative Court (OVG) of North Rhine-Westphalia, 11 February 1992, ILR 94 (1994), 597–608, 602. Decision of the Federal Administrative Court. (BVerwGE 100, 300).

[17] Ibid., 605; Koskenmäki, "Legal Implications", 10.

[18] Decision of the Federal Administrative Court of 29 February 1996 (BVerwG 5 C 23.95) (BVerwGE 100, 300).

[19] Koskenmäki, "Legal Implications", 7; Herdegen, "Der Wegfall effektiver", 52; Dahm et al., *Völkerrecht*, 245; Eileen Denza, *Diplomatic Law: Commentary on the Vienna Convention on Diplomatic Relations*, 2nd edition (Oxford: Clarendon Press, 1998), 395.

Chapter Seven

The Hypocritical Approach of the North to Solving the Absence of Effective Government: State Reconstruction

The end of the Cold War had two major consequences for public international law. The first was the global aspiration that the United Nations could finally play its role in providing collective security and peace in the world.[1] The second was the ability of the United States to act as a sole superpower to pursue its political and economic interests without the opposition of the Soviet Union.

U.S. President George H.W. Bush declared a "New World Order" immediately after the end of the Cold War in 1990. His son, President George W. Bush, stated the role of the United States in a speech on 26 February 2003 on the eve of the U.S. attack on Iraq: 'We meet here during a crucial period in the history of our nation and of the civilized world. Part of that history was written by others; the rest will be written by us'.[2]

The absence of effective government became a popular issue with the appearance of the 'failed state' concept in the beginning of the 1990s, but public international law lacked sufficient legal means to deal with the phenomenon. The reaction of the international community was shaped mainly in this context, chiefly influenced by the 'failed state' paradigm. Because Chapter VII of the UN Charter identified the absence of effective government as a threat to peace, the solution was sought in the measures set out in this document.

While Chapter VII was invoked as a legal platform for the efforts of the international community, many different solutions were proposed, including political trusteeship, nation building, and state building. International transitional administration emerged as one of the main elements of state reconstruction. These solutions were attempted under the claim of instituting democracy, protecting human rights, or forming constitutions. This approach was put into

1 *An Agenda for Peace*, A/47/277 S/24111 of 17 June 1992; Security Council Meeting on 31 January 1992, S/PV 3046.

2 Francis Fukuyama, *State-Building: Governance and World Order in the 21st Century* (Ithaca, New York: Cornell University Press, 2004), 95.

practice at the beginning of the 1990s in Somalia. The international community mounted a military intervention to bring this 'failed state', which had been identified as a threat to international peace and security, into line.

Almost two decades later, the concept of state reconstruction still gives rise to many questions in international law. This chapter first presents the main claims and elements of the concept of state reconstruction on the legal basis of Chapter VII of the UN Charter and then examines the aim and content of state reconstruction and its suitability for solving the absence of effective government in the practice of international law.

International Involvement from Technical Assistance to International Transitional Administration

The lack of adequate instruments in traditional international law to deal with the absence of effective government was foremost on the agenda of the Summit Meeting of the Security Council on 31 January 1992 on "The Responsibility of the Security Council in the Maintenance of International Peace and Security".[3] Secretary-General Boutros-Ghali was entrusted with the task of preparing a report consisting of

> [...] analysis and recommendations on ways of strengthening and making more efficient within the framework and provisions of the Charter the capacity of the United Nations for preventive diplomacy, for peacemaking and for peacekeeping.[4]

The resulting *Agenda for Peace: Preventive Diplomacy and Related Matters* of 17 June 1992[5] was in fact the first policy-setting UN document to set out a graduated reaction to internal conflict and its consequences according to Chapters VI and VII of the UN Charter.[6] This report influenced subsequent UN efforts to address internal conflict and the absence of effective government and foresaw post-conflict peacekeeping as the centre of the international community's efforts.[7] A number of UN Security Council resolutions and international law documents in line with the '*Agenda for Peace*' appeared in the following years.

3 S/PV. 3046 of 31 January 1992.
4 Ibid.
5 *An Agenda for Peace*, A/47/277—S/24111 of 17 June 1992.
6 Markus Benzing, "Midwifing a New State: The United Nations in East Timor", *Max Planck Yearbook of United Nations Law* 9 (2005), 297.
7 *An Agenda for Peace*, A/47/277—S/24111 of 17 June 1992.

In Resolutions 1265 (1999),[8] 1296 (2000),[9] and 1674 (2006)[10] on the protection of civilians in armed conflict, the Security Council signalled that targeting civilians or impeding humanitarian access could in themselves constitute a threat to international peace and security. The report on the 'Responsibility to Protect' of the International Commission on Intervention and State Sovereignty (ICISS) in 2001[11] and the 2005 World Summit document[12] more clearly invoke the use of Chapter VII of the UN Charter in states dealing with the absence of effective government. Both of these documents are categorised as soft law.

Since 1945 both the scope for implementing Chapter VII of the UN Charter and the content of peacekeeping operations have changed. The international community initially restricted its efforts to technical assistance but after 1990 began to take on more difficult tasks.

The changing peacekeeping role of the United Nations can be analyzed as falling into three stages. In the first stage, the traditional peacekeeping operations between 1945 and 1987, the United Nations highlighted the principles of the equal sovereignty of states, non-intervention, and non-force. In this context only 13 peace-keeping operations were mounted over a span of more than 40 years. Because these operations dealt with conflicts between states, the United Nations at first played the role of a neutral party, with restricted tasks. Chapter VI of the UN Charter defined the legal basis of the traditional peacekeeping operation, mainly conducted by unarmed or lightly armed personnel.[13] Simon Chesterman has described traditional UN peacekeeping operations as 'non-threatening and impartial, governed by the principles of consent and minimum force'.[14]

The second generation of UN peacekeeping operations took place between 1987 and 1992. The 13 UN peacekeeping operations established during this short period were influenced by the end of the Cold War and the changing character of conflict—more *within* states than *between* states. They differed from the traditional operations in their multidimensionality. International engagement became more complex and frequent, involving not only military but also civic functions. In fact, peacekeeping efforts in this generation were described mainly as technical assistance.

---

8 S/Res/1265 (1999) of 17 September 1999.

9 S/Res/1296 (2000) of 21 April 2000.

10 S/Res/1674 (2006) of 28 April 2006.

11 http://www.iciss.ca/report-en.asp.

12 A/Res/60/1 of 24 October 2005; http://www.un.org/summit2005/, especially outcomes 9 and 138.

13 An Agenda for Peace, A/47/277—S/24111 of 17 June 1992.

14 Simon Chesterman, *You, the People, The United Nations, Transnational Administration, and State-Building* (Oxford: Oxford University Press, 2004), 238.

The third generation of UN peacekeeping operations that arose after *An Agenda for Peace* was issued in 1992 differed in several ways from those described above. The operations have been mounted within states under Chapter VII of the UN Charter, without the consent of all parties[15] and have involved more than mere technical assistance. The United Nations or its Member States have taken over legislative, executive, and even juridical power in third countries, as in the case of international transitional administration. This generation of peacekeeping operations was the main determinant of the international community's approach to solving the phenomenon of the absence of effective government.[16]

International Transitional Administration

International transitional administration was an invention of international law after the Cold War,[17] although the approach originated in the idea of political trusteeship[18] under British colonial policy in the late 18th and 19th centuries.[19] This concept influenced the mandate system of the League of Nations after the First World War[20] and the trusteeship system of the United Nations after the Second World War.

Both of these systems were conceived for dependent territories, but when legal scholars placed the political trusteeship system back on the international law agenda almost 50 years after the establishment of the United Nations, the

15 Ibid.; Boutros Boutros-Ghali, introduction to *The United Nations and Somalia 1992–1996*, United Nations Blue Books Series, Volume VIII (New York: United Nations 1996), 33.

16 Carsten Stahn, *The Law and Practice of International Territorial Administration, Versailles to Iraq and Beyond* (Cambridge: Cambridge University Press, 2008), 9.

17 The legal question for international administration is covered in Chapter 5.

18 Henry H. Perritt, "Structures and Standards for Political Trusteeship", *UCLA Journal of International Law and Foreign Affairs* 8 (2003), 385; Michael Bothe and Thilo Marauhn, "The United Nations in Kosovo and East Timor: Problems of a Trusteeship Administration", *International Peace-keeping* 6 (2000), 152; Brian Deiwert, "A New Trusteeship for World Peace and Security: Can an Old League of Nations Idea Be Applied to a First Century Iraq?", *Indiana International and Comparative Law Review*. 14 (2004), 771 et. seq.; Joshua S. Miller, "Putting Iraq in Trust: Reviving the UN International Trusteeship under General Principles of the International Fiduciary Obligation to Manage the Natural Resources of a Post-Saddam Iraq", *Suffolk Transnational Law Review* 27 (2003–2004), 1, 37 et. seq.

19 Nele Matz, "Civilization and Mandate System under the League of Nations as the Origin of Trusteeship", *Max Planck Yearbook of United Nations Law* 9 (2005), 50.

20 Article 22 of the League of Nations stated that the people in the territories were 'not yet able to stand by themselves under the strenuous conditions of the modern world'.

targets were not dependent territories but sovereign states. The absence of effective government arose as an important issue in the discussion of political trusteeship. After the end of the Cold War, the Security Council first attempted to implement such a broad mandate in Somalia, but when this endeavour failed, the United Nations and the North quickly gave up the larger claims of establishing effective government or reconstructing the state.[21] Subsequently, the United Nations partly administered most territories based on technical assistance[22] and implemented full-fledged administration only in East Timor and Kosovo.[23] The U.S. and UK civil administration of Iraq, the CPA, was also a full-fledged administration.[24]

The Definition and Content of International Transitional Administration in Cases of the Absence of Effective Government

Carsten Stahn describes international transitional administration as a 'sleeping beauty' in international law.[25] Scholars have approached with subject from different perspectives,[26] but many related issues remain open questions in international law.[27] Brett H. McGurk, who served as Special Assistant to the President and Senior Director for Iraq and Afghanistan, Strategic Planning and Policy Development under U.S. President George W. Bush pointed out that

21 The case studies in Chapter 5 contain more detail on the military intervention.

22 The important third generation peace-keeping operations included the United Nations Transitional Authority in Cambodia (UNTAC) between 1992 and 1993 (S/Res/745 [1992] of 28 February 1992), the United Nations Operation in Somalia (UNOSOM II) in 1993 (S/Res/814 [1993] of 26 March 1993), the Institution of the High Representative for Bosnia-Herzegovina in 1995 (S/Res/1031 [1995] of 15 December 1995, para. 27), and the United Nations Transitional Authority in Eastern Slavonia, Baranja, and Western Sirmium (UNTAES) (S/Res/1037 [1996] of 15 January 1996 and Doc.S/1995/951).

23 The United Nations Interim Administration Mission in Kosovo (UNMIK) in 1999 (S/Res/1244 [1999] of 10 June 1999, paragraphs 1 et. seq.) and the United Nations Transitional Administration in East Timor (UNTAET) (S/Res/1272 [1999] of 25 October 1999, para. 1 et. seq.).

24 S/Res/1483 (2003) of 22 May 2003, paragraph 4.

25 Stahn (*The Law and Practice*, 3–4) deals in detail with international territorial administration.

26 Steven R. Ratner, *The New UN Peacekeeping: Building Peace in Lands of Conflict after the Cold War* (New York: St. Martin's Press, 1995); various articles on this issue in *Max Planck Yearbook of the United Nations Law*, Vol. 9 (2005); Frank-Erich Hufnagel, *UN-Friedensoperationen der zweiten Generation. Vom Buffer zur Neuen Treuhand* (Berlin: Duncker & Humblot, 1996).

27 In Chapter 5 the legal basis of the international transitional administration is adequately demonstrated.

> [...] the international law of state-building in failed and post-conflict states does not exist. Instead, most state-building efforts have relied entirely on ad hoc UN Security Council Resolutions, which are often adopted in haste, with no overarching theme or consistency.[28]

This assertion is borne out clearly in the case of the absence of effective government.

The first unresolved question in international law about international transitional administration is its definition and content in cases of the absence of effective government. In each case the content of the UN mandate was sui generis, with enormous scope and complexity where the mandate authority assumed legislative, executive, and judicial authority over the territory.[29] International law takes a general approach regarding the content of international transitional administration. The United Nations has settled for reviewing individual missions rather than undertaking a comprehensive assessment.

International documents did not substantially clarify the ambiguity of the content of international transitional administration. 'Transitional civil administration' was mentioned for the first time in the Brahimi Report of 2000 on the future of the UN peace operations, but no effort was described in detail.[30] The *Report of the High-Level Panel on Threats, Challenges and Change* and the Outcome Document of the High-Level Plenary Meeting of the General Assembly in September 2005 recommended institutions for the international transitional administration and favored the establishment of a Peacebuilding Commission but left open the tasks the commission would perform.[31] As with the notion of the 'failed state', scholars formed their own definitions of the concept and content of international transitional administration.[32] For example, Ralph Wilde defines territorial administration as 'a formally constituted, locally-based management structure operating with respect to a particular territorial unit,

---

28 Brett H. McGurk, "Revisiting the Law of Nation-Building: Iraq in Transition", *Virginia Journal of International Law* 45 (2005), 453.

29 Michèle Griffin and Bruce Jones, "Building Peace through Transitional Authority: New Directions, Major Challenges", *International Peacekeeping* 7 (2000), 3, 77; Stahn, *The Law and Practice*, 369–371.

30 See paras. 76–83 of the *Report of the Panel on the United Nations Peace Operations* (Brahimi Report), UN Doc. A/55/305, S/2000/809 (21 August 2000).

31 See *A More Secure World: Our Shared Responsibility. Report of the Secretary-General's High-level Panel on Threats, Challenges and Change*, UN Doc. A/59/565 (2 December 2004), paras. 262–264 and GA Resolution 60/1 (World Summit Outcome) of 24 October 2005, paras. 97–105. Paragraph 98 of this resolution specifies that '[t]he Commission should focus attention on the reconstruction and institution-building efforts necessary for recovery from conflict and support the development of integrated strategies in order to lay the foundation for sustainable development'.

32 For a different definition, see Stahn, *The Law and Practice*, 44.

whether a state, a sub-state unit or a non state territorial entity'. However, even Wilde describes his definition as artificial.[33] In this lacuna the character of international transitional administration as a long-term or short-term solution cannot be adequately established.

Moreover, the duration of the mandate changes from one transitional administration to another. For example, the UN Transitional Administration in East Timor (UNTAET) lasted for more than three years, ending in May 2002, the UN Interim Administration Mission in Kosovo has been in place since 1999 in spite of Kosovo's declaration of independence on 17 February 2008, and the CPA began on 21 April 2003 and was dissolved on 28 June 2004. The limit of the authority and accountability of international transitional administration also remain unanswered in international law.[34]

The international administration in Iraq clearly showed the ambiguous content, complexity, and unresolved international legal questions of international transitional administration. Security Council Resolution 1483 (2003) decreed the status, responsibilities, and state-building efforts of the United States and UK as an occupying power[35] for the purpose of promoting 'the welfare of the Iraqi people through the effective administration of the territory'. However, providing security and stability and establishing conditions 'in which the Iraqi people can freely determine their own political future' in paragraph 4 and establishing 'national and local institutions for representative governance' in paragraph 8(c) went beyond the customary responsibilities of an occupying power[36] under international law, especially the Geneva Conventions of 1949 and the Hague Regulations of 1907.

Along with the law of occupation, paragraphs 8 and 9 of Resolution 1483 (2003) address the other legal regime, state building. Operational paragraph 8 refers to the responsibility of the UN Special Representative for Iraq, and operational paragraph 9 refers to an interim administration. In spite of these references to the two parallel legal regimes, the Security Council did not deal sufficiently with their correlation and limits.[37]

---

33 Ralph Wilde, *International Territorial Administration. How Trusteeship and the Civilizing Mission Never Went Away* (Oxford: Oxford University Press, 2008), 21.

34 Stahn, *The Law and Practice*, 3–4.

35 Para. 13 of the preamble of SC Res. 1483 (2003) of 22 May 2003, UN Doc. S/RES/1483 (2003).

36 Stahn, *The Law and Practice*, 143–144; Adam Roberts, "Transformative Military Occupation: Applying the Laws of War and Human Rights", *American Journal of International Law* 100 (2006), 613.

37 Stahn, *The Law and Practice*, 143–144; See UK Ministry of Defense, "The Manual of the Law of Armed Conflict" (2004), para.11.11, note 5.

Adequacy of International Transitional Administration as a Solution to the Absence of Effective Government

The adequacy of international transitional administration to solve the problem of the absence of effective government can be evaluated only by determining the character of international transitional administration in such cases. In other words, because the content of international transitional administration has not been defined generally in international law, its adequacy as a long-term or short-term solution is undetermined open. Therefore, it is impossible to answer this question through general practice in international law.

If transitional administration is assumed to be a long-term-solution for the absence of effective government, it has to pass the test of effectiveness. The most important reason for this is the discrepancy between the pragmatic concept of the international community and the historical and global economic and political context linked to the roots of the phenomenon. If the concept is accepted as a short-term solution, the international community has to define its aim. An international transitional administration could be justified after a military intervention in the case of genocide or human rights violations but could not solve the problem of the absence of effective government.

Practical Impossibility

Moreover, the international community does not have the capacity to implement international administration in every state dealing with the absence of effective government. The United Nations is the world's hope to realise international peace and security, but its financial and organizational capacity is limited.[38] Western countries have continually reduced foreign aid since the end of the Cold War. Despite promises in international forums, only a few small states have devoted as much as 1 percent of their gross domestic product to international development aid. The United States, which is eager to appear as a rescuer of Southern states, spends only 0.1 percent of its GDP on foreign aid.[39] The gap between the reduced financial capacity of the United Nations and the unwillingness of the Northern countries to contribute to foreign aid on the one hand and the UN aim of establishing international territorial administration with broad authority to reconstruct states on the other hand has been shown

[38] Jan Cristian Hildenbrand, *Zur Krisenaktionsfähigkeit der Friedenstruppen der VN, Notwendigkeiten, Konzepte und Perspektiven ihrer Verbesserung* (Baden-Baden: Nomos Verlagsgesellschaft, 2001), 93 et. seq.

[39] Michael Ignatieff, *Empire Lite: Nations Building in Bosnia, Kosovo and Afghanistan* (New York: Vintage Books, 2003), 93.

in Kosovo and East Timor. Even with these states' small populations and territories, the United Nations faced such a daunting challenge that it radically turned away from the concept of full-fledged international administration to a so-called 'light footprint' in Afghanistan.[40]

Paradigms of State Reconstruction

The concept of state reconstruction is based on diverse paradigms. The first is the definition of the absence of effective government as a threat to international peace under Chapter VII of the UN Charter. This paradigm made it possible to combine the solution approach with military intervention in practice.[41] The efforts of the international community to address the absence of effective government also have been determined by 1) the assumption of the incapacity of the state as virtually the sole cause of the problem and the inability of such states to sustain themselves as members of the international community[42] and 2) the appearance of the international community as the main actor in state reconstruction.[43]

The literature on UN peacekeeping operations is abundant.[44] If the United Nations' military intervention in Somalia in 1993 is accepted as the beginning of the implementation of the paradigm of state reconstruction, it is important to look at the discrepancies between the claim and actual practice of state reconstruction during the past 15 years.

40 Ebrahim Afsah and Alexandra H. Guhr, "Afghanistan: Building a State to Keep the Peace", *Max Planck Yearbook of United Nations Law* 9 (2005), 382.

41 The legal discussion concerning the international administration and Chapter VII of the UN Charter is found in Chapter 5.

42 Gerard Helman and Steven B. Ratner, "Saving Failed States", *Foreign Policy* 89 (1992–1993), 3.

43 Henry J. Richardson, "Failed State, Self-Determination, and Preventive Diplomacy: Colonialist Nostalgia and Democratic Expectations", *Temple International and Comparative Law Journal* 10 (1996), 18; Madeleine Albright, "Yes, There Is a Reason to Be in Somalia", *New York Times*, August 10, 1993, A19.

44 Michael Bothe, ed., *UN Peacekeeping, A Documentary Introduction*, The Hague: Kluwer Law International, 1999; Seref Aksu, *The United Nations, Intra-state Peacekeeping and Normative Change* (Manchester: Manchester University Press, 2003); Wolfgang Biermann, ed., *UN Peacekeeping in Trouble* (Aldershot, UK: Ashgate Publishing, 1998); Boris Kondoch, ed., *International Peacekeeping* (Aldershot, UK: Ashgate Publishing, 2007); Ray Murphy, *UN Peacekeeping in Lebanon, Somalia and Kosovo* (Cambridge: Cambridge University Press, 2007); Norrie MacQueen, *Peacekeeping and the International System* (London: Routledge Publishing, 2006); Andrzej Sitkowski, *UN Peacekeeping, Myth and Reality* (Westport, Connecticut: Praeger Security International, 2006).

State Building and Nation Building

The different terms used by Security Council and General Assembly resolutions to describe state reconstruction include 'reconstruction of the country', 'rebuilding the country', and 'assisting the process of national rapprochement'.[45] However, legal scholars have mainly discussed state reconstruction in terms of nation building and state building. The Bonn Agreement on Afghanistan, for example, was considered a nation-building effort.[46] Most international legal literature describes state building as the restructuring of the political and administrative institutions that are the infrastructure of a state. In contrast, common values such as culture, history, and language are central to the concept of nation building. Many authors agree with the claim that state building is a fundamental step in nation building.[47] In fact, these two notions have not differed explicitly either in practice or in theory. They are sometimes used interchangeably, sometimes expressed as two different concepts, and sometimes used as complementary concepts. In summary, both notions are at the centre of efforts at state reconstruction but neither has been clearly defined.

The Concept of State Reconstruction

Under the rubric of state reconstruction, the international community posits a long-term solution dealing with political, administrative, economic, and security issues. Many state reconstruction concepts, however, suffer from the lack of a clear concept or method. Making the nation-state the final step in state reconstruction does not help clarify the concept. In spite of the claim that state reconstruction is a long-term solution to the absence of effective government, an overview shows that measures taken even in the case of security appear short sighted because of the complexity and variety of problems involved.

---

[45] A/Res/47/119 of 2 April 1993, A/Res/48/208 of 21 December 1993.

[46] Barry E. Carter, Phillip R. Trimble, and Curtis Bradley, *International Law* (New York: Aspen Publishers, 2003), 83.

[47] Rüdiger Wolfrum, "International Administration in Post-conflict Situations by the United Nations and Other International Actors", *Max Planck Yearbook of United Nations Law* 9 (2005), 654; Raphael Utz, "Nations, Nation-Building, and Cultural Intervention: A Social Science Perspective", *Max Planck Yearbook of United Nations Law* 9 (2005), 616; Armin von Bogdandy, Stefan Häußler, Rafael Utz, and Felix Hanschmann, "State-Building, Nation-Building, and Constitutional Politics in Post-Conflict Situations: Conceptual Clarifications and an Appraisal of Different Approaches", *Max Planck Yearbook of United Nations Law* 9 (2005), 613.

The Concept of the Nation-State

The aim of state reconstruction is usually described as re-establishing a nation-state,[48] but the notion of the nation-state as the goal complicates the issue. Public international law accepts the nation-state as the core of the Westphalia system, but the historical phenomenon of the nation-state appeared much earlier,[49] and even after the establishment of the Westphalia system, many empire states or post-feudal political entities such as the Ottoman Empire, Hungary, Germany, and Italy appeared in the international order. Neither the Soviet Union nor Yugoslavia were established as nation-states.[50] From both historical and social standpoints, the concept and development of the nation-state in Europe is sui generis. It did not appear in pre-colonial Africa or America because of colonial politics. Very few states in Arab countries or in Asia were established under the nation-state concept, with the exception of Iran, Japan, Burma, and Thailand.[51]

Another problem arises in the different interpretations of the concept of the nation-state. Alfred Coban expressed this aptly, writing that 'Institutions change, but the terms used to describe them remain the same [...] their real meaning is apparent only in their history'.[52] Today 'nation-state' frequently appears in political and social science as well as international law, but its meaning changed drastically between the 17th and 21st centuries. Therefore, almost every author who uses the term in the context of state building or nation building feels a need to define the term.

The final issue is that public international law does not use the term 'nation-state' even though the current international order is based on the Westphalia system, of which the nation-state was once the core. In public international law the state has three main elements—government, territory, and people. International law specifies the characteristics of neither the state nor the people.

---

48 Helman and Ratner, "Saving Failed States", 3 et. seq.

49 Alfred Cobban, *The Nation State and National Self-determination* (London: Harper Collins Publishers, 1969), 24. The state is some 10,000 years old, appearing in Mesopotamia's 'first agricultural societies' and in China with its highly trained bureaucracy. In fact, the main characteristics of the nation-state are seen in the pre-classical world—Sumerian from the mid 4th millennium BCE until the late 3rd millennium BC and Egypt. In the West there were several nation-states in the 12th and 13th centuries. The 14th century was the high point of nation-states, which found their roots in the political, social, and economic context of the Middle Age.

50 Jeffrey Herbst, "Global Change and the Future of Existing Nation-States", in *The Self-Determination of Peoples, Community, Nation, and State in an Interdependent World*, ed. Wolfgang Danspeckgruber (London: Lynne Rienner Publishers 2002), 13–15.

51 Cobban, *The Nation State*, 24.

52 Ibid., 23.

Because the attempt to define 'people' in public international law reaches a dead end, the term 'nation-state' does not make the concept of state reconstruction any clearer.

Political Issues

Democracy, a constitution, and human rights appear as political elements of almost every state reconstruction project. In Afghanistan, for example, a constitution was one of the main aims of nation building. This approach has been adopted mainly because of the North's assumption that it should teach these values to the Southern countries. However, this is nothing new; it is rooted in the colonial system.[53] In the League of Nations, the attitude of Western supremacy was expressed in a distinction between 'civilized' and 'non-civilized' people.[54] In the Cold War era, the jargon of the North changed from civilising the South to modernising it through democracy, development of a market economy, and westernisation.[55]

Various aspects of the international community's assumption that democracy, human rights, and constitutions are part of state reconstruction can be criticised in practice. The first issue is the way constitutions are made and the values of democracy or human rights are implemented. Despite Europe's long and difficult progress toward realising these values, the international community has tried to institute them in the South in a matter of years, contradicting the very spirit of these hard-won achievements. In the same paradigm, the North indexes democracy in the South almost exclusively to 'free and fair' elections,[56] but holding elections alone cannot solve the whole problem and even gives winners and losers a fresh reason to fight each other.[57]

---

53 Many ex-colonial powers saw establishing constitutions for their former colonies as part of the process of decolonisation, for example, Great Britain's idea of sharing the Lancaster model of constitution making; Sujit Choudhry, "Old Imperial Dilemmas and the New Nation-Building: Constitutive Constitutional Politics in Multinational Polities", *Connecticut Law Review* 37 (2004–2005), 933; Louis Aucoin, Karl F. Inderfurth, and Howard J. Wiarda, "Building the Institutions of the Nation (Panel II)", *Georgia Journal of International and Comparative Law* 33 (2004–2005), 171.

54 Article 22 of the Covenant of the League of Nations.

55 Ruth E. Gordon, "Saving Failed States: Sometimes A Neo-colonialist Notion", *American University Journal of International Law and Policy* 12 (1997), 6, 960.

56 James Crawford and Susan Marks, "The Global Democracy Deficit: An Essay in International Law and its Limit", in *Re-imaging Political Community: Studies in Cosmopolitan Democracy*, ed. Daniel Archiburgi, David Held, and Martin Köhler (Cambridge, UK: Polity Press, 1998), 72, 80.

57 Griffen and Jones, "Building Peace through Transitional Authority", 81.

Similar hypocrisy is evident in the international community's recognition of the governments in these states, despite the fact that these governments are not accepted by all parts of the countries, as in case of Afghanistan after the military intervention or the Transitional Federal Government of Somalia. The aim of keeping states dealing with the absence of effective government under the international legal system plays an important role in this policy. On this basis the Security Council adopted various resolutions with the consent of Somalia to enter into the country's territorial waters and 'use all necessary means' to fight piracy and armed robbery.[58] However, the capacity of Somalia's government to provide this consent is questionable. Although the sovereignty, self-determination, territorial integrity, and political independence of states are referenced in almost all Security Council resolutions, the international community in fact exploits existing governments to take measures that serve its interests.

Democracy, human rights, and a constitution cannot be implemented from outside or by force.[59] The concept of state reconstruction is usually invoked just after military intervention, as in Afghanistan. Even this attitude is nothing new. Woodrow Wilson expressed the aim of U.S. military intervention at the beginning of the 20th century as follows: 'I am going to teach the South American Republics to elect good men'.[60] No matter what claims countries have made for occupying Afghanistan throughout history, the people have made it clear that they do not welcome outside interference. The North's desire to implement its values in non-European states almost by force is none other than cultural intervention in the South, by which 'the centre establishes a particular identity for the rest of the population'.[61]

Another questionable issue is the relationship between political and economic liberalisation. Political liberalisation followed economic development in the North, but this progression has been turned almost upside down in the South, where international financial organisations impose a precondition of political liberalisation for economic development.[62] The UK representative in a Security Council Meeting of 31 January 1992 described democracy as 'a delicate

---

58 S/Res/1846 (2008) of 2 December 2008, S/Res/1816(2008) of 2 June 2008, S/Res/1851 (2008) of 16 December 2008, S/Res/1846 (2008) of 2 December 2008.

59 Ignatieff, *Empire Lite*, 85; Howard Wiarda, "Building the Institutions", 193.

60 Leo Panitch and Sam Gindin, "Theorizing American Empire", in *Empire's Law: The American Imperial Project and the War to Remake the World*, ed. Amy Bartholomew (London: Pluto Press, 2006), 29.

61 Utz, "Nations", 638.

62 Caroline Thomas, "International Financial Institutions and Social and Economic Human Rights: An Exploration", in *Human Rights Fifty Years On: A Reappraisal*, ed., Tony Evans (Manchester: Manchester University Press, 1998), 166.

plant that needs the nourishing soil of peace, security and economic development'.[63] As long as the people in the South have to struggle for survival, political liberalisation will remain ephemeral.

The final issue is that the North's claim of fostering democracy and human rights or making constitutions to institute civilisation, modernisation, and development has been refuted in practice. The mandate system, through which the 'civilised nations' aimed to place the 'uncivilised nations' under their tutelage, functioned differently in the end than the formal aim set out in Wilson's principles and by the League of Nations. The mandate powers used the system for their economic and geostrategic interests. Many independence movements were crushed, and people's will to govern was worn down through the well-known policy of divide and rule, as in the Category A mandate territories of Iraq and Palestine under the mandate regime of the League of Nations. Iraq took 12 years to gain its independence because of the repressive policy of Great Britain, and the latter imposed a divide and rule tactic in Palestine.[64] A similar policy was seen in the French mandate territories. France suppressed the nationalist movement in Syria and exploited the nationalist movement in Lebanon for its own aims and sent native troops from Cameroon and Togoland to fight in wars in other countries.[65]

During the Cold War the two superpowers often supported or even imposed dictatorial regimes to serve their own political and economic interests. As a result, the the democratic legitimisation of new governments, human rights, and attempts to dissolve political corruption played subordinate roles in international law, and the international community frequently ignored repression and genocide throughout the 1970s and 1980s.[66] With the help of the CIA, the United States brought down democratically elected governments in the Congo, Iran, Guatemala, and Liberia that tried to create popular movements or nationalise industries and installed notoriously repressive regimes in their place.[67] The

63 Security Council Meeting of 31 January 1992, S/PV. 3046, 8–9.

64 Frederick S. Northedge, *The League of Nations, Its Life and Times 1920–1946* (Leicester: Leicester University Press, 1986), 195.

65 Dharam C. Gupta, *The League of Nations* (Delhi: Vikas Publishing House, 1974), 51; Michael Dennis Callahan, *Mandates and Empire: The League of Nations in Africa 1914–1931* (Brighton, UK: Sussex Academic Press, 1999), 188.

66 Helmut Strizek, *Ruanda und Burundi: von der Unabhängigkeit zum Staatszerfall: Studie über eine gescheiterte Demokratie im afrikanischen Zwischengebiet* (Munich: Weltforum-Verlag, 1996), 25.

67 Ronald E. Powaski, *The Cold War: The United States and the Soviet Union, 1917–1991* (New York: Oxford University Press, 1998), 105, 106, 131, and 223; Adekeye Adebajo, *Liberia's Civil War: Nigeria, ECOMOG, and Regional Security in West Africa* (Boulder, Colorado: Lynne Rienner Publishers, 2002), 21.

political influence sometimes went so far that multinational enterprises directly determined the political situation in countries in the South. ITT Corporation, a large U.S. conglomerate, played an important role in the overthrow of the democratically elected government of Salvador Allende by a military coup in Chile, and the influence of the United Fruit Company in Central America is well known.[68]

The discrepancy between the international community's aim and methods in state reconstruction has been evident since the end of the Cold War. To succeed, such efforts require maximum consensus among the population in the territory to bridge ethnic and religious dissimilarities and search for a 'we' that defines a people. Without this consensus, neither minimal peace nor order can be established or endure. The international community's approach, however, has mostly been to destroy a state's remaining sense of commonality at the same time as it promotes the drafting of constitutions. In most multilateral and unilateral military interventions, the intervening power has destroyed existing or residual common bases. UNITAF and UNOSOM II singled out Mohammed Farah Aidid's USC/SNA, one of the two most important parties in the Somali conflict, as an enemy instead of trying to reconcile it with the other party. In Afghanistan the nation-building project was implemented parallel to a 'war on terror' to destroy 'enemies'. Claiming to make war against the Taliban, the North ignored this entity in the reconstruction process even though the Taliban was an important part of the conflict as well as of the population of Afghanistan.[69] The civil war between Shiites and Sunnites in Iraq began after the U.S. occupation and took on an important dimension when Saddam Hussein was taken to the gallows one day before the most important religious feast in the Islamic world, Eid-al-Adha.[70]

The international community's policy of pinpointing one part of the community as an enemy has other consequences that affect state reconstruction. In every instance of state reconstruction, United Nations resolutions maintain that the people of the country should be the main actor in re-establishing the state. However, attempts to keep the 'enemy' out of power has made the international community so blind that it has either killed or captured their elites while outlawing or disbanding armies or political parties,[71] as in Iraq.[72]

---

68 Jost Berstermann, *Das Einmischungsverbot im Völkerrecht*, Europäische Hochschulschriften, Reihe 2, Rechtswissenschaften (Frankfurt: Verlag Peter Lang, 1991), 49.

69 Afsah and Guhr, "Afghanistan", 411.

70 Ibid.

71 Oren Barak, "Dilemmas of Security in Iraq", *Security Dialogue* 38 (2007), 4, 460.

72 Ibid., 461.

In such situations, the international community usually establishes puppet governments and promotes elections with often questionable legitimacy.[73] The initial political engagement and aid policy of the international community may appear substantial, but over the long term, the praxis has been shown to be ineffective in many countries. In 2006 Amrullah Saleh, director of Afghanistan's National Intelligence Agency, pointed out the lack of effective political progress in the country.[74] In Iraq, as well, it is difficult to identify positive political achievements.

Administrative Structure

The international community continually stresses the need for the 'transfer of strong institutions' to states dealing with the absence of effective government, but its paradigms and efforts to establish administrative structures fall short in various ways.

The 'lack of strong institutions' is cited in almost every case of the absence of effective government, but it is not clear what the international community means by this. In practice, it seems to mean public services such as schools and hospitals. Rebuilding or establishing such structures have been cited as evidence of the success of the international effort. In reality, these short-term achievements cannot help establish strong institutions in states dealing with the absence of effective government. Taking over these institutions from a state makes the state idle and causes it to loose prestige among its people. These activities originate in the independence of a state and have to be provided by the state.[75] Over the long term, if the state is not able to provide the political goods, establishment of schools or hospitals by the international community cannot solve the problem. What does it mean to establish a school when people are unable to send their children there or the state is unable to provide the basic services?

The effort of the international community does not appear as an integral concept in international law practice. Besides the United Nations, many other

---

73 Barnett R. Rubin, "Saving Afghanistan", *Foreign Affairs* 86 (2007), 1, 69. Rubin points out that the government is ineffective against the insurgency because it lacks popular support.

74 Rubin, "Saving Afghanistan", 59. For detailed information, see Hamish Nixon and Richard Ponzio, "Building Democracy in Afghanistan: The Statebuilding Agenda and International Engagement", *International Peacekeeping* 14 (2007), 1, 26–40 and Barnett R. Rubin and Humayun Hamidzada, "From Bonn to London: Governance Challenges and the Future of State-building in Afghanistan", *International Peacekeeping* 14 (2007), 1, 8–26.

75 Erica Harper, "United Nations Transitional Administration: Missions in State or Nation-Building?", in *Post-Conflict Reconstruction: Nation-and/or State-Building*, ed., Horst Fischer and Noëlle Quénivet (Berlin: Wissenschaftlicher Verlag, 2005), 33.

international organisations and NGOs take a role in such activities, but with little organized collaboration or effective division of labor. Second, although the re-establishment of effective government is the main target of the international community's efforts, the international actors ignore the governmental authority within the state territory while attempting to establish administrative structures. The following passage by an officer in charge in Afghanistan illustrates this:

> Not a single one of the more than 350 projects submitted by international organizations and NGOs actually promised to consult the Afghan interim administration. How can the Afghan government coordinate reconstruction when every day NGOs arrive, fan out into the countryside and find a school to rebuild, an orphanage to establish or an orthopaedic centre to reconstruct, all without telling the Kabul government anything?[76]

Economic Issues

Economic issues should be a key and urgent element in a concept of state reconstruction for a long-term solution to the absence of effective government. The first reason for this is that the phenomenon itself depends directly on economic issues. Second, while a state appears as a political, historical, social, and economic unity, economic issues directly affect political and social issues. Third, every state has unique historical, social, cultural, political, and economic characteristics that interrelate in complex ways. In spite of this diversity and complexity, states are interdependent economically, and technology and globalisation strengthen this interdependence.

In practice, however, economic efforts have fallen short in state reconstruction. In many cases of the absence of effective government, such measures are short sighted, usually limited to financial assistance. In Somalia, where the international community used force without restraint, UNOSOM's economic measures were transient and superficial because they focused on subsistence, logistical needs, and external dependence. This was also the case in Kosovo, where the fourth pillar of UNMIK was the reconstruction of the economy under the management of the European Union.[77] In spite of nearly 10 years of international transitional administration, Kosovo still suffers from major economic problems, including 60–70 percent unemployment.[78] Nor in Afghanistan has the international community begun to take long-term

[76] Quoted in Ignatieff, *Empire Lite*, 100.

[77] S/Res/1244 (1999) of 10 June 1999, paragraph 11.

[78] Jürgen Friedrich, "UNMIK in Kosovo: Struggling with Uncertainty", *Max Planck Yearbook of United Nations Law* 9 (2005), 265.

measures to address economic issues. Rubin described Afghanistan in 2007 as the poorest country in the world outside of sub-Saharan Africa.[79] Opium production has increased since 2002 and reached record levels in 2007.[80] Because of the aid expenditures by foreign forces, international organizations, and NGOs, non-drug growth averaged more than 15 percent between 2002 and 2007, but this growth was only temporary. In spite of the apparent economic growth, the government failed to meet the basic needs of the population. Measures to revitalise agriculture and the rural economy or increase the quota for available energy have been very limited. Electricity is still one of the most important needs in the country, but no major power projects were completed until 2007. In fact, the capital city, Kabul, had more electricity in 2002 than in 2007.[81] In such a situation, U.S. pressure to eradicate opium poppy cultivation remains a short-sighted measure when the people seek aid from the drug traffickers and unemployment is so high.[82]

When the international community has seemed to take long-term measures, such measures have been based not on local historical, social, and cultural realities but on the values and interests of the North. They have followed the Washington Consensus[83] of market privatisation and liberalisation. This was clearly evident in the case of Iraq.[84] Because it was impossible to implement the Washington Consensus under Saddam Hussein, the United States and its allies established conditions to do so after Saddam's overthrow. The CPA's efforts were driven not by the economic reconstruction needs of Iraq or the country's cultural, social, and political identity but by the economic interests and political values of the United States and the UK.[85]

Authorised by the Security Council, the CPA attempted to transform the country's 'socialist economy' into a free market economy with privatisation and foreign direct investment at the centre.[86] Even primary schools were privatised

---

79 Rubin, "Saving Afghanistan", 66–67.
80 Ibid., 69.
81 Rubin, "Saving Afghanistan", 66–67.
82 Ibid., 57–78.
83 This is explained in Chapter 8 in detail.
84 Antonio F. Perez, "Legal Framework for the Economic Transition in Iraq—Occupation under the Law of War vs. Global Governance under the Law of Peace", *The Transnational Lawyer* 18 (2004), 53–54.
85 S/Res/1483 (2003) of 22 May 2003.
86 Judith Richards Hope and Edward N. Griffen, "The New Iraq: Revising Iraq's Commercial Law Is a Necessity for Foreign Direct Investment and the Reconstruction of Iraq's Decimated Economy", *Cardozo Journal of International Law and Comparative Law* 11 (2003–2004), 875, Rüdiger Wolfrum, "Iraq from Belligerent Occupation to Iraqi Exercise of Sovereignty: Foreign Power versus International Community Interference", *Max Planck Yearbook of United Nations Law* 9 (2005), 22–23.

as part of this policy. As early as the U.S. and UK invasion in April 2003, the United States sought sole authority for decisions on the future sale of Iraqi oil and many other economic issues. Security Council Resolution 1483 (2003) of 22 May 2003 authorised the CPA to reform the laws, infrastructure, and economy.[87] The free market economy, which had been impossible to impose during the Saddam period, quickly replaced the existing economic system.[88] Foreign ownership of business was permitted by a proclamation on the 'radical reform of the Iraqi legislation concerning foreign investment' on 19 December 2003.[89] The CPA cancelled the state-controlled banking system and designed a new system to be established by up to six foreign banks over five years. Foreign investment in the sale of Iraqi oil was made for an initial 30-year period.[90] Making no effort to rebuild the state in the absence of effective government, the international community dealt with neither the causes of the economic problems nor their link to the global economic context, with the exception of realising the Washington Consensus.

The international community is still very far from dealing with the contradiction between the claim of the economic and government recovery of states in the South and the process of the global economy. Today many Southern countries have lost their authority in the political and social as well as economic spheres through globalisation and privatisation,[91] increasingly handing over their economic decision-making authority to international actors.

Security

The stated aim of the international community's efforts to address the absence of effective government is international peace and security. Establishing safe conditions within the state has determined both short-term and long-term measures, because without minimal conditions for peace, neither political institutions nor civic institutions can evolve. This aim has been at the centre of every international reconstruction project and peacekeeping operation,[92] in Afghanistan and Iraq[93] as well as in Somalia. As a result, security has accounted

87 S/Res/1483 (2003) of 22 May 2003; Najam Rafique, *U.S. Iraq Policy: From Hesitation to Occupation*, www.issi.org.pk/journal/2003_files/no_2/article/2a.htm.06. 06.2007, 12.

88 Hope and Griffen, "The New Iraq", 875; Wolfrum, "Iraq from Belligerent Occupation", 23.

89 Wolfrum, "Iraq from Belligerent Occupation", 22; Rafique, *U.S. Iraq Policy*, 12.

90 Rafique, *U.S. Iraq Policy*, 12.

91 Thomas, "International Financial Institutions", 162; Johan Galtung, "The Third World and Human Rights in the Post-1989 World Order", in *Human Rights Fifty Years on: A Reappraisal*, ed., Tony Evans (Manchester: Manchester University Press, 1998), 211, 215.

92 Ignatieff, *Empire Lite*, 32.

93 Ibid, 85; Wiarda, "Building the Institutions", 193.

for a huge part of the budget in state reconstruction projects. Nevertheless, the international community's praxis has not been successful in any of these countries.

The first problem is that the aim is not necessarily to provide security for the people in the state but rather to create essential security conditions for the powerful states in the North.[94] Ignatieff translates the nation-building effort of the international community in Afghanistan, for example, as 'creating a state strong enough to keep al-Qaeda from returning'[95] in order to prevent further attacks against the North. In the post-Yugoslavia Balkan states and the Caucasus, the interests of the North determined not only the choice of states in which to intervene but also the duration of military measures taken under Chapter VII of the UN Charter. This has also been true in Somalia, Afghanistan, and Iraq. The international community did not end the military intervention in Somalia because the problem was solved or because minimum security had been established for the people, but because it did not want to risk losing any more forces. In Afghanistan and Iraq, military measures will not end because the situation has improved or the international community rethinks the policy through which so many people have died or become permanently incapacitated. It will end when the international community cannot tolerate any more loss of its troops or no longer wants to finance the operation.

The second problem is the way the international community tries to achieve security, choosing one conflict party to fight the others. This strategy has destroyed any remaining sense of commonality in Somalia (where Mohammed Farah Aidid's USC/SNA was chosen over its rival) and in Afghanistan (where the Taliban was identified as the enemy in the 'war on terror').[96] The international national community's policy in Iraq has resulted in a civil war between the Shiite and Sunni, which appears to be the main obstacle to stability and security in the country. The international community in every instance fights against part of the people in a country in order to rescue the country.

The third problem is the authority and lack of accountability of foreign forces in the country, as well as their limitations and relations with the local security forces. The Karzai government was established in Afghanistan in 2003, but the forces of the United States and its allies still operate under the principle of 'freedom of action'.[97] The concurrent operation of the coalition forces and International Security Assistance Force (ISAF) makes it difficult for the Afghan people to distinguish between them. The situation in Iraq seems no better.

---

94 Ibid., 109.
95 Ibid., 79.
96 Afsah and Guhr, "Afghanistan", 384–385. 411; Rubin, "Saving Afghanistan", 57–78.
97 Rubin and Hamidzada, "From Bonn to London", 13.

The practice of the international community has not shown success in establishing safe conditions within states dealing with the absence of effective government. Conditions in Somalia have not changed since the military intervention of the international community, whose policy has been to close its eyes. Today Somalia appears as a threat to the international community in terms of the dire humanitarian situation and international terrorism through piracy in the Gulf of Aden.[98] The picture is not so different in Afghanistan in spite of two international military commands, the United States-led coalition and ISAF.[99] The country now has its own army and policy but is unable to provide internal security because of rampant corruption and the impotence of the Ministry of the Interior and the judiciary.[100]

In spite of years of the 'war on terror', the insurgency has grown in Afghanistan, with local government and U.S. casualties reaching their highest level in 2008.[101] Moreover, the claim that Pakistan actively supports the Taliban seems no less true today than when the 'war on terror' began.[102]

In conclusion, although the international community made legal space for the paradigm of state reconstruction through a broad interpretation of Chapter VII of the UN Charter, this technocratic paradigm of going into a foreign country to re-establish the state has come to an end in practice. The discrepancy between the economic geopolitical interests of the intervening countries, as in Afghanistan and Iraq, and their claim of rebuilding states brings this double-think into strong relief. While technocratic paradigm of re-establishing a state from the outside is superficial if not hypocritical,[103] using the term 'nation-building' for one-to-five-year initiatives is nothing short of ironic[104] and

98 Douglas Guilfoyle, "Piracy off Somalia: UN Security Council Resolution 1816 and IMO Regional Counter-Piracy Efforts", *International and Comparative Law Quarterly*, 57(2008), 691. S/Res/1838(2008) of 7 October 2008.

99 Rubin and Hamidzada, "From Bonn to London", 11.

100 Rubin, "Saving Afghanistan", 74.

101 iCasualties.org. Operation Enduring Freedom (http://icasualties.org/OEF/DeathsByYear.aspx) lists fatalities in Afghanistan by nationality and year. The total number of casualties in 2008 was 294, 155 of those among U.S. troops, The rise in civilian deaths from US and NATO airstrikes, which nearly tripled from 2006 to 2007, has fueled a public backlash, according to "'Troops in Contact': Airstrikes and Civilian Deaths in Afghanistan" (New York: Human Rights Watch, 2008).

102 Rubin, "Saving Afghanistan", 59.

103 Mohammed Ayoob, *The Third World Security Predicament: State Making, Regional Conflict and the International System* (Boulder, Colorado: Lynne Rienner Publishers, 1995), 32; (Richardson 1996, 18); Volker Böge, *Von Muschgeld und Blutdiamenten. Traditionale Konfliktbearbeitung in zeitgenössischen Gewaltkonflikten* (Hamburg: Schriften des Deutschen Übersee-Instituts Hamburg, 2004), 8; Ignatieff, *Empire Lite*, 85.

104 Seth G. Jones and James Dobbins, "The UN's Record in Nation Building", *Chicago Journal of International Law* 6 (2005–2006), 703–723, The authors describe as nation-building the

neither fits the reality nor respects states and people in the South.[105] This does not mean that the international community will throw the lessons of the past to the winds—unless international law cannot rescue itself as a means to effect international policy.

efforts of the United Nations in the Congo (1960–1964), Namibia (1989–1990), El Salvador (1991–1996), Cambodia (1991–1993), and Mozambique (1992–1994).

105 This is explored in detail in Parts I and II. William L. Zartman, "Introduction: Posing the Problem of State Collapse", in *Collapsed States: The Disintegration and Restoration of Legitimate Authority*, ed., William. L. Zartman, (Boulder, Colorado: Lynne Rienner Publishers, 1995), 2, 3; Daniel Thürer, "Der Wegfall effektiver Staatsgewalt 'the Failed State'", in *Der Wegfall effektiver Staatsgewalt: "The Failed State"*, Berichte der Deutsche Gesellschaft für Völkerrecht 34, ed. Daniel Thürer, Matthias Herdegen, and Gerhard Hohloch (Heidelberg: Müller, 1996), 11.

Chapter Eight

The Hypocritical Approach of the North to Solving the Absence of Effective Government: The Economic and Social Approach as a Long Term Solution

> 'Of course I wish I were in school. I want to learn to read and to write [...] But how can I? My mother needs me to get water'.[1]
>
> Yeni Bazan, age 10, El Alto, Bolivia

The link between peace and economic and social issues has been expressedd since the establishment of the League of Nations, and current international law offers many means to implement the economic and social approach. In cases of the absence of effective government, an alternative view, which appears as both a long-term solution and a preventive measure, is based on the economic and social approach in the global context.

As shown in Chapter 7, the concept of state reconstruction covers economic and social issues but these are not addressed as thoroughly as the issue of security, and their solution is restricted to measures within the state or the liberalisation of the global economy.

The United Nations and various international organisations, as well as international lawyers, have pointed out the economic, political, and social causalities of the absence of effective government and linked a solution to these causalities. Although this view has been promulgated in reference to the states in South since the establishment of the United Nations, it has found little resonance in the face of the absence of effective government.

This chapter focuses on two interlinked issues, advocating for an attempt to address economic and social issues in a global context for a long-term solution to the absence of effective government and examining the North's implementation of the economic and social approach to serve its own interests. The link between economic and social approaches and international peace and the legal basis for such an approach are explained. The approach, efforts, and

---

1 UNDP, *Human Development Report* (New York, 2006), 1.

success of the international community in this area are determined mainly by the foundations and tendencies of international law and by the relationship between the needs of the South and the model used by the North to address economic and social problems. This analysis allows an exploration of obstacles to the effectiveness of the international community in meeting economic and social needs.

Economic and Social Problems and International Peace

Economic factors are the most important determinants of state as a political, economic, social, cultural, and historical unity.[2] Increasing poverty and the widening gap between the North and the South link the absence of effective government to the international context. This link argues for an economic and social approach to dealing with poverty and reducing economic inequality to achieve international peace in the long term.

Increasing Poverty and the Widening Gap between North and South

Two contrary tendencies characterise present global development. The first is usually described as globalisation, in a positive sense, with technology and other political and economic development eroding distance and state borders. The other is the rising incidence of poverty in the South and the widening gap between North and South. According to the UNDP, in 1960 the income of the 20 percent of the world's people living in the richest countries was 30 times greater than that of the 20 percent living in the poorest countries. This proportion increased to 82 percent greater in 1995.[3] This increasing trend was confirmed in the United Nations Conference on Trade and Development (UNCTAD) *Least Developed Countries Report* of 2002.[4] Obijafar Aginom describes the contradiction between the positive and negative consequences of globalisation as 'the paradox of a global village in a divided world'.[5]

---

2 Olusegun Yerokun, *Legal Aspects of Structural Adjustment Programme in Nigeria* (Oya, Nigeria: University of Ilorin, 1989), 3.

3 UNDP, *Human Development Report*, (New York, 1998), 29–33.

4 United Nations Conference on Trade and Development (UNCTAD), *The Least Developed Countries Report 2002: Escaping the Poverty Trap*, Geneva, 16 June 2002, 101. Similar data are described by many authors, including Obijiofar Aginam, "Global Village, Divided World: South-North Gap and Global Health Challenges at Century's Dawn", *Indiana Journal of Global Legal Studies* 7 (2000), 603 and 607 and Vijanarayana Reddy, *Third World Development and the New International Economic Order* (New Delhi: Deep & Deep, 1994), 9.

5 Aginam, "Global Village, Divided World", 603, 607.

Economic problems and poverty appear in almost every country as structural violence, intensified by inequality between states and within states.[6] Most states dealing with the absence of effective government are in the South, and poor countries and poor people in these countries are the first to be affected by the phenomenon.[7]

The Link between Economic and Social Issues and International Peace

Traditional international law, as well as modern public international law, describes peace and security in a narrow sense as primarily the absence of war.[8] A broader definition is found in international agreements and resolutions of international organisations, especially after the Second World War. The expressed aim of the League of Nations and the United Nations was to secure international peace and security, but both organisations saw a direct or indirect link between economic and social issues and international peace and security. Solving economic tensions between states was one of the main goals of the League of Nations foreseen in Article 23 of the UN Charter. Article 22 settled some economic and social issues in the mandate system, and the need to settle economic relations between states for international peace was the most important reason for the establishment of the Bretton Woods institutions after the Second World War.

The link between collective security and economic and social issues is stated directly in Article 55 and the preamble of the UN Charter and indirectly in Article 1[9] and has been expressed by UN organs in numerous meetings and resolutions.[10] Since 1945 the General Assembly and Economic and Social Council, in particular, have focused on this link, for example, in the 1948

6 Johan Galtung, *Strukturelle Gewalt*, Beiträge zur Friedens-und Konfliktforschung (Hamburg: Rowohlt Verlag, 1975).

7 Johan Galtung, *Peace Development in the Pacific Hemisphere*, (Honolulu: University of Hawaii Institution for Peace, 1989), 2; Gerhard Alt, ed., *Armut im Süden durch Wohlstand im Norden, Nachträge und Schlaglichter zur Dependenz-Theorie* (Munich: Hanns-Seidel Stieftung, 1998); Jean Ziegler, *Das Imperium der Schande, der Kampf gegen Armut und Unterdrückung* (Munich: Pantheon, 2007); J. Dine, "Multinational Enterprises: International Codes and the Challenge of Sustainable Development," *Non-State Actors and International Law 1* (2001), 81–106.

8 Galtung, *Peace Development*, 9.

9 Article 55 of the UN Charter poses 'the creation of the condition of stability and well-being' as a precondition for peaceful and friendly relations among nations.

10 A/Res/198(III) of 4 December 1948 on the Economic Development of under-Developed Countries; A/Res/623 (VII) 21 December 1952; A/Res/1710 (XVI) of 19 December 1961 on the United Nations Development Decade, A Program for International Economic Co-operation. King Hassan II of Morocco described the underdevelopment found mostly in the South as 'the greatest threat to world peace and security' in the Security Council Meeting of 31 January 1992, S/PV. 3046, 38.

General Assembly Resolution on the Economic Development of Under-Developed Countries quoted below. This was the first resolution concerning economic conditions in the South.

> [...] the low standards of living existing in Member States have bad economic and social effects in the countries directly concerned and on the world as a whole, and create conditions of instability which are prejudicial to the maintenance of peaceful and friendly relations among nations and to the development of conditions of economic and social progress [...].[11]

Former Secretary-General Boutros-Boutros Ghali pointed out in *An Agenda for Peace* that 'the deepest causes of conflict [are] economic despair, social injustice and political oppression'.[12] This link has underlaid the agenda of various international organisations and was the source of the Doha Development Agenda (DDA) in the Doha Trade Round in 2001.[13]

Addressing poverty and reducing economic inequality are the most powerful instruments for a long-term solution to the absence of effective government for two reasons. The first is the link between peace and the economic and social issues. Hans Kelsen describes peace as the 'absence of force',[14] and Galtung defines peace broadly as the 'absence of direct and structural violence between and within the states, realizing survival + well-being + identity + freedom for all; in other words, satisfaction of human needs and in addition, ecological balance'.[15] A long-term solution for the absence of effective government, and hence peace, can be found only when economic and social problems are alleviated in poor countries. The second reason is that countries are economically interdependent despite their diverse history, politics, cultures, and social structures.

---

11 A/Res/198(III) of 4 December 1948 on the Economic Development of Under-developed Countries.

12 *An Agenda for Peace*, A/47/277 S/24111 of 17 June 1992; Security Council Meeting on 31 January 1992, S/PV 3046.

13 "Development: Annan Calls For 'Development Round' of Trade Talks", UN WIRE, Sept.19.2000; IMF/WORLD BANK: "Wolfensohn promotes Equitable Growth", UN WIRE, Sep. 22, 2000; Press Release, ILO/04/36, August 11, 2004, http://www.ilo.org/public/english/bureau/inf/pr/2004/36.htm; "Worldwatch Insitute Warns of Threat to Global Stability", UN WIRE, May 23, 2003. Sungjoon Cho, "Doha's Development", *Berkeley Journal of International Law* 25 (2007), 169.

14 Hans Kelsen, "General International Law and the Law of the United Nations" in *The United Nations: Ten Years' Legal Progress*, ed. H. Gesina, J. Van Der Molen, et al. (The Hague: Publisher unknown, 1956), 1. Kelsen writes, "By 'use of force' or 'enforcement action', not only the employment of physical and especially armed force but any action taken by one person against, and means to the disadvantage of, another person, without consent of the latter, in particular any violation of the right of a person, may be understood".

15 Galtung, *Peace Development*, 2.

Many meetings of international organisations and international legal documents describe dealing with economic problems and reducing economic inequality between and within states and between the North and South as a critical part of establishing peace and collective security. In 1949 the Economic and Social Council announced that the solution to economic and social problems was a precondition for securing freedom.[16] The General Assembly stated on 24 October 1970 that 'the success of international development activities will depend on the promotion of equal political, economic, social, and cultural rights for all members of society'.[17] The General Assembly frequently pointed out that 'revitalising the economy' was a precondition for 'ensuring peace and normalcy'[18] in Afghanistan in the 1990s. The UK representative to the Security Council Meeting of 31 January 1992 stated that

> [...] peace and prosperity are indivisible and [...] lasting peace and stability require effective international cooperation for the eradication of poverty and the promotion of a better life for all in larger freedom.[19]

The UN Secretary-General's Millennium Report of 2000 included the statement that 'strategies of prevention must address the root causes of conflicts, not simply their violent symptoms [...] the majority of wars today are wars among the poor'.[20]

In summary, putting economic and social problems in the forefront, redressing poverty, and diminishing inequality are the only ways to achieve a long-term solution to the absence of effective government. These realities affirm the importance of international cooperation in the economic and social fields.

The Legal Basis of the Economic and Social Approach

International law focused on economic and social issues early in its existence.[21] The international legal order after the Second World War was established on

---

16 United Nations Economic and Social Council, Reference Pamphlet No. 2, Geneva 1949.

17 International Development Strategy for the Second United Nations Development Decade, GA/Res/2626 (XXV) of 24 October 1970.

18 A/Res/48/208 of 21 December 1993; A/Res/51/195 of 13 February 1997.

19 First Security Council Meeting of 31 January 1992, S/PV. 3046.

20 Roderic Alley, *International Conflict and the International Community: War without End?* (Aldershot, UK: Ashgate Publishing, 2004), 17.

21 The International Labour Organization (ILO) was established through the Treaty of Versailles in 1919. The International Narcotics Board has been active since the time of the League of Nations.

the twin pillars of the world economic system and the world political system.[22] The Soviet Union proposed a third international organisation to rule on social issues in the Dumbarton Oaks Conference in 1944 during the preparatory phase of the UN Charter, but when this approach did not find broad acceptance, social and economic issues were incorporated into the UN Charter.[23]

The proposal for the United Nations was first drafted by the United States, then submitted to other powerful countries, and finally brought before delegates of Southern countries in the 1951 San Francisco Conference. The way the UN Charter was drafted had consequences for the sections that concerned economic and social issues. At the San Francisco Conference the South raised a number of important issues for debate, including the aims and principles of the organisation, peace and justice, and economic and social problems in the South. But because the content of the UN Charter had been largely defined before the conference by the powerful states, the Northern perspective overshadowed the economic and social problems of the South.[24] Anthony Dolman describes this omission below.

> In short, the Charter of the United Nations, whilst being less offensive to the developing countries than the Covenant of the League of Nations, had little to offer them. Their needs went unheard, their aspirations unrecognized. The Charter was not a mandate for development [...] The San Francisco conference gave little articulation to the requirements of the poor world; its needs and aspirations did not figure prominently—if indeed at all—in the grand institutional design then drawn up.[25]

In the following decades, however, the international institutions and states established new instruments to deal with economic and social problems.

---

[22] The World Bank, IMF, and other international financial institutions determined the world economic system, and the United Nations decided international political issues; Georg Dahm, *Völkerrecht*, Volume II (Stuttgart: Kohlhammer Verlag, 1961), 590; Sundhya Pahuja, "Technologies of Empire: IMF Conditionality and the Reinscription of the North/South Divide", *Leiden Journal of International Law* 13 (2000), 756. Because international security was the most important aim of the establishment of the United Nations, the first name suggested for the organisation was the International Security Organization. Vlademir Trukhanovsky, *British Foreign Policy during World War II, 1939–1945* (Moscow: Progress Publishers, 1970), 441–445.

[23] Detlev Christian Dicke, *Die administrative Organisation der Entwicklungshilfe durch die Vereinten Nationen* (Frankfurt: Athenaeum-Verlag, 1972), 8; Nikolaj Mironov, *Law, Progress and Peace: A Journalist's Observations on the Influence of Soviet Law on the Progressive Development of International Law* (Moscow: Novosti Press Agency Publishing House, 1971), 88.

[24] Antony J. Dolman, *Resources, Regimes, World Order* (New York: Pergamon Press, 1981), 166.

[25] Ibid.

The Legal Basis and Normative Function of the Economic and Social Approach

In the UN Charter, which is the legal basis of the economic and social approach in current international law, the preamble and Articles 1(2), 1(3), 13 (1), 55, 62 deal directly or indirectly with economic and social issues.[26] Chapters IX and X define the responsibility of the organisation concerning economic and social problems. Article 55 contains circumstantial details about consensus on the economic and social approach in the Charter.[27] Besides the creation of conditions of stability and well-being, Article 55 calls for

> [...] a) high standards of living, full employment, and conditions of economic and social progress and development and b) solutions to international economic, social, health, and related problems and international cultural and educational co-operation.[28]

The resolutions of the responsible organs of the United Nations and their subsidiary organs are also legal sources for the economic and social approach regarding Articles 10, 13, and 62.[29] Different aspects of economic and social issues are addressed in other international documents and the establishment agreements of the international organisations. For example, the Articles of Agreement of the International Bank for Reconstruction and Development (IBRD) states as one of the Bank's aims the integration of Southern countries into the global economy,[30] and Article XXXVI of the General Agreement

---

26 Benedetto Conforti, *The Law and Practice of the United Nations* (Leiden: Martinus Nijhoff Publishers, 2005), 241–242. The preamble, which contains other elements regarding human rights, generally includes two references to economic and social issues: 'to promote social progress and better standards of life in larger freedom' employing 'international machinery for the promotion of the economic and social advancement of all peoples'. Article 1/3 of the UN Charter is ambiguous about economic and social matters, vaguely mentioning 'achieving international co-operation in solving international problems of an economic, social, cultural, or humanitarian character'. Article 13/b of the UN Charter describes the responsibility of the General Assembly 'in the economic, social, cultural, educational and health fields'.

27 Erskine Childers, "The United Nations System", in *Challenges to the United Nations, Building a Safer World*, ed. Erskine Childers (London: Catholic Institute for international Relations and St. Martin's Press, 1994), 14.

28 Article 55 of the UN Charter.

29 Conforti, *Law and Practice of the United Nations*, 241–242. Permanent Sovereignty over Natural Resources (GA/Res/ 1803 [XVII] of 14 December 1962); International Covenant on Economic, Social and Cultural. Rights (GA/Res/3281 [XXIX] of 12 December 1974), entry into force 3 January 1976; Charter of the Economic Rights and Duties Resolution (3281 [XXIX] of 12 December 1974); International Pact on Economic, Social and Cultural Rights, signed on 19 December 1966, entry into force 31 December 1998 (135 states).

30 Articles of Agreement of the International Bank for Reconstruction and Development, July 22, 1944, Article I. Purposes. Ibrahim F. Shihata, *The World Bank in a Changing World: Selected Essays and Lectures*, Volume II (Dordrecht: Martinus Nijhoff Publishers, 1995), 62.

on Tariffs and Trade contains social targets such as raising standards of living and ensuring full employment.[31]

Actors

The actors for economic and social issues include institutions within the UN system, international organisations such as intergovernmental organisations and NGOs, regional organisations, and individual states.[32] The UN system plays the most important role in economic and social cooperation. According to Article 60 of the UN Charter, the General Assembly and the Economic and Social Council are principally responsible for the activity of the United Nations in this area.[33] The General Assembly is at the top of this system, and the Economic and Social Council is under the General Assembly. All other subsidiary organs, commissions, programs, and funds act under these two main UN organs.[34] The Secretary-General is also indirectly responsible for the activity of the United Nations in the field of economic and social cooperation.[35]

The various special agencies ruled on by Articles 57 and 59 of the UN Charter are the other actors for economic and social cooperation.[36] The international financial institutions are among the specialised UN agencies.[37] The United Nations has generally accepted NGOs as partners in providing relief supplies.[38] Chapter VIII of the UN Charter describes regional organisations as responsible organs in the area of economic and social cooperation, and Articles 2(3) and 56 denote every state as responsible for such cooperation.[39]

---

[31] General Treaty on Tariffs and Trade, Geneva 1947, Article XXIX.

[32] Article 56 of the UN Charter for the members, Article 57 of the UN Charter for the specialized Agencies, and article 52 for the regional agencies. Muthiah Alagappa, "Regional Arrangements, the UN, and International Security: A Framework for Analysis", in *Beyond UN Subcontracting, Task-Sharing with Regional Security Arrangements and Service-Providing NGOs*, ed. Thomas G. Weiss (London: Macmillan Publishers, 1998), 3.

[33] For the General Assembly, Articles 13 and 60 of the UN Charter and for the Economic and Social Council, Articles 62–66 of the UN Charter; Dicke, *Die administrative Organisation*, 16.

[34] Conforti, *Law and Practice of the United Nations*, 241.

[35] Ibid.

[36] UN Charter. The 14 Special Organisations include the FAO, IAEA, ICAO, IBRD, IDA, IFC, IMF, ILO, IMCO, ITU, UPU, UNESCO, WHO, and WMO; Dicke, *Die administrative Organisation*, 13.

[37] http://www.un.org/aboutun/chart.html.

[38] A/Res/43/206 of 20 December 1988; A/Res/44/178 of 19 December 1989; A/Res/45/229 of 21 December 1990; A/Res/46/176 of 19 December 1991.

[39] Hans Kelsen, *The Law of the United Nations, A Critical Analysis of Its Fundemental Problems* (London: Stevens & Sons Ltd, 1950), 99.

Legally Binding Force

The question whether the rules and decisions of the international organisations are legally binding is a crucial point in economic and social efforts. The UN organs responsible for economic and social issues have no law-making power, and their decisions are no more than recommendations.[40] Moreover, the measures laid out in various parts of the UN Charter concerning economic and social issues have no legally binding force,[41] as will be discussed later.

Uther intergovernmental organisations that deal to some extent with economic and social problems were mainly established in the North or vest decision-making power in the North. Like the international organisations, most NGOs originate in and are financed in the North. Consequently, their approach is mainly determined by the North.

Few states in the South are able to take an active role in the economic and social approach to states dealing with the absence of effective government. Only the regional organisations in the South can appear as actors for economic and social cooperation. Although they have some advantages over other regional and international organisations in the North in terms of human resources, experience, and knowledge, they lack the capacity to do more than support the United Nations.[42]

Efforts of the International Community

Since the establishment of the United Nations, the international community has taken different approaches to solving the problem of the absence of effective government and implemented various measures concerning the world political and economic context. However, its approach, efforts, and success in this area have been influenced mainly by the form and trends of international law, the South's approach to the issue and the demands of the South, and the North's approach and model to address economic and social problems. An overview of the shape and trends of international law and the divergence between the approaches of the South and the North will help to both explain the failure of the international community to deal with the absence of effective government and suggest solutions.

---

40 Article 13, 62 of the UN Charter; Conforti, *Law and Practice of the United Nations*, 242; Dicke, *Die administrative Organisation*, 26; Childers, "The United Nations System", 16.

41 Article 56 of the UN Charter.

42 Alagappa, "Regional Arrangements", 4.

Form and Trends of International Law

The form and trends of international law have important effects on economic, political, and social problems in the Southern countries, the international community's efforts to address these problems, and the probability of their success. As Shadrack Gutto persuasively argues, in all relationships, 'either at the national or international levels, the dialectic relation between economic structures, institutions, and norms is decisive'.[43] The shape and tendency of international law concerning the absence of effective government can be analysed under four categories: 1) the structure and tendency of international economic law, 2) development policy, 3) international organisations, and 4) different application of the principle of sovereignty in the North and South.

The Structure of International Economic Law

Many international law scholars consider trade central to international law.[44] In the 19th century, Antoine Pillet saw 'commerce as the cause of international law rather than as a fundamental right'.[45] International economic law originated in the Middle Ages, when commercial and maritime law started to develop with instruments such as mercantile courts at the international level, which Shaw describes as 'an embryonic international trade law'.[46]

Current international economic law took shape mainly after the Second World War, with the liberalisation of the world economic order at the core of this system. The liberalisation of the world economic order was realised in two different ways. Equal opportunity for free trade is the basis of economic relations between countries in the North, but the Open Door Policy mainly determines economic relations between the North and South. Jürgen Habermas

---

[43] Shadrack B.O. Gutto, *Human and Peoples' Rights for the Oppressed: Critical Essays on Theory and Practice from Sociology of Law Perspectives* (Lund, Sweden: University of Lund, 1993), 100; Shedrack Agbakwa, "A Line in the Sand: International (Dis)order and the Impunity of Non-State Corporate Actors in the Developing World", in *The Third World and International Order: Law, Politics and Globalisation*, Developments in International Law 45, eds. Anghie Antony, Chimni Bhupinder, Karin Mickelson, and Obiaora Okafor (The Hague: Martinus Nijhoff Publishers, 2003), 8.

[44] Ellery C. Stowell, *International Law, A Restatement of Principles, in Conformity with Actual Practice* (New York: Henry Holt, 1931), 138.

[45] Antoine Pillet, *Recherches sur les droits fondamentaux des etats* (Paris: A Pedone, 1899), 8–9; Antony Anghie, "Colonialism and the Birth of International Institutions: Sovereignty, Economy and the Mandate System of the League of Nations", *New York University Journal of International Law and Politics* 34 (2002), 3, 534.

[46] Malcholm N. Shaw, *International Law*, 4th edition (Cambridge: Cambridge University Press, 1997), 17.

describes this discrepancy as follows: 'The by now fashionable talk of the "globalisation of markets" needs to be rendered more precise. Naturally, there is no such a thing as the "universal market"'.[47]

Equal Opportuniy for Free Trade among States in the North

In the 18th and 19th centuries, the liberal economic theory of Adam Smith succeeded the mercantilism of the 16th century and the free trade of the 17th century. It was first practiced in Europe in the second part of the 19th century with the Cobden-Chevalier Treaty of 23 January 1860 between France and Great Britain.[48] Trade pacts were later established based on free trade in Europe, but the United States stayed outside free trade because it wanted to protect its young industry against Europe, especially England.[49] Most European states, however, including England, Germany, and Italy, returned to economic protectionism between 1870 and the First World War. The main reason for the policy change was the need to establish their own industries and therefore to protect their internal markets from competition. In spite of their protectionist policies, the common need to expand markets, exploit natural resources, and feed their populations bound these states together.

These needs assumed a political and economic dimension in imperialism and colonialism.[50] The First World War was rooted in increasing political antagonism between states because of the focus on national economies and unlimited competition.[51] Cordell Hull, U.S. Secretary of State under President Franklin Roosevelt, described the link between the First World War and trade as follows:

> When the war came in 1914, I was very soon impressed by two points. The first was its terrific commercial impact on the United States. I saw that you could not separate the idea of commerce from the idea of war and peace. You could not have serious war anywhere in the world and expect commerce to go on as before. And the second was that wars were often largely caused by economic rivalry conducted unfairly.[52]

---

47 Jürgen Habermas, "Beyond the Nation-State? On Some Consequences of Economic Globalization", in *Democracy in the European Union: Integration through Deliberation*, eds. Erik Eriksen and John Fossum (London: Routledge, 2000), 31.

48 www.britannica.com/eb/topric-12335/Anglo-French-Agreement of1869–1827.

49 Dahm, *Völkerrecht*, 586.

50 Ibid.

51 Ibid.

52 Cordell Hull, *The Memoirs of Cordell Hull*, Volume I (New York: Macmillan Publishers, 1948), 84.

After the end of the First World War, states attempted to build a world order according to the principle of free trade. Point III of Wilson's principles[53] and Article 23 of the League of Nations[54] attest to this attempt. In the years following the establishment of the League of Nations, various conferences were held to deal with economic problems, including finance and currency conferences in 1922, a raw steel conference in 1926, and a world economic conference in 1927.[55]

Economic interests and the hope of avoiding conflict later led the League of Nations to concentrate on economic issues. By the time the League of Nations ended, a commission had been established to explore the possibility of states working together on such issues.[56] However, the states failed to deal with the causes of the economic problems for various reasons, including the abandonment of the gold standard and the onset of the Depression.[57] In the decade before the Second World War, protectionist policy took on a more complicated dimension through trade restrictions and competitive exchange controls by the states. This protectionist approach was one of the most important reasons for the Great Depression of the 1930s and the Second World War.[58]

With the Second World War, the United States sought to create a global trade regime to prevent such mutually destructive tariffs and increase international trade. Cordell Hull, one of the designers of the Bretton Woods institutions, wrote,

> If there is anything certain in this world, it is that, after present hostilities come to an end, there will be an even more desperate need than there was in recent years for vigorous action designed to restore and promote healthy and mutually beneficial trade among nations.[59]

The United States, which held the most powerful position in the economic arena during this time, played an important role in rebuilding the international economic order after the Second World War. Already during the war, the country had taken the initiative of proposing institutions for the new international

---

53 President Woodrow Wilson's Fourteen Points, 8 January 1918.

54 Article 23 of the Covenant of the League of Nations.

55 Dahm, *Völkerrecht*, 587–588; Christian Gloria, "Internationales Wirtschaftsrecht", in *Völkerrecht*, ed. Knut Ipsen, 3rd edition (Munich: C.H. Beck, 1999), 545.

56 The Bruce Commission, "Le développement de la coopération internationale dans le domaine economique et social (Rapport Bruce)", Genf 1939, S.s.N.Doc. 1939, General 3; Dicke, *Die administrative Organisation*, 6.

57 Dahm, *Völkerrecht*, 587–588; Gloria, "Internationales Wirtschaftsrecht", 545.

58 *The New Encyclopaediea Britannica*, 15th edition (London: Encyclopaedia Britannica (UK) Ltd., 2005), "Capitalism", 832; Pub. L. No. 71–361, 46 Stat. 590 (1930); Pahuja, "Technologies of Empire", 756–757.

59 Hull, *The Memories of Cordell Hull*, 747.

economic order.[60] In the Atlantic Charter of 14 August 1941, U.S. President Franklin Roosevelt and British Prime Minister Winston Churchill declared free trade as one of the eight common principles in their national policies.[61]

When the world economic system was first shaped after the Second World War, three institutions were conceived. As a consequence of the Bretton Woods Conference, the IBRD and IMF were established in 1945. The effort to establish an international organisation to regulate international trade was not successful.[62] At the Havana Conference of 1947, the conference states decided to establish an International Trade Organization (ITO), but it did not come into force because the U.S. Congress did not ratify it on the grounds that it was too interventionist.[63] In the end, 23 countries signed the General Agreement on Tariffs and Trade (GATT), the preliminary document to establish the ITO, in 1947. GATT came into force on 1 January 1948.[64]

The context of the Second World War and the reconstruction of post-war Europe determined the goals of the World Bank and IMF. Article 1 of the Articles of Agreement of the IBRD identified the purposes of the World Bank as assisting the development and reconstruction of developing countries and countries in Europe destroyed by war and facilitating and promoting international trade.[65] Article 1 of the Articles of Agreement of the IMF identified its aims as promoting international monetary cooperation, exchange stability, and international trade and providing financial assistance to member states with payment difficulties.[66]

GATT was established mainly to liberalise international trade without discrimination.[67] The World Bank and IMF appeared as full-fledged international organisations to implement these articles, but GATT lacked an institutional framework from 1948 to 1995.[68] Almost 50 years later, the Uruguay Round

60 Dahm, *Völkerrecht*, 590.

61 Atlantic Charter of 14 August 1941. For example, Article V described preventing discrimination, and Article VI described the equal right to the trade and the raw materials of the world.

62 Dolman, *Resources*, 168.

63 Said El-Naggar, "Developing Countries and the International Trading System", in *Law in the Service of Human Dignity*, ed. Steve Charnovitz, Debrap P. Steger, and Peter van Den Bossche (Cambridge: Cambridge University Press, 2005, 59).

64 Sheikh R. Ali, *The International Organizations and World Order Dictionary* (Santa Barbara, California: ABC-CLIO, 1992), 69.

65 *Articles of Agreement of the International Bank for Reconstruction and Development.*

66 *Articles of Agreement of the International Monetary Fund*; Pahuja, "Technologies of Empire", 757; Sabine Schlemmer-Schulte, "Global Business and Development," (speech given at the University of the Pacific McGeorge School of Law, Sacramento, California, 20 January 2006), 13.

67 El-Naggar, "Developing Countries", 59–63.

68 Ibid., 59.

of trade negotiations resulted in the establishment of the World Trade Organization (WTO) in 1995. The WTO has three main tasks: to implement the Uruguay Round Agreements, to resolve disputes under the agreements, and to cooperate with the IMF and World Bank.[69] The relationship between the Bretton Woods institutions and WTO has been getting closer since the post-war. The establishment of these three institutions allowed the powerful countries to take measures to ensure their own equal opportunities for free trade among themselves.

The Open Door Policy

Equal opportunity for free trade among the powerful states and the rules for trade between the powerful countries and other countries are based on the Open Door Policy. The idea originated in British commercial relations with the Qing Dynasty in China, which opened the territory to foreign trade in the first part of the 19th century.[70] The powerful states instituted the Open Door Policy to provide equal opportunity for commerce and navigation in 'undeveloped regions and in less powerful states' in the same century.[71] Since then, the policy has been implemented in parallel with the historical context.

---

[69] *Agreement between the International Monetary Fund and the World Trade Organization* and *Agreement between the International Bank for Reconstruction and Development, the International Development Association, and the World Trade Organization*; John W. Head, *The Future of the Global Economic Organizations, An Evaluation of Criticism Levelled at the IMF, the Multilateral Development Banks, and the WTO* (Aldertshot, UK: Transnational Publications, 2005), 57; Jan Wouters and Dominic Coppens, "International Economic Policy-Making: Exploring the Legal Linkages between the World Trade Organization and the Bretton Woods Institutions", *International Organizations Law Review* 3 (2006), 267–315.

[70] A half century later, American business circles saw market possibilities in the Chinese Empire as a way to rescue them from overproduction after an enormous growth in industry. Through the Connecticut State Board of Trade in 1898, the United States implemented its Open Door Policy in China. One year later, in 1899, U.S. Secretary of State Jon Hay asked other powerful states including France, Germany, Italy, Japan, and Russia to assume a common policy on trade and navigation in China to avoid a favored position for any of these nations. These states accepted Hay's proposal in the Washington Conference on the Limitation of Armaments of 1921–1922. A series of three articles on the American 'dilemma of having a productive capacity far in excess of ability to consume' in the *Journal of Commerce and Commercial Bulletin*, May 25, 26, and 27, 1897, cited in Charles S. Campbell, *Special Business Interests and the Open Door Policy* (New Haven: Yale University Press, 1951), 1; *Proceedings of the Connecticut State Board of Trade, 1891–1906* (New Haven, Connecticut 1908), Ninth Annual Meeting, October 19, 1898, 24 cited in Campbell, Special Business Interest and Open Door Policy, 1; Conference on the Limitation of Armaments (Government Printing Office, Washington 1922), 1625–626, cf. 1268 et seq.; Stowell, *International Law*, 144.

[71] Stowell, *International Law*, 144; Benjamin Gerig, *The Principle of Equal Economic Opportunity before and since the Establishment of the Mandates System: A Study of the Open Door Policy as a Colonial Trade Policy* (London: G. Allen & Unwin, 1930), 15.

Between the 15th and 18th centuries, when first Spain, then Portugal, and then the Netherlands, France, and Great Britain discovered territories in South America, the principles of monopoly and exclusion drove colonial policy. As a consequence of world historical events, economic liberalism began to have a stronger influence on this policy in the 19th century.[72] The General Act of the Berlin Conference of 1885 through which European powers carved up Africa was a milestone for colonial policy. The European powers and the United States signed the first multilateral treaty that instituted the Open Door Policy, ruling on free trade and navigation for all nations in the Basin of the Congo, the vast territory in Central Africa.[73]

The Open Door Policy can be understood more clearly in light of the need of the powerful countries' for markets, labour, and raw materials,[74] which was pointed out by many colonial politicians.[75] The need for equal opportunity for the colonial powers and the United States in the dependent territories can be seen in the language of the General Act of the Berlin Conference, in which the words 'perfect equality', 'without discrimination', 'no differential treatment', and 'no exclusive privileges' or their equivalents appear at least 15 times.[76]

The Open Door Policy played a determining role in Wilson's Fourteen Points after the First World War. Wilson's Points II, III, IV, and V established the rules for trade between the colonial powers and the United States. Point V, which appeared later in Article 22 of the Covenant of the League of Nations as the Mandate System,[77] focused on the Open Door Policy in the colonial territories as part of free and equal trade among the powerful countries.[78] Benjamin Gerig explains the implementation of the Open Door Policy through the Mandate System below.

> From all this came the Mandate System from the desire that none of the claimants should derive superior advantages over the other in the dismembered territories. Economic rivalries were so keen that only equality of economic opportunity could avert conflicts among them.[79]

---

[72] Gerig, *The Principle of Equal Economic Opportunity*, 16–19.

[73] Ibid., 31. On page 34 Gerig writes, 'The Conventional Basin of the Congo includes, besides the Congo Free State, parts of Cameroon, of French Equatorial Africa, Portuguese Angola, Kenya, Uganda, Nyasaland, Ruanda-Urundi, Tanganyika, parts of Rhodesia, and of Italian Somaliland'.

[74] Ibid., 32–33.

[75] Ibid.

[76] Ibid., 39, President Woodrow Wilson's Fourteen Points, 8 January, 1918, Points II, III, VI and V.

[77] Ibid., 85.

[78] President Woodrow Wilson's Fourteen Points.

[79] Gerig, *The Principle of Equal Economic Opportunity*, 45.

Gerig describes the Mandate System as the introduction of 'a new method in Open Door administration' through the Mandate Commission but sees the system more as a 'practical device for giving effect to an economic principle in particular situations' than a legal instrument.[80]

Before and after the First World War, many authors saw the refusal to open the trade door to powerful states as a breach of international law or grounds for war.[81] According to Ellery Stowell, states have a right to use force to compel an 'unsocial community' to enter into commerce.[82] In 1925 R.L. Buel described the need for equal opportunity for powerful states in the 'non-civilized Nations' as part of the Open Door Policy as follows:

> One of the greatest possible steps toward world peace would be a treaty signed by the ten leading colonial powers, not only in their own colonies, but in the independent countries of the world, such as China, Turkey, Mexico, Siam, Liberia, Abyssinia, Persia, and Afghanistan, and placing the supervision of such an agreement in the hands of some impartial international tribunal.[83]

When the world economic system was established after the Second World War, the Open Door Policy, already legitimised in practice by the powerful states for decades, was legalised and institutionalised in international law. Three issues facilitated the implementation of this policy.

First, the long pursuit of an economic protectionist policy by the European states and United States was one of the reasons for the First and Second World Wars, as explained above. However, when international economic law was established based on free trade, the weaker economic and social conditions in the Southern countries and new countries after independence vis à vis the more powerful states were ignored. Instead, the international financial institutions based their decisions on the principle of equal treatment, although the North had supremacy because of its economic and technological advantages.[84]

Second, the North still implements a protectionist policy over the South when Southern products endanger Northern products, especially agricultural or textile products.[85] To protect their agricultural industries from foreign competition, rich countries expend nearly one billion dollars a day, which contributes to driving farmers in poor countries out of the global markets.[86]

80 Ibid., 9.

81 Franz von Liszt, *Völkerrecht* (Berlin: Verlag von O. Härig, 1913), 7, 71; (Stowell 1931, 137).

82 Stowell, *International Law*, 137–139.

83 Raymond Leslie Buell, *International Relations* (New York: Henry Holt and Company, 1925), 441, cited in Gerig, *The Principle of Equal Economic Opportunity*, 16.

84 Fr. Noel Dias, "The NIEO Revisited", *Sri Lanka Journal of International Law* 8 (1996), 38.

85 Schlemmer-Schulte, "Global Business", 12.

86 Cho, "Doha's Development", 166.

Third, the North has most of the decision-making power in international economic law. In this picture, the Southern countries appear in the international arena not as part of the world economic order but as markets for Northern countries. Even sellers of natural resources and raw products have little authority to determine terms of trade.

In current international law, many economic rules serve to legitimise the Open Door Policy, and various instruments appear as means for its implementation.[87] Almost all international economic rules were established after the Second World War, based mainly on the principles of equality in trade that enabled the North's access to the territories of the South, equality in trade among the Northern states, and equal opportunities for the Northern states in the Southern states.[88]

Property rights are among the international economic rules that serve this paradigm. International economic law has tended to transfer authority to rule on property rights from domestic law to international law. One of the main instruments for this policy is privatisation, in which the international financial institutions play an important role.[89]

International trade and investment law are other important international economic rules that serve the Open Door Policy. The exclusion of foreign investment rights from domestic law arose at the same time as decolonisation,[90] and foreign investment law assumed tremendous importance in the late 1980s and early 1990s.[91] Investment law involves many rules on equal trade between states, and the WTO is the main international organisation facilitating

---

87 Bhupinder S. Chimni, "Third World Approaches to International Law: A Manifesto", in *The Third World and International Order: Law, Politics and Globalisation*, Developments in International Law 45, ed. Anghie Antony, Chimni Bhupinder, Karin Mickelson, and Obiaora Okafor (The Hague: Martinus Nijhoff Publishers, 2003), 47.

88 Fenner Brockway, *The Colonial Revolution* (London: Hart-Davis, 1973), 598.

89 Chimni ("The World Trade Organization", 47) describes four other instruments that facilitate the internationalisation of property rights: 1) the international specification and regulation of intellectual property rights, 2) the adoption of a network of international laws that lift constraints on the mobility and operation of the transnational corporate sector, 3) the definition of sustainable development in a manner which implies the redistribution of property rights between the North and South and also imposes some conditions, 3) the regulation of process and production methods and 4) the metamorphosis of the area of common heritage of humankind into a system of corporate property rights.

90 Muthucumaraswamy Sornarajah, "Economic Neo-Liberalism and the International Law on Foreign Investment", in *The Third World and International Order: Law, Politics and Globalisation*, Developments in International Law 45, ed. Anghie Antony, Chimni Bhupinder, Karin Mickelson, and Obiaora Okafor (Leiden: Martinus Nijhoff Publishers, 2003), 175.

91 Edward Graham, "Should There be Multilateral Rules on Foreign Direct Investment?", in *Governments, Globalization and International Business*, ed. John Dunning (Oxford: Oxford University Press, 1997), 481.

trade based on the equality of states.[92] However, most rules concerning equal trade between states are theoretical rather than functional. Because the parties to the agreements and their various economic interests and capacities determine the content of the treaties, most general rules of equality, such as non-discrimination and reciprocity, are not enforceable. Only a few clear normative standards, such as banning export subsidies, can be substantively implemented.[93]

The Open Door Policy can be seen clearly in international finance and development law, where the charters of institutions including the Bretton Woods institutions constitute its legal basis. Through their conditionality policy, the IMF and World Bank have pushed states in the South to take measures including privatisation, free trade, and welcoming foreign investment to implement the liberal economy. It is worth mentioning that the policy of conditionality applies only to the South and that both these institutions have focused only on Southern countries since the 1970s.[94]

Sabine Schlemmer-Schulte sees two main differences in the regulation of global and regional economies based on the example of the European Union. First, economic rules within the European Union are based on comprehensive regulations and the establishment of a 'fair level playing field for all market players', but the economic policy of the financial institutions toward the South involves no such elements. The second difference appears in the content and quality of the rules of trade. Economic rules in the European Union have clear content and uniform standards, unlike the rules determined by the financial institutions for the South.[95]

The Open Door Policy is implemented in the Southern countries through various actors.[96] The Bretton Woods institutions have been the main actors of this policy for four decades.[97] The World Bank and IMF became involved in the South in different historical contexts. The World Bank was involved first in the reconstruction of the European states after the Second World War and later in the South, but the breakdown of the par value system was the turning point for the IMF's shift from monetary powers to lending to

92 Schlemmer-Schulte ("Global Business", 15, 16) also describes bargaining for exchanges of liberalisation commitments, enforceable commitments, and safety valves as principles that aim to realise equal treatment in trade.

93 Ibid.

94 Ibid., 17–18.

95 Ibid., 19–20.

96 The actors are complex issues of international law which cannot be dealt with adequately here.

97 Ibid., 14; John Head, *The Future of the Global Economic Organizations, An Evaluation of Criticism Levelled at the IMF, the Multilateral Development Banks, and the WTO* (Aldershot, UK: Transnational Publications, 2005), 3.

Southern countries. Especially after the Mexican debt crisis in 1980, both institutions were the main instruments for the debt management strategy for the South. The IMF established conditionalities for states asking for help to address balance of payment deficits and debt crises. The relation between the financial institutions and the states is determined through their adjustment programs, which Carolina Thomas has described as 'spoken agreements'.[98] Economic conditionalities not only pertain to balance of payments difficulties but also facilitate international trade, privatisation, and foreign investment. In many cases, private investment follows the Southern states' acceptance of the adjustment programs of the IMF.[99] The other important influence of the IMF and World Bank on the Southern economy is in their role as 'gatekeeper' for other bilateral aid. The World Bank is the gatekeeper for 75 percent of the aid to sub-Saharan Africa.[100]

The international financial institutions influence economic, social, and political issues in Southern countries under the claim of integrating these countries into the global economy.[101] However, the policy of the Bretton Woods institutions implemented through conditionalities pushes the South to open its doors to the North without reciprocation. The WTO is as much an instrument of the Open Door Policy as the Bretton Wood institutions in spite of its fundamental goal of 'improving the welfare of the people of the member countries'.[102] Chimni describes the WTO as a 'key institution to sustain the global capitalist order to the advantage of an emerging transnational capitalist class (TCC) whose interests are articulated by powerful states'.[103]

When the WTO was established in 1995, the needs of the Southern countries played little role, as was the case in the establishment of the Bretton Woods institutions. For example, the Uruguay Round did not deal with the protectionism policy of the rich countries in trade sectors where poor countries have

---

98 Caroline Thomas, "International Financial Institutions and Social and Economic Human Rights: An Exploration", in *Human Rights Fifty Years on: A Reappraisal*, ed. Tony Evans (Manchester: Manchester University Press, 1998), 167.

99 Schlemmer-Schulte, "Global Business", 14.

100 David Williams, "Aid and Sovereignty: Quasi-States and the International Financial Institutions", *Review of International Studies* 26 (2000), 567.

101 Shihata, *The World Bank*, 62.

102 World Trade Organization, "The Multilateral Trading System—Past, Present and Future", http: www.wto.org/wto/multilateral/trading/HTML, visited April 26, 1999; Marrakesh Agreement Establishing the World Trade Organization, Legal Instruments—Results of the Uruguay Round, 33 I.L.M 1125 (1994), Preamble and art. III:3; Timothy Stostad, "Trappings of Legality: Judicialization of Dispute Settlement in the WTO, and its Impact on Developing Countries", *Cornell International Law Journal* 39 (2006), 3.

103 Bhupinder S. Chimni, "The World Trade Organization, Democracy and Development: A View from the South", *Journal of Trade* 40 (2006), 1, 5.

an advantage, such as agriculture and textiles.[104] In spite of the one-country-one-vote system and the fact that the developing countries make up 75 percent of the membership in the WTO, they have much less influence on the decision-making process[105] than the Organisation for Economic Cooperation and Development (OECD) countries.[106] Global enterprise is marked by a disproportionate distribution of profits for the benefit of the rich countries, except for a few developing countries, and the WTO serves this disproportion.[107] Vis à vis global economic complexity and interdependence, the Southern countries are faced with the dilemma of taking part in either the entire set of the agreements or none of them. They have little choice but to accept the whole settlement.[108]

Multinational enterprises (MNE), with their enormous economic potential, are influential powers in the international economic order[109] and an important instrument for the Open Door Policy.[110] Many scholars describe MNE as 'cornerstones of modern imperialism and neo-colonialism'.[111] Three features of the MNE make them the main instrument of the Open Door Policy: 1) their

---

[104] Cho, "Doha's Development", 168.

[105] Sonia E. Rolland, "Developing Country Coalitions at the WTO: In Search of Legal Support", *Harvard International Law Journal* 48 (2007), 483; Cho, "Doha's Development", 168.

[106] Rolland, "Developing Country Coalitions", 483. The Green Room is one of the instruments that preclude the developing countries from the decision making process. http://www.wto.org/englishtratop_e/dda_e/meet08_org_e.htm.

[107] Cho, "Doha's Development", 165.

[108] Chimni, "The World Trade Organization", 53.

[109] Cristina Baez, Michele Dearing, Margaret Delatour, and Christine Dixon, "Multinational Enterprises and Human Rights", *International and Comparative Law Review* 8 (1999–2000), 184; Tania Voon, "Multinational Enterprises and State Sovereignty under International Law", *Adelaide Law Review* 21 (1999), 219; Sarah Joseph, "Taming the Leviathans: Multinational Enterprises and Human Rights", *Netherlands International Law Review* XLVI (1999), 1, 172.

[110] Multinational enterprises appeared on the international scene as early as the 15th century and were the most important instruments of colonialism beginning in the 17th century. With the Industrial Revolution, their focus changed from retail market-factory-national concerns to multinational concerns. From the beginning of the 20th century, Europe and the United States established large corporations to control natural resources and markets in the Southern countries and colonial territories. Jost Berstermann, *Das Einmischungsverbot im Völkerrecht*, Europäische Hochschulschriften, Reihe 2, Rechtswissenschaften (Frankfurt: Peter Lang Publishing Group, 1991), 49; Mark B. Baker, "Tightening The Toothless Vise: Codes of Conduct and the American Multinational Enterprise", *Wisconsin International Law Journal* 89 (2001–2002), 141; Agbakwa, "A Line in the Sand", 4; Steven Hymer, "Multionationale Konzerne und das Gesetz der ungleichen Entwicklung", in *Imperialismus und strukturelle Gewalt*, ed. Dieter Senghaas (Frankfurt: Suhrkamp Verlag, 1972), 201–202.

[111] Gutto, *Human and Peoples' Rights*, 97, 104–105; Agbakwa, "A Line in the Sand", 6, 8; Norman Girvan, *Corporate Imperialism: Conflict and Expropriation, Essays in Transnational Corporations and Economic Nationalism in the Third World* (New York: M.E. Sharpe, 1976), 11–12; Paul M. Sweezy, "Corporation, the State, and Imperialism", *Monthly Review* 30 (1978), 1–10.

goal of economic prosperity, 2) their economic power base in the North,[112] and 3) their transfer of wealth to home states in the North. The MNE are more powerful than Southern governments and determine the content of agreements that serve their own interests.[113] For example, the U.S. Firestone Tire and Rubber Company opened a rubber plantation in Liberia in 1926 and was exempt from duties and taxes until 2005.[114] The MNE are almost the only actors that determine the market even for raw materials and semi-finished products in the Southern countries.[115] Their dominant position gives them impunity in the South[116] and de facto economic as well as political authority.[117] Instead of setting up their activities under existing rules in host states, the MNE compel the host states to either adjust their domestic law or overlook violations of domestic law.[118] The larger MNE owned by Northern states deal directly with the governments of the South 'in a new form of diplomacy'.[119] Baez et al. write, 'Multinationals find developing countries desirable because they provide the most efficient production in today's market. This source of abundant and cheap labor is the prime interest of the MNE'.[120]

Development Policy as an Instrument of the Open Door Policy

An historical survey since the end of the Second World War confirms that development policy has directly or indirectly served the political and economic interests of powerful states and is in fact an instrument of the Open Door Policy. Development policy first appeared during the Cold War, and its shape and content has since changed with the economic and political world order. It served the United States as a Cold War policy and the former colonial powers

---

112 Ninety percent of all MNE originate in developed countries. Most ownership is national, and only a few have multinational partners. Baez et al., "Multinational Enterprises", 187.

113 Agbakwa, "A Line in the Sand", 4; Baez et al., "Multinational Enterprises",185.

114 Fred van der Kraaij, "The Open Door Policy: Past, Present and Perspectives of the Liberian Concept of Foreign Investment", in *Liberia: Underdevelopment and Political Rule in a Peripheral Society*, ed. Robert Kappel, Werner Korte, and Friedegund R. Mascher (Hamburg: Institut für Afrika-Kunde, 1986), 215.

115 Reddy, *Third World Development*, 28.

116 Habermas, "Beyond the Nation-State?", 31.

117 Agbakwa, "A Line in the Sand", 32.

118 Elisa Westfield, "Globalization, Governance, and Multinational Enterprise Responsibility: Corporate Codes of Conduct in the 21st Century", *Virginia Journal of International Law* 42 (2001–2002), 1077.

119 Lung-Chu Chen, "An Introduction to Contemporary Law: A Policy-Oriented Perspective", *International Law*, ed. Barry Carter and Philip Trimble (Boston: Aspen Law & Business, 1999), 137.

120 Baez et al, "Multinational Enterprises", 230.

as a way to keep their former colonies under their control.[121] When the United States and European countries put the Open Door Policy into effect through the international financial institutions and international economic law, they used development policy to camouflage its consequences.

International Organisations

States began to use multilateral means to rule their relations in the 19th century[122] and with the establishment of the League of Nations at the Paris Peace Conference of 1919–1920 for the first time settled their political relations through an international organisation.[123] The number of international organisations has grown rapidly after the Second World War, and they increasingly regulate issues in the economic, political, and social field in the international arena.[124]

Today the international organisations, in their current form and with their current international legal personality,[125] capacity, and responsibility, play a very important role in the international legal order. Consequently, their composition and practice have an important effect on the absence of effective government and the international community's effectiveness in finding economic and social solutions for the phenomenon. Issues ranging from the construction to the responsibility of the international organisations are briefly analysed below using the United Nations and the Bretton Woods institutions as examples.

The French Marxist Nicos Poulantzas described international institutions as lacking powers of their own but instead reinforcing class powers.[126] The following quotation from an article by the environmental legal scholar Daniel Esty expresses another aspect of the character of international organisations:

> I argue that the WTO stands at a watershed. The Post-World War II international order centered on issue-based 'decomposable hierarchies' has begun to break down. A new, more complex and fluid international system is beginning to

---

[121] Dicke, *Die administrative Organisation*, 8–9; Adekeye Adebajo, *Liberia's Civil War: Nigeria, ECOMOG, and Regional Security in West Africa* (Boulder, Colorado: Lynne Rienner Publishers, 2002), 27; Brockway, *Colonial Revolution*, 600.

[122] Examples are the Congress of Vienna in 1814–1815 and the Universal Postal Union in 1863.

[123] Ian Brownlie, *Principles of Public International Law* (Oxford: Oxford University Press, 1998), 677.

[124] There is a correlation between the appearance and expansion of the international organisations and the independence of the colonial territories, which appear equal and sovereign in the international legal order.

[125] Shaw, *International Law*, 909.

[126] Chimni, "The World Trade Organization", 7; Nicos Poulantzas, *Classes in Contemporary Capitalism* (London: New Left Books, 1975), 70.

> emerge. But the new architecture has structural flaws. In particular, little attention has been paid to what is required to establish the legitimacy of international organizations in general and the WTO in particular.[127]

Especially since the end of the Cold War, the international community has been sensitive to the need to implement democracy and establish constitutional systems in the South. At the same time, the North has interfered increasingly in the internal issues of the South, demanding democratisation in developing countries[128] and even intervening militarily with the justification of supporting democracy.[129] Nonetheless, the Northern countries have not shown the same sensitivity to the need for democratic structures in all international regimes.[130]

The Establishment of the International Organisations

This undemocratic tendency first appeared during the establishment of the international organisations, when the North disregarded the ideas of the South. The United States drafted the UN Charter after entering the Second World War and presented it to the other Big Four countries, the Soviet Union, France, the Republic of China, and Great Britain.[131] These countries came together at the Dumbarton Oaks Conference in 1944 to finalise the Charter. When the text was presented to Southern countries at the United Nations Conference in San Francisco on 25 April 1945, they had little opportunity to influence the content.[132]

The establishment of the Bretton Woods institutions, whose content was determined almost exclusively by the United States and Great Britain to serve

127 Daniel C. Esty, "The World Trade Organization's Legitimacy Crisis", *World Trade Review* 1 (2002), 8.

128 Conforti, *The Law and Practice of the United Nations Law and Practice of the United Nations*, 250.

129 Chapter 5 describes this in detail.

130 The president of the Security Council Meeting of 31 January 1992 described the necessity of such democratisation at the international level as well as within states as follows: "The contours of the global order to which it will lead are not yet clearly perceivable. But several lessons are already being driven home: Democratisation at the national level dictates a corresponding process at the global level. At both levels, it aims at the rule of law [...] For global society, it means democratisation of international relations and the participation of all States in developing new norms of international life. Small States can play large constructive roles at both levels". S/PV 3046 of 31 January 1992, 8–9.

131 Alf Ross, *Constitutions of the United Nations: Analysis of Structure and Function* (Copenhagen: Munksgaard, 1950), 19. Before Dumbarton Oaks, conferences were held in Moscow, Cairo, and Tehran.

132 Ibid.; Trukhanovsky, *British Foreign Policy*, 1–5, 44; Dolman, *Resources*, 167. The states in the South included 20 in Latin America, 9 in Asia, and 3 in Africa.

their economic interests, was equally undemocratic.[133] Developing countries were in fact excluded from the establishment of the economic and financial institutions during the Second World War.[134] Only 9 of the 45 countries at the United Nations Monetary and Financial Conference in 1944 were non-European, and only 29 states had signed the Articles of Agreement.[135]

The Composition of the Organs of the International Organisations

The organs of the international organisations also were established undemocratically, with the Northern countries making the decisions that affected the Southern countries. A comparison of the three principal organs of the United Nations—the General Assembly, Security Council, and Economic and Social Council—shows this clearly.[136] The General Assembly is the highest decision-making body for international economic and social co-operation, according to Article 60 of the UN Charter. Every state has one vote,[137] but in spite of full membership in this 'supreme decision-making body', the decisions of the General Assembly are not automatically binding for states unless they become treaties ratified in international law.[138] The Economic and Social Council has neither binding power nor ultimate decision-making power.[139]

However, the Security Council differs from the General Assembly and Economic and Social Council in many respects. First, the Security Council has only 15 members[140] and the five so-called 'Great Powers' have permanent membership.[141] Under Article 27 of the UN Charter, no decision concerning international peace and security can be adopted unless the five permanent mem-

[133] Ibid., 12; Pahuja, "Technologies of Empire", 755.

[134] International Monetary Fund Records Office (April 1942), cited in Edward S. Mason and Robert E. Asher, *The World Bank since Bretton Woods* (Washington, DC: The Brookings Institution, 1973), 15.

[135] Egypt, Ethiopia, Liberia, and South Africa in Africa and China, India, Iran, Iraq, and the Philippines in Asia (Shihata, *The World Bank*, 2).

[136] Article 7 of the United Nations Charter.

[137] Childers, "The United Nations System", 15; Article 18/1 of the UN Charter.

[138] Ibid.; Conforti, *Law and Practice of the United Nations*, 242.

[139] Dicke, *Die administrative Organisation*, 26; Conforti, *Law and Practice of the United Nations*, 242; Childers, "The United Nations System", 16.

[140] The number of Member States in the Security Council increased only once after decolonisation, from 11 to 15, with General Assembly Resolution 1991 (XVIII) of 17 December 1963. The current number of states in the world is 192. The restricted number of Member States in the Security Council is one of the main criticisms of international law.

[141] The Republic of China, France, Russia, the UK, and the United States. Article 23 of the UN Charter; General Assembly Resolution 1991 (XVIII) of 17 December 1963. Ten other members are elected by the General Assembly for periods of two years.

bers agree.[142] Second, the Security Council has the power to make decisions that Member States must carry out under the United Nations Charter according to Article 25 of the UN Charter, while the resolutions of the General Assembly are only recommendations to states.[143] Beatrice Heuser described this as a 'paradoxical fusion of realism and idealism, for a ruling oligarchy, for a concert of powers within a system of collective security, ostensibly among equals'.[144]

Among the Bretton Woods institutions, the IMF currently has 185 members, most of them Southern countries, but this majority plays little role in the decision-making process. The IMF takes decisions not according to the one state—one vote system, but according to the weighted-vote system, through which voting power remains in a handful of countries.[145] The United States has 17.55 percent of the votes, while India has only has 1.98 percent.[146] Consequently, the developed countries govern the decision-making process and the Southern countries only appear to participate.[147]

The Northern states' decision-making power in the Bretton Woods institutions contradicts the premise that the Southern countries are these institutions' only area of operation. In other words, the people who are affected by the decisions of the Bretton Woods institutions have no say in these decisions.[148] Moreover, these institutions are criticised as secretive and non-transparent in spite of their insistence on transparency in the governments of the South. Documents containing policies, decisions, and plans or minutes of closed meetings are disclosed arbitrarily.[149]

---

142 Article 27/2–3 of the UN Charter.

143 Article 13 of the UN Charter; (Kelsen 1950, 95–97); Yoram Dinstein, "Sovereignty, the Security Council and the Use of Force", in *Redefining Sovereignty: The Use of Force After the Cold War*, ed. Michael Bothe, Mary Ellen O'Connell, and Natalino Ronzitti (Aldershot, UK: Transnational Publishers, 2005), 115.

144 Beatrice Heuser, "Sovereignty, Self-determination, and Security", in *State Sovereignty, Change and Persistence in International Relations*, ed. Sohail H. Hashmi (Philadelphia: University of Pennsylvania Press, 1997), 88.

145 IDA Article VI, § 3; IBRD Articles Article V, § 3; Conforti, *Law and Practice of the United Nations*, 250.

146 http://www.guardian.co.uk/theguardian/2002/jul/18/guardianletters2, November 2008.

147 Reddy, *Third World Development*, 27.

148 Jo Marie Griesgraber and Bernard G. Gunter, introduction to *The World Bank: Lending on a Global Scale*, ed. Jo Marie Griesgraber and Bernhard G. Gunter (London: Pluto Press, 1996), xv.

149 Joseph E. Stiglitz, "Failure of the Fund: Rethinking the IMF Response", *Harvard International Review* 23 (2001), 14; Andrew Balls and George Parker, "Europe Likely to Select Candidate by Next Week for IMF Vacancy", *Financial Times*, 17 April 2004, 8.

The Law-Making Power of the International Organisations

The international organisations are the foremost law-making powers in current international law. The constituent documents set the legal space for these powers, from treaty making to decision making.[150] The organs of the international organisations can either implement an article of the constituent document or use their authority to interpret the main document and take a decision. Because the decision-making powers are given to organs dominated by the Northern states, the law-making power is used almost exclusively by those states.

The North has exploited the law-making power of the international organisations to promote its interests through the range of interpretation. The Security Council is the only UN law-making power that gives only five states decision-making authority. This main body responsible for maintaining international peace and security adopts its resolutions on the legal basis of the UN Charter.[151] Since the end of the Cold War, the Security Council has extended its legal authority through interpretation. Many internal issues, including human rights and democracy, have fallen under the Security Council's mandate through the wide interpretation of the phrase 'threat to peace', but the Security Council interprets the content of these internal issues.[152] Moreover, the concept of international administration appeared through the wide interpretation of Chapter VII by the Security Council.

The law-making power of the Bretton Woods institutions appears through the influence of the regional banks, and the capacity of the decision-making powers through the implementation and interpretation of their articles.[153] The broad law-making power of these institutions is clearly seen in their policy in the South. The conditionality policy of the Bretton Woods institutions in the Southern countries is one of their main means to use their law-making power.[154]

---

[150] Shaw, *International Law*, 914; Ian Brownlie, *The Rule of Law in International Affairs: International Law at the Fiftieth Anniversary of the United Nations* (London: Martinus Nijhoff Publishers, 1998), 682; Articles 82, 83 of the Vienna Convention of 21 March 1986.

[151] Article 24 of the UN Charter.

[152] Sean D. Murphy, *Humanitarian Intervention: The United Nations in an Evolving World Order* (Philadelphia: University of Pennsylvania Press, 1996), 392; Jennifer L. Czernecki, "The United Nations Paradox: The Battle between Humanitarian Intervention and State Sovereignty", *Duquesne Law Review* 41 (2002–2003), 391–407, 401.

[153] Williams, "Aid and Sovereignty", 567; Article IX. Interpretation of the Articles of the Agreement of the International Bank for the Reconstruction and Development, Article XVIII, Interpretation of the Articles of Agreement of the International Monetary Fund.

[154] Pahuja, "Technologies of Empire", 758.

Limited Responsibility and Accountability
The principle of state responsibility is a basic concept of customary public international law.[155] Judge Max Huber elegantly defined the correlation between rights and responsibilities in international law in the *Spanish Zone of Morocco Claims* case of 1925. He wrote that

> Responsibility is the necessary corollary of a right. All rights of international character involve international responsibility. If the obligation in question is not met, responsibility entails the duty to make reparation.[156]

With an increasing focus on state responsibility,[157] the responsibility of international organisations remains almost a black hole[158] despite their broad capacity in international law. In spite of the predominance of only five powerful states in decision making, the Security Council is responsible to no other institution. Neither any UN organ nor any single state or group of states has the legal means to act against its resolutions or activities.[159] There is no mechanism to hold the United Nations responsible for human rights violations that occur during its military interventions.[160] Moreover, the international transitional administration of the United Nations has immunity. For nearly 10 years UNMIK has functioned undemocratically. As Friedrich says, 'No democratic state government in the world accords itself immunity from any responsibility as does UNMIK'.[161] This is shown in the 2001–2002 report of the Ombudsperson in Kosovo quoted below:

> UNMIK is not structured according to democratic principles, does not function in accordance with the rule of law, and does not respect important international

155 Brownlie, *Principles of Public International Law*, 79.

156 Spanish Zone of Morocco Claims Case (1925), 2 RIAA 615 at 641.

157 Malcolm Evans, ed. *International Law*, 2nd edition (Oxford: Oxford University Press, 2006), 452.

158 International law has only recently dealt with the responsibility of the international organisations. A Committee on Accountability of International Organizations was established after the decision of the International Law Association's Executive Council in May 1996, and the Committee published its first report on the Conference of the ILA in Taipei in 1998. See ILA Report of the Sixty-Eighth Conference, Taipei, May 24–30, 1998; Eisuke Suziki and Suresh Nanwani, "Responsibility of International Organizations: The Accountability Mechanisms of Multilateral Development Ranks", *Michigan Journal of International Law* 27 (2005–2006), 178–179.

159 Heuser, "Soverignty, Self-determination, and Security", 89.

160 This is also true of unilateral military intervention by the other international organisations. The large-scale NATO bombing of Yugoslavia between 24 March and 10 June 1999 (Operation Allied Force) that aimed to protect Kosovo Albanians through humanitarian intervention caused extensive loss of life and destroyed the country's civil and military infrastructure.

161 Jürgen Friedrich, "UNMIK in Kosovo: Struggling with Uncertainty", *Max Planck Yearbook of United Nations Law* 9 (2005), 285.

> human rights norms. The people of Kosovo are therefore deprived of protection of their basic rights and freedoms three years after the end of the conflict by the very entity set up to guarantee them.[162]

According to the Articles of Agreement of the IMF and the World Bank, the legal space for imposing conditions on borrowing countries is restricted to economic issues. But the Bretton Woods institutions determine not only economic but also social and political issues in the borrowing countries under the Washington Consensus and have no legal obligation for the negative outcomes of their policies. The negative consequences of their policies, which will be cited later, have been public knowledge since the 1980s.[163]

Different Application of the Concept of Sovereignty in the North and South

Developments such as the establishment of the regional and international organisations, the tremendous growth in technology, and globalisation have altered the concept of sovereignty. The term has a different meaning under globalisation than it did when Jean Bodin conceived it in the late 16th century.[164] Especially since the end of the Second World War, when the former colonial territories appeared as new states sovereign and equal under the international legal order, international law has applied the concept of sovereignty differently in the North and South.[165] Interestingly, the United Nations mentions the 'sovereignty, independence, territorial integrity and unity of the states' in almost every resolution, but takes decisions for many states in the South under Chapter VII of the UN Charter.[166] The sovereignty of the Southern

---

[162] Ombudperson Institution in Kosovo, Second Annual Report 2001–2002, www.ombudspersonkosovo.org; Raphael Utz, "Nations, Nation-Building, and Cultural Intervention: A Social Science Perspective", *Max Planck Yearbook of United Nations Law* 9 (2005), 644.

[163] Sigrun I. Skogly, "The Position of the World Bank and the International Monetary Fund in the Human Rights Field", in *An Introduction to the International Protection of Human Rights*, ed. Raija Hanski and Markku Suksi (Turku, Finland: Åbo Akademi University Institute for Human Rights, 1997), 194.

[164] Ruth E. Gordon, "Some Legal Problems with Trusteeship", *Cornell International Law Journal* 28 (1995), 314; Christian Tomuschat, "How the Classical Concept of Sovereignty Has Evolved", in *The International and the National: Essays in Honour of Vojin Dimitrijević, ed.* Milica Delević Đilas amd Vladimir Đjerić (Belgrade: Belgrade Center for Human Rights 2003), 21.

[165] Christian Tomuschat, "Völkerrecht ist kein Zweiklassenrecht, Der Iraq-Krieg and seine Folgen", *Vereinten Nationen* 51 (2003), 2, 41; Gordon, "Some Legal Problems with Trusteeship", 316.

[166] S/Res/1657 (2006) of 6 February 2006 and S/Res/1665 (2006) of 29 March 2006 on Côte d'Ivoire; S/Res/1667 (2006) of 31 March 2006 on Liberia; S/Res/1669 (2006) of 10 April

countries has diminished mainly through 1) the restriction of 'intervention or interference' to military intervention and 2) the erosion of the prohibition against military intervention through a broad interpretation of self-defence in Article 51 and the requirement of enforcement measures under Chapter VII.

Legitimisation of Economic, Social, and Political Intervention through International Law

Two developments have legitimised intervention in the economic, social, and political affairs of states. The first was the appearance after the end of the Second World War of the many international actors that have taken an active role in the states. The second was the tendency of international law, especially since the end of the Cold War, to transfer internal issues such as human rights, democracy, and the form of the political and economic structure of government from municipal law to international law.

The policy of the Bretton Woods institutions is the best example of the gradual legitimisation of the interference of international actors in the internal political and economic affairs of states. Although many paragraphs of the Articles of Agreement implicitly or explicitly restrict the activities of the World Bank and IMF to economic issues and prohibit political and non-economic interference,[167] the international financial organisations have increasingly used credits since the 1970s to influence economic and later social and political issues in the South.[168] In the 1990s the Bretton Woods institutions focused on good governance, which has not only economic but also political and social dimensions such as human rights, democracy, and the environment.[169] Joseph Gold describes conditionality in the IMF as a 'portmanteau word that encompasses all the policies that the Fund wishes a member to follow [...]'.[170] Tony Evans describes structural adjustment programmes (SAP) as '[...] the redistribution of structural decision-making powers away from states and

2006 on Burundi; S/Res/1654 (2006) of 31 January 2006 on the Democratic Republic of the Congo; and S/Res/1658 (2006) of 14 February 2006 on Haiti.

167 Articles of Agreement of the IBRD, Art III/Sec 5/b, Art IV/Sec 10, IBRD Article IV§ 10; IDA Article V§ 6; IBRD Article III, § 10; IBRD Article V§ 5 (c); Article V/Sec.3 of the Articles of Agreement of the IMF.

168 Mark E. Wadrzyk, "Is It Appropriate for the World Bank to Promote Democratic Standards in a Borrower Country?", *Wisconsin International Law Journal* 17 (1999), 561.

169 Ibid.

170 Joseph Gold, *Conditionality* (Washington: International Monetary Fund, 1979) cited in Pahuja, "Technologies of Empire", 758.

into global economic institutions [...]'.[171] Their economic weakness gives the Southern states no option but to accept the policy of the international financial institutions.[172]

Hypocritical Approach to Sovereignty

The North's license to intervene military in Southern countries in the context of environmental and human rights violations appeared in the political realm during the Cold War. As explained in Part II, however, in the 1990s the international community held that the concepts of human rights and democracy in international law were more important than the sovereignty of states. At the same time, unilateral and multilateral military intervention in the Southern countries has been debated on humanitarian or security grounds,[173] and many states have experienced intervention since the 1990s.[174]

The international community's hypocritical approach to sovereignty can be seen clearly in the context of environmental and human rights violations. The United States consistently resists the rulings of the International Court of Justice, and the North guards its sovereignty against possible measures to restrict environmental pollution.[175] The international community shows the same double face concerning human rights violations, citing such violations as a reason for military intervention in the South but referring to them superficially in the cases of China and Russia, two permanent members of the Security Council. The 'interest, power and hegemony'[176] of Northern states determine their reaction to democracy, human rights, and collective security in the South. For example, although NGOs openly criticised the human rights abuses during the regime of President Olusegun Obasanjo in Nigeria, the United States and other Western countries maintained diplomatic relations. A week after a massacre of civilians in Benue State by the military, U.S. officials met with Obasanjo to discuss measures to fight terrorism without touching on the massacre.[177]

171 Tony Evans, introduction to "Power, Hegemony and the Universalization of Human Rights", in *Human Rights Fifty Years, A Reappraisal*, ed. Tony Evans (Manchester: Manchester University Press, 1998), 15.

172 Jedediah Purdy, "A World of Passions: How to Think About Globalization Now", *Indiana Journal of Global Legal Studies* 11 (2004), 1, 23–28.

173 Murphy, *Humanitarian Intervention*, 393.

174 See Chapter 5.

175 Kurt Mills, *Human Rights in the Emerging Global Order: A New Sovereignty* (Basingstoke, UK: Macmillan Publishers, 1998), 1.

176 Evans, introduction to "Power, Hegemony and the Universalization of Human Rights", 1.

177 Philip C. Aka, "Nigeria since May 1999: Understanding the Paradox of Civil Rule and Human Rights Violations under President Olusegun Obasanjo", *San Diego International Law Journal* 4 (2003), 209, 257.

While the United States initiated military intervention in Haiti before Aristide's election ostensibly to protect democracy, it had protected the Duvalier dictatorship from 1957 to 1990.[178]

Contradiction between the Demands of the South and the Model of the North

Under current international law, the South's demand for solutions to its economic and social problems and the North's model for solving those problems determine the international community's efforts and effectiveness in this area. The North applies its model through international organisations and institutions, while the South expresses its grievances mainly through the General Assembly, the Economic and Social Council, and ad hoc conferences. The following sections attempt to illustrate the contradiction between these two positions as well as their enforcement in international law during and after the Cold War.

During the Cold War

The new international legal order after the Second World War and the appearance of new states, especially after decolonisation and the Cold War, were the main determinants of the model of the North and the demands of the South. The approaches of the North and the South can be analyzed under two Cold War periods, between 1945 and 1970 and between 1970 and 1990.

Between 1945 and 1970

The establishment of the new international legal order that spotlighted the United Nations as bringing in a peaceful world order and economic independence influenced the demands and approach of the South, but development policy as an instrument of the Cold War shaped the model of the North.

As mentioned earlier, the UN Charter does not deal specifically with the economic situation of the South; the international community uses international economic and social cooperation in Article 55 and other articles as the legal basis for their efforts. The General Assembly first placed the South and its

[178] W.Q. Beardslee, "The United State's Haiti Intervention: The Dangers of 'Redefined' National Security Interests", *Denver Journal of International Law and Policy* 25 (1994), 1, 193.

problems on its agenda with Resolution 198 (III) of 4 December 1948.[179] Afterward its approach to the South's economic and social development shifted gradually. The United Nations Development Decades I[180] and II,[181] UNCTAD I in Geneva in 1964[182] and UNCTAD II in New Delhi in 1968, the Declaration of the Permanent Sovereignty over Natural Resources in 1962, and the Joint Declaration of the Developing Countries with regard to the United Nations Conference on Trade and Development made at the 18th Session of the General Assembly in 1963 were important forums for the Southern countries to articulate their recommendations for solving their problems.[183] The elements of the approaches of the Southern counties described in General Assembly resolutions between 1945 and 1970 are summarised below.

The principles of sovereignty, self-determination, and the economic and political independence of the developing states have been demonstrated consistently in these resolutions.[184] For example, from the first the General Assembly resolutions, political and economic interference through technical and financial assistance is prohibited.[185] The 1962 Declaration of Permanent Sovereignty over Natural Resources cited the principles of equality and self-determination as the basis for economic and financial agreements between developed and developing countries and prohibited exploitation and misuse in international cooperation for the economic development of developing countries.[186]

Beginning in 1949, General Assembly resolutions linked international economic and commercial policy and the economic development of the South,[187] and the importance of this link was increasingly emphasized. The link springs from the belief that the economic development of the South can be realised only if economic development is seen as part of international economic and commercial policy. In other words, the 'less developed countries' can finance their economic development by being part of the international economy. According to the 1963 Joint Declaration of the Developing Countries with regard to

[179] GA/Res/198 (III) of 4 December 1948: Economic Development of Underdeveloped Countries.

[180] GA/Res/1710 (XV) of 19 December 1961.

[181] GA/Res/2626 (XXV) of 24 October 1970.

[182] UNCTAD was established through General Assembly Resolution 1995 (XIX) of 30 December 1964.

[183] GA/Res/1803(XVII) of 14 December 1962; GA/Res/1897(XVIII) of 11 November 1963.

[184] GA/Res/2200(XXI) of 16 December 1966: International Covenant on Economic, Social and Cultural Rights and on Civil and Political Rights; G/Res/2525 (XXV) 24 October 1970: Declaration on Principles of International law Concerning Friendly Resolutions.

[185] GA/Res/200(III) 4(d) of 4 December 1948.

[186] Paragraph 7 of GA/Res/1803(XVII) of 14 December 1962: Permanent Sovereignty over Natural Resources.

[187] GA/Res/307(IV) of 16 November 1949; GA/Res/404(V) of 20 November 1950.

the United Nations Conference on Trade and Development, only under this condition can developing countries realise their economic independence in an interdependent and integrated world economic system.[188]

The significance of imports and exports for the economic welfare of states was clear by the end of the 1940s.[189] In 1952 the General Assembly mentioned financing the economic development of the developing countries through trade,[190] and it continued to refer to this issue in various resolutions. The appearance of new states and the economic, social, and political weakness of the South influenced international trade measures. National economic development measures in fact aimed to protect the young states from the political and economic interference of powerful states. Other measures with the same intent included establishing a market in which the South could sell its primary commodities at fair and equitable international prices and giving the South an equitable share of the earnings from its natural resources extracted and marketed by foreign capital.[191] Putting trade at the centre of financing for economic development was based on the philosophy of 'self-sustaining growth'.[192] In the 1963 Joint Declaration of the Developing Countries with regard to the United Nations Conference on Trade and Development, the Southern countries demanded that UNCTAD help them 'reach the stage of self-sustaining growth' through trade.[193] The same declaration argued that the patterns and principles of world trade are determined mainly by the interests of powerful states and negatively affect—even frustrate—the attempts of the South to grow more rapidly. It was for this reason that the Southern countries called for reconstruction of the economic system as the main basis for UNCTAD.[194]

UNCTAD I, held between 23 March and 16 June 1964, stressed the importance of trade for economic development in the South. The phrase 'equality of treatment between unequals is itself inequality' set the tone of subsequent UNCTAD conferences.[195] Southern countries considered UNCTAD a hope for restructuring world trade to facilitate their self-sustaining economic growth.[196]

---

188 GA/Res/1897(XVIII) of 11 November 1963: Joint Declaration of the Developing Countries with regard to the United Nations Conference on Trade and Development.

189 GA/Res/307(IV) of 16 November 1949; GA/Res/404(V) of 20 November 1950.

190 GA/Res/623 (VII) of 21 December 1952.

191 GA/Res/623 (VII) of 21 December 1952; GA/Res/1027(XI) of 20 February 1957; GA/Res/1519, 20, 22, 24 (XV) of 15 December 1960; paragraph 2 of GA/Res/1710 of 19 December 1961.

192 GA/Res/1710 (XV) of 19 December 1961: Declaration of the United Nations Development Decade in 1961.

193 GA/Res/1897(XVIII) of 11 November 1963.

194 Ibid.

195 El-Naggar, "Developing Countries", 73.

196 Reddy, *Third World Development*, 68.

The conference participants committed to establishing a concept of world trade that would diminish the gap between the developing and developed countries. In this sense, UNCTAD is an alternative to GATT. GATT was an instrument to realise free trade through trade agreements based on the principle of equality of treatment between unequals, while the South hopes that UNCTAD would be 'a forum for the definition of principles and broad policy measures on trade, aid and development'.[197] Since the end of the 1940s, the General Assembly has consistently cited technical and financial assistance as a means for the economic development of the South. Vehicles and methods for technical and financial assistance have changed and been refined.[198] The General Assembly defined technical assistance as the provision of expert personnel and technical organisation in Southern countries where their lack obstructs economic development.[199] The important point was, however, that the Southern countries perceived the financial and technical assistance as only a short-term solution.

The General Assembly focused on the roots of economic and social problems in the South and called for long-term measures to address them, including industrialisation, land reform, and rights over natural resources. Unequal development of technology increased the South's dependence on the North and widened the gap between economic development in the North and South. Beginning in the late 1950s, the General Assembly described technology as a main instrument for the economic development of the South.[200] Regrettably, the North's response to the South's demand for industrialisation reinforced the South's dependence on Northern technology and industry and limited technology transfer to old, expensive, or experimental technologies.

The General Assembly first called for land reform in 1952 and continued to draw attention to this issue in following years,[201] but its implementation has faced obstacles not only within states but also in the face of the Open Door

[197] Ibid., 68–69. Under General Assembly Resolution 2205 (XXI) of 17 December 1966, UNCTAD appears as an organ of the General Assembly.

[198] GA/Res/198(III) of 4 December 1948; GA/Res/400(V) of 20 November 1950; GA/Res/305–307 (IV) of 16 November 1949; GA/Res/518, 521(VI) of 12 January 1952; GA/Res/622 (VII) of 21 December 1952; GA/Res/831 (XI) of 26 November 1954; GA/Res/1023 (XI) of 21 December 1956; GA/Res/1215 (XII) of 14 December 1957; GA/Res/2087–2088, 2090 (XX) of 20 December 1965; GA/Res/2169 (XXI) of 11 December 1966; GA/Res/2276 (XXII) of 4 December 1967; GA/Res/2401 (XXIII) of 13 December 1968.

[199] GA/Res/200 (III) of 4 December 1948.

[200] GA/Res/1033 (XI) of 26 February 1957; GA/Res/2089–2091 (XX) of 20 December 1965; GA/Res/2259 (XXII) of 25 October 1967; GA/Res/1710 of 19 December 1961, 4 (a): *Declaration of the Development Decade.*

[201] GA/Res/521 (IV) of 12 January 1952; GA/Res/625 of 21 December 1952.

Policy. When land reform has threatened their economic interests, Northern states have used almost any means to obstruct the process, pointed out in Chapter 3 in the case of Guatemala.

Another important issue was the legal rights of the Southern countries over their natural resources. The General Assembly described these rights as one of the main instruments of these states' economic independence and development. Resolution 523 (VI) of 12 January 1952 contained the following statement:

> [...] the under-developed countries have a right to determine freely the use of their natural resources and [...] must utilize such resources in order to be in a better position to further the realization of their plans of economic development in accordance with their national interest and to further the expansion of the world economy.[202]

Various other resolutions mentioned rights over natural resources,[203] but the 1962 Declaration of the Permanent Sovereignty over Natural Resources was the most detailed and comprehensive.[204] The General Assembly pointed out the 'inalienable sovereignty of States over their natural wealth and resources' and called for the implementation in good faith of related foreign investment agreements.[205] Several resolutions brought a new dimension to the protection of the South's rights over its natural resources,[206] for example, General Assembly Resolution 2158 (XXI) of 25 November 1966, which pointed out the responsibility of foreign investors who exploit natural resources in the South to train local people.[207] However, the issue of rights over natural resources came up against a closed Open Door Policy many times. The example of Iran is described in Chapter 5.

From 1945 to 1970 the North used development assistance as a Cold War instrument and kept the formal colonial territories economically dependent on the former colonial powers. Development assistance was designed to further the Cold War aims of the United States immediately after the Second World

202 GA/Res/523(VI) of 12 January 1952.

203 General Assembly Resolution 1314 (XIII) of 1958 foresaw the establishment of the Commission on Permanent Sovereignty over Natural Resources; GA/Res/1515 (XV) of 15 December 1960; GA/Res/2158 (XXI) of 25 November 1966; GA/Res/2173 (XXI) of 12 December 1966; GA/Res/2386 (XXIII) of 14 November 1968.

204 GA/Res/1803 (XVII) of 14 December 1962.

205 Paragraph 8 of GA/Res/1803 (XVII) of 14 December 1962.

206 GA/Res/2173 (XXI) of 12 December 1966; GA/Res/2386 (XXIII) of 14 November 1968; GA/Res/1897 (XVIII) of 11 November 1963: Joint Declaration of the Developing Countries with regard to the United Nations Conference on Trade and Development.

207 GA/Res/2158 (XXI) of 25 November 1966.

War. On 12 March 1947, U.S. President Truman declared that the United States would support Greece and Turkey economically and militarily to keep those countries out of the Soviet sphere of influence, a position that became known as the Truman Doctrine.[208] Two years later, with Truman's speech marking the foundation of NATO, the Truman Doctrine had turned into U.S. development policy. 'Foreign aid' programs were put into place alongside military support from the early 1950s to support anti-Communist governments, especially in the Middle East and Asia.[209] The U.S. Government's Strategic Hamlets program in Vietnam is a prime example.

The United States claimed that the main motive for its development assistance was to help the Third World develop economically and socially, following the U.S. example.[210] Because of the Cold War, bilateral aid was the centre of development policy in the first decades after the establishment of the United Nations. U.S. foreign credit and investment rose to approximately US$ 5.4 million between 1946 and 1952, while World Bank borrowing lending remained at US$ 1.5 million in the same period.[211]

After the 1960s U.S. development policy shifted from bilateral aid to multilateral aid.[212] The United States had tried to implement the changing policy through its alliances and regional and international organisations including NATO and the Organization for European Economic Cooperation (OEEC), which was established in 1948 and became the OECD in 1961.[213] The World Bank was already involved in the Southern countries in the 1950s and established the International Development Association (IDA) on 24 September 1960 to channel funding to the poorest countries.[214] Before the 1970s the IMF took steps that signalled its involvement in the South, including changing its policy on enforcing conditions attached to its finance facilities and changing the juridical nature of its monetary powers.[215] Nonetheless, U.S. development policy until the end of the 1960s was mainly characterised by bilateral aid. Such

---

208 Truman Doctrine, http://www.yale.edu/lawweb/avalon/trudoc.htm.

209 Cheryl Payer, "Causes of the Debt Crisis", in *The IMF, the World Bank and the African Debt, Volume 2, The Social and Political Impact*, ed. Bade Onimode (London: Zed Books, 1989), 8.

210 Pahuja, "Technologies of Empire", 762.

211 Georg Erler, "Internationale Finanz- und Wirtschaftshilfe als politisches und völkerrechtliches Problem", *Sonderdruck aus Menschen und Staat in Recht und Geschichte* (Berlin: Dt. Zentraldr, 1953), 31–32.

212 Pahuja, "Technologies of Empire", 762.

213 Ibid.

214 Ibid., 760–761.

215 Scott R. Sidell writes in *The IMF and Third-World Political Instability: Is There a Connection* (New York: St. Martin's Press, 1988) that the roots of the IMF policies go back to 1952; Pahuja, "Technologies of Empire", 760–780.

aid was almost 90 percent of official development assistance in 1967.[216] But by the end of the 1960s, the U.S. Congress was questioning the effectiveness of bilateral aid as a foreign policy.[217]

During the same period, the United States participated in the exploitation of the former colonial territories through various agreements with the former colonial powers. Through the Marshall Plan and the Mutual Security Act, the country gained concessions to extract strategic raw materials. U.S. private investment in the South increased from US$ 130 million to US$ 774 million between 1943 and 1955. During the height of independence movements between 1945 and 1960, the United States gave US$ 835 million in aid for military purposes to the major ex-colonial powers.[218]

After decolonisation European countries appeared on the scene as donors of bilateral aid or credits to the South, but these initiatives mainly served their economic interests and their desire to retain their economic hegemony over their former colonial territories. In the 1960s Britain and France provided aid and loans almost exclusively to their ex-colonies.[219] Victor Israelyan describes the influence of the colonial powers on their ex-territories as follows:

> [...] the metropolitan countries have saddled some of the young states with unequal military and political agreements. France, for example, has made many of her former possessions accept the commitment to stay in the franc zone and to conclude no economic agreements with third countries before consulting France. Military bases remained on their territories. Similar commitments were wrested from some of her ex-colonies by Britain. With foreign advisers installed in government offices and foreign monopolies dominant in their economy, such commitments are making big inroads into the independence of the young states.[220]

The North maintained its control over the economies of the former colonial territories by withdrawing capital, refusing credit, and restricting commerce. Israelyan describes these moves as 'collective colonialism'.[221] French and West German monopolies obliged the new African countries to buy their manufactured goods at high prices and to sell raw materials at low prices.[222] The ex-colonial powers also served their own interests through export credits.[223] The developed countries transferred real resources and grants for the purchase of

---

216 Lester B. Pearson, *Partners in Development: Report of the Commission on International Development* (New York: Praeger Publishers, 1969), 209.

217 Pahuja, "Technologies of Empire", 762.

218 Victor Israelyan, ed. *Soviet Foreign Policy* (Moscow: Progress Publishers, 1967), 152.

219 Pahuja, "Technologies of Empire", 761.

220 Israelyan, ed., *Soviet Foreign Policy*, 151.

221 Ibid.

222 Ibid.; Brockway, *Colonial Revolution*, 599.

223 International Monetary Fund, Staff Papers Vol. XVII, at 89–90 (1970).

equipment at very high costs as part of such credits.[224] Thus the seeds of the debt problems of the developing counties were sown immediately after their independence. The total debt of the developing countries was rose from US$ 18 billion in 1960 to US$ 75 billion in 1970 and US$ 112.4 billion after the oil crisis of 1973.[225] Profitable investment by the developed countries also played an important role in their relations with the new states.[226]

Inspired by the new international law order, the Southern countries consistently followed measures for self-sustaining economic growth in this period. The principles of sovereignty, self-determination, and economic and political independence had been at the centre of their demands since the establishment of the United Nations. The links among international economic and commercial policy and economic development, attempts to address the roots of the problems, and the search for long-term solutions were the main paradigms for self-sustaining economic growth.

The approaches of the South differed from those of the superpower countries and former colonial powers soon after the end of the Second World War. During the Cold War the superpowers defined their policy toward the Southern countries in reference to the conflict. The former colonial powers searched for ways to gain economic and political control of their former territories. Both used aid to achieve their own aims. This was also true of development policy.

Between 1970 and 1990

The hope for a 'braver world order' after the establishment of new international laws and the independence of the colonial territories soured in the 1970s, by which time the South had begun to recognise the inequality between states and their former colonists' reluctance to grant them economic independence. Gro Harlem Brundtland, Chairman of the report "Our Common Future", described the decades of the 1960s and 1970s as follows:

> There was a time of optimism and progress in the 1960s, when there was greater hope for a braver new world and for progressive international ideas. Paradoxically, the 1970s slid slowly into moods of reaction and isolation while at the same time a series of conferences offered hope for greater co-operation on major issues.[227]

224 Pahuja, "Technologies of Empire", 764.
225 Reddy, *Third World Development*, 28.
226 Brockway, *Colonial Revolution*, 17.
227 Gro Harlem Brundtland, Chairman's Foreword to *Our Common Future*, http://www.un-documents.net/ocf-cf.htm.

Between 1970 and 1990, the demands of the New International Economic Order was the impetus for the approach of the Southern countries, while the liberalisation of the global economy and development policy (which was also Cold War Policy) shaped the model of the North.

The South's demand for a restructuring of the economic and political world order was expressed in the 1960s and 1970s in several publications, including the first Club of Rome "Limits to Growth" report in 1972.[228] In spite of its much-debated content, two issues in this report found general acceptance. The first was the recognition of problems in the Southern countries and the need to solve those problems in an international context. The second was the belief that solving the problems was impossible under the existing international order without new market mechanisms.

The goals of the Second Development Decade made the antagonism between the contemporary international institutional structure and the demands of the South more visible.[229] The 1974 NIEO was their most important vehicle to voice proposals to redress their disadvantages in the global economic and political system.[230] Documents after 1974 either confirmed the issues described in the NIEO or brought them wider attention. The Declaration on the Right to Development adopted by the General Assembly in 1986[231] recognised development as an inalienable human right and stated that 'equality of opportunity for development is a prerogative both of nations and of individuals who make up nations'.[232] Many UNCTAD conferences organised between the 1970s and 1990s[233] generated instruments and solutions to economic and social problems

---

[228] The Club of Rome was founded by Aurelio Peccei, Hasan Özbekhan, Erich Jantsch, and Alexander Christakis in 1968 to focus on a variety of international political issues.

[229] A/Res/2626 of 24 October 1970, *International Development Strategy for the Second United Nations Development Decade*. These issues were stressed by Jan Tinbergen, the main architect of the International Development Strategy for the Second Development Decade of the United Nations. (Reddy, *Third World Development*, 6–7).

[230] Dolman, *Resources*, 85–86.

[231] A/Res/41/128 of 4 September 1986.

[232] A/Res/41/128 of 4 September 1986 describes development as "a comprehensive economic, social, cultural and political process, which aims at the constant improvement of the well-being of the entire population and of all individuals on the basis of their active, free and meaningful participation in development and in the fair distribution of benefits resulting there from". The Right of Development was described in many later international law documents, including A/42/117 of 7 December 1987: Vienna Declaration and Programme of Action; A/Conf. 157/23 of 12 July 1993: United Nations Millennium Declaration; and A/55/2 of 8 September 2000. Samuli Seppänen, *Good Governance in International Law* (Helsinki: University of Helsinki, 2003), 74–75; Schlemmer-Schulte, "Global Business", 7.

[233] For example, UNCTAD III in Santiago, Chile, from 13 April 13 to 17 May 1972, UNCTAD IV in Nairobi, Kenya, from 3 to 31 May 1976, and UNCTAD V in Manila, Philippines from 7 May to 3 June 1979; Reddy, *Third World Development*, 69–75.

in the South. The central issues of these conferences were a new trade policy to facilitate development in the Southern countries, structural reform, and debt repayment.[234]

The NIEO evolved piece by piece from various General Assembly resolutions and events. Its importance lay in the declaration of unity of the Southern countries and the creation of a movement to express their demands. Antony Dolman described the NIEO as 'a reaction to colonialism and neo-colonialism and to mounting frustration and alienation with two decades of development efforts and of debates on the need for economic reforms'.[235] The General Assembly adopted three documents to define the content of the NIEO: the Declaration on the Establishment of a New International Economic Order,[236] the Program of Action on the Establishment of a New International Economic Order,[237] and the Charter of Economic Rights and Duties of the States.[238]

The Declaration on the Establishment of a New International Economic Order (NIEO) identifies the 'alien and colonial domination, foreign occupation, racial discrimination, apartheid and neo-colonialism' in the South as the most important barriers to economic, social, and political progress, exacerbated by inequitable distribution of the benefits of technological development.[239] The Declaration also noted the enormous income gap between developing and developed countries: at the time, the developing countries contained 70 percent of the world's population but earned only 30 percent of the world's income. Most important, the Declaration asserted that it was impossible to achieve economic and social development in the South within the existing international economic order. Contemporary international political and economic law established before the appearance of many new Southern states appeared to be in direct conflict with their demands.[240]

Based on the principles of the sovereign equality of states, self-determination of all peoples, non-interference, territorial integrity, and independence,[241] the NIEO declared that states' full permanent sovereignty over their natural resources epitomised economic independence.[242] The General Assembly prohib-

---

[234] Reddy, *Third World Development*, 69–75.
[235] Dolman, *Resources*, 82.
[236] GA/Res/3201(S-VI) of 1 May 1974: *Declaration of the Establishment of a New International Economic Order.*
[237] GA/Res/3202(S-VI) of 1 May 1974.
[238] GA/Res/3281(XXIX) of 12 December 1974; Reddy, *Third World Development*, 4.
[239] GA/Res/3201(S-VI) of 1 May 1974: *Declaration on the Establishment of a New International Economic Order.*
[240] Ibid., para. 1.
[241] Ibid., paras. 4(b) and 4(d).
[242] Ibid., para. 4(e).

ited developed states from setting preconditions for technical and financial assistance and transfer of modern science and technology to the Southern states and from mounting interference to exploit them.[243]

The core elements of the NIEO's philosophy were its inclusion of the economic and social problems of the South as part of the world economy and its link between the interests of the developed and developing countries.[244] The need to accelerate development in the South[245] and urge cooperation between developing countries drove this approach.[246] The first precondition for such development and cooperation was a just and equitable trade relationship between the developing and developed countries, especially concerning 'the prices of raw materials, primary commodities, [and] manufactured and semi-manufactured goods'.[247] The General Assembly also posited that 'subordination of the exercise of sovereignty' from colonial domination to coercion could be realised through this means.[248]

Another precondition for the NIEO was the 'active, full and equal participation' of the developing countries in decision-making in international law. The South, for example, had cited the weighted voting system as an obstacle to equal power in the international organisations.[249] The Declaration on the Establishment of a New International Economic Order called for restructuring the international organisations to meet the South's demands for a greater voice. The NIEO also called for reshaping international organisations such as the IMF to focus on the needs of the South to promote 'the development of the developing countries and the adequate flow of real resources to them'.[250] Dolman noted at the time that 'the developing countries seek to redress institutional distortions in international economic relations which may cost them $ 100 billion a year [...]'.[251]

The Declaration also focused on the activities, competence, authority, and responsibility of the MNE. With their economic and political weaknesses and lack of institutions and legal arrangements, the South was vulnerable to exploitation by the profit-oriented and well-endowed corporations based in the

243 Ibid., paragraphs 4 (k), 4 (o), and 4 (p).
244 *Preamble of the Declaration on the Establishment of a New International Economic Order*, A/Res/S-6/3201 of 1 May 1974, paragraph 4 (b).
245 Ibid., para. 4 (t).
246 Ibid., paras. 4 (n), 4 (s), and 4 (r).
247 Ibid., para. 4 (j).
248 Ibid., para. 4 (h) and 4 (i).
249 Karen A. Mingst and Margaret P. Karns, *The United Nations in the Post-Cold War Era* (Boulder, Colorado: Westview Press, 1995), 33.
250 Reddy, *Third World Development*, 8.
251 Dolman, *Resources*, 82.

North.[252] The Southern countries described these corporations as an obstacle to their development because they served as instruments of the Open Door Policy, as explained earlier, and violated political and economic sovereignty, basic human rights, and economic and social rights.[253] The Declaration on the New International Economic Order Programme of Action and Charter of Economic Rights and Duties included among its goals the regulation and supervision of the MNE to avoid their negative effects in the South.[254] This regulation had long been a demand of the Southern countries.[255]

Although the South expressed its demand for economic development through many UN documents and ad hoc instruments from the 1970s to the 1990s, the measures and institutions adopted through General Assembly resolutions have no legally binding force. For this reason, it was impossible to realise the goals of the NIEO or implement the Charter of Economic Rights and Duties of States.[256] The United States, Japan, and many European states reacted reluctantly to the NIEO.[257] UNCTAD and the Economic and Financial Committee have little influence on the economic world order and could only reiterate the orthodox position they had taken since 1954.[258]

The most important NIEO demand, a restructuring of the international organisations, received little attention. There were several attempts to 'revitalise' the UN Economic and Social Council (ECOSOC) to give it a greater role in global macroeconomic issues, but the opposition of the industrial states forestalled those efforts.[259] The call to reorganise power in the international financial institutions also fell on deaf ears. After the breakdown of the par

---

[252] Milton Friedman, in "Social Responsibility of Business", *New York Times*, September 13, 1970, §6 at 32, wrote, 'There is one and only one social responsibility of business: to increase its profits'; Baker, "Tightening The Toothless Vise", 95, 141.

[253] Baker, "Tightening The Toothless Vise", 97–99, 103; Kebebew Ashagrie, *Statistics on Working Children and Hazardous Child Labor in Brief* (1998), www.ilo.org/public/english/standards/ipec/simpoc/stats/child/stats.htm; Agbakwa, "A Line in the Sand", 4, 7; Westfield 2001–2002, 1077.

[254] Gutto, in *Human and Peoples' Rights*, 97–98, describes the MNE as a means of antidevelopment and therefore responsible for the economic problems in the Southern countries. GA Res. 3281 (XXIX), UN GAOR, Supp. No. 31 (1974), 50, Article 2 of Chapter II of the Charter of Economic Rights and Duties of States, paragraph 4(g) of the NIEO, and Part V of the Programme of Action.

[255] Gloria, "Internationales Wirtschaftsrecht", 558; Voon, "Multinational Enterprises", 242; Baker, "Tightening The Toothless Vise", 107–141.

[256] Agbakwa, "A Line in the Sand", 8.

[257] Dolman, *Resources*, 84, 95, 96; Reddy, *Third World Development*, 6.

[258] Alan Oxley, "North/South Dimensions of a New World Order", in *Whose New World Order, What Role for the United Nations?*, ed. Mara R. Bustelo and Philip Alston (Sydney: The Federation Press, 1991), 103 et. seq.

[259] Childers, "The United Nations System", 17.

value system, the new monetary system exacerbated economic instability in the South and the changing policy of the World Bank and IMF intensified the inequality.

The effort to establish an international instrument to prevent the negative effects of the MNE and make them accountable for their activities had a similar fate. Such attempts had been made in 1970 by the Andean Group,[260] which proposed a code to regulate foreign investors, and in 1976 by the OECD, which developed guidelines for MNE.[261] In 1972 ECOSOC looked into the role and impact of the MNE and their accountability to host countries. Three years later, in 1975, the Commission on International Investment and Transnational Corporations seemed to answer the South's demands.[262] The Commission's main task was to draft a code of conduct for relations between MNE and host states and for corporate accountability.[263] Its Draft Code of Conduct on Transnational Corporations, finalised in 1990, was opposed by the Northern countries in 1992.[264] Various international institutions have drafted voluntary codes of conduct both within and outside UN machinery,[265] but MNE still operate outside international and domestic law. Shedrack Agbakwa describes this situation as 'induced and typical of the current Northern-dominated global order'.[266]

Consequently, the only opening for the United Nations to take measures to promote economic and social cooperation was through providing humanitarian assistance or acting as an instrument for the development policy of the North.

The approach of the North to the economic and social problems of the South was determined by the Cold War and the liberalisation of the global economy between the 1970s and 1990s. The changing tasks of the Bretton Woods institutions and increasing focus on Southern countries actually facilitated the

---

[260] The Andean Group is a trade organisation established by the Treaty of Cartagena in 1969 and including Bolivia, Chile, Colombia, Ecuador, and Peru. Venezuela joined in 1973, and Chile and Peru have since left the group. The group created a free trade area called the Andean Pact in 1992.

[261] Gutto, *Human and Peoples' Rights*, 98; Baker, "Tightening The Toothless Vise", 107–141.

[262] Chen, "Introduction to Contemporary Law", 138.

[263] Gloria, "Internationales Wirtschaftsrecht", 558; Voon, "Multinational Enterprises", 242.

[264] The latest draft is in UN Doc E/1990/94 (1990).

[265] Examples are Consumer Protection Guidelines, the World Health Organization (WHO) International Code of Marketing of Breast-Milk Substitutes, and the international Tripartite Declaration of Principles concerning Multinational Enterprises and Social Policy. Voon, "Multinational Enterprises", 243; Fiona Macmillan, "Making Corporate Power Global", *International Trade Law Review* 1999, 9, cited in: Voon, "Multinational Enterprises", 242.

[266] Agbakwa, "A Line in the Sand", 4.

liberalisation of the global economy and the U.S. Cold War policy. In 1990 former World Bank President Barber Conable described the main paradigm for linking development policy to the global liberal economy as follows:

> If I were to characterize the past decade, the most remarkable thing was the generation of a global consensus that market forces and economic efficiency were the best was to achieve the kind of growth which is the best antidote to poverty.[267]

As mentioned above, Tthe Cold War partners directly used military, financial, and economic aid to Southern countries to further their interests, while the former colonial powers used bilateral strategies in their relations with their former territories after the end of the Second World War. However, after the re-examination of its Cold War policy in the 1960s, the United States and former European colonial powers began to shift from bilateral to multilateral strategies.

The shift in focus of the Bretton Woods institutions away from post-war reconstruction and the breakdown of the par value system allowed the United States to implement its development policy through the international financial institutions in the 1970s. When they began to focus on the South, these institutions based their operations on the liberal economic ideology established by the Group of Seven (the United States, UK, Canada, France, Germany, Italy, and Japan).[268] Claiming to find a solution for the economic problems of the South through the liberal economy, the international financial institutions used credits and long-term projects to enforce macroeconomic policies.[269]

The conditions they imposed were influenced by the complementary principles of stabilisation and structural adjustment. Stabilisation focused on short- to medium-term measures, for example, reducing expenditures to address balance of payment problems, while structural adjustment focused on long-term economic issues.[270]

The conditions of the Bretton Woods institutions are based on free trade and laissez-faire capitalism.[271] Liberalisation, privatisation, and the creation of laws that facilitate commercial transactions and foreign investment are

[267] R.J. Douthwaite, *The Growth Illusion: How Economic Growth Has Enriched the Few, Impoverished the Many, and Endangered the Planet* (Dartington, UK: Green Books, 1998), 63.

[268] Thomas, in "International Financial Institutions", 166, describes the international financial institutions as looking 'through neo-liberal tinted glasses' for their policy in the South.

[269] Pahuja, "Technologies of Empire", 758; Thomas, "International Financial Institutions", 167.

[270] Georges Chapelier and Hamid Tabatabai, "Development and Adjustment, Stabilization, Structural Adjustment and UNDP Policy," UNDP Policy Discussion Paper (New York: United Nations Development Program, 1989), 19; Griesgraber and Gunter, introduction to *The World Bank: Lending on a Global Scale*, xiv.

[271] World Bank, *World Development Report 1991*, Oxford: Oxford University Press 1991, 152; David Williams, "Aid and Sovereignty: Quasi-States and the International Financial Institutions," *Review of International Studies* 26 (2000), 567.

the cornerstones of their policy.[272] Reform of fiscal policy and the financial sector, such as exchange rate liberalisation, and reform of the state tax and transfer system are important conditions for financial liberalisation, while deregulation of trade and the investment regime is an important condition for trade liberalisation. Liberalisation foresees sectoral reform in the agricultural, industrial, and social sectors.[273]

The Bretton Woods institutions use privatisation as one of their main instruments for restructuring Southern economies.[274] Privatisation reduces states' role in determining economic issues, opens states to foreign investment, and replaces the ruling powers with the market. Since the 1980s privatisation has been implemented as a macroeconomic policy even for the main political goods such as health care, education, and security.[275] While the North has been unwilling to establish effective international laws to control the activities of the MNE,[276] as demanded by the South, it has made more and more room for foreign investment and MNE in international law through its liberal policies.[277]

With the push to abandon their own economic policies and accept the macroeconomic policies prescribed by the North, little by little the Southern countries lost their decision-making power over their economies, and their governments became instruments for the implementation of the Open Door Policy. In fact, these policies indirectly handed over the economic decision-making power of the developing countries to the international financial institutions dominated by the North.[278]

Although the stated aims of the Bretton Woods institutions were to implement macroeconomic policy and improve conditions in the South, the reality since the late 1970s has been different. The protectionist policy of the powerful countries was the most important cause of both World Wars, but the Bretton

---

[272] Antony Anghie, "Time Present and Time Past: Globalization, International Financial Institutions and the Third World", *New York University Journal of International Law and Politics* 32 (2000), 2, 247.

[273] Giovanni Andre Cornia and Julius Court, *Inequality, Growth and Poverty in the Era of Liberalisation and Globalisation*, Policy Brief No. 4 (Helsinki: United Nations University World Institute for Development Economic Research, 2001), 17; Griesgraber and Gunter, introduction to *The World Bank: Lending on a Global Scale*, xiv; Conforti, *Law and Practice of the United Nations*, 241; Baker, "Tightening The Toothless Vise", 92.

[274] Schlemmer-Schulte, "Global Business", 5.

[275] Thomas, "International Financial Institutions", 168; Berstermann, *Das Einmischungsverbot im Völkerrecht*, 48; Saladin Al-Jurf, "Good Governance and Transparency: Their Impact on Development", *Transnational Law and Contemporary Problems* 9 (1999), 193, 206; Graham Bird, "Reforming the IMF: Should the Fund Abandon Conditionality?" *New Economy* 7 (2000), 214.

[276] Girvan, *Corporate Imperialism*, 11–12; Sweezy, "Corporation, the State, and Imperialism", 2.

[277] Baker, "Tightening The Toothless Vise", 104.

[278] Ibid.

Woods institutions and other international economic organisations barely considered the traditional economic structures of the Southern states or their weak economies compared with those of the North. Their policy has contradicted the demands of the South since the Second World War and actually hinders their natural economic process.[279]

Despite the fact that self-determination of political, social, and economic issues is one of the main principles of international law, the Bretton Woods institutions have increasingly influenced the economies of the Southern countries. Ignoring its demands to protect its economies, the international economic organisations and international economic law have facilitated foreign investment and the penetration of the MNE into the markets of the South. Hence, the principle of equality among unequals has turned the South into a market for the North.

In contrast, the North uses its protectionist policies in areas where the Southern countries appear to threaten Northern markets.[280] The prices of major commodities sold by the South, such as copper, sugar, rubber, iron ore, timber, and cotton, have fallen considerably since the implementation of the Bretton Woods policies. As a consequence, countries in Latin America and Africa lost more than US$ 55 billion in export earnings between 1980 and 1984.[281]

The model of the North—linking liberalisation of the global economy to development policy—facilitated the Open Door Policy through the international economic organisations and international economic law. This policy had economic, political, and social consequences for the South from the 1970s to the 1990s,[282] contributing to political instability throughout the 1980s. The international financial institutions claimed to instil political liberalisation through economic liberalisation, but their policies undermined the establishment of democracy and played a part in the appearance of anarchy and civil war in Angola, Sudan, Rwanda, Sierra Leone, and Latin America between 1950 and 1980.[283] Some international lawyers maintain that the policies of the Bretton Woods institutions are an important causal factor in the absence of effective

[279] Timothy A. Canova, Claire Moore Dickerson, and Katherine V.W. Stone, "Labor and Finance as Inevitably Transnational: Globalization Demands a Sophisticated and Transnational Lens", *San Diego Law Review* 41 (2004), 109.

[280] UN World Commission on Environment and Development, *Our Common Future*, (Oxford: Oxford University Press 1987), para. 19.

[281] Ibid., paragraph 35.

[282] Baker, "Tightening The Toothless Vise", 104; Mark E. Denham and Mark Owen Lombardi, "Perspectives on Southern Sovereignty: Problems with(out) Borders", in *Perspectives on Southern Sovereignty, The Postmodern Paradox*, ed. Mark E. Denham and Mark Owen Lombardi (New York: Macmillan Publishers, 1996), 7.

[283] Thomas, "International Financial Institutions", 166; Denham and Lombardi, "Perspectives on Southern Sovereignty", 7.

government. Michel Chossudovsky argues that structural adjustment programs in the 1980s were a factor in the appearance of the phenomenon in Somalia and Rwanda, and Anne Orford sees the policies of the international financial institutions as contributing to ethnic tensions in Yugoslavia.[284] Rodwan Abourharb and David Cingranelli examine political destabilisation, including anti-government protests and riots, resulting from the Bretton Woods policies in the 131 developing countries since 1981.[285]

The economic consequences of the Bretton Woods policies are clearer than their political consequences.[286] The effect of the Northern economic model on the Southern states was first evident in August 1982, when Mexico failed to pay either the interest or the principal on its foreign debt. State bankruptcy also appeared in many countries in Africa and Asia.[287] The Southern debt crisis mainly influenced the structural adjustment policy of the Bretton Woods institutions in the 1980s but also made the debt crisis more difficult to correct. Sub-Saharan Africa's external debt was US$6 billion in 1970, US$80 billion by the mid-1980s, and more than US$112 billion by 1989, after the Bretton Woods institutions took measures against the debt crisis.[288] The increasing debt has brought economic consequences including hyperinflation, declining production, and fiscal imbalance.[289] The per capita GDP of Southern countries declined by approximately 10 percent in the 1980s.[290]

Liberal economic policies such as privatisation, which ignored states' unique political and economic features, had direct and indirect social consequences. For example, the budget cuts in social and health services that were part of many macroeconomic reforms hit the poor hard and increased inequalities within states.[291]

---

284 Cited in Anghie, "Time Present and Time Past", 263.

285 Rodwan Abourharb and David Cingranelli, *Human Rights and Structural Adjustment* (Cambridge: Cambridge University Press, 2006).

286 Bade Onimode, Introduction to *The IMF, the World Bank and the African Debt, Volume 2, The Social and Political Impact*, ed. Bade Onimode (London: Zed Books, 1989), 3.

287 Mingst and Karns, *The United Nations in the Post-Cold War Era*, 355, 465.

288 World Bank, *World Development Report 1990*, Washington 1990, 225.

289 Trevor Parfitt, "The Politics of Adjustment in Africa with Special Reference to Egypt", Cairo Papers in Social Science, The Economics and Politics of Structural Adjustment in Egypt, Third Annual Symposium, Monograph 16 (1993), 3, 3.

290 UN World Commission on Environment and Development, *Our Common Future*, (Oxford: Oxford University Press 1987), para. 36.

291 Shihata, *The World Bank*, 9; Evans, Introduction, 15; Baker, "Tightening The Toothless Vise", 104; Gopal Garuda, "Lender of Last Resort: Rethinking IMF Conditionality", *Harvard International Law Review* 20 (1998), 36, 38; Jason Morgan-Foster, "The Relationship of IMF Structural Adjustment Programs to Economic, Social and Cultural Rights: The Argentine Case Revisited", *Michigan Journal of International Law* 24 (2003), 577, 583; Mark Weisbrot, "Another IMF Crash", *The Nation*, 19 December 2001, 6–7; Ross P. Buckley, "A Tale of

After the Cold War

The hope for a more effective role for the United Nations in promoting international peace, security, and economic and social prosperity on the one hand and the single superpower position of the United States on the other have been the major influences on the content, effort and consequences of the international community's economic and social approach since the Cold War. Many paradigms—good governance, the Washington Consensus, sustainable development, humanitarian assistance—arose or were refined during this period, but the Washington Consensus and sustainable development were the most prominent and far-reaching. The former clearly was the model for the North, based on the liberalisation of the global economy, but the latter is murkier.

The post-Cold War period ushered in a more systematic application of the North's concept and measures and a clearer discrepancy between the model of the North and the demands of the South to address the economic and social problems of the South. The section below describes the international community's approach and efforts driven by the concepts of sustainable development and the Washington Consensus.

Sustainable Development and the Demands of the South

Sustainable development links environmental and development issues and is one of the most interesting concepts in international law. The link was pointed out as early as 1962, although the term was first used in 1980.[292] The 1987 report of United Nations World Commission on Environment and Development (WCED), or Brundtland Commission, entitled "Our Common Future", which was based on General Assembly Resolution 38/161 (1983), popularised the concept.[293] In the beginning sustainable development aimed to relate development to the environment, mainly in reference to the North. Since then, however, it has evolved to cover development policy concerning

---

Two Crises: The Search for the Enduring Reforms of the International Financial System", *UCLA Journal of International Law and Foreign Affairs* 6 (2001), 1, 42–43; John. V. Paddock, "Comment, IMF Policy and the Argentine Crisis", *University of Miami Inter-American Law Review* 34 (2002), 155, 158–159.

[292] National Strategies for Sustainable Development, World Conservation Strategy: Living Resource Conservation for Sustainable Development, Sustainable Development timeline, http://www.iisd.org/rio+5/timeline/sdtimeline.htm. This Web page provides general information about the progress of the link between development and the environment.

[293] GA/Res/38/161 of 19 December 1983: *Process of Preparation of the Environmental Perspective to the Year 2000 and Beyond*. "Our Common Future" was annexed to A/42/427: Development and International Co-operation: Environment of 11 December 1987.

the South.[294] In the 21st century the importance of establishing a global policy for environmental problems has loomed increasingly larger, calling for a clear legal space in international law.[295]

There is clearly an important link between the economic and social problems in the South and global environmental issues.[296] However, changing the original version of the concept of sustainable development so that Southern economic and social problems take the stage alongside global environmental issues makes the concept more ambiguous, even if it is still appealing.[297] In fact, this retouching has diminished attention to environmental issues in the North and to the link between the economic world order and environmental damage. It has also camouflaged the role of the North in the economic problems of the South.

The first UN conference on environmental issues, the United Nations Conference on the Human Environment, was held in Stockholm in 1972. The regional environmental problems of northern Europe, including acid rain, were the main impetus for the event. The conference's declaration clearly linked development and the environment in terms of the impacts of industrialisation and technological development.[298] Paragraph 4 pointed out that underdevelopment in the South was also a reason for environmental problems.[299]

Few Southern countries took part in the Stockholm conference. A consortium of countries calling themselves the Group of 77, a caucus organisation that helps developing states pursue common goals and develop leverage in UN deliberations, maintained that 'environmental concerns diverted attention from the need for changes in the international power structure'.[300] This concern was regrettably borne out in the following decades.

Our Common Future further clarified the link among development, the environment, and the concept of sustainable development, as well as the link

---

294 Mingst and Karns, *The United Nations in the Post-Cold War Era*, 467.

295 Conforti, *Law and Practice of the United Nations*, 241; Peter Malanczuk, "Sustainable Development: Some Critical Thoughts in the Light of the Rio Conference", in *Sustainable Development and Good Governance*, ed. Konrad Ginther (Dordrecht, Germany: Martinus Nijhoff Publishers, 1995), 23, 25; Chimni, "The World Trade Organization", 71.

296 Stéphanie Giry, *The New York Times Magazine*, December 9, 2007. Climate change has even been cited as a reason to advocate for military policies to deal with the increased danger of conflict and war over dwindling resources A retired U.S. admiral wrote in a military officers' report on incorporating the destabilising effect of climate change in weak states into U.S. defence strategy, 'Climate change will provide the conditions that will extend the war on terror'.

297 GA/Conf.151/26 (Volume I) of 12 August 1992. The Rio Conference on the Environment and Development (UNCED) took place from 3 to 14 June 1992.

298 Declaration of the United Nations Conference on Human Environment, paragraphs 3 and 4.

299 Ibid.

300 Mingst and Karns, *The United Nations in the Post-Cold War Era*, 465.

between sustainable development and the South.[301] The following definition of sustainable development in Part II of this report may be the clearest explanation of the concept and for this reason is repeated here.

> Humanity has the ability to make development sustainable to ensure that it meets the needs of the present without compromising the ability of future generations to meet their own needs. The concept of sustainable development does not imply limits—not absolute limits but limitation imposed by the present state of technology and social organization on environmental resources and by the ability of the biosphere to absorb the effects of human activities.[302]

Until now this has been the only attempt to define 'sustainable development'. It raises a number of questions—for example, the meaning of 'needs', the place for such a concept in a capitalist economic world order, the linking of sustainability to the causality of under-development in the South, neo-colonialist policies, and the sin quo non link between development and democracy.[303] Nevertheless, *Our Common Future*, including the excerpt quoted above, was significant in many respects and sent a message to the North that it should consider future generations and other societies and economies when promoting development. The report pointed out the following environmental damage caused by the North in the South: 1) the use of natural resources, industry, and technology with no regard for people in other parts of the world, 2) unrestricted environmental damage, especially in the South, and 3) exacerbation of economic, social, and political problems in the south in the name of profit for the North. The only responsibility that the report attributes to the South is the environmental damage resulting from poverty,[304] as explained in paragraph 8 quoted below.

> But poverty itself pollutes the environment, creating environmental stress in a different way. Those who are poor and hungry will often destroy their immediate environment in order to survive. They will cut down forests; their livestock will overgraze grasslands; they will overuse marginal land; and in growing numbers they will crowd into congested cities.[305]

---

[301] Brundtland described development and the environment as inseparable: 'The "environment" is where we all live; and 'development' is what we all do in attempting to improve our lot within that abode'. Gro Harlem Brundtland, Chairman's Foreword to *Our Common Future*, http://www.un-documents.net/ocf-cf.htm.

[302] UN World Commission on Environment and Development, *Our Common Future*, (Oxford: Oxford University Press 1987), para. 27.

[303] Eren Kirmizialtin, "Sürdürülebilir Kalkinma", in *Ekonomik Kurumlar ve Kavramlar Sözlügü, Elestirel Bir Giris*, ed. Fikret Başkaya and Aydın Ördek (Ankara: Özgür Üniversite Yayınları, 2008), 1059–1063.

[304] Gro Harlem Brundtland, Chairman's Foreword, *Our Common Future*, http://www.un-documents.net/ocf-cf.htm.

[305] Ibid.

Since the 1992 United Nations Conference on Environment and Development in Rio de Janeiro and the resulting Rio Declaration, intended to guide sustainable development around the world, the link between development and the environment has taken on a different dimension. First, environmental issues in the North have taken a back seat to those in the South. One of the most important reasons for this was the North's reluctance to jeopardise its profits and economic sovereignty. Another was the North's exploitation of the notion of sustainable development in order to implement its development policy concerning the South. This tendency was clearly demonstrated first in the Rio Declaration[306] and later in other international conferences and documents on sustainable development.[307]

Today sustainable economic and social development appear mainly as a new version of the development policy of the North with a 'sustainable' dimension. The meaning of 'sustainability' is still an open question and will remain so until current global economic policy is examined as a cause of those economic and social problems. While the North mostly uses the notion as an instrument of its development policy, the measures called for by the South are given lip service but rarely taken seriously. It is no accident that measures to address environmental issues have often met the same fate as measures to address economic and social problems in the South: they have no legally binding force.[308]

The Model of the North—The Washington Consensus

The liberalisation of the global economy according to neoliberal policies was one of the main targets of the new international legal order after the end of the Cold War. With the dissolution of the Soviet Union's alternative political and economic ideology, the main barrier to the liberalisation of the global economy disappeared.[309] This historical fact facilitated the North's access to Southern countries. Under these circumstances, the Washington Consensus appeared

---

[306] GA/Conf.151/26 (Volume I) of 12 August 1992. The Rio Conference on the Environment and Development (UNCED) took place from 3 to 14 June 1992.

[307] Examples are the 1995 Social Summit in Copenhagen, 1995 Fourth Women's Conference in Beijing, 1996 Habitat II Conference in Istanbul, United Nations Millennium Declaration of 8 September 2000, and Johannesburg Declaration on Sustainable Development of September 2002.

[308] Mingst and Karns, *The United Nations in the Post-Cold War Era*, 467. The most important exception to this rule concerning environmental issues may be the Kyoto Protocol, which was negotiated in December 1997 and became legally binding on February 16, 2005.

[309] Bahram Ghazi Shariat Panahi, *The IMF, the World Bank Group and the Question of Human Rights* (Ardsley, New York: Transnational Publishers, 2005), 46.

as a package presenting neoliberal policies.[310] U.S. dominance was made clear when the Washington-based institutions (IMF, World Bank, and U.S. Treasury Department) were presented as the main actors to implement the measures foreseen under this concept.[311]

The term 'Washington Consensus' was first used in the 1970s in order to implement the neoliberal policy of stability and structural adjustment.[312] In the 1990s John Williamson put the notion on the international agenda. His article[313] on economic policies in Latin America defined the common denominators of stability and structural adjustment policies based on the free market, which were to be implemented in the less-developed countries by the Washington-based institutions. The article identifies the main elements or preconditions of the neoliberal stability and structural adjustment policies as

> [...] fiscal discipline, a redirection of public expenditure priorities towards fields offering both high economic return and potential to improve income distribution, such as primary health care, primary education, and infrastructure, tax reform, interest rate liberalization, a competitive exchange rate, trade liberalization, liberalization of inflows of foreign direct investment, privatization, deregulation and secure property rights.[314]

The WTO and MNE are considered cooperating institutions with the actors of the Washington Consensus.[315] The measures of the Washington Consensus, which affected not only economic but also political and social issues, differed from practice during the Cold War.[316]

310 Francis Fukuyama, *State-Building: Governance and World Order in the 21st Century* (Ithaca, New York: Cornell University Press, 2004), 5; Thomas, "International Financial Institutions", 166.

311 Panahi, *The IMF*, 46; John Williamson, "From Reform Agenda to Damaged Brand Name," *Finance and Development*, September 2003, 10.

312 Metin Altıok, "Washington Konsensüsü", in *Ekonomik Kurumlar ve Kavramlar Sözlügü, Elestirel Bir Giris*, ed. Fikret Başkaya and Aydın Ördek (Ankara: Özgür Üniversite Yayınları, 2008), 1297.

313 John Williamson, *The Progress of Policy Reform in Latin America, Policy Analyses in International Economics* (Washington: D.C: Institute for International Economics1990), 9; Panahi, *The IMF*, 46.

314 Panahi, *The IMF*, 46.

315 World Bank, *Reforming Public Institutions and Strengthening Governance: A World Bank Strategy*, Washington, DC, 2000; World Bank, *World Development Report 2002*, Washington, DC, 2002, 99.

316 World Bank, *Accelerated Development in Sub-Saharan Africa* (Washington, DC, 1981); World Bank, *Toward Sustained Development in Sub-Saharan Africa*, (Washington, DC, 1984); World Bank, *The Sub-Saharan Africa Long-Term Perspective Study* (Washington, DC, 1989), cited in Shihata, *The World Bank*, 55; World Bank, *Development and Human Rights: The Role of the World Bank*, (Washington, DC, 1992), 63.

At the end of the 1990s, when the negative consequences of the neoliberal policies began to appear, the international community tried to 'fix' the Washington Consensus through additional reforms.[317] In addition to a number of economic measures, the reforms included the requirement of a functional government as a precondition for effective implementation of the measures promoted by the Bretton Woods institutions. Ibrahim F. Shihata explained this as follows:

> The World Bank's current attention to governance issues grew in part out of the expansion of its structural adjustment lending operations in the 1980s. Through these experiences, the Bank came to realize that the ability of developing countries to engage in structural adjustment depended on the quality of the government carrying out the adjustment program.[318]

The notion of 'good governance', also used by advocates of sustainable development, appeared as part of the Washington Consensus.[319] In practice this meant states' ability to carry out the decisions of the Bretton Woods institutions and implement liberal policies. Efficiency, transparency, and political liberalisation (democracy, participation, and attention to human rights) were defined as criteria for good governance.[320] The international financial institutions and the Northern states have often imposed political liberalisation as a prerequisite for funding.[321] As a consequence of its liberalisation policy, the North also interferes in social issues within states, for example, by demanding cuts in government employees' wages and other social benefits.[322]

Today, almost 20 years after the implementation of the Washington Consensus and the paradigm of sustainable development, the world is little better

---

317 Dani Rodrik, "After Neoliberalism, What?" Remarks at a Conference on Alternatives to Neoliberalism, Washington DC, 22–23 June 2002, http:/kgshome.harvard.edu/~Sdrodrik/shortpieces.-html (visited 31 March 2007).

318 Shihata, *The World Bank*, 54–55.

319 Seppänen, *Good Governance*, 16.

320 World Bank, *World Development Report 2002*, 104; IMF, "The Role of the IMF in Governance Issues: Guidance Notes accepted by the IMF Executive Board on 4 August 1997", www.imf.org/external/np/sec/nb/1997/nb9715.htm#13, visited on 3 December 2002; World Bank, *World Development Report 2002*, 99–104. Seppänen, in *Good Governance*, 19–20, describes good governance under the Washington Consensus as 'state policies that best enable the functioning of the market economy and free global competition'.

321 Thomas, "International Financial Institutions", 166. Some international organisations established by the Northern countries also made the link between political and economic liberalisation. For example, the Development Assistance Committee of the OECD pointed out 'a vital connection between open, democratic and accountable political systems, individual rights and the effective and equitable economic systems' in 1989.

322 Seppänen, *Good Governance*, 87–88; World Bank, *Reforming Public Institutions and Strengthening Governance: A World Bank Strategy*, Washington, DC 2000, and *World Development Report 2002*, 99, 105.

off than before the 1990s. Nearly 11 million people died in 2002 alone from infectious diseases, and at least as many people died in natural catastrophes or war.[323] Twenty percent of the world's population lives on less than one dollar a day.[324]

While one of the most important aims of proponents of both the Washington Consensus and sustainable development is the improvement of economic and social conditions in the developing countries, many scholars interpret these concepts as contradictory. The measures taken under the aegis of development do not automatically promote economic, social, and cultural rights.[325] Marie Claire Cordonier has pointed out the incompatibility between the current international trade debate and environmental and social concerns,[326] and Middleton and O'Keefe (2003) have described the discrepancy between neoliberal policy and sustainable development.[327]

Sustainable development alone was regrettably not successful in changing the rhetoric of the development policy of the North. Since Rio de Janeiro, few planned measures have been realized.[328] On the contrary, the concept of sustainable development, even though it contains many elements of the NIEO, has undermined and diluted the demands of the South.

Practice has shown that the North continues to ignore demands from the South to change the economic and political world order to solve its problems. Although Southern countries see financial and technical aid as a short-term measure for economic development, the North has put such aid at the centre of its development policy.[329] Many advocate for Northern countries to devote even larger percentages of their GNP to development assistance. But even aid policy is hypocritical in many respects. In fact, the Northern countries have invested less and less in foreign aid since the Cold War. Except during the Cold War, financial assistance from the rich countries to the poor countries

[323] Muna Ndulo, "Imagine a World without Hunger: The Hurdles of Global Justice", *Cornell International Law Journal* 39 (2006), 3, 781.

[324] Cho, "Doha's Development", 166.

[325] CESCR General Comment 2 on International technical assistance measures (Art. 22), E/1990/23, Fourth session, 02/02/90, para.7; Panahi, *The IMF*, 40.

[326] Marie-Claire Cordonier Segger, "Integrating Social and Economic Development and Environmental Protection in World Trade Law", in *Sustainable Development in World Trade Law*, ed. Markus W. Gehring and Marie-Claire Cordonier Segger (The Hague: Kluwer Law International, 2005), 129–152, 633; Cho, "Doha's Development", 167.

[327] N. Middleton and P. O'Keefe, *Rio Plus Ten: Politics, Poverty and Environment* (London, Sterling, VA, 2003).

[328] Ibid; Alan Terry, Jennifer Hill and Wendy Woodland, "Uniting National Aspirations and Local Implementation in Sustainable Development: An Introduction", in *Sustainable Development: National Aspirations, Local Implementation*, ed. Jennifer Hill, Alan Terry and Wend Woodland (Aldershot, UK: Ashgate Publishing, 2006), 2.

[329] Schlemmer-Schulte, "Global Business", 10.

has remained mostly a promise which has not been delivered. In 1961 the wealthy states promised to invest 0.7 per cent of their GNP in poor countries as 'official development assistance', but only four small countries, Denmark, the Netherlands, Norway, and Sweden, fulfilled this commitment.[330] The current global average for overseas development assistance is only 0.28 percent.[331] The hypocrisy of Northern development policy is also clearly seen in its protection of domestic trade through the Open Door Policy. According to the 2005 Human Development Report, the rich countries invest $ 1 billion *a year* in agriculture in poor countries but spend nearly $ 1 billion a *day* to subsidise overproduction in agriculture domestically.[332]

As a consequence of neoliberal policies both under and since the Washington Consensus, the prospects of development by the Bretton Woods institutions are criticized from different quarters.[333] While democracy and development increasingly appear as important issues for the activities of the financial institutions as well as the WTO, few if any reforms have taken place in this area.[334]

Jean-Marc Coicaud and Veijo Heiskanen maintain that measures under the Washington Consensus actually increase inequalities.[335] Joseph E. Stiglitz, former Chief Economist of the World Bank, describes the IMF's policy of liberalisation in the Southern countries as premature and undemocratic and points out that it has caused economic crisis and instability.[336] He reproaches the IMF as causing the Asian financial crises of 1997 and bringing political destabilization because of its lack of accountability and non-democratic operation.[337] The policies of the Bretton Woods institutions have led to rapid increases in both the amount of debt and the number of indebted states. The debt of the developing

330 Dolman, *Resources*, 85.

331 Schlemmer-Schulte, "Global Business", 10.

332 World Bank, *Human Development Report 2005*, Washington, DC 2005, 75.

333 Antonio F. Perez, "Legal Framework for the Economic Transition in Iraq—Occupation Under the Law of War vs. Global Governance Under the Law of Peace", *The Transnational Lawyer* 18 (2004), 53; Daniel Daianu, "Institutional and Policy Variety, the Role of IFIs and Economic Development", in *International Institutions and Multinational Enterprises, Global Players—Global Markets*, ed. John-ren Chen (Cheltenham, UK: Edward Elgar, 2004, 196).

334 Chimni, "The World Trade Organization", 6, 34; Rolland, "Developing Country Coalitions", 550–551.

335 Jean-Marc Coicaud and Veijo Heiskanen, Conclusion of "International Organisations, The Evolution of international Politics, and Legitimacy", in *The Legitimacy of International Organisations*, ed. Jean-Marc Coicaud and Veijo Heiskanen (Tokyo: The United Nations University Press, 2001), 54.

336 Joseph E. Stiglitz, "Failure of the Fund: Rethinking the IMF Response," Harvard International Review 23 (2001), 14.

337 Joseph E. Stiglitz, *Globalization and its Discontents* (New York: Norton, 2003), 251–252.

countries amounted to US$ 567 billion in 1980 and rose to US$ 1.6 trillion in 1997 and US$ 2.2 trillion in 2000.[338] Consequently, capital flowed from the North to the South in 1981 but from the South to the North by the end of the 1990s. In 1998, the sum of US$ 30 billion moved from the Southern countries to the Northern countries.[339] Examples abound of the negative effects of World Bank projects on local populations.[340]

The most critical issues in the WTO have not been addressed, and there is no will among state parties to do so. Despite the fact that developing countries constitute the majority in the WTO, their 'relatively marginalized position'[341] makes it difficult to link development to world trade. Because of a growing consensus on the insufficiency of trade liberalisation[342] for development and the active role of trade in development since 11 September 2001, the members of the WTO have focused on development issues in the Doha Development Round, the trade-negotiation round of the WTO that began in November 2001, and opted for a trade negotiation agenda named the 'Doha Development Agenda' (DDA).[343] While the Agenda put the needs of the developing countries into the centre, Paragraph 2[344] pointed out the important role of trade in the promotion of economic development and alleviation of poverty.[345] The major elements of the Doha Development Agenda are trade liberalisation for agricultural products and services, market access for non-agricultural products, a review of existing rules on subsidies and trade agreements, trade facilitation, intellectual property, dispute settlement procedures, trade and the envi-

[338] Mingst and Karns, *The United Nations in the Post-Cold War Era*, 355, 465.

[339] Oxley, "North/South Dimensions of a New World Order", 104.

[340] Panahi, *The IMF*, 40–44. Examples include the Land Bank Program in Brazil at the end of the 1990s, the Kedung Ombo Project in Indonesia between 1985 and1989, the Quinghani Project in 1999, and oil projects in Africa.

[341] Rolland, "Developing Country Coalitions", 483.

[342] Henning Jessen, "Trade and Development Law", in *Sustainable Development in World Trade Law*, ed. Markus W. Gehring and Marie-Claire Cordonier Segger (The Hague: Kluwer Law International, 2005), 73–126.

[343] WTO, Ministerial Declaration, 14 November 2001, WT/MIN(01)/DEC/1(20 November 2001), para. 2; Wouters and Coppens, "International Economic Policy-Making", 277; *Simon Lester*, "Aid for More Than Just Trade: The Case for a Role for the WTO in Development Aid", *University of New South Wales Law Journal* 30 (2007), 2, 332; Markus W. Gehring, Marie-Claire Cordonier Segger, and Martin Endicott, "Conclusion" in *Sustainable Development in World Trade Law*, edited by Markus W. Gehring and Marie-Claire Cordonier Segger (The Hague: Kluwer Law International, 2005), 632, 642.

[344] Ministerial Declaration, Ministerial Conference—Fourth Session, Doha, Qatar (14 November 2001), WTO Doc. WT/MIN(01)/DEC/W/1, para.2.

[345] Jessen, "Trade and Development Law" 73–126; Gehring, Segger and Endicott, "Conclusion", 632–633.

ronment, and a review of special and differential treatment provisions.[346] The developed nations pushed for including the so-called 'Singapore issues' (transparency in government procurement, trade facilitation, trade and investment, and trade and competition) in any new trade negotiations despite the opposition of most developing countries.[347]

There was little progress concerning development issues in the Doha Round ministerial meetings in Cancún, Mexico, in 2003 or in Hong Kong in 2005.[348] A typical example was the continual shifting of agricultural measures. At the ministerial meeting in Hong Kong, states promised to eliminate agricultural export subsidies by the year 2013, but they still do not agree on plans to realise this promise.[349] The North has weakened the approach of the developing country coalition[350] for a more effective role in the WTO by promoting the issue of 'aid for trade'.[351]

Today the 'development deficiency'[352] of the WTO is still acute.[353] In fact, according to developing countries, the organisation still works for the benefit of the developed countries while complicating the developing countries' access to international markets.[354]

The activities, economic and political power, and human rights violations of the MNE cause considerable concern in Southern countries,[355] but in spite

---

346 Cho, "Doha's Development", 169–170; *Doha Ministerial Declaration*, paras. 27 and 38–41; WTO Secretariat, *World Trade Report 2003*, xix; Wouters and Coppens, "International Economic Policy-Making", 278.

347 Ian F. Fergusson, *World Trade Organization Negotiations: The Doha Development Agenda*, CRS Report for Congress, January 18, 2008, Congressional Research Service, http://www s.nationalaglawcenter.org/assets/crs/RL32060.pdf.

348 Cho, "Doha's Development", 171.

349 Judith Wise, "Hunger and Thieves: Anticipating the Impact of WTO Subsidies Reform on Land and Survival in Brazil," *American Law Review* 31 (2006–2007), 2, 531.

350 Roland, *The African Exprerience*, 550; Lester, in *Partners in Development*, 347, writes, '[...] a narrow aid initiative that is limited to "trade issues" is the wrong approach. If trade ministers want to take development seriously, they cannot just carve out a safe of aid to operate in. Development aid is not a full solution to the problem of underdevelopment'.

351 Wouters and Coppens, "International Economic Policy-Making", 278, 314.

352 Celso L.N. Amorim, "The WTO from the Perspective of a Developing Country", *Fordham International Law Journal* 24 (2000), 95 ff.

353 Cho, "Doha's Development", 166.

354 Faizel Ismail, "How Can Least-Developed Countries and Other Small, Weak and Vulnerable Economies Also Gain from the Doha Development Agenda on the Road to Hong Kong?", *Journal of World Trade* 40 (2006), 1, 3, 51; Cho, "Doha's Development", 166.

355 Marion Weschka, "Human Rights and Multinational Enterprises: How Can Multinational Enterprises Be Held Responsible for Human Rights Violations Committed Abroad?" *Zeitschrift für ausländisches öffentliches Recht und Völkerrecht* 66 (2006), 626; *Commentary on the Norms on the Responsibilities of Transnational Corporations Business Enterprises with Regard to Human Rights*, UN Doc.E/CN.4/Sub.2/2003/38/Rev.2, 26/08/2003, http://documents-dds-ny.un.org/UNDOC/GEN/G03/160/18/pdf/G0316018, visited July 7, 2006; Joseph, "Taming

of various international guidelines and codes promulgated by international organisations, no international legal measures to protect weak states against the MNE and no 'new international law of multinational enterprises'[356] appear on the horizon.

In fact, the policies under the Washington Consensus have acted as none other than an instrument for the Open Door Policy. Sabine Schlemmer-Schulte describes this situation as follows:

> [...] this financing leads the Southern countries to open themselves up to the North, while there is no reciprocal opening of the North to the South, since only Southern countries ask for IMF financing to address balance of payments difficulties.[357]

the Leviathans", 172; The coup against Salvador Allende, President of Chile, in 1973 and the killing of 2,000 Ogoni people and destruction of approximately 30 villages in Ogoniland and the role of the Royal Dutch Shell in Nigeria show how far the MNE have been willing to go; Anthony Sampson, *Weltmacht ITT: die politische Geschäfte eines multinationalen Konzerns*, (Frankfurt: Büchergilde Gutenberg, 1975); Baez et al., "Multinational Enterprises", 185, 233.

356 Dine, "Multinational Enterprises", 81.

357 Schlemmer-Schulte, "Global Business", 14.

Conclusion

The Cold War shaped international law for more than 40 years, and its end in the 1990s brought the aspiration for a more peaceful world order based on law and a more effective role for the United Nations. Twenty years later, the international legal order is more complex than ever. This more complex construct has hardly ushered in a more peaceful world. On the contrary, the process and practices of international law have shown so many inconsistencies that they cast doubt on the legitimacy of both international law and the United Nations.

After the 1990s the influence on international law switched from the Cold War to the United States as the sole superpower. Especially after 11 September 2001, the world saw a new configuration in which the United States more clearly determines the process and context of international relations but also international law.

In the age of globalisation, states with effective governments are still the most important precondition for the stability of the international order. This work makes numerous arguments to support this assertion and examines various complications in cases of the absence of effective government, but it primarily questions the international community's recognition and definition of the phenomenon, its proposed solutions, and its praxis.

The notion of the 'failed state' captures the international community's paradigm for the absence of effective government. It is also a prototype that illustrates how political issues influence international law, how they are interpreted, to what extent power and international politics determine international law, and how successful such a paradigm can be as a long-term solution for international peace and security.

The preceding chapters illustrate that the absence of effective government cannot be defined in an internal context alone and is not a new phenomenon, despite the attention it has drawn from the international community at the beginning of the 21st century. The United States first put the issue on the international legal agenda to facilitate its foreign policy, and the international community's recognition of the phenomenon in each country has largely depended on that policy. Both Somalia and Afghanistan experienced the absence of effective government to varying degrees in the beginning of the 1990s, but with guidance from the U.S. Government, the international community intervened militarily in Somalia while ignoring Afghanistan for another decade.

The 'failed state' paradigm clearly shows how terms used to describe states with ineffective governments originate and how they are transferred from international policy to international law. 'Failed state', 'rogue state', and 'the war on terror' have been used so often that we take them for granted without questioning their pejorative meanings or their fragility vis à vis states' right to honour and equal sovereignty in international law.

This work argues that although the international community has confronted the absence of effective government for many years (almost every country in the South has experienced it), it is impossible to group the phenomenon in all countries under one definition. Nor is it possible to identify the international community's typical reaction under international law to countries with ineffective governments. Each case needs to be assessed according to its unique features.

The international community has never questioned the subjectivity of states dealing with the absence of effective government in international law. However, here arises the question of the consistency of the international system and the capacity of the international community to play a more important role in such states than invoking the principles of state sovereignty and self-determination. The recognition of Afghanistan's government after the U.S. military intervention and the Somali government in the context of piracy in the Gulf of Aden rather serve more to this paradigm.

Since the fall of the Soviet Union, political, economic, and military intervention in the South has been justified on the grounds of promoting values such as democracy, human rights, and economic liberalisation instead of 'saving the world from communism'. Under these colours the North has posed as the saviour of the Southern countries while depriving them of their sovereignty. On the one hand the United States, France, and the UK provide the largest amount of bilateral and multilateral foreign aid and loans to the South,[1] but on the other hand they are the largest exporters of arms to the South. In fact, non-intervention—the sine qua non of the principle of sovereignty—has been reduced in praxis to military intervention since the Cold War. Especially since the liberalisation of the global economy, political and economic intervention de facto remain outside the principle of non-intervention.

As a rule, the principle of non-intervention under Article 2/7 of the UN Charter is accepted in cases of the absence of effective government, but exceptions arise in the international community's interpretation of the conditions for applying the principle. The Security Council has not hesitated to interpret

[1] N. Ball, J.D. Friedman, and. C.S. Rossiter, "The Role of International Financial Institutions in Preventing and Resolving Conflict", in David Cortright, ed., *The Price of Peace, Incentives and International Conflict Prevention* (Lanham, Maryland: Rowman & Littlefield, 1997), 260.

cases of the absence of effective government under Chapter VII of the UN Charter, especially when military intervention and international territorial administration are proposed. Generally, Chapter VII is considered applicable when a 'threat to the peace' is identified. Although the Security Council opened the door to military intervention in states dealing with the absence of effective government by referring to Chapter VII, the absence of effective government is not a threat which can be avoided through measures foreseen in Chapter VII. Experience since the 1990s has proven that interpreting the situation in such states as a 'threat to the peace' under Chapter VII is neither adequate nor effective to solve the problem.

The legal basis of international transitional administration is a most important question. The international community used a broader interpretation of Chapter VII to justify international transitional administration, but in fact there is no legal place for it in current international law.

The principle of non-force is also accepted as valid in cases of the absence of effective government, but two issues are problematic in such states. The first is self-defence. In Article 51 of the UN Charter, states dealing with the absence of effective government appear as the actors in 'armed attack' but also as the victims of such attacks. The role of states with ineffective governments as actors in 'armed attack' arose as a major issue in international law after the end of the Cold War, especially after 11 September 2001. Legal analysis shows the fragility of defining the consequences of the absence of effective government as 'armed attack', but in many states dealing with the phenomenon military intervention is exempt from sanction on the grounds of self-defence. This was the case when Israel intervened in Lebanon in 2006 and the Gaza Strip in 2009, the United State intervened in Afghanistan in 2001, and Turkey intervened in Iraq in 2008.

The positions of the international community and the United Nations have been inconsistent and ineffectual in such cases. When Israel bombed the militant group Hamas in the Gaza Strip in December 2008, killing hundreds of Palestinians, UN Secretary-General Ban Ki-moon called for an immediate ceasefire and condemned Israel's 'excessive use of force' but at the same time recognised its right to defend itself from earlier Hamas rocket attacks.[2] Not all Palestinians had supported Hamas, but the Israeli attacks served as a unifying force, at least temporarily.

On the other hand, international law chooses to keep silent about protecting states dealing with the absence of effective government when they are victims of 'armed attack'. In these cases international lawyers call into question the sovereignty of the 'failed states' and fail to address the question of who protects

---

2 "Israel Vows War on Hamas in Gaza", BBC News, 29 December 2009, http://news.bbc.co.uk/2/hi/middle_east/7803711.stm.

such states from military intervention. It is not surprising; therefore, that Turkey sought legitimacy to enter Iraqi Kurdistan militarily in recent years through the permission of the United States rather than through international law.

In cases of military intervention in countries experiencing the absence of ineffective government, the teleological interpretation (reference to the ultimate purpose) of the principle of non-force has no place. Except in instances of multilateral intervention, the interests of third countries are considered more important than the principle of non-force, as in Afghanistan and Iraq.

The right of self-determination in international law is also problematic in the case of states dealing with the absence of effective government. First, it is invoked as a justification for military intervention. From a legal perspective, it is impossible to argue that either unilateral or multilateral military intervention further the internal aspect of self-determination. Praxis also brings this claim into question. Second, the issue of secession as a solution to the absence of effective government, analysed in detail in Chapter 5, has been met with closed eyes by the international community. An example is Somaliland, whose independence is still not recognised even though it is more stable than the rest of Somalia.

Complications in international relations arise consistently in cases of the absence of effective government, although they are different in each case. In harmony with its policy of keeping states within the international law order, the international community has paid lip service to overcoming these complications, but it has mainly ignored the negative effects rather than taking active measures. Especially when complications arise in diplomatic relations as a result of economic problems, every state could take measures to avoid the negative effects, but in practice this does not happen.

The international community's approach to solving the problem of the absence of effective government has taken two forms, state-building and economic and social measures. International transitional administration was actually the end goal of the 'failed state' paradigm, to be accomplished by state-building, nation-building, and attempts to institute democracy, respect for human rights, and self-determination. This work does not cover international transitional administration extensively but raises the question of its adequacy to solve the problem of the absence of effective government in the short or long term because of its ambiguous aims. Without resolving this issue, international transitional administration cannot be an effective solution. In practice, implementation in each case of international transitional administration is sui generis.

Praxis has clearly shown that trying to solve the absence of effective government through military intervention and international transitional administration has no chance of success because the North's approach—easily dismantling states on the one hand and mounting ambitious 'nation-building' projects on the other—takes the interests of the South lightly. Sixteen years after the 1992 U.S. military intervention, Somalia is again on the agenda of the international community and the United Nations because of the rampant piracy in the Gulf of Aden. Such incidents have threatened international shipping since the beginning of the civil war in the early 1990s, and since 2005 international organizations including the International Maritime Organization have expressed concern over their increase. On 7 October 2008 the Security Council adopted Resolution 1838 (2008) under Chapter VII of the UN Charter, which calls on states to

> [...] use, on the high seas and airspace off the coast of Somalia, the necessary means to repress acts of piracy in a manner consistent with the 1982 United Nations Convention on the Law of the Sea.[3]

The most recent resolutions concerning Somalia, however, show that nothing has changed in either the country's situation or the international community's paradigm for the absence of effective government. The complaint that it is difficult for the international community to provide humanitarian assistance in Somalia and act as necessary under Chapter VII of the UN Charter has appeared in every Security Council resolution on the country since the 1990s. Regrettably, these serves neither address the situation nor rescue the international community from the problem.

> While foreigners and wealthy Afghans power air conditioners, hot-water heaters, computers and satellite televisions with private generators, average Kabulis suffered a summer without fans and face a winter without heaters.[4]

This excerpt from an article by Barnett Rubin in 2007 may seem out of place in a work on international law, but it is useful to ask how effective international law can be if the international community is unable to understand what people face in 'a winter without heaters'.

Article 1 of the Universal Declaration of the Human Rights proclaims that

> All human beings are born free and equal in dignity and rights. They are endowed with reason and conscience and should act towards one another in a spirit of brotherhood.[5]

---

3 UN Security Council Department of Public Information, "Security Council Asks Nations with Military Capacity in Area to 'Actively Fight Piracy' on High Seas off Somalia", 7 October 2008, http://un.org/News/Press/docs/2008/sc9467.doc.htm.

4 Barnett R. Rubin, "Saving Afghanistan", *Foreign Affairs* 86 (2007), 1, 66–67.

5 Adopted and proclaimed by General Assembly Resolution 217 A (III) of 10 December 1948.

Forty years after this was written, it is evident in many of the countries the international community triumphantly entered under the banner of reconstruction, including Somalia, Iraq, and Afghanistan, that their people are neither free nor equal nor treated in a spirit of brotherhood. The international community has shown insensitivity to the continual loss of life of people in these territories while mourning the death of each soldier recruited by the foreign powers. Human rights violations have been presented as a justification for military intervention since the 1990s, but the international community has closed its eyes to its own human rights violations in countries such as Afghanistan and Iraq.

Today there are two different legal languages in the international order. The North consigns every incident in the Middle East to the magic category of 'terrorism' to legitimise its actions in these territories. Meanwhile, in the South these incidents are often perceived as heroic attempts to repel foreign invaders or attain justice. The North's increasing use of military intervention to solve the absence of effective government has in fact facilitated the imposition of the Open Door Policy.

This work has shown that an analysis of the historical and international context is indispensable to examine the absence of effective government. Consequently, the solution to the problem can only be found through an economic and social approach concerning the historical and international context. International law has pointed out the role of economic and social measures in securing international peace and security. Yet Chapter 8 argues in detail that the current economic and social approach to solving the absence of effective government is futile in many senses. Its enforcement is mainly determined through the shape and trend of the international law, and it is not the affected states who have the instruments in international law to implement the measures.

Almost every state dealing with the absence of effective government was subsumed under an international legal system established before it came into existence. Few states played any role in establishing this system, which did not consider their cultural, political, or social characteristics. In other words, they were pushed to adopt a system which is alien for them.

The current system of international law is structured neither to protect the political, social, and cultural identity of all states nor to promote their well-being. This can be seen clearly in the structure of this system. Its raison d'être is to eliminate conflict between powerful states. The argument that it serves these powerful states is borne out by the structure and composition of the UN Security Council, the principle of equal opportunity among the powerful states that is the basis of the international economic system, and the Open Door Policy. The North has created the international law-making power, and states dealing with the absence of effective government have recourse to no independent international organization to manage their economic and social problems and no instrument in the international legal system to redress their economic and political grievances. The demands of the South remain demands.

Development policy attempts to address these issues but can work only within the space the international political and economic system allows. It is therefore formulated and primarily serves to camouflage the damage done by the political and economic policy of the powerful states. In this process the North perceives Southern claims such as 'a common heritage' through the lens of colonialism and suspects notions such as aid for trade and, sadly, sustainable development as attempts to subvert its own aims.

The effectiveness of any legal order rests on its recognition by its subjects. If international law does not succeed and continues to be applied differently for the North and the South, it will lose its legitimacy. Without legitimacy, it can only be implemented by force. For many years we have seen the futility of the politics of force in the world. Today the Security Council legitimises military intervention in many states in the South under Chapter IV of the UN Charter on the ever-expanding grounds of confronting 'threats to the peace', but legitimising military intervention is not making the world any safer.

Peace can only be established once international law protects the interests of all nations, respecting and responding to their different cultural values. This ideal can be realised not through aristocracy but through democracy in international law, with the Southern countries taking the stage alongside the Northern lawmakers.

Bibliography

Abdullahi, Mohamed. D. *Fiasco in Somalia: US—UN Intervention*. Occasional Paper 61. Pretoria: Africa Institute of South Africa, 1995.

Abouharb, Rodwan, and David Cingranelli. *Human Rights and Structural Adjustment*. Cambridge: Cambridge University Press, 2006.

Acevedo, Domingo E. "The Haitian Crisis and the OAS Response: A Test of Effectiveness in Protecting Democracy." In *Enforcing Restraint: Collective Intervention in Internal Conflicts*, edited by Lori F. Damrosch, 119–155. New York: Council on Foreign Relations Press, 1993.

Adams, Nassau. "The UN's Neglected Brief—The Advancement of All Peoples." In *Challenges to the United Nations, Building a Safer World*, edited by Erskine Childers, 26–50. London: Catholic Inst. for International Relations, 1994.

Adebajo, Adekeye. *Liberia's Civil War: Nigeria, ECOMOG, and Regional Security in West Africa*. Boulder, Colorado: Lynne Rienner Publishers, 2002.

Adetoun, Bolanle Akande. "The Role and Function of Research in a Divided Society: A Case Study of Niger Delta Region of Nigeria." In *Researching Conflict in Africa, Inside and Experience*, edited by Elisabeth Porter, Gillian Robinson, Marie Smyth, Albrecht Schnabel, and Eghosa Osaghae, 47–58 New York: United Nations University Press, 2005.

Afsah, Ebrahim, and Alexandra H. Guhr. "Afghanistan: Building a State to Keep the Peace." *Max Planck Yearbook of United Nations Law* 9 (2005), 373–456.

Agbakwa, Shedrack. "A Line in the Sand: International (Dis)order and the Impunity of Non-State Corporate Actors in the Developing World." In *The Third World and International Order: Law, Politics and Globalization*, Developments in International Law 45, edited by Antony Anghie, Bhupinder Chimni, Karin Mickelson, and Obiaora Okafor, 1–18. The Hague: Martinus Nijhoff Publishers, 2003.

Aginam, Obijiofor. "Global Village, Divided World: South-North Gap and Global Health Challenges at Century's Dawn." *Indiana Journal of Global Legal Studies* 7 (2000), 603–628.

Ahmed, Ismail I., and Reginald Herbold Green. "The Heritage of War and the State: State Collapse in Somalia and Somaliland: Local-Level Effects, External Interventions and Reconstruction." *Southern Quarterly* 20 (1999), 1, 113–127.

Aka, Philip C. "Nigeria since May 1999: Understanding the Paradox of Civil Rule and Human Rights Violations under President Olusegun Obasanjo." *San Diego International Law Journal* 4 (2003), 209–276.

——. "The Military, Globalization, and Human Rights in Africa." *New York Law School Journal of Human Rights* 18 (2002), 3, 361–438.

Aksu, Seref. *The United Nations, Intra-state Peacekeeping and Normative Change*. Manchester: Manchester University Press, 2003.

Alagappa, Muthiah. "Regional Arrangements, the UN, and International Security: A Framework for Analysis." In *Beyond UN Subcontracting, Task-Sharing with*

Regional Security Arrangements and Service-Providing NGOs, edited by Thomas Weiss, 1–18. London: Macmillan, 1998.

Albright, Madeleine K. "Statement before the Subcommittee on Foreign Operations, Export Financing, and Related Programs of the House Appropriations Committee, March 12, 1993." *Department of State Dispatch*, April 5, 1993.

Alexander, Klinton W. "NATO's Intervention in Kosovo: The Legal Case for Violating Yugoslavia's National Sovereignty in the Absence of Security Council Approval." *Houston Journal of International Law* 22 (2000), 3, 403–449.

Alexandrov, Stanimir. A. *Self Defence against the Use of Force in International Law*. The Hague: Kluwer Law International, 1996.

Ali, Sheikh R. *The International Organizations and World Order Dictionary*. Santa Barbara, California: ABC-CLIO, 1992.

Alie, Joe A. *A New History of Sierra Leone*. London: Macmillan, 1990.

Al-Jurf, Saladin. "Good Governance and Transparency: Their Impact on Development." *Transnational Law and Contemporary Problems* 9 (1999), 175–191.

Alley, Roderic. *Internal Conflict and the International Community: Wars without End?* Aldershot, UK: Asghate Publishing, 2004.

Alt, Gerhard, editor. *Armut im Süden durch Wohlstand im Norden, Nachträge und Schlaglichter zur Dependenz-Threorie*, 5th edition. Munich: Hanns-Seidel-Stieftung, 1998

Altıok, Metin. "Washington Konsensüsü." In *Ekonomik Kurumlar ve Kavramlar Sözlügü, Eleştirel Bir Giriş*, edited by Fikret Başkaya and Aydın Ördek, 1297–1304. Ankara: Özgür Üniversite Yayınları, 2008.

Alvarez, José E. "Constitutional Interpretation in International Organisations." In *The Legitimacy of International Organizations*, edited by Jean-Marc Coicaud and Veijo Heiskanen, 104–154. Tokyo: The United Nations University Press, 2001.

Amorim, Celso L.N. "The WTO from the Perspective of a Developing Country." *Fordham International Law Journal* 24 (2000), 1–2, 95–106.

Anghie, Antony. "Colonialism and the Birth of International Institutions: Sovereignty, Economy and the Mandate System of the League of Nations." *New York University Journal of International Law and Politics* 34 (2002), 3, 513–633.

——. "Finding the Peripheries: Sovereignty and Colonialism in Nineteenth-Century International Law." *Harvard International Law Journal* 40 (1999), 1, 1–80.

——. *Imperialism, Sovereignty and the Making of International Law*. Cambridge: Cambridge University Press, 2005.

——. "Time Present and Time Past: Globalization, International Financial Institutions and the Third World." *New York University Journal of International Law and Politics* 32 (2000), 2, 243–290.

Aucoin, Louis, Karl F. Inderfurth, and Howard J. Wiarda. "Building the Institutions of the Nation (Panel II)." *Georgia Journal of International and Comparative Law* 33 (2004–2005), 171–194

Ayoob, Mohammed. *The Third World Security Predicament: State Making, Regional Conflict and the International System*. Boulder, Colorado: Lynne Rienner Publishers, 1995.

Azzellini, Dario. "Kolumbien: 100 Jahre Krieg gegen die Bevölkerung." In *Politische*

Ökonomie der Gewalt, Staatszerfall und die Privatisierung von Gewalt und Krieg, edited by Werner Ruf, 235–267. Opladen: Leske + Budrich, 2003.

Baade, Hans W. "The Legal Effects of Codes of Conduct for Multinational Enterprises." In *Legal Problems of Codes of Conduct for Multinational Enterprises*, edited by Norbert Horn, 3–38. London: Kluwer, 1980.

Baez, Cristina, Michele Dearing, Margaret Delatour, and Christine Dixon. "Multinational Enterprises and Human Rights." *International and Comparative Law Review* 8 (1999–2000), 183–338.

Baker, Mark B. "Tightening the Toothless Vise: Codes of Conduct and the American Multinational Enterprise." *Wisconsin International Law Journal* 20 (2001), 1, 89–142.

Baldus, Manfred. "Extraterritoriale Intervention der Bundeswehr zur Rettung von fremden und deutschen Staatsangehörigen." In *Frieden und Recht*, edited by Ingo Erberich, Ansgar Hörster, Michael Hoffmann, Thorsten Kingreen, Hermann Pünder, and Rainer Störmer, 259–295. Münster: Richard Boorberg Verlag, 1998.

Ball, N., Jordana D. Friedman, and Caleb S. Rossiter. "The Role of International Financial Institutions in Preventing and Resolving Conflict." In *The Price of Peace, Incentives and International Conflict Prevention*, edited by David Cortright, 243–264. Lanham, Maryland: Rowman & Littlefield, 1997.

Barak, Oren. "Dilemmas of Security in Iraq." *Security Dialogue* 38 (2007), 4, 455–475.

Bartl, Jürgen. *Die Humanitäre Intervention durch den Sicherheitsrat der Vereinten Nationen in "Failed State": Das Beispiel Somalia*, Schriften zum Staats-und Völkerrecht 82, Frankfurt: Peter Lang, 1999.

Beardslee, W.Q. "The United State's Haiti Intervention: The Dangers of 'Redefined' National Security Interests." *Denver Journal of International Law and Policy* 25 (1994), 1, 189–197.

Becker, Tal. *Terrorism and the State, Rethinking, the Rules of State Responsibility*. Oxford, UK: Hart Publishing, 2006.

Benton, Lauren A. *Law and Colonial Cultures: Legal Regimes in World History, 1400–1900*. Cambridge: Cambridge University Press, 2002.

Benzing, Markus. "Midwifing a New State: The United Nations in East Timor." *Max Planck Yearbook of United Nations Law* 9 (2005), 295–372.

Berber, Friedrich. *Lehrbuch des Völkerrechts, Allgemeines Friedensrecht. Volume I*. Munich: C.H. Beck, 1975.

Beres, Louis René, and Yoash Tsiddon-Chatto. "In Support of Anticipatory Self-Defense: Israel, Iraq and International Law." *Contemporary Security Policy* 19 (1998), 2, 111–114.

Berstermann, Jost. *Das Einmischungsverbot im Völkerrecht*, Europäische Hochschulschriften, Reihe 2, Rechtswissenschaften, Frankfurt: Peter Lang, 1991.

Biermann, Wolfgang, editor. *UN Peacekeeping in Trouble*. Aldershot, UK: Ashgate Publishing, 1998.

Bilgrami, Syed J.R. "United Nations: With and Without Cold War." *Indian Journal of International Law* 35 (1995), 143–156.

Bird, Graham. "Reforming the IMF: Should the Fund Abandon Conditionality?" *New Economy* 7 (2000), 214–218.

Birnbaum, Michael. Krisenherd Somalia: *Das Land des Terrors und der Anarchie*. Munich: Heyne Verlag, 2002.

——. "Somalia." In *Die Arabische Staaten, Geschichte, Politik, Religion, Gesellschaft, Wirtschaft*, edited by Walter M. Weiss, 287–300. Heidelberg: Palmyra, 2007

Blay, Sam, Ryszard Piotrowicz, and Martin Tsamenyi, editors. *Public International Law: An Australian Perspective*. Melbourne: Oxford University Press, 1997.

Bledsoe, Robert L., and Boleslaw A. Boczek. *The International Law Dictionary*. Santa Barbara, California: ABC-CLIO, 1987.

Bluntschli, Johan Kaspar. *Das moderne Völkerrecht der zivilisierten Staaten*. Nördlingen, Germany: C.H. Beck, 1868.

Boahen, Albert A., editor. *Africa under Colonial Domination 1880–1935*. London: John Curry, 1990.

Boczek, Boleslaw A. *International Law: A Dictionary*. Lanham, Maryland: The Scarecrow Press, Inc., 2005.

Bogdandy, Armin von, Stefan Häussler, Rafael Utz, and Felix Hanschmann. "State-Building, Nation-Building, and Constitutional Politics in Post-Conflict Situations: Conceptual Clarifications and an Appraisal of Different Approaches." *Max Planck Yearbook of United Nations Law* 9 (2005), 579–613.

Bosi, Tanya Domenica. "Post-Conflict Reconstruction: The United Nations' Involvement in Afghanistan." *New York Law School Journal of Human Rights* 19 (2003), 3, 819–831.

Bothe, Michael. "Militärische Gewalt als Instrument von Konfliktregelung: Versuch einer rechtlichen und politischen Ordnung zehn Jahre nach dem Ende des Ost-West-Konflikts." In *Praxishandbuch UNO, Die Vereinten Nationen im Lichte globaler Herausforderungen*, edited by Sabine von Schorlemer, 13–26. Berlin: Springer-Verlag, 2003.

—— editor. *UN Peacekeeping, A Documentary Introduction*. The Hague: Kluwer Law International, 1999.

Bothe, Michael, and Thilo Marauhn. "The United Nations in Kosovo and East Timor: Problems of a Trusteeship Administration." *International Peace-keeping* 6 (2000), 152–156.

Boutros-Ghali, Boutros. "Concluding Statement by the Secretary-General: Towards the Twenty-First Century: International Law as a Language for International Relations." United Nations Congress on Public International Law, New York, March 13–17, 1995.

——. Introduction to *The United Nations and Somalia, 1992–1996*. United Nations Blue Book Series. Volume III, 3–87. New York: United Nations, 1996.

Bowden, Brett. "The Colonial Origins of International Law: European Expansion and the Classical Standard of Civilization." *Journal of the History of International Law* 7 (2005), 1, 1–23.

Bowett, Derek W. *Self-Defence in International Law*. Manchester: Manchester University Press, 1958.

Boyle, Joseph. "Traditional Just War Theory and Humanitarian Intervention." In *Humanitarian Intervention*, edited by Terry Nardin and Melissa S. Williams, 31–57. New York: New York University Press, 2006.

Böge, Volker. *Muschelgeld und Blutdiamanten. Traditionale Konfliktbearbeitung in zeitgenössischen Gewaltkonflikten*. Hamburg: Schriften des Deutschen Übersee-Instituts Hamburg, 2004.

Brahimi, Lakhdar. Briefing tot he Security Council, Transcript from 13 November 2001, http://www.un.org/News/dh/latest/afghan/Brahimi-sc-briefing.html.

Braun, Dieter, and Karlernst Ziem. *Afghanistan: Sowjetische Machtpolitik—Islamische Selbstbestimmung—Innenafghanische Prozesse, Regionale Konfliktfolgen, Internationale Verflechtungen*. Baden-Baden: Nomos Verlagsgesellschaft, 1988.

Brierly, James Leslie. The Law of Nations, an Introduction to the International Law of Peace. Oxford, UK: Clarendon Press, 1955.

Brilmayer, Lea. "Secession and Self-Determination: A Territorial Interpretation." In *Self-Determination in International Law* (Library of Essays in International Law), edited by Robert McCorquodale, 451–476. Aldershot, UK: Dartmouth Publishing Co., Ltd., 2000.

Brockway, Fenner. *The Colonial Revolution*. London: Hart-Davis, 1973.

Brown, Bartram S. "Human Rights, Sovereignty, and the Final Status of Kosovo." *Chicago-Kent Law Review* 80 (2005), 1, 235–272.

Brownlie, Ian. *Principles of Public International Law*. 6th ed. Oxford: Oxford University Press, 2003.

——. *Principles of Public international Law*. Oxford: Oxford University Press, 1998.

——. *The Rule of Law in International Affairs: International Law at the Fiftieth Anniversary of the United Nations*. London: Martinus Nijhoff Publishers, 1998.

——. "The Use of Force in Self Defence." *British Year Book of International Law* 37 (1961), 183–268.

Bruha, Thomas, and Markus Krajewski. "Bürgerkrieg." In *Lexikon des Rechts—Völkerrecht*, edited by Ignaz Seidl-Hohenveldern, 46–49. Neuwied, Germany: Luchterhand, 2001.

Buckley, Ross. P. "A Tale of Two Crises: The Search for Enduring Reforms of the International Financial System." *UCLA Journal of International Law and Foreign Affairs* 6 (2001), 1, 1–43.

Buell, Raymond Leslie. *International Relations*. New York: Henry Holt and Company, 1925.

Calic, Marie-Janine. "Die Jugoslawienpolitik des Westens seit Dayton." *Aus Politik und Zeitgeschichte* 34 (1999), 22–32.

Callahan, Michael D. *Mandates and Empire, The League of Nations and Africa, 1914–1931*. Brighton, UK: Sussex Academic Press, 1999.

Campbell, Charles S. *Special Business Interests and the Open Door Policy*. New Haven: Yale University Press, 1951.

Canova, Timothy A., Claire Moore Dickerson, and Katherine V.W. Stone. "Labour and Finance as Inevitably Transnational: Globalization Demands a Sophisticated and Transnational Lens." *San Diego Law Review* 41 (2004), 109–113.

Caplan, Richard. *A New Trusteeship? The International Administration of War-Torn Territories*. New York: International Institution for Strategic Studies, 2002.

Carter, Barry E., Phillip R. Trimble, and Curtis A Bradley. *International Law*. New York: Aspen Publishers, 2003.

Cassese, Antonio. *International Law*. Oxford: Oxford University Press, 2001.

——. *Self Determination of Peoples, A Legal Reappraisal*. Cambridge, UK: Cambridge University Press, 1995.

——. "Self Determination Revisited." In *International Law in an Evolving World. Liber Amicorum in Tribute to Professor Eduardo Jiménez de Aréchaga*, 229–240. Montevideo, Uruguay: Fundación de Cultura Universitaria, 1994.

Chapelier, Georges, and Hamid Tabatabai. *Development and Adjustment, Stabilization, Structural Adjustment and UNDP Policy*. UNDP Policy Discussion Paper. New York: United Nations Development Program, 1989.

Chen, Lung-Chu. "An Introduction to Contemporary Law: A Policy-Oriented Perspective." In *International Law*, edited by Barry Carter and Philip Trimble. Boston: Aspen Law & Business, 1999.

Chesterman, Simon. *You, The People: The United Nations, Transnational Administration, and State-Building*. Oxford: Oxford University Press, 2004.

Childers, Erskine. Introduction to *Challenges to the United Nations, Building a Safer World*, edited by Erskine Childers, 1–13. London: Catholic Institute for International Relations and St. Martin's Press, 1994.

——. "The United Nations System." In *Ibid*, 14.

Chimni, Bhupinder S. "Third World Approaches to International Law: A Manifesto." In *The Third World and International Order: Law, Politics and Globalisation*. Developments in International Law 45, edited by Antony Anghie, Bhupinder S. Chimni, Karin Mickelson, and Obiaora Okafor, 47–95. The Hague: Martinus Nijhoff Publishers, 2003.

——. "The World Trade Organization, Democracy and Development: A View from the South." *Journal of Trade* 40 (2006), 1, 5–36.

Cho, Sungjoon. "Doha's Development." *Berkeley Journal of International Law* 25 (2007), 2, 165–202.

Choudhry, Sujit. "Old Imperial Dilemmas and the New Nation-Building: Constitutive Constitutional Politics in Multinational Polities." *Connecticut Law Review* 37 (2004–2005), 4, 933–945.

Clapham, Christopher. *Africa and the International System: The Politics of State Survival*. Cambridge: Cambridge University Press, 1996.

——. "Failed States and Non-States in the Modern International Order." Third Conference on Failed States: Globalization and the Failed State, Purdue University, West Lafayette, Indiana, April 7–10 2000.

Cobban, Alfred. *The Nation State and National Self-Determination*. London: Harper Collins Publishers, 1969.

Coicaud, Jean-Marc. Conclusion: "International Organizations, The Evolution of international Politics, and Legitimacy." In *The Legitimacy of International Organisations*, edited by Jean-Marc Coicaud and Veijo Heiskanen, 259–262. Tokyo: The United Nations University Press, 2001.

Collier, Paul, Anke Hoeffler, and Mans Söderbom. *On Duration of Civil War*, Policy Research Working Paper Series 2681. Washington: The World Bank, 2001. Available at www.econ.worldbank.org/programmes/conflict.

Conforti, Benedetto. *The Law and Practice of the United Nations*. Leiden: Martinus Nijhoff Publishers, 2005.

Cooper, Robert. "Gibt es eine neue Welt-Ordnung." *Europa-Archive* 18 (1993), 507–517.

Cornia, Giovanni Andrea, and Court Julius. *Inequality, Growth and Poverty in the*

Era of Liberalisation and Globalisation. Policy Brief No. 4. Helsinki: United Nations University and World Institute for Development Economic Research (WIDER), 2001

Craven, Matthew C.R. "The Problem of State Succession and Identity of States under International Law." *European Journal of International Law* 9 (1998), 1, 142–162.

Crawford, James R. *The Creation of States in International Law*. 2nd ed, Oxford: Clarendon Press, 2006.

——. *The Creation of States in International Law*. Oxford: Clarendon Press, 1979.

——. "Report, State Practice and International Law in Relation to Unilateral Secession." In *Self-Determination in International Law, Quebec and Lessons Learned*, edited by Anne F. Bayefsky, 1–67. The Hague: Kluwer Law International, 2000.

——. "The ILC's Articles on Responsibility of States." *American Journal of International Law* 96 (2002), 4, 874–890.

——. "Responsibility to the International Community as a Whole." *Indiana Journal of Global Legal Studies* 8 (2000–2001), 302–322.

Craven, Matthew C.R., and Susan Marks. "The Global Democracy Deficit: An Essay in International Law and its Limit." In *Re-imaging Political Community: Studies in Cosmopolitan Democracy*, edited by Daniele Archibugi, David Held, and Martin Köhler, 72–90. Cambridge, UK: Polity Press, 1998.

Czernecki, Jennifer L. "The United Nations' Paradox: The Battle between Humanitarian Intervention and State Sovereignty." *Duquesne Law Review* 41 (2002–2003), 2, 391–407.

Daase, Christopher. *Kleine Kriege—Große Wirkung. Wie unkonventionelle Kriegsführung die internationale Politik verändert*. Baden-Baden: Nomos Verlagsgesellschaft, 2002.

Dahm, Georg. *Völkerrecht. Volume II*, Stuttgart: Kohlhammer Verlag, 1961.

——. *Völkerrecht. Volume I*. Stuttgart: Kohlhammer Verlag, 1958.

Dahm, Georg, Jost Delbrück, and Rüdiger Wolfrum. *Völkerrecht, Volume 1/3*. Berlin: Walter de Gruyter, 2002.

Daianu, Daniel. "Institutional and Policy Variety: The Role of IFIs and Economic Development." In *International Institutions and Multinational Enterprises, Global Players-Global Markets*, edited by Joh-Ren Chen, Cheltenham, UK: Edward Elgar, 2004.

D'Amato, Anthony. "The Invasion of Panama Was a Lawful Response to Tyranny." *American Journal of International Law* 84 (1990), 2, 516–524.

Daramy, Sheikh Batu. "Constitutional Development in the Post-Colonial State of Sierra Leone 1961–1984." *African Studies* 30. Lewiston, New York: Edwin Mellen Press, 1993.

Davidson, Basil. *Modern Africa: A Social and Political History*. London: Longman, 1994.

Davies, V.A.B. "Sierra Leone: Ironic Tragedy." *Journal of African Economies* 9 (2000), 3, 349–369.

De Almada, José, Robert Godding, Lord Hailey, A.M. Joekes and H. Laurentie. *Colonial Administration by European Powers*. London: Royal Institute of International Affairs, 1947.

Deiwert, Brian. "A New Trusteeship for World Peace and Security: Can an Old League of Nations Idea Be Applied to a First Century Iraq?" *Indiana International and Comparative Law Review* 14 (2004), 3, 771–806.

Denham, Mark E., and Mark Owen Lombardi. "Perspectives on Southern Sovereignty: Problems with(out) Borders." In *Perspectives on Southern Sovereignty: The Postmodern Paradox*, edited by Mark E. Denham and Mark Owen Lombardi, 1–12. New York: Macmillan, 1996.

Denza, Eileen. *Diplomatic Law: Commentary on the Vienna Convention on Diplomatic Relations*. 2nd ed. Oxford: Clarendon Press, 1998.

Despagnet, Frantz. *Cours de Droit International Public*. 2nd ed, Paris, 1893.

Dias, Fr. Noel. "The NIEO Revisited." *Sri Lanka Journal of International Law* 8 (1996), 27–57.

Dicke, Detlev Christian. *Die administrative Organisation der Entwicklungshilfe durch die Vereinten Nationen*. Frankfurt: Athenaeum-Verlag, 1972.

Dine, J. "Multinational Enterprises: International Codes and the Challenge of 'Sustainable Development'." *Non-State Actors and International Law* 1 (2001), 2, 81–106.

Dinstein, Yoram. "Sovereignty, the Security Council and the Use of Force." In *Redefining Sovereignty, The Use of Force After the Cold War*, edited by Michael Bothe, Mary Ellen O'Connell, and Natalino Ronzitti, 111–122. Aldershot, UK: Transnational Publishers, 2005.

——. *War, Aggression and Self Defence*. Cambridge, UK: Grotius Publications Limited, 1994.

——. *War, Aggression and Self Defence*. 3rd ed. Cambridge, UK: Cambridge University Press, 2001.

Dixon, Martin. *Textbook on International Law*. 4th ed. Oxford: Oxford University Press, 2005.

Doehring, Karl. *Allgemeine Staatslehre: Eine systematische Darstellung*. 3rd ed. Heidelberg: Müller, 2004.

——. "Effectiveness." *Encyclopedia of Public International Law* 7 (1984), 70–74.

——. *Völkerrecht, Ein Lehrbuch*. 2nd ed. Heidelberg: Müller, 2004.

Dolman, Antony J. *Resources, Regimes, World Order*. New York: Pergamon Press, 1981.

Dore, Isaak I. "Constitutionalism and the Post-Colonial State in Africa: A Rawlsian Approach." *Saint Louis University Law Journal* 41 (1997), 4, 1301–1318.

Douthwaite, Richard J. *The Growth Illusion: How Economic Growth Has Enriched the Few, Impoverished the Many, and Endangered the Planet*. Dartington, UK: Green Books, 1999.

Drumbl, Mark A. "Punishment, Post-Genocide: From Guilt to Shame to Civis in Rwanda." *New York University Law Review* 75 (2000), 5, 1221–1326.

Dugard, John. *International Law: A South African Perspective*. 2nd ed. Capetown: Juta and Company Ltd., 2000.

Eikenberg, Kathrin. "Die UNO in Somalia." *Blätter für deutsche und internationale Politik* 38 (1993), 9, 1061–1069.

El-Naggar, Said. "Developing Countries and the International Trading System." In *Law in the Service of Human Dignity*, edited by Steve Charnovitz, Debra P. Steger, and Peter van den Bossche, 58–75. Cambridge: Cambridge University Press, 2005.

Epping, Volker. "Völkerrechtssubjekte." In *Völkerrecht*, edited by Knut Ipsen, 3rd ed. 52–93. Munich: C.H. Beck, 1990.

Erler, Georg. "Internationale Finanz- und Wirtschaftshilfe als politisches und völkerrechtliches Problem." *Sonderdruck aus Menschen und Staat in Recht und Geschichte.* Berlin: Dt. Zentraldr, 1953.

Esty, Daniel C. "The World Trade Organization's Legitimacy Crisis." *World Trade Review* 1 (2002), 1, 7–22.

Evans, Malcolm D., editor, *International Law.* 2nd ed. Oxford: Oxford University Press, 2006.

Evans, Tony. Introduction: "Power, Hegemony and the Universalization of Human Rights." In *Human Rights Fifty Years on: A Reappraisal*, edited by Tony Evans, 1–23 Manchester: Manchester University Press, 1998.

Ezetah, Chinedu Reginald. "Legitimate Governance and Statehood in Africa: Beyond the Failed State and Colonial Self- Determination." In *Legitimate Governance in Africa, International and Domestic Legal Perspectives*, edited by Kofi Edward Quashigah, 419–459. The Hague: Kluwer Law International, 1999.

Fastenrath, Ulrich. "States, Extinction." *Encyclopaedia of Public International Law* 10 (1987), 465–467.

Fieldhouse, David K. *The Colonial Empires: A Comparative Survey from the Eighteenth Century.* 2nd ed. London: Macmillan, 1982.

Fielding, Lois E. "Taking the Next Step in the Development of New Human Rights: The Emerging Right of Humanitarian Assistance to Restore Democracy." *Duke Journal of Comparative and International Law* 5 (1995), 2, 329–377.

Fink, Udo. *Kollektive Friedenssicherung, Kapitel VII UN-Charta in der Praxis des Sicherheitsrates der Vereinten Nationen. Volume II.* Frankfurt: Peter Lang, 1999.

Fischer, Horst. "Diplomatische und konsularische Beziehungen." In *Völkerrecht*, edited by Knut Ipsen, 432–487. Munich: C.H. Beck, 1990.

Franck, Thomas M. "The Emerging Right to Democratic Governance." *American Journal of International Law* 86 (1992), 1, 46–91.

Friedrich, Jürgen. "UNMIK in Kosovo: Struggling with Uncertainty." *Max Planck Yearbook of United Nations Law* 9 (2005), 225–293.

Fröhlich, Dieter. *Nationalismus und Nationalstaat in Entwicklungsländern: Probleme der Integration ethnischer Gruppen in Afghanistan.* Meisenheim am Glan, Germany: Hain Verlag, 1970.

Fukuyama, Francis. *State-Building. Governance and World Order in the 21st Century.* Ithaca, New York: Cornell University Press, 2004.

Galtung, Johan. *Peace and Development in the Pacific Hemisphere.* Honolulu: University of Hawaii Instition for Peace, 1989.

——. *Strukturelle Gewalt. Beiträge zur Friedens-und Konfliktforschung.* Hamburg: Rowohlt Verlag, 1975.

——. "Eine strukturelle Theorie des Imperialismus." In *Imperialismus und strukturelle Gewalt Analysen über abhängige Reproduktion*, edited by Dieter Senghaas, 29–104. Frankfurt: Suhrkamp Verlag, 1972.

——. "The Third World and Human Rights in the Post-1989 World Order." In *Human Rights Fifty Years on: A Reappraisal*, edited by Tony Evans, 211–232. Manchester: Manchester University Press, 1998.

Garcia-Mora, M.R. *International Responsibility for Hostile Acts of Private Persons against Foreign States.* The Hague: Martinus Nijhoff Publishers, 1962.

Gardner, Richard N. "Neither Bush nor the 'Jurisprudes'." *American Journal of International Law* 97 (2003), 585–589.
Garuda, Gopal. "Lender of Last Resort: Rethinking IMF Conditionality." *Harvard International Law Review* 20 (1998), 36–39.
Garwood-Gowers, Andrew. "Pre-emptive Self Defence: A Necessary Development or the Road to International Anarchy." *Australian Year Book of International Law* 23 (2004), 51–72.
Gehring, Markus W., Marie-Claire Cordonier Segger, and Martin Endicott. "Conclusion." In *Sustainable Development in World Trade Law*, edited by Markus W. Gehring and Marie-Claire Cordonier Segger, 631–643. The Hague: Kluwer Law International, 2005.
Geiger, Rudolf. *Grundgesetz und Völkerrecht, die Bezüge des Staatsrechts zum Völkerrecht und Europarecht.* 2nd ed. Munich: C.H. Beck, 1994.
Geiß, Robin. *"Failed States", Die normative Erfassung gescheiterter Staaten.* Berlin: Duncker & Humblot, 2005.
Gerig, Benjamin. *The Principle of Equal Economic Opportunity before and since the Establishment of the Mandates System: A Study of the Open Door as A Colonial Trade Policy.* London: G. Allen & Unwin, 1930.
Ghazi Shariat Panahi, Bahram. *The IMF, the World Bank Group and the Question of Human Rights.* Ardsley, New York: Transnational Publishers, 2005.
Girvan, Norman. *Corporate Imperialism: Conflict and Expropriation. Essays in Transnational Corporations and Economic Nationalism in the Third World.* New York: M.E. Sharpe, 1976.
Giry, Stéphanie. "Climate Conflicts." *The New York Times Magazine*, December 9, 2007.
Gloria, Christian. "Die Grundprinzipien des Völkerrechts über die Beziehungen zwischen den Staaten.". In *Völkerrect*, edited by Knut Ipsen, 3rd ed. 330–345. Munich: C.H. Beck, 1990.
——. "Internationales Wirtschaftsrecht." In *Völkerrect*, edited by Knut Ipsen. 3rd ed. 544–625. Munich: C.H. Beck, 1990.
——. "Der Staat im Völkerrecht." In *Völkerrect*, edited by Knut Ipsen. 3rd ed. 227–345. Munich: C.H. Beck, 1990.
Gold, Joseph. *Conditionality.* Washington: International Monetary Fund, 1979.
Goldmann, Matthias. "Sierra Leone: African Solutions to African Problems?" *Max Planck Yearbook of United Nations Law* 9 (2005), 457–515.
Gordon, Ruth E. "Saving Failed States: Sometimes a Neocolonialist Notion." *American University Journal of International Law and Policy* 12 (1997), 6, 903–974.
——. "Some Legal Problems with Trusteeship." *Cornell International Law Journal* 28 (1995), 2, 301–347.
Graham, Edward. "Should There Be Multilateral Rules on Foreign Direct Investment?" In *Governments, Globalization and International Business*, edited by John Dunning, 481–506. Oxford: Oxford University Press, 1997.
Gray, Christine D. *International Law and the Use of Force.* 2nd ed. Oxford: Oxford University Press, 2004.
Griesgraber, Jo Marie, and Bernhard G. Gunter, editors. *The World Bank: Lending on a Global Scale.* London: Pluto Press, 1996.

Griffin, Michelle, and Bruce Jones. "Building Peace through Transitional Authority: New Directions, Major Challenges." *International Peacekeeping* 7 (2000), 3, 75–90.

Grzeszick, Bernd. "Staatsgewalt in der UN-Charta zwischen Gewaltverbot und Selbstverteidigung." *Archiv des Völkerrechts* 41 (2003), 4, 484–505.

Guilfoyle, Douglas. "Piracy off Somalia: UN Security Council Resolution 1816 and IMO Regional Counter-Piracy Efforts." *International and Comparative Law Quarterly* 57 (2008), 3, 690–699.

Gupta, Dharam C. *The League of Nations*. Delhi: Vikas Publishing House, 1974.

Gutto, Shadrack B.O. *Human and Peoples' Rights for the Oppressed: Critical Essays on Theory and Practice from Sociology of Law Perspectives*. Lund, Sweden: Lund University Press, 1993.

Habermas, Jürgen. "Beyond the Nation-State? On Some Consequences of Economic Globalization." In *Democracy in the European Union Integration through Deliberation?*, edited by Erik Eriksen and John Fossum, 29–41. London: Routledge, 2000.

Hacke, Christian. "Amerikas Krieg gegen Terror—Die Operation 'Enduring Freedom' in Afghanistan." *Jahrbuch internationale Politik* 25 (2004), 11–21.

Hailbronner, Kay. "Der Staat als primäres Völkerrechtssubjekt." In *Völkerrecht*, edited by Wolfgang Graf Vitzthum. 2nd ed. 161–265. Berlin: Walter de Gruyter, 2001.

Hanski, Raija, and Markku Suksi, editors. *An Introduction to the International Protection of Human Rights*. Turku, Finland: Åbo Akademi University Institute for Human Rights, 1997.

Harper, Erica. "United Nations Transitional Administration: Missions in State or Nation-Building?" In *Post-Conflict Reconstruction: Nation-and/or State-Building*, edited by Horst Fischer and Noëlle Quénivet, 33–55. Berlin: Wissenschaftlicher Verlag Berlin, 2005.

Harris, D.J. *Cases and Materials on International Law*. 6th ed. London, Sweet & Maxwell, 2004.

Haverland, Christine. "Secession." *Encyclopaedia of Public International Law* 10 (1987), 384–389.

Head, John W. *The Future of the Global Economic Organizations: An Evaluation of Criticism Levelled at the IMF, the Multilateral Development Banks, and the WTO*. Aldershot, UK: Transnational Publications, 2005.

Helman, Gerald B., and Steven B. Ratner. "Saving Failed States." *Foreign Policy* 89 (1992), 3–20.

Henning Jessen. "Trade and Development Law." In *Sustainable Development in World Trade Law*, edited by Markus W. Gehring and Marie-Claire Cordonier Segger, 77–101. The Hague: Kluwer Law International, 2005.

Herbst, Jeffrey. "African Peacekeepers and State Failure." In *Peacekeeping and Peace Enforcement in Africa: Methods of Conflict Prevention*, by Robert I. Rotberg, Erika Albaugh, Happyton Bonyongwe, Christopher Clapham, Jeffrey Herbst, and Steven Metz, 16–34. Cambridge: World Peace Foundation, 2000.

——. "Global Change and the Future of Existing Nation-States." In *The Self-Determination of Peoples: Community, Nation, and State in an Interdependent World*, edited by Wolfgang Danspeckgruber, 13–31. London: Lynne Rienner Publishers, 2002.

Herdegen, Matthias. "Der Wegfall effektiver Staatsgewalt im Völkerrecht: 'The Failed State'". In *Der Wegfall effektiver Staatsgewalt: "The Failed State"*, edited by Daniel Thürer, Matthias Herdegen, and Gerhard Hohloch, 49–85. Heidelberg: Müller, 1996.

Heuser, Beatrice. "Sovereignty, Self-determination, and Security." In *State Sovereignty, Change and Persistence in International Relations*, edited by Sohail H. Hashmi, 81–105. Philadelphia: University of Pennsylvania Press, 1997.

Hildenbrand, Jan Cristian. *Zur Krisenaktionsfähigkeit der Friedenstruppen der VN, Notwendigkeiten, Konzepte und Perspektiven ihrer Verbesserung*. Baden-Baden: Nomos Verlagsgesellschaft, 2001.

Hobsbawm, Erich J. *Das Gesicht des 21. Jahrhunderts, Hat der Staat noch einen Sinn*. Munich: Carl Hanser Verlag, 2000.

Holsti, Kalevi J. *Peace and War: Armed Conflict and International Order 1648–1989*. Cambridge: Cambridge University Press, 1991.

——. *Political Sources of Humanitarian Disasters*. Research for Action Paper 36, Helsinki: United Nations University and World Institute for Development Economic Research (WIDER), 1997.

Hooper, James R., and Paul R. Williams. "Earned Sovereignty: Political Dimension." *Denver Journal of International Law and Policy* 31 (2003), 3, 355–372.

Hope, Judith R., and Edward N. Griffen. "The New Iraq: Revising Iraq's Commercial Law is a Necessity for Foreign Direct Investment and the Reconstruction of Iraq's Decimated Economy." *Cardozo Journal of International and Comparative Law* 11 (2003–2004), 3, 875–902.

Hoyle, Peggy. "Somaliland: Passing the Statehood Test." *IBRU Boundary and Security Bulletin* 8 (2000), 3, 80–91.

Hubel, Helmut. *Das Ende des Kalten Kriegs im Orient, die USA, die Sowjetunion und die Konflikte in Afghanistan, am Golf und im Nahen Osten, 1979–1991, Auswirkungen für Europa und Deutschland*. Munich: Oldenbourg-Verlag, 1995.

Hufnagel, Frank-Erich. *UN-Friedensoperationen der zweiten Generation, vom Puffer zur neuen Treuhand*. Berlin: Duncker & Humblot, 1996

Hull, Cordell. *The Memoirs of Cordell Hull*. Volume I, New York: Macmillan, 1948.

Hymer, Steven. "Multinationale Konzerne und das Gesetz der ungleichen Entwicklung". In *Imperialismus und strukturelle Gewalt Analysen über abhängige Reproduktion*, by Dieter Senghaas, 201–239. Frankfurt: Suhrkamp Verlag, 1972.

Ignatieff, Michael. *Empire Lite: Nation Building in Bosnia, Kosovo, and Afghanistan*. New York: Vintage Books, 2003.

——. "State Failure and Nation-building." In *Humanitarian Intervention: Ethical, Legal and Political Dilemmas*, edited by J.L. Holzgrefe and Robert O. Keohane, 299–321. Cambridge: Cambridge University Press, 2003.

Ipsen, Knut. *Völkerrecht*. 3rd ed. Munich: C.H. Beck, 1990.

Ismail, Faizel. "How Can Least-Developed Countries and Other Small Weak and Vulnerable Economies also Gain from the Doha Development Agenda on the Road to Hong Kong?" *Journal of Trade* 40 (2006), 1, 37–68.

Israelyan, Victor, editor. *Soviet Foreign Policy*. Moscow: Progress Publishers, 1967.

Jackson, Robert H. *Quasi-States, Sovereignty, International Relations and the Third World*. Cambridge: Cambridge University Press, 1993.

Jackson, Robert H., and Carl G. Rosberg. "Why African's Weak States Persist: The Empirical and the Juridical in Statehood." *World Politics* 35 (1982), 1, 1–24.

Jellinek, Georg. *Allgemeine Staatslehre*. 4th ed. Berlin: Springer Verlag, 1922.

Jones, Seth G., and James Dobbins. "The UN's Record in Nation Building." *Chicago Journal of International Law* 6 (2005–2006), 2, 703–723.

Joseph, Sarah. "Resolving Conflicting Claims of Territorial Sovereignty and External Self-Determination, Part I: A Proposed Formula." The *International Journal of Human Rights* 3 (1999), 1, 40–61.

——. "Taming the Leviathans: Multinational Enterprises and Human Rights." *Netherlands International Law Review* XLVI (1999), 2, 171–203.

Kaldor, Mary. *Neue und alte Kriege, Organisierte Gewalt im Zeitalter der Globalisierung*. Frankfurt: Suhrkamp Verlag, 2000.

Kaplan, Robert D. *The Ends of the Earth: A Journey at the Dawn of the 21st Century*. New York: Random House, 1996.

Karns, Margaret P., and Karen A. Mingst. The United Nations in the Post-Cold War Era. Boulder, Colorado: Wesview Press, 1995.

International Organisations: The Politics and Processes of Global Governance. Boulder, Colorado, Lynne Rienner Publishers, 2004.

Kelsen, Hans. "Collective Security and Collective Self-Defense under the Charter of the UN." *American Journal of International Law* 42 (1948), 4, 783–796.

——. "General International Law and the Law of the United Nations." In *The United Nations—Ten Years' Legal Progress*, edited by H. Gesina, J. Van Der Molen, et al, 1–16. The Hague, 1956.

——. *The Law of the United Nations, A Critical Analyses of Its Fundamental Problems*. London: Stevens & Sons Ltd., 1950.

——. *Principles of International Law*. 2nd ed. New York: Henry Holt, 1967.

Kennedy, David. "New Approaches to Comparative Law: Comparativism and International Governance." *Utah Law Review* 2 (1997), 545–637.

Kibble, Steve. "Somaliland: Surviving Without Recognition; Somalia: Recognised but Failing?" *International Relations* XV (2001), 5, 255.

Kimminich, Otto, and Stephan Hobe. *Einführung in das Völkerrecht*. 7th ed. Tübingen, Germany: A. Francke Verlag, 2000.

Kirmizialtin, Eren. "Sürdürülebilir Kalkinma." In *Ekonomik Kurumlar ve Kavramlar Sözlügü, Elestirel Bir Giris*, edited by Fikret Başkaya and Aydın Ördek, 1059–1063. Ankara: Özgür Üniversite Yayınları, 2008.

Kiza, Ernosto. "Polit-ökonomische Wege zur Analyse von Staatszerfall: Die Sozialistische Föderative Republik Jugoslawien—Ein Beispiel." In *Politische Ökonomie der Gewalt. Staatszerfall und die Privatisierung von Gewalt und Krieg*, edited by Werner Ruf, 185–217. Opladen, Germany: Leske + Budrich, 2003.

Knubben, Rolf. *Die Subjekte des Völkerrechts—allgemeine Lehre von der vollen und beschränkten völkerrechtlichen Rechts—und Handlungsfähigkeit*. Stuttgart: Kohlhammer, 1928.

Kolb, Robert. "Self-Defence and Preventive War at the Beginning of the Millennium." *Zeitschrift für öffentliches Recht* 59 (2004), 2, 111–134

Kondoch, Boris, editor. *International Peacekeeping*. Aldershot, UK: Ashgate Publishing, 2007.

Koskenmäki, Riikka. "Legal Implications Resulting from State Failure in Light of the Case of Somalia." *Nordic Journal of International Law* 73 (2004), 1, 1–36

Krajewski, Markus. "Humanitarian Intervention and Other Use of Force? Preventive Use of Force and Military Actions against Non-State Actors: Revisiting the Right of Self-Defense in Insecure Times." *Baltic Yearbook of International Law* 5 (2005), 1–26.

——. "Selbstverteidigung gegen bewaffnete Angriffe nicht staatlicher Organisationen: Der 11 September 2001 und seine Folgen." *Archiv des Völkerrechts* 40 (2002), 2, 183–214.

Krech, Hans. *Der Bürgerkrieg in Somalia (1988–1996)*. Berlin: Verlag Köster, 1996.

Kreijen, Gerard. *State Failure, Sovereignty and Effectiveness: Legal Lessons from the Decolonization of Sub-Saharan Africa*. Leiden: Martinus Nijhoff Publishers, 2004.

Kress, Claus. *Gewaltverbot und Selbstverteidigungsrecht nach der Satzung der Vereinten Nationen bei staatlicher Verwicklung in Gewaltakte Privater*. Berlin: Duncker & Humblot, 1995.

Krieger, Heike. *Das Effektivitätsprinzip im Völkerrecht*. Berlin: Duncker & Humblot, 2000.

Laurantie, H. "Recent Developments in French Colonial Policy." In *Colonial Administration by European Powers*, edited by José de Almada, Robert Godding, Lord Hailey, A.M. Joekes, and H. Laurentie, 1–19. London: Royal Institute of International Affairs, 1947.

Hersh Lauterpacht. *Recognition in International Law*. Cambridge: Cambridge University Press, 1948.

Lester, Simon. "Aid for More than Just Trade: The Case for a Role for the WTO in Development Aid." *University of New South Wales Law Journal* 30 (2007), 2, 332–348.

Lewis, Paul. "UN Lists Four Nations at Risk because of Wide Income Gaps." *New York Times*, June 2, 1994.

Liebach, Ingo. *Die unilaterale humanitäre Intervention im "zerfallenen Staaten" ("Failed State")*. Cologne: Carl Heymanns Verlag, 2004.

Lloyd, David O. "Succession, Secession, and State Membership in the United Nations." *New York University Journal of International Law and Politics* 26 (1994), 4, 761–796.

Lyons, Gene M., and Michael Mastanduno. Introduction: "International Intervention, State Sovereignty, and the Future of International Society." In *Beyond Westphalia? State Sovereignty and International Intervention*, edited by Gene M. Lyons and Michael Mastanduno, 1–18. Baltimore: Johns Hopkins University Press, 1995.

McCalmon, Brian K. "States, Refugees, and Self Defence." *Georgetown Immigration Law Journal* 10 (1996), 2, 215–239.

McGurk, Brett. "Revisiting the Law of Nation-Building: Iraq in Transition." *Virginia Journal of International Law* 45 (2005), 2, 451–465.

Mcmahan, Jeff. "Intervention and Collective self-determination." *Ethics & International Affairs* 10 (1996), 1–24.

MacQueen, Norrie. *Peacekeeping and the International System*. London: Routledge, 2006.

Maass, Citha D. "Der Afghanistan-Konflikt: Konfliktmerkmale als Ansatz für ein UN-Vermittlungskonzept." In *Afghanistan in Geschichte und Gegenwart, Beiträge zur*

Afghanistan, edited by Conrad J. Schetter and Almut Wieland-Karimi, 153–173. Frankfurt: Verlag für Interkulturelle Kommunikation, 1999.

Magner, Tara. "Does a Failed State Country of Origin Result in a Failure of International Protection? A Review of Politics toward Asylum-Seekers in Leading Asylum Nations." *Georgetown Immigration Law Journal* 15 (2001), 4, 703–726.

Mahoney, Richard D. *JFK: Ordeal in Africa, The Ordeal of Power*. New York: Oxford University Press, 1983.

Makinda, Samuel M. *Seeking Peace from Chaos: Humanitarian Intervention in Somalia*. Boulder, Colorado: Lynne Rienner Publishers, 1993.

Malanczuk, Peter. *Akehurst's Modern Introduction to International Law*. London: Routledge, 1997.

——. "Sustainable Development: Some Critical Thoughts in Light of the Rio Conference." In *Sustainable Development and Good Governance*, edited by Konrad Ginther, 23–52. Dordrecht: Martinus Nijhoff Publishers, 1995.

Mamdani, Mahmood. "From the Zaire to the Democratic Republic of the Congo." In *Crisis in the Democratic Republic of Congo*, edited by Mwesiga L. Baregu, 45–55. Harare, Zimbabwe: SAPES, 1999,

Marek, Krystyna. *Identity and Continuity of States in Public International Law*. Geneva: Librairie Droz, 1968.

Marston, Geoffrey, "United Kingdom Materials on International Law." *Baltic Yearbook of International Law* 56 (1985), 460–.

Mason, Edward S., and Robert E. Asher. *The World Bank since Bretton Woods*. Washington: The Brookings Institution, 1973.

Matthies, Volker. "Regionale Anarchie als globales Problem". In *Weltpolitik in neuen Jahrhundert*, edited by Karl Kaiser and Hans-Peter Schwarz, 222–231. Bonn: Bundeszentrale für Politische Bildung, 2000.

Matthiessen, Kalala Ilunga. *Die Demokratische Republik Kongo, eine Analyse aus staatstheoretischer, verfassungsrechtlicher und völkerrechtlicher Sicht*. Münster: Waxmann Verlag, 2005.

Mutua, Makua wa. "Why Redraw the Map of Africa: A Moral and Legal Inquiry." *Michigan Journal of International Law* 16 (1995), 4, 1113–176.

Matz, Nele. "Civilisation and the Mandate System under the League of Nation as Origin of Trusteeship." *Max Planck Yearbook of United Nations Law* 9 (2005), 47–95.

Menzel, Eberhard. *Völkerrecht*. Munich: C.H. Beck, 1962.

Middleton, Roger. "Piracy in Somalia Threading Global Trade, Feeding Local Wars," Chatham House Briefing Paper. London: Royal Institute of International Affairs, 2008, www.chathamhouse.org.uk

Middleton, N and O'Keefe, P., Rio Plus Ten: Politics, Poverty and the Environment. London: Sterlin, VA, 2003.

Miller, Joshua S. "Putting Iraq in Trust: Reviving the UN International Trusteeship under General Principles of the International Fiduciary Obligation to Manage the Natural Resources of a Post-Saddam Iraq." *Suffolk Transnational Law Review* 27 (2003–2004), 1, 37–76.

Mills, Kurt. *Human Rights in the Emerging Global Order: A New Sovereignty*. Basingstoke, UK: Macmillan, 1998.

Mingst, Karen A., and Margaret P. Karns. *The United Nations in the Post-Cold. War Era*. Boulder, Colorado: Westview Press, 1995.

Minnerop, Petra. "The Classification of States and the Creation of Status within the International Community." *Max Planck Yearbook of United Nations Law* 7 (2003), 79–182.

Mironov, Nikolaj. *Law, Progress and Peace: A Journalist's Observations on the Influence of Soviet Law on the Progressive Development of International Law*. Moscow: Novosti Press Agency Publishing House, 1971.

Moore, Margaret, editor. *National Self-Determination and Secession*. Oxford: Oxford University Press, 1998.

Morgan-Foster, Jason. "The Relationship of IMF Structural Adjustment Programs to Economic, Social and Cultural Rights: The Argentine Case Revisited." *Michigan Journal of International Law* 24 (2003), 2, 577–646.

Mujaju, Akiki B. "The Regional Response in Eastern and South Africa." In *Crisis in the Democratic Republic of the Congo*, edited by Mwesiga Laurent Baregu, 83–90. Harare, Zimbabwe: SAPES Books, 1999.

Murphy, Ray. *UN Peacekeeping in Lebanon, Somalia and Kosovo*, Cambridge: Cambridge University Press, 2007.

Murphy, Sean D. *Humanitarian Intervention, The United Nations in an Evolving World Order*. Philadelphia: University of Pennsylvania Press, 1996.

——. "Nation-Building: A Look at Somalia." *Tulane Journal of International and Comparative Law* 3 (1995), 1–2, 19–43.

——. "Terrorism and the Concept of Armed Attack in Article 51 of the UN Charter." *Harvard International Law Journal* 43 (2002), 1, 41–51.

Murswiek, Dietrich. "Souveränität und humanitäre Intervention." *Der Staat* 35 (1996), 1, 31–44.

Mutharika, A. Peter. "The Role of International Law in the Twenty-First Century: An African Perspective." *Fordham International Law Journal* 18 (1995), 1706–1719.

Nardin, Terry. Introduction to *Humanitarian Intervention*, edited by Terry Nardin and Melissa S. Williams, 1–26. New York: New York University Press, 2006.

National Conference of All Liberian National Parties, Patriotic Fronts, Interest Groups and Concerned Citizens. "Final Communiqué of The National Conference of All Liberian National Parties, Patriotic Fronts, Interest Groups and Concerned Citizens of 29 August 1990." In *Regional Peace-Keeping and International Enforcement: The Liberian Crisis*, edited by Marc Weller, 89–. Cambridge: Cambridge University Press, 1994.

Ndulo, Muna. "Imagine a World without Hunger: The Hurdles of Global Justice". *Cornell International Law Journal* 39 (2006), 3, 779–787.

Nelson, Harold D., editor. *Somalia: A Country Study*. Washington: American University Press, 1982.

Nixon, Hamish, and Richard Ponzio. "Building Democracy in Afghanistan: The State Building Agenda and International Engagement." *International Peacekeeping* 14 (2007), 1, 26–40.

Nojumi, Neamatollah. *The Rise of the Taliban in Afghanistan: Mass Mobilisation, Civil War, and the Future of the Region*. New York: Palgrave Macmillan, Ltd., 2002.

Northedge, Frederick S. *The League of Nations, Its Life and Times 1920–1946*. Leicester: Leicester University Press, 1986.
Nowrot, Karsten, and Emily W. Schacabker. "The Use of Force to Restore Democracy: International Legal Implications of the ECOWAS Intervention in Sierra Leone." *American University International Law Review* 14 (1998–1999), 2, 321–412.
O'Connell, Mary Ellen. "The Myth of Preemptive Self-Defense." American Society of International Law Task Force Paper, August 2002. Washington, DC: American Society of International Law.
Oliver, Roland. *The African Experience: Major Themes in African History from Earliest Times to the Present*. London: Harper Collins Publishers, 1991.
Onimode, Bade, editor. *The IMF, the World Bank and the African Debt. Volume II. The Social and Political Impact*, London: Zed Books, 1989.
Oppenheim, Lassa F.L. *International Law*. 4th ed. Edited by Sir Arnold D. McNair. London: Longmans, 1928.
Oxley, Alan. "North/South Dimensions of a New World Order." In *Whose New World Order?* edited by Mara R. Bustelo and Philip Alston, 101–. Sydney: The Federation Press, 1991.
Paddock, John V. "Comment, IMF Policy and the Argentine Crisis." *University of Miami Inter-American Law Review* 34 (2002), 1, 155–187.
Pahuja, Sundhya. "Technologies of Empire: IMF Conditionality and the Reinscription of the North/South Divide." *Leiden Journal of International Law* 13 (2000), 749–813.
Panitch, Leo, and Sam Gindin. "Theorizing American Empire." In *Empire's Law: The American Imperial Project and the War to Remake the World*, edited by Amy Bartholomew, 44–51. London: Pluto Press, 2006.
Papastavridis, Efthymios. "Security Council Resolution 1368/2001 and 1378/2001: Collective Security or the Right of Self Defence?" *Reveu Hellénique de Droit International* 55 (2002), 2, 501–512.
Parfitt, Trevor. "The Politics of Adjustment in Africa with Special Reference to Egypt", In *The Economics and Politics of Structural Adjustment in Egypt*, edited by H. Löfgren. Cairo Papers in Social Science, Volume XVI, (1993), 3, 4–19.
Parsons, Anthony. *From Cold War to Hot Peace, UN Intervention 1947–1995*. London: Penguin Books, 1995.
Partan, Daniel G. "Peaceful Settlement and the Cold War." *Cincinnati Law Review* 34 (1965), 293–340.
Payer, Cheryl. "Causes of the Debt Crisis." In *The IMF, the World Bank, and African Debt. Volume II: The Social and Political Impact*, edited by Bade Onimode. London: Zed Books, 1989.
Pearson, Lester B., editor. *Partners in Development: Report of the Commission on International Development*. New York: Praeger, 1969.
Perez, Antonio F., "Legal Framework for the Economic Transition in Iraq—Occupation under the Law of War vs. Global Governance under the Law of Peace." *The Transnational Lawyer* 18 (2005), 1, 53–72.
Perritt, Henry H. "Structures and Standards for Political Trusteeship." *UCLA Journal of International Law and Foreign Affairs* 8 (2003), 2, 385–472.
Philipp, Christiane E. "Somalia—A Very Special Case." *Max Planck Yearbook of United Nations Law* 9 (2005), 1, 517–554.

Pillet, Antoine. *Recherches sur les Droits Fondamentaux des Etats*. Paris: A. Pedone, 1899.

Piotrowicz, Ryszard. "The Structure of the International Legal System." In *Public International Law: An Australian Perspective*, edited by Sam Blay, Ryszard Piotrowicz, and Martin Tsamenyi. Melbourne: Oxford University Press, 1997.

Piquard, Brigitte. "Understanding the Afghan Conflict Heritage: A Key for a Sustainable Process of Peace Settlement and Rehabilitation." *Humanitäres Völkerrecht* 17 (2004), 2, 73–78.

Poulantzas, Nicos. *Classes in Contemporary Capitalism*. London: New Left Books, 1975.

Powaski, Ronald E. *The Cold War: The United States and the Soviet Union, 1917–1991*. New York: Oxford University Press, 1998.

Pradetto, August. "Internationaler Terror, forcierter Regimewechsel und die UNO: Der Fall Afghanistan." *Aus Politik und Zeitgeschichte* 51 (2001), 24–35.

Purdy, Jedediah. "A World of Passions: How to Think About Globalization Now." *Indiana Journal of Global Legal Studies* 11 (2004), 2, 1–49.

Quashigah, Edward Kofi, and Obiora Chinedu Okafor, editors. *Legitimate Governance in Africa: International and Domestic Legal Perspectives*. The Hague: Kluwer Law International, 1999.

Rafique, Najam. U.S. Iraq Policy: From Hesitation to Occupation, www.issi.org.pk/journal/2003_filed/no_2/article/2a.htm.06.06.2007.

Raič, David. *Statehood and the Law of Self-Determination*. The Hague: Kluwer Law International, 2002.

Randelzhofer, Albrecht. "Commentary on Article 51." In *The Charter of the United Nations*. Volume II, ed. Bruno Simma, 2nd ed. Oxford: Oxford University Press, 2002.

Ratner, Steven R. *The New UN Peacekeeping: Building Peace in Lands of Conflict after the Cold War*. New York: St. Martin's Press, 1995.

Reddy, Vijayanarayana. *Third World Development and New International Economic Order*. New Delhi: Deep & Deep, 1994.

Reisman, W. Michael. "Coercion and Self Determination: Construing Charter Article 2(4)." *American Journal of International Law* 78 (1984), 3, 642–645.

Reuter, Jens. "Die politische Entwicklung in Kosovo 1992/1993." *Südosteuropa* 43 (1994), 1–2, 18–30.

Richardson, Henry J. " 'Failed State', Self-Determination, and Preventive Diplomacy: Colonialist Nostalgia and Democratic Expectations." *Temple International and Comparative Law Journal* 10 (1996), 1, 1–11.

Roberts, Adam. "Transformative Military Occupation: Applying the Laws of War and Human Rights." *American Journal of International Law* 100 (2006), 3, 580–622.

Rolland, Sonia E. "Developing Country Coalition at the WTO: In Search of Legal Support." *Harvard International Law Journal* 48 (2007), 2, 483–551.

Ross, Alf. *Constitutions of the United Nations: Analysis of Structure and Function*. Copenhagen: Munksgaard, 1950.

Ross, Michael L. "How Do Natural Resources Influence Civil War? Evidence from Thirteen Cases." *International Organisations* 58 (2004), 35–67.

Rotberg, Robert I. "Failed State in a World of Terror." *Foreign Affairs* 81 (2002), 4, 127–140.

———. "The Failure and Collapse of Nation-States: Breakdown, Prevention, and Repair." In *When States Fail, Causes and Consequences*, edited by Robert I. Rotberg, Princeton: Princeton University Press, 2004.

Rotberg, Robert I., Erika Albaugh, Happyton Bonyongwe, Christopher Clapham, Jeffrey Herbst, and Steven Metz. *Peacekeeping and Peace Enforcement in Africa: Methods of Conflict Prevention*, Cambridge, Massachusetts: World Peace Foundation, 2000.

Rotter, Manfred. "Staat". In *Völkerrecht*, edited by Ignaz Seidl-Hohenveldern, 380–, 3rd edition, Neuwied, Germany: Luchterhand, 2001.

Rubin, Barnett R. *The Fragmentation of Afghanistan: State Formation and Collapse in the International System*. New Haven, Connecticut, Yale University Press, 1995.

———. Saving Afghanistan, Foreign Affairs 86 (2007), 1, 57–78.

Rubin, Barnett R., and Humayun Hamidzada. "From Bonn to London: Governance Challenges and the Future of State building in Afghanistan." *International Peacekeeping* 14 (2007), 1, 8–25.

Ruf, Werner, editor. *Politische Ökonomie der Gewalt, Staatszerfall und die Privatisierung von Gewalt und Krieg*. Friedens und Konfliktforschung 7. Opladen, Germany: Leske + Budrich, 2003.

Samatar, Ahmed I., *Socialist Somalia, Rhetoric and Reality*. London: Zed, 1988.

Sampson, Anthony. *Weltmacht ITT: Die Politische Geschäfte eines Multinationalen Konzerns*. Hamburg: Rowohlt Verlag, 1973.

Sarwari, Mohammad Sadiq. *Afghanistan zwischen Tradition und Modernisierung*. Bern: Peter Lang, 1974.

Schaller, Cristian. *Internationales Sanktionsmanagement im Rahmen von Artikel 41Charta*. Baden-Baden: Nomos Verlagsgesellschaft, 2003.

Schetter, Conrad. "Der Krieg in Afghanistan und seine regionale Dimension." In *Jahrbuch Internationale Politik 1997/1998* (2000), 211–221.

Schiedermair, Hartmut. "Effektive Herrschaftsgewalt und Rechtsfähigkeit im Völkerrecht." *Juristische Arbeitsblätter* 16 (1984), 638–641.

Schindler, Dietrich. "Different Types of Armed Conflicts according to the Geneva Conventions and Protocols." *Recueil des Cours de l'Académie de droit international* 163 (1979), 2, 121–163.

Schlemmer-Schulte, Sabine, "Global Business and Development", speech given at the University of the Pacific McGeorge School of Law, Sacramento, California, January 20, 2006.

———. "The World Bank and Human Rights." *Austrian Review of International and European Law* 4 (1999), 230–268.

Schmidt, Siegmar. "Ambivalente Entwicklungen in Afrika und die internationale Gemeinschaft." *Jahrbuch Internationale Politik* 25 (2001–2002), 295–302.

Schoiswohl, Michael. *Status and (Human Rights) Obligations of Non-Recognized* De Facto *Regimes in International Law: The Case of "Somaliland."* Leiden: Martinus Nijhoff Publishers, 2004.

Scholler, Heinrich. "Somalias langer Weg zur neuen Staatlichkeit." *Recht in Afrika* 7 (2004), 2, 229–242.

Schroeder, Emily. "The Kosovo Crisis: Humanitarian Imperative versus International Law." *The Fletcher Forum of the World Affairs* 28 (2004), 1, 179–200.

Schweitzer, Michael. *Staatsrecht III, Staatsrecht, Völkerrecht, Europarecht*. 7th ed. Heidelberg: Müller, 2000.

Scott, George. The Rise and Fall of the League of Nations. London: Hutchinson, 1973.

Segger, Marie-Claire Cordonier. "Integrating Social and Economic Development and Environmental Protection in World Trade Law." In *Sustainable Development in World Trade Law*, edited by Markus W. Gehring and Marie-Claire Cordonier Segger, The Hague: Kluwer Law International, 2005.

Seidl-Hohenveldern, Ignaz. *Völkerrecht, Lexikon des Rechts*. 3rd ed. Neuwied, Germany: Luchterhand, 2001.

——. "Souveränität." In *Völkerrecht, Lexikon des Rechts*. 3rd ed., Neuwied, Germany: Luchterhand, 2001.

Selassie, Bereket Habte. "Self-Determination in Principle and Practice: The Ethiopian-Eritrean Experience." *Columbia Human Rights Law Review* 29 (1997), 1, 92–142.

Senghaas, Dieter, editor. *Imperialismus und strukturelle Gewalt Analysen über abhängige Reproduktion*. Frankfurt: Suhrkamp Verlag, 1972.

Seppänen, Samuli. *Good Governance in International Law*. Helsinki: University of Helsinki, 2003.

Shaw, Malcolm N. *International Law*, 4th ed. Cambridge, UK: Cambridge University Press, 1997.

Shehadi, Kamal S. *Ethnic Self-Determination and the Break-up of States: The Power of Ethnic Responses to Creating New States, Redrawing International Borders and Salvaging Failed States*. London: Brassey's Ltd., 1993.

Shihata, Ibrahim F. *The World Bank in a Changing World, Selected Essays and Lectures*. Volume II. Dordrecht: Martinus Nijhoff Publishers, 1995.

Sidell, Scott R. *The IMF and Third World Political Instability: Is There a Connection?* New York: St. Martin's Press, 1988.

Simma, Bruno, editor. *The Charter of the United Nations: A Commentary*. Volumes I and II. 2nd edition. Oxford: Oxford University Press, 2002.

Šimonović, Ivan. "State Sovereignty and Globalization: Are Some States More Equal?" *Georgia Journal of International and Comparative Law* 28 (2000), 3, 381–404.

Simpson, Gerry J. "The Diffusion of Sovereignty: Self-determination in the Post-Colonial Age." *Stanford Journal of International Law* 32 (1996), 2, 255–286.

Sitkowski, Andrzej. *UN Peacekeeping, Myth and Reality*. Westport, Connecticut: Praeger Security International, 2006.

Skogly, Sigrun I. "The Position of the World Bank and the International Monetary Fund in the Human Rights Field." In *International Protection of Human Rights Field*, edited by Raija Hanski and Markku Suksi, 193–205. Turku, Finland: Åbo Akademi University Institute for Human Rights, 1997

Sollis, Peter. "Partners in Development? The State, NGOs, and the UN in Central America." In *NGOs, the UN, and Global Governance*, edited by Thomas G. Weiss and Leon Gordenker, 189–206. Boulder, Colorado: Lynne Rienner Publishers, 1996.

Sornarajah, Muthucumaraswamy. "Economic Neo-Liberalism and the International Law on Foreign Investment." In *The Third World and International Order: Law, Politics and Globalisation*, Developments in International Law 45, edited by Antony Anghie, Chimni Bhupinder, Karin Mickelson, and Obiaora Okafor, 172–. Leiden: Martinus Nijhoff Publishers, 2003.

Stahn, Carsten. "Collective Security and Self-Defence after the September 11 Attacks." *Tilburg Foreign Law Review* 10 (2002), 1, 10–42.

———. The Law and Practice of International Territorial Administration, Versailles to Iraq and Beyond. Cambridge, UK: Cambridge University Press, 2008.

Stein, Torsten, and Christian von Buttlar. *Völkerrecht*. 11th ed. Munich: Heymann, 2005.

Stevenson, Jonathan. "Hope Restored in Somalia?" *Foreign Policy* 91 (1993), 138–154.

Stiglitz, Joseph E. "Failure of the Fund: Rethinking the IMF Response." *Harvard International Review* 23 (2001), 2, 14–18.

———. *Globalization and its Discontents*. New York: Norton, 2003.

Stostad, Timothy. "Trappings of Legality: Judicialization of Dispute Settlement in the WTO and Its Impact on Developing Countries." *Cornell International Law Journal* 39 (2006), 3, 811–845.

Stowell, Ellery C. *International Law: A Restatement of Principles in Conformity with Actual Practices*. New York: Henry Holt, 1931.

Strizek, Helmut. *Ruanda und Burundi: von der Unabhängigkeit zum Staatszerfall: Studie über eine gescheiterte Demokratie im afrikanischen Zwischenseengebiet*. Munich: Weltforum-Verlag, 1996.

Suzuki, Eisuke, and Suresh Nanwani. "Responsibility of International Organizations: The Accountability Mechanisms of Multilateral Development Banks." *Michigan Journal of International Law* 27 (2005–2006), 1, 177–225.

Sweezy, Paul M. "Corporations, the State, and Imperialism." *Monthly Review* 30 (1978), 1–10.

Tainter, Joseph A. *The Collapse of Complex Societies*. Cambridge: Cambridge University Press, 1988.

Talmon, Stefan. "Recognition of Government: An Analysis of the New British Policy and Practice." *British Yearbook of International Law* 63 (1992), 231–297.

Tandon, Yash. "Globalization and the Great Lakes Regional Crisis." In *Crisis in the Democratic Republic of the Congo*, edited by Mwesiga Baregu, 42–. Harare: Sapes Books, 1999.

Terry, Alan, Jennifer Hill, and Wendy Woodland. "Uniting National Aspirations and Local Implementation in Sustainable Development: An Introduction." In *Sustainable Development: National Aspirations, Local Implementation*, edited by Alan Terry, Jennifer Hill, and Wendy Woodland, 1–13. Aldershot, UK: Ashgate Publishing, 2006.

Tesón, Fernando R. *Humanitarian Intervention: An Inquiry into Law and Morality*. Dobbs Ferry, New York: Transnational Publishers, 1997.

Tetzlaff, Rainer. "Der Wegfall effektiver Staatsgewalt in den Staaten Afrikas." *Internationale Politik* 55 (2000), 8–16.

Thomas, Carolina. "International Financial Institutions and Social and Economic Human Rights: An Exploration." In *Human Rights Fifty Years on: A Reappraisal*, edited by Tony Evans, 161–187. Manchester: Manchester University Press, 1998.

Thürer, Daniel. "Modernes Völkerrecht: Ein System im Wandel und Wachstum- Gerechtigkeitsgedanke als Kraft der Veränderung." *Zeitschrift für ausländisches und öffentliches Recht und Völkerrecht* 60 (2000), 3–4, 557–604.

——. "Der Wegfall effektiver Staatsgewalt: 'Failed State'". In *Der Wegfall effektiver Staatsgewalt "The Failed State"* Berichte der Deutsche Gesellschaft für Völkerrecht 34, by Daniel Thürer, Matthias Herdegen, and Gerhard Hohloch, 9–. Heidelberg: Müller, 1996.

Tomaševski, Katarina. *Responding to Human Rights Violations, 1946–1999*. The Hague: Martinus Nijhoff Publishers, 2000.

Tomuschat, Christian. "How the Classical Concept of Sovereignty Has Evolved." In *The International and the National: Essays in Honour of Vojin Dimitrijević*, edited by Milica Delević Đilas and Vladimir Đerić, 21–34. Belgrade: Belgrade Center for Human Rights, 2003.

——. "Völkerrecht ist kein Zweiklassenrecht, Der Irak-Krieg und seine Folgen." *Vereinten Nationen* 51 (2003), 2, 41–46.

Triggs, Gillian D. *International Law: Contemporary Principles and Practice*. Chatswood, Australia: LexisNexis Butterworths, 2006.

Trukhanovsky, Vladimir. *British Foreign Policy during World War II*. Moscow: Progress Publishers, 1970.

Truman, Harry S. *Memoirs, Volume II: Years of Trial and Hope*. London: Hodder and Stoughton, 1956.

Türk, Danilo. "Recognition of States: A Comment." *European Journal of International Law* 4 (1993), 1, 66–71.

Umozurike, Umozurike Oji. *Self-Determination in International Law*. Hamden, Connecticut: Shoe String Press, 1972.

Utz, Raphael. "Nations, Nation-Building, and Cultural Intervention: A Social Science Perspective." *Max Planck Yearbook of United Nations Law* 9 (2005), 615–647.

Van den Boom, Dirk. *Bürgerkrieg in Liberia: Chronologie—Protagonisten—Prognose*. Münster: LIT Verlag, 1993.

Van der Kraaij, Fred. "The Open Door Policy of Liberia: Past, Present and Perspectives of the Liberian Concept of Foreign Investment." In *Liberia: Underdevelopment and Political Rule in a Peripheral Society*, edited by Robert Kappel, Werner Korte, and Friedegund R. Mascher, 150–191. Hamburg: Institut für Afrika-Kunde, 1986.

Van Eijk, Ryan. "The United Nations and Reconstruction of Collapsed States in Africa." *African Journal of International and Comparative Law* 9 (1997), 3, 573–599.

Van Hippel, Karin, and Alexandros Yannis. "The European Response to State Collapse in Somalia." In *European Approaches to Crisis Management*, edited by Knud Erik Jorgensen, 65–83. The Hague: Kluwer Law International, 1997.

Väyrynen, Raimo. "*The Age of Humanitarian Emergencies*." Helsinki: World Institute for Development Economic Research (WIDER) Research for Action 25, 1996.

Verdross, Alfred. *Völkerrecht*. Vienna: Springer, 1964.

Verdross, Alfred, and Bruno Simma. *Universelles Völkerrecht*. Berlin: Duncker & Humblot, 1984.

Volker, Matthies. "Die UNO am Horn von Afrika: Die Missionen in Somalia (UNOSOM I, UNITAF; UNOSOM II) und Äthiopien (UNMEE)." In *Praxishandbuch UNO, Die Vereinten Nationen im Lichte globaler Herausforderungen*, edited by Sabine von Schorlemer, 41–63. Heidelberg: Springer, 2003.

Von der Heydte, Friedrich August Freiherr. *Völkerrecht: Ein Lehrbuch, Volume I*, Köln: Verlag für Politik und Wirtschaft, 1958.

Von Liszt, Franz. *Völkerrecht*. Berlin: Verlag von O. Härig, 1913.

Von Schorlemer, Sabine, editor. *Praxis-Handbuch UNO, Die Vereinten Nationen im Lichte globaler Herausforderungen*. Heidelberg: Springer, 2003.

Voon, Tania. "Multinational Enterprises and State Sovereignty under International Law." *Adelaide Law Review* 21 (1999), 2, 219–252.

Wadrzyk, Mark E. "Is It Appropriate for the World Bank to Promote Democratic Standards in a Borrower Country?" *Wisconsin International Law Journal* 17 (1999), 553–577.

Wallace, Rebecca M.M. *International Law*. London: Sweet & Maxwell, 2005.

Wallace-Bruce, Nii Lante. "Of Collapsed, Dysfunctional and Disoriented States: Challenges to International Law." *Netherlands International Law Review* 47 (2000), 53–73.

——. "Taiwan and Somalia: International Legal Curiosities." *Queens Law Journal* 22 (1997), 2, 453–485.

Waters, Malcolm. *Globalization*. New York: Routledge, 1995.

Weber, Max. *The Theory of Social and Economic Organisation*. Oxford: Oxford University Press, 1947.

Weber, Sebastian. "Das Sezessionsrecht der Kosovo-Albaner und seine Durchsetzbarkeit." *Archiv des Völkerrechts* 43 (2005), 494–512.

Weiss, Thomas G., editor. *Beyond UN Subcontracting: Task-Sharing with Regional Security Arrangements and Service-Providing NGOs*. Basingstoke, UK: Macmillan, 1998.

Weiss, Thomas, and Leon Gordenker, editors. *NGOs, the UN, and Global Governance*. Boulder, Colorado: Lynne Rienner Publishers, 1996.

Weller, Marc, editor. *Regional Peace-Keeping and International Enforcement: The Liberian Crisis*. Cambridge, UK: Cambridge University Press, 1994.

Wellhausen, Malte. *Humanitäre Intervention, Probleme der Anerkennung des Rechtsinstituts unter besonderer Berücksichtigung Kosovo-Konflikts*. Baden-Baden: Nomos Verlagsgesellschaft, 2002.

Weschka, Marion. "Human Rights and Multinational Enterprises: How Can Multinational Enterprises Be Held Responsible for Human Rights Violations Committed Abroad?" *Zeitschrift für Ausländisches Öffentliches Recht und Völkerrecht* 66 (2006), 3, 625–661.

Westfield, Elisa. "Globalization, Governance, and Multinational Enterprise Responsibility: Corporate Codes of Conduct in the 21st Century." *Virginia Journal of International Law* 42 (2001–2002), 4, 1075–1108.

Wilde, Ralph. *International Territorial Administration: How Trusteeship and the Civilizing Mission Never Went away*. Oxford: Oxford University Press, 2008.

Williams, David. "Aid and Sovereignty: Quasi-States and the International Financial Institutions." *Review of International Studies* 26 (2000), 557–573

Williamson, John. "The Progress of Policy Reform in Latin America." *Policy Analysis in International Economics* 28 (1990), 353–380.

Wippman, David. "Defending Democracy through Foreign Intervention." *El papel del derecho internacional en América. La soberanía nacional en la era de la integración regional*, 121–149. México City: Universidad Nacional Autonomo de Mexico Instituto de Investigaciones Jurídicas, 1987.

Wise, Judith. "Hunger and Thieves: Anticipating the Impact of WTO Subsidies Reform on Land and Survival in Brazil." *American Indian Law Review* 31 (2006–2007), 2, 531–551.

Wolfrum, Rüdiger. "International Administration in Post-Conflict Situations by the United Nations and Other International Actors." *Max Planck Yearbook of United Nations Law* 9 (2005), 649–696.

——. "Iraq—from Belligerent Occupation to Iraqi Exercise of Sovereignty: Foreign Power versus International Community Interference." *Max Planck Yearbook of United Nations Law* 9 (2005), 1–45.

Wolfrum, Rüdiger, and Christiane Philipp. "Die Taliban: ein Subjekt des Völkerrechts?" In *Praxis Handbuch UNO: Die Vereinten Nationen im Lichte globaler Herausforderungen*, edited by Sabine von Schorlemer, 145–157. Heidelberg: Springer Verlag, 2003.

Woolsey, Theodore D. Introduction to *the Study of International Law*. 6th ed. New York: Scribner's. 1892.

Wouters, Jan, and Dominic Coppens. "International Economic Policy-Making: Exploring the Legal Linkages between the World Trade Organization and the Bretton Woods Institutions." *International Organizations Law Review* 3 (2006), 2, 267–315.

Yannis, Alexandros. *State Collapse and the International System: Implosion of Government and the International Legal Order from French Revolution to the Disintegration of Somalia*. Geneva: Graduate Institute of International Studies, 2000.

——. "State Collapse and Prospects for Political Reconstruction and Democratic Governance in Somalia." *African Yearbook of International Law* 5 (1997), 23–47.

Yansané, Aguibou Y. *Decolonization in West African States with a French Colonial Legacy: Comparison and Contrast, Development in Guinea, the Ivory Coast, and Senegal (1945–1980)*. Cambridge, Massachusetts: Schenkman Publishing, 1984.

Yerokun, Olusegun. *Legal Aspects of Structural Adjustment Programme in Nigeria*. Oya, Nigeria: University of Ilorin, 1989.

Yoffee, Norman, and George L. Cowgill, editors. *The Collapse of Ancient States and Civilizations*. Tucson, Arizona: University of Arizona Press, 1988.

Yoo, John C. "International Law and the War in Iraq." *American Journal of International Law* 97 (2003), 563–576.

Yusuf, Abdulqawi A. "Government Collapse and State Continuity: The Case of Somalia." *Italian Yearbook of International Law* 13 (2003), 11–33.

Zartman, I. William. Introduction: Posing the Problem of State Collapse to *Collapsed States: The Disintegration and Restoration of Legitimate Authority*, edited by I. William Zartman, 1–11. Boulder, Colorado: Lynne Rienner Publishers, 1995.

Zemanek, Karl. "Self-Defence against Terrorism: Reflections on an Unprecedented Situation." In *El Derecho Internacional en los albores del siglo XXI, Homenaje Al Profesor Juan-manuel Castro-rial Canosa*, edited by Fernando M. Mariño, *695–714. Madrid: Editorial Trotta, 2002.*

Zenk, Peter-Michael. *Auf dem Weg zur Weltinnenpolitik? Zur Problematik militärischer Interventionen bei innerstaatlichen Konflikten*. Hamburg: Institut für Friedensforschung und Sicherheitspolitik, 1994.

Ziegler, Jean. *Das Imperium der Schande, der Kampf gegen Armut und Unterdrückung*. Munich: Pantheon, 2007.

Zimmermann, Andreas and Carsten Stahn. "Yugoslav Territory, United Nations Trusteeship or Sovereign State? Reflections on the Current and Future Legal Status of Kosovo." *Nordic Journal of International Law* 70 (2001), 423–460.

Zippelius, Reinhold. *Allgemeine Staatslehre*. 14th ed. Munich: C.H. Beck, 2003.

Zischg, Robert. *Nicht-internationaler bewaffneter Konflikt und Völkerrecht, Zur Zulässigkeit der Konfliktparteien durch dritte Staaten*. Baden-Baden: Nomos Verlagsgesellschaft, 1996.

INDEX

www.ingramcontent.com/pod-product-compliance
Lightning Source LLC
LaVergne TN
LVHW080847300926
849162LV00003B/359
9789004178120